THE THIRD MILLENNIUM

A HISTORY OF THE WORLD: AD 2000–3000

THE THIRD MILLENNIUM

A HISTORY OF THE WORLD : AD 2000–3000

BRIAN STABLEFORD AND DAVID LANGFORD

Alfred A. Knopf, Inc., New York

I would like to dedicate this exercise in future history to my children, Leo Michael Stableford and Katherine Margaret Stableford, who I hope will have a better opportunity to check up on its reliability than I will. BMS

My part in this book is for my younger brother, Jon Langford, who according to the best statisticians should be seeing four and a half more years of the future than me. DL

This is a Borzoi Book
published by Alfred A. Knopf, Inc.

Published in the United States by Alfred A. Knopf, Inc., New York. Distributed by Random House, Inc., New York.

Library of Congress Cataloguing
in Publication Data
Stableford, Brian M.
The Third Millennium
Includes index.
1. Twenty-first century – forecasts.
I. Langford, David. II. Title.
CB161.568 1985 909.83 85-156
ISBN 0-394-53980-X
ISBN 0-394-74151-X
Manufactured in Italy
First American Edition

CONTENTS

THE PERIOD OF TRANSFORMATION 2400 TO 2650

Left, **Gantz organic home,** twenty-second century (see Chapter Thirteen).

CREATION OF THE NEW WORLD 2650 TO 3000

PROLOGUE

When people look back over the last thousand years (AD 2000-3000), the first reaction is always, "What enormous changes!" A closer look produces a second shock – how slowly in hindsight, the changes came! With better management in the chaotic aftermath of the twentieth and twenty-first centuries the level of civilization today could have been reached in half, or even a quarter of the time.

However, the history of mankind stretches back for eight hundred millennia, to that uncertain era when *Homo sapiens* gradually evolved from *Homo erectus*. Through more than seven hundred and fifty of those millennia, alterations in the human condition were so slow as to be imperceptible. Even the first technological revolution – the revolution that introduced basic agricultural methods and primitive metallurgy – produced a transformation in human lifestyles that took tens of thousands of years to evolve. We can speak of the last thousand years as the *third* millennium not simply because of the dating system linked to the birth of Jesus Christ, but because each of the three millennia mapped by modern calendars has seen greater change than the whole of previous human history. They have been the millennia of accelerating technological progress, while all the thousands of years that we now mark BC were periods when such progress was at most fitful and at least non-existent.

The history of the third millennium may come to have special importance because the period of accelerating progress is now coming to an end. The rate of change seems to be slowing again, and the graph of human achievement reaching a new plateau. We might be wrong in thinking so – after all, we can no more predict our future with certainty than the people of the twentieth century could predict theirs – but, just as they had good grounds for anticipating a new millennium of unprecedented technological achievement and social change, so we have firm indications of a millennium of relative stability. When historians in the forty-first century try to summarize the fourth millennium, they may well report far less dramatic transformations than those recorded here.

We are well aware in introducing our book, therefore, that we face a uniquely difficult task. In condensing the achievements of the third millennium into a few hundred pages we can hardly do them justice. At the same time we are immensely fortunate in being able to record the most interesting times that the human race has lived through. To live in interesting times, it was said, is to be burdened by a terrible curse; to tell the story of interesting times is a different matter. There is a great deal of suffering in our record, but we can take pride and comfort in the fact that the suffering was not all in vain.

In recalling these past times, we must remember that we are the heirs not only of our parents, grandparents and the many generations of our individual bloodlines, but of *all* the men and women who lived and died in those turbulent years. Nothing that has ever happened to human beings in the past is irrelevant and although we can only paint a word-picture of the last thousand years with the broadest of brush-strokes, concealing the lives and deaths of billions of individuals within the cold reach of our general statements, this coolness is by no means callous. It is a history which should engage the emotions. We believe that if the people of the twentieth century could glimpse this record of what happened to the world they bequeathed to their descendants, they too could feel proud of it, despite its moments of tragedy. The achievements of the third millennium were built on foundations laid by them, just as their own achievements were founded in those of earlier generations.

When the year which we now call 1 AD began, civilization had come to all the continents of the world except one. There were permanent settlements established in large tracts of cultivated land in the Americas, in Europe, in Africa and in Asia. Many great cities had already fallen into ruins; numerous cultures had suffered virtual obliteration. It was an era of cultural imperialism, when several political communities were striving to extend their dominion to absorb others.

In the recent past, Alexander III of Macedon had hugely extended the empire founded in Greece by his father. That empire was short-lived, but its brief presence encouraged the Greeks to begin to talk of the *Oikoumenê* – "the World". They did not mean the world in its physical sense, but an assembly of human cultures ripe for consolidation. Though ignorant of the world's real extent, in either sense, they nurtured the dream of its union by conquest. The idea passed to the Romans, who were already establishing a new empire as the first millennium began. It is logical, therefore, to call the period covered by our calendars "the history of the world", because the *idea* of the world was but newly born.

The first millennium has been frequently represented as a Dark Age, an age of barbarian victories against the march of civilization: the era of the Huns and the Vikings. It was also the era of the great religions, however, when the ends of cultural imperialism were carried forward by means of conversion to various faiths rather than by military conquest and domination. In Europe, the Christian empire of faith was much more diffuse, in political terms, than the Roman Empire which it replaced, but it proved far less easy to dislodge. In Asia, three great religious empires were formed, competing where their borders overlapped. The great religions proved well able to survive the destruction and renewal of states, and endured with great resilience the endless clashing of armies. The communities created by the empires of faith paved the way for the technological progress of the second millennium. Some historians still see the tight grip on human consciousness exerted by the first-millennium faiths as counter-progressive, but we contend that without the relative social stability brought about by these moral commonwealths, the eventual technological revolutions could not have taken place. Large-scale organized religion permitted the development of literacy and a sense of history, the elaborate division of labour, and the formation of communities of nations.

By 1000 AD Christianity was at its height in Europe. Western Europe entered a phase of rapid technological change and although progress was interrupted by depopulation due to the Black Death in the fourteenth century, there was continual innovation during the seven hundred years preceding the explosive Industrial Revolution of the eighteenth century.

The pattern of human life was severely altered in those communities which pioneered the Industrial Revolution. The rhythms of day and night and of seasonal change were supplanted by the rhythms of clocks and pistons. A boundary was crossed which divorced people from their marriage with nature and made them a new marriage with machinery. A gap opened between the "developed" parts of the world and the "undeveloped" – or, more tellingly, the "underdeveloped". The empires of faith came under stress, and in due course broke apart, although their resilience was such that they continued to live in spite of their internal injuries and loss of power. Slowly but surely they were displaced by new economic and technological empires whose power was even greater. But the marriage of man and machine was to prove a troublesome one, and as the second millennium moved to its close it was reaching a period of crisis. At last it was possible to speak of there being an *Oikoumenê* – a whole world, an entire human community – but there seemed every chance that it would suddenly destroy itself and undo the whole pattern of human progress. With humanity poised on this dangerous brink, the third millennium began.

CHAPTER ONE
THE WORLD IN THE YEAR 2000

The rapid acceleration of technological development in the last quarter of the second millennium had many consequences, most unintended and some highly problematic. The world's population increased dramatically, especially in the twentieth century. In 1900 there were less than two billion people; by 2000 there were nearly five billion. This expansion had been permitted by an equally dramatic increase in food supplies resulting from new agricultural techniques, and from advances in medical science and hygiene.

Earth's ecosystem under threat

Five billion people put an enormous strain on the Earth's ecosystem. Intensive crop cultivation threatened the long-term viability of the soil in the most fertile regions. Heavy industries were polluting the biosphere: sulphurous fumes released by burning coal eventually fell back to the surface as acid rain; heavy metals and non-biodegradable organic poisons were beginning to destroy vulnerable links in the ecological chain of eaters and eaten. Both industry and agriculture were dependent on energy generated from non-renewable resources: fossil fuels, coal and oil.

Of the world's five billion people, more than a billion were subsistence farmers, and a further billion were poor farmers struggling to reach a viable standard of living by raising cash crops. This remained the case despite the trend of the previous two centuries toward large-scale monoculture farming, with its absence of crop rotation and consequent dependence on chemical nutrients. The poor farmers, still increasing in number although their lands were shrinking rapidly, constituted an even greater threat to the ecosphere than did technology. Their sheer numbers made them major contributors to soil erosion, and their dependence on wood for fuel denuded their lands of trees. They threatened to turn huge areas into desert.

Humanity close to extermination

In the world at this time inequalities between nations and individuals were more striking than ever before. This was not simply due to vast differences of wealth and income, but because technology had created so many things that could be possessed. There were numerous opportunities for the rich – nations as well as individuals – to convert their wealth into exotic, showy lifestyles. At the same time, the expansion of mass communication publicized these inequalities. Resentment and anguish were everywhere, and were manifested in worldwide civil strife. Most poor nations were constantly racked with civil war, their conflicts exacerbated by the activities of the two great empires of economic ideology, centred in the USA and the USSR, which were hungry to absorb the nations of the so-called Third World.

Two world wars had already been fought in the twentieth century. No type of technology had evolved more rapidly than the technology of mass destruction; by the year 2000 several nations possessed the theoretical capacity to exterminate the entire human race. It seemed highly probable that a third world war – or any conflict involving the two great "superpowers" – would precipitate immediate total devastation of the ecosphere. It was not simply humankind which was under threat, but almost every living species.

Sufficient resources to solve all problems

It may seem that the world in the year 2000 was in a desperate plight, and that the prospects for mankind were poor. With the

In the year 2000 humanity faced tremendous problems. Industrial pollution had killed and was killing entire ecosystems; atomic warfare was an ever-present potential catastrophe – the world might end at any minute; overpopulation placed intolerable stress on world economies; while the rapidly growing deserts reduced the area available for food production.

benefit of hindsight, however, we can see that there were two aspects to the situation. The problems were, in a sense, the accidental corollaries of great achievements. The poorest people, living on the margin of survival, were more numerous than ever before, but at the same time more people were living more comfortably than ever before, and mankind had the means – at least potentially – to meet the dire threats to its future. Resources were available that could solve all the problems confronting the world. The difficulty lay in forging the collective will to deploy them.

It was vital for the world, as it moved into the third millennium, to find a new ecological balance. Humanity had somehow to stabilize its relationship with the environment – to regulate the energy-economy and escape dependence on fossil fuels. They had to reorganize the agricultural base so that it could operate efficiently and indefinitely. They had to keep conflict to a level that did not threaten the survival of the species.

Appropriate technologies were already under investigation – and in some cases under development – that could meet these needs if only an international meeting of minds could be arranged. Investigation of new methods of energy-generation, like fusion power, was proceeding. A brand-new biological technology was already in its infancy, an organic technology in which living things were used as machines – an early example being the modified bacteria which synthesized interferon. A new approach to inter-community relations, assisted by new communications systems, was slowly emerging to fill the gaps opened by the decline of religion and ideology. It took time for the people of the third millennium to exploit these technologies, but the seeds were there for a revolution.

Anxiety tempered by hope

Inevitably, the turn of the millennium was an anxious time. It is difficult for us to appreciate the anxiety of those days. We are not unacquainted with fear and horror, but we can hardly imagine the burden of everyday fears and horrors that those people must have carried. Of course they adapted, as people always have, and were probably unaware for the most part, of the efforts that they made in so doing.

As the Christian empire approached the year 1000 many people believed that the world would surely end. They believed in the magic of numbers, and supposed that Christ would come again to supervise a day of judgment and establish the Kingdom of God. In the event no one came, but the millenarianism of those days, though tinged with fear and doubt, was essentially hopeful. The new millenarianism current as the year 2000 approached gave much freer rein to fear and doubt. There was no refuge to be found in prayer, no ideal Kingdom to which the virtuous could look forward. Nevertheless there was hope, and hope legitimately entertained. The people had no option but to put their trust in one another, no matter how uneasily, and that trust proved not to be misplaced. The nations, in becoming inextricably bound together politically, economically and communicatively, were already moving away from the suicidal contemplation of total war.

Salvation by technology and will power

We are inclined today to think of the salvation of that world of long ago in primarily technological terms. We look back at the effects of new communications technology, which eliminated distances and broke through language barriers, slowly binding together a world community; at the development of fusion power, which gave people control of the most powerful energy-producing process permitted by their physical circumstances, and saved them from dependence on the sun's energy; and at the increasing command over the fundamental processes of life which allowed genetic engineers to find countless ways of answering human needs precisely and efficiently. However, we tend to forget – and we dishonour the people of that time by so doing – that behind the development of those technologies was a powerful will, an indomitable desire possessed by innumerable men and women to secure not just their own well-being but the well-being of their children and their neighbours. If that had been lost, then "the one world" would have ended before it had even been created.

Of course, not all the people of the year 2000 were prepared to trust in their fellows. For many, the desire to contribute to the general well-being was confused by deep-rooted resentments and hatreds. Just as the technologies of survival were slow to develop, so was the collective will of the world community. We begin our history of the third millennium by demarcating a Period of Crisis covering the year 2000 to about 2180, when the fate of the world lay in the balance.

THE PERIOD OF CRISIS

2000 TO 2180

CHAPTER TWO

WAR AND PEACE IN THE TWENTY-FIRST CENTURY

When the new millennium began, three-quarters of the world's nations were involved in wars of one kind or another. Some were being fought with tanks, shells, rifles, rockets and bombs; others with political propaganda and economic sanctions. Wherever there were religious boundaries, ethnic boundaries or boundaries separating opposing political ideologies, there was tension. Such tensions were arguably not the principal causes of wars, but merely provided fault-lines which could divide nations or communities into factions. Today we can see that the real war underlying most of these conflicts was the war between the rich and the poor. During the period of crisis this became more evident in the changing realignment of nations and their elites, and in the changing nature of the wars that they fought.

The threat of global holocaust

Until partially displaced by plague warfare, nuclear war was the cardinal source of anxiety in the twenty-first century, at least in the developed nations. It is difficult today to appreciate how real the threat of global holocaust was, for the simple reason that if it had ever happened this history could not have been written. For fifty years before and after the beginning of the third millennium there was a real danger that the two superpowers, the USA and the USSR, might launch their vast armouries of missiles at one another. The mutual hatred of these powers, and the apparent opposition of their political ideals, seemed quite fierce enough to spark such an orgy of mutual annihilation. The fact that no such conflict did occur, and that the threat receded during the twenty-first century, reflects the growing realization by the people of both powers that their true interests as developed nations were very similar, and that their real enemy was poverty and disadvantage, both at home and abroad. The major nuclear incidents that did occur forced the two superpowers together rather than apart, although it might have been a different story had the "unthinkable" happened in their own countries, or in Europe.

16 June 2011: an atomic bomb was detonated in anger for the first time since 1945. A few seconds after the explosion, the Libyan city of Sabha was a radioactive wasteland and 78,000 people died.

By January 2001 thirty nations* claimed to possess nuclear weapons and the capability of delivering them. Opinions were frequently divided as to the latter part of each claim.

With that many nuclear weapons and that many fingers on the trigger, it was surely only a matter of time before a bomb went off. The fate of the world hung on the issue of where the explosion would take place, and who would cause it.

The first Arab-Israeli incident

No threat of nuclear action was made until 2007, when an ultimatum was issued by an alliance of Arab countries to Israel, demanding withdrawal of Israeli forces from several occupied territories by 1 May. If no such withdrawal took place, the alliance warned, there would be a nuclear attack on Tel Aviv. Thanks to strong diplomatic pressure from other nations, the threat was not carried out, even though the Israelis stood firm. When the situation again deteriorated, and diplomatic moves had once more failed to break the long-standing impasse, a second ultimatum was issued by the same allied nations in 2010. Diplomatic intervention by the superpowers, this time through the medium of a joint communiqué, again secured a cooling-off.

On 7 June 2011 the Israeli air force attacked installations in Saudi-Arabia, Egypt and Libya where, allegedly, nuclear missiles were being readied for launch. The attack used only conventional weapons. On 9 June the forces of six Arab nations began a massive invasion of three disputed territories. Within four days, after fierce fighting and heavy casualties on both sides, the Israelis were retreating on all fronts. Jerusalem fell on 13 June; on 15 June Tel Aviv was threatened from the south. On that day prime minister Solomon Thanesar declared that unless the invaders immediately withdrew he would order a nuclear strike against an unnamed target. At 4 a.m. on 16 June a 50-kiloton nuclear warhead was detonated 800 metres above the Libyan city of Sabha. The destruction was limited – less than a hundred thousand people died – but no one in the world

*The USA, the USSR, China, India, Pakistan, France, Germany, Britain, Spain, Italy, Australia, Canada, Libya, Egypt, Israel, Saudi-Arabia, Kuwait, the United Arab Emirates, Iraq, Turkey, Mexico, Brazil, Argentina, Chile, Indonesia, Bolivia, Zaire, Kenya, South Africa and New Zealand.

Computerised infantryman, year 2000. Soldiers were personally equipped with highly complex weaponry. The nerve centre was the helmet. It included an infra-red nightsight, head-up aiming display and battle computer for tactical information. The backpack included a launcher for two fire-and-forget homing missiles.

doubted the seriousness of the situation; it was the first nuclear attack in sixty-six years.

President Austen immediately warned that the USA would not tolerate reprisal against Israel, and the Politburo of the USSR issued a strong statement to the effect that further Israeli use of nuclear missiles would provoke "severe repercussions". The two superpowers instructed the UN security council to order all fighting in Israel to cease. There was no clear declaration by either nation of what would happen if their instructions were defied, but their resolve was not tested. In the negotiations to draw up acceptable boundaries for the state of Israel which followed, however, it was noticeable that both the USA and the USSR took an active role, arguing that when the adherence of nations or peoples to the principle of self-determination led them to use nuclear weapons, that principle had to be set aside in favour of enforced arbitration.

Nuclear sabotage in Zaire

The second nuclear incident of the twenty-first century involved the detonation of a nuclear device in Zaire on 24 December 2020, in the region north of the Congo river. The warhead exploded in its own silo, but this was clearly an act of sabotage rather than a freak accident. It never became clear who the saboteurs were nor how they carried out their mission. No evidence remained, encouraging the belief that it was a domestic matter. Only seven thousand people were killed by the 80-kiloton blast itself, but nuclear fall-out contaminated a wide region from Gabon to Kenya, and many more deaths followed in the next few months.

The so-called Christmas explosion lent force to a United Nations campaign for the setting up of an international corps whose task would be to place observers in all establishments where nuclear weapons were kept, everywhere in the world. The USA and the USSR, initially hostile, eventually offered to supply personnel to carry out such a role in all nations except their own, but no such corps was ever actually formed. The USA/USSR nuclear policing talks can, however, be identified as the birthplace of the accord by which the two nations appointed themselves joint custodians of world nuclear peace.

The second Arab-Israeli incident

On 4 April 2037 Israel again attacked her Arab neighbours with nuclear weapons, this time without warning, a pre-emptive strike in response to the perceived threat of further invasion. This time Benghazi, Riyadh and Aleppo were all hit, and the loss of life was enormous. The response of the Arab nations seemed likely to be uncontainable, leading to all-out nuclear war, but the two superpowers issued an undertaking to the UN that they would supervise not only the nuclear disarmament of all the Middle Eastern nations, but also draw up definitive borders for the state of Israel. Presidents Konrad and Kamenov agreed that their "solution" to the territorial problems would be arbitrary but that the matter must be ended. Deliberately ignoring the representations of all the contending parties, Konrad and Kamenov drew up their proposals and presented them to the United Nations as something not open to negotiation. Israel and her neighbours objected strenuously – perhaps for the first time finding something on which they could agree – but the settlement was imposed. It cannot be said that resentments died away quickly; strife continued for more than a century and a half, but the control exercised by the superpowers was eventually extended to conventional weaponry too. Large-scale conventional war could be as locally destructive as a nuclear exchange – compare the 1940s firestorms at Hiroshima and at Dresden. More than a century after, the same controls were finally applied to the technology of both forms of holocaust.

For many years it seemed that the "declaration of the two Presidents", otherwise known as the "2K Command", had established a pattern that would secure world-wide nuclear peace. Although relationships between the USA and the USSR continued to fluctuate, the two nations seemed inextricably bound together in preventing other nations from imperilling the world. It was inevitable, though, that while the extent of their resolve remained untested, there *had* to be at least one more nuclear exchange.

Desperation in Brazil

The interference of the more powerful nations in the affairs of the smaller ones, overtly as well as covertly, continued to increase throughout the twenty-first century. The growing awareness of the ecological crisis made it obvious – even in 2001 – that what nations did within their own boundaries was a legitimate concern of other nations. It was evident that some countries were "exporting" their industrial pollution via the prevailing winds, and that for example the USSR's plan to divert the flow of some of its rivers could have climactic consequences for the whole northern hemisphere.

The nation which suffered most from the efforts of the world community to govern its ecology was Brazil, custodian of the forest. As anxiety about rising levels of carbon dioxide in the atmosphere increased, so did concern about the Brazilians' destruction of the Amazon rain forest, for the simple reason that the forest was an enormous biomass and a vast exchange-system, taking carbon dioxide out of the atmosphere and releasing oxygen into it.

Brazil was one of the largest nations in the world and thus faced exceptional difficulties in adapting to the communications revolution. To bring together the scattered Brazilian population into the kind of information network that had already grown up in the developed countries would have been very difficult in any case. The limitations placed on the ecological development of the country compounded these problems. In terms of its natural resources Brazil was very rich, but its dominance in South America was lost early in the twenty-first century when its neighbours – particularly Argentina – began to benefit far more from the agrarian revolution stimulated by the genetic engineers, and from the communications revolution. While the Argentinian pampas was being turned into a vast granary, the Brazilian wilderness was protected by outsiders.

Brazil's attempts to remain a key force in South American politics became increasingly desperate. In exchange for conceding control of their country's development (or lack of it) to outsiders, successive Brazilian governments attempted to obtain trade concessions which their neighbours were increasingly unwilling to allow. As Brazil came to seem more and more like a backwater in a world that was beginning to get on top of its problems, her neighbours began to resent her demands for special treatment. So she remained obstinately locked into a pattern of economic decline and political instability.

By 2060 Argentina was clearly in control of the economic development of the South American sub-continent. Backed by the USA and other major powers, the Argentines eagerly took the leading role in "bringing South America into the twenty-first century". The Brazilians, feeling themselves the victims of a conspiracy of nations, elected increasingly radical and militant governments whose relations with the rest of the world deteriorated rapidly. In April 2078 the Brazilian President Jerome finally brought his country to the brink of confrontation when he authorized an Amazon Basin Development Scheme in direct contradiction of United Nations resolutions. Argentina was eventually persuaded to accept responsibility for exercising control over her neighbour, and it was Argentine troops who moved in, in December 2078, to stop the symbolic opening of the Development Scheme in Itaituba. Jerome, with public support at an almost hysterical level, announced within five days that bombers would attack Buenos Aires if the troops were not withdrawn.

The evidence now suggests that this ultimatum was a bluff – that Jerome hoped thereby to secure special attention from the superpowers, and to negotiate new and advantageous trade arrangements. But the USA and the USSR, not wishing to be used in this way, took a firm line with Jerome, and public sentiment in Brazil was thus confirmed in the belief that the whole world was against them. When Jerome despatched his air force, including several nuclear-armed bombers, he was probably still hoping to force swift action from the superpowers rather than attempting to destroy Argentina. His own troops did not see matters that way, however, and nor did the Argentines. They sent their planes to stop the Brazilian fleet.

Buenos Aires destroyed

The two air fleets clashed over Uruguay, and once the battle began events moved too quickly for any effective control. Jerome, in the end, did try to call off his bombers, but it was too late. Two planes reached Buenos Aires and dropped their bombs. The explosions, totalling forty megatons, destroyed the city and rendered the countryside inhabitable for many miles around. Fall-out later carried death and destruction of the land into Uruguay and Chile as well as other regions of Argentina. Radioactive rain was eventually to fall in New Zealand, Australia and South Africa. Estimates of the number of deaths due to the Jerome strike can only be approximate, but they probably approached forty million.

President Jerome, having overplayed his hand disastrously, was dead by 4 January 2079, less than forty-eight hours after the bombs fell. American forces established a temporary government in Rio de Janeiro on 12 January, and President Percival quickly invited the USSR to send units of the Red Army to help in the pacification. Emergency aid for victims of the catastrophe was recruited from all nations south of the Tropic of Capricorn. All nuclear weapons on the subcontinent were seized by the two superpowers and removed and no one attempted to prevent them from so doing. Brazil ceased to exist as a nation, her territory being divided into four administrative zones, each one controlled by UN managers for a period of ten years until they could be handed back to representatives of their own people.

This stern resolve was strengthened by climatological observations which tended to confirm the possibility of the long-dreaded "nuclear winter". Previous nuclear incidents of that century had been "insignificant" despite all their horror. Even counting Buenos Aires, the total megatonnage of nuclear weapons used in anger throughout the twenty-first century was less than some *individual* atmospheric tests of the Cold War. But directed against a great city and its surrounds, the 40-megaton blasts led to firestorms, erupting smoke and dust – which not only coloured the world's sunsets for months afterward but did indeed screen off sunlight to produce tiny yet measurable effects of chill and gloom. The threshold of eco-disaster had not, it seemed, been so very far away. After nearly a century of debate and retreat, the remaining "survivalists" were forced to concede that nuclear winter and its potential extinction of humanity were not "just theories". The final confirming data had been gathered, at a hideous cost.

It took more than thirty years to clear up the peripheral damage caused by the Buenos Aires explosions; the area around the city itself remained unsettled for more than a century. Not until the middle of the twenty-fifth century, by which time a fairly substantial local population had re-established itself, was the city rebuilt and given back its old name. By that time the rebuilding was symbolic of the certainty that there never would be another nuclear incident. Indeed, after 2079 no nuclear device was ever again detonated in an act of war.

CHAPTER THREE

THE END OF THE ARMS RACE

The arms race was a legacy of the twentieth century which went hand in hand with twentieth-century "doublethink". Both the USA and the USSR entered the twenty-first century with a massive commitment to the unthinkable – to the major nuclear war which had been fended off for 55 years, rather than to the conventional wars still sprouting everywhere like weeds. The dividing line between a supposedly acceptable conventional war and an escalating nuclear spasm had become very nearly sacred; had in fact acquired the status of a taboo on thought as well as action. Politicians found it useful to exploit the superstition in bravura displays of brinkmanship – President Kennedy with the 1962 Cuban missile crisis, Premier Vershinin with the Iranian confrontation of 1997, and so on – relying on the "unthinkable" status of nuclear war to provide a safety-net.

So far the situation they created makes reasonable sense. The peculiarity of the first century of nuclear weapons was that, even while depending ultimately on the magic conventional/nuclear borderline as a barrier no one would dare cross, the politicians and strategists of the time eagerly supported weapons research that would lead to the blurring and erosion of this distinction.

For example, there was much talk about tactical as opposed to strategic nuclear use. The theory was that a nuclear strike against, say, a conventional army in the field could be defined as a tactical attack which need not necessarily lead to full-scale nuclear exchange. "In the field" here implied Europe, since World War III was then expected to start with large-scale conventional war there – partly because of the NATO/Warsaw Pact borders, and partly thanks to a semi-rational sense of historical inevitability. The notion of slugging it out in Europe was attractive at first sight to the USA and the USSR; and through the last quarter of the twentieth century and some years into the twenty-first, everyone in Europe felt the point of the German black joke that a tactical nuclear weapon was one that landed on Germany.

Tactical nuclear weapons

What were the tactical weapons which seemed likely to have such an irresponsibly destabilizing effect? Some were much the same as the big strategic weapons, the difference having a sort of theological subtlety – a matter of intention rather than construction – it depended where the weapon was aimed. Some were smaller versions of the big bombs, a few kilotons' explosive yield aimed to knock out a crucial unit, an armoured column, a communications centre, rather than whole armies or whole cities. Very tiny nuclear yields were possible even then, down to just a few equivalent tons of TNT (although at this lowest level the effective cost per unit energy release was prohibitive and futile). The infamous neutron bomb, or reduced-blast/enhanced-radiation weapon, was actually deployed as a tactical weapon by the USA, the USSR, Britain, France, Israel and some other countries. In spite of the popular folklore of the time, it was still not possible to do more than *boost* the neutron radiation output of a small but powerful nuclear weapon. The n-bomb remained an atomic bomb with all the usual flash, blast and fall-out – but the boosted radiation increased the lethal radius of the weapon.

In the "micro-nuke" area, some American work was even done on the possibility of a bullet-sized warhead using the highly fissionable element californium. Since californium could then only be produced in tiny amounts through nuclear transmutation at a cost of millions of dollars per gram, and since it was not even prepared in metallic form until the end of the twentieth century, the strange urge to blur the line marking the nuclear threshold was quite evident.

Massive "conventional" warheads

More than one nation (for example, Sweden with its "No Nuclear Weapons" policy) chose to creep up on the nuclear threshold from the opposite direction, with fuel-air-explosive (FAE) warheads. These large conventional devices relied on the release of volatile fuel which mingled with a relatively large volume of air to give the effect of an explosive charge many metres across. The blastwave from this huge "virtual warhead" was comparable to that from micro-nukes: FAE offered a strictly conventional and therefore non-escalatory weapon whose explosion could, in the event, be quite easily mistaken for a nuclear one. Air-to-ground missiles with massive FAE warheads were indeed used during the first Israeli assault in the ten-day war of 2011: the result was that half the nuclear-armed world went into red alert. Several commentators argued at the time that this nuclear mobilization helped stiffen Thanesar's resolve to threaten an Israeli nuclear strike. Others held that the real lesson was a truism: the world dare not let any nuclear-owning nation be threatened with extinction even by conventional means, since every such nation was positioned to throw the switches for the long-delayed World War III. The idea that large-scale conventional war could win major victories died with the traumatic shock of the 2011 fireball over Libya.

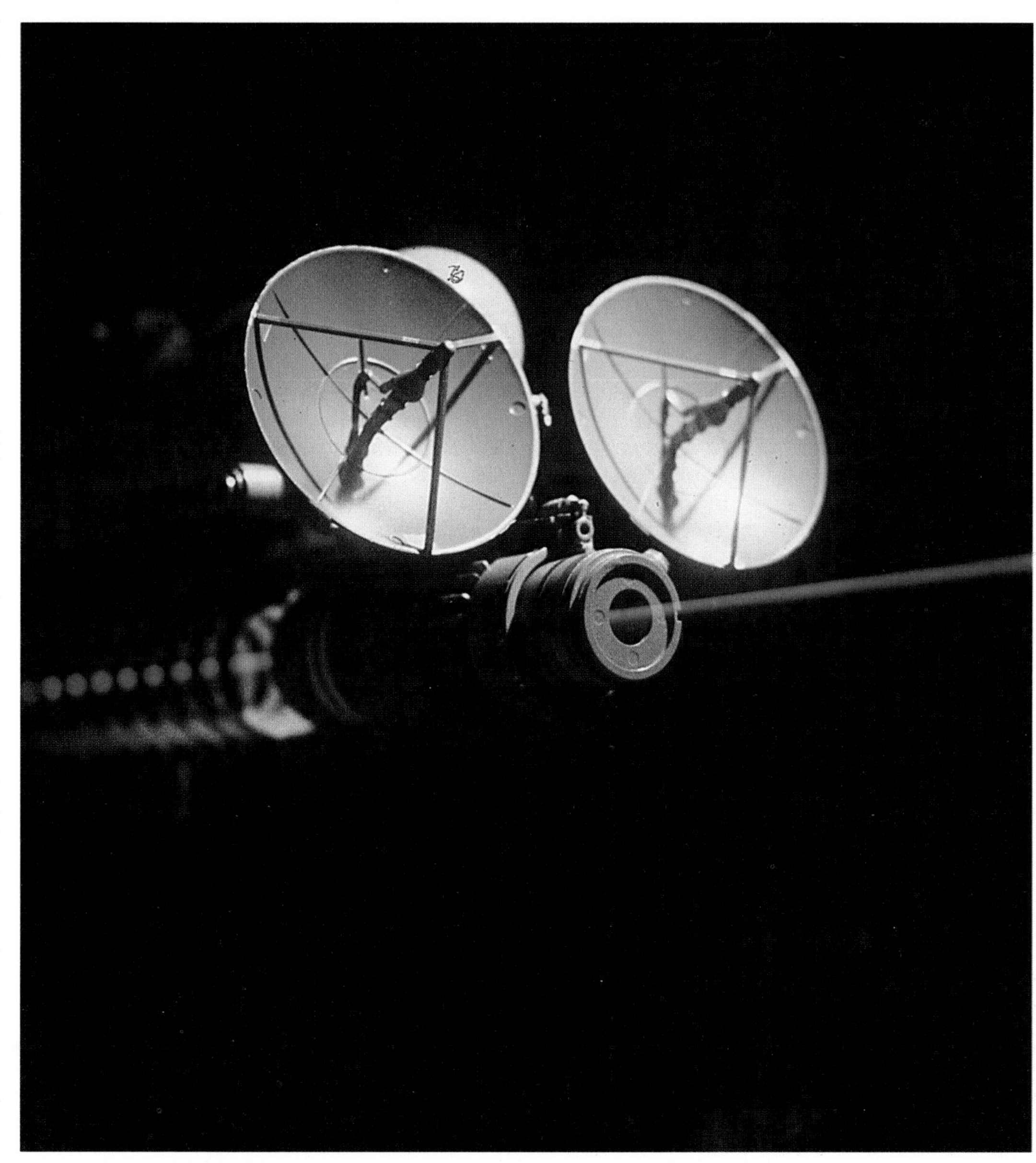

Satellite warfare

Doublethink was visible again in the superpowers' enthusiasm for extending the battlefield into near space. American and Russian delegates said concerned things to each other over conference tables, proposing various ineffectual curbs on the growing nuclear stockpiles – these Strategic Arms Limitation Talks (SALT) went on in desultory fashion throughout the century. Meanwhile, back at home, their scientists were working on advanced charged-particle, neutral-particle and laser weapons intended to counter an "inter-continental ballistic missile" (ICBM) strike: at the high point of ICBM's trajectories, the satellite-mounted energy weapons would destroy or incapacitate them. These weapons, which at the time were more science-fictional than practical, merely accelerated the arms race.

In the first place, there was already a standard strategic answer to any defence of less than 100 per cent efficiency: simply increase the scale of the attack until the requisite number of ICBMs can be expected to slip through the barrier. None of the Starwars, Sipapu or Molnya (Russian for "lightning") energy weapon systems approached 100 per cent efficiency (indeed they were a good deal less reliable than advertised, and so provoked excessive counter-measures). ICBM manufacture took a steep upward turn to take advantage of the loophole. In the second place, these new systems meant proliferation at a new level – weaponry for intersatellite warfare beyond the atmosphere. "Warsat"

Laser space weapons were standard issue to US and Soviet forces by 2001. This model was nuclear-powered, and could destroy virtually anything in its line-of-sight. Reflector armour and chameleon shields, introduced in the 2020s, severely reduced laser effectiveness.

and "Killsat" deployment would have been expensive enough if the only cost were in making the laser-armed or explosive satellites; far more energy and thus much more money went into boosting them into orbit via shuttle craft.

The culmination of this came in 2009 when US President Foxx announced the Cataract system, a network of orbiting nuclear mines with enhanced radiation output, whose simultaneous detonation would in theory blind every satellite eye for long enough to provide a launch window for America's ICBM strike. Within three weeks Premier Azov reported a very similar Soviet system; a speech from Chairman Chen implied that China had anticipated both the USA and the USSR; and so on. History does not record whether all three claims were true; certainly there was by then an incredible amount of hardware in orbit, and such accidents as the Argentine-USSR satellite collision of 2018 were perhaps inevitable.

Economic warfare

What was, of course, happening beneath the technological glitter was the translation of the arms race still further into economic war. It is quite certain from disks released in the latter twenty-first century that the USA at least was aware of and encouraged this (Pentagon Database 1998:20563 *et seq.*), secure in the belief in its own limitless resources. Ironically, the USSR appears to have had a similar confidence, though founded more on historical imperatives, and to have played much the same game. The weapons need never be fired. The opposition need only be made to bleed itself dry keeping up with the latest fashion in weapons technology. The victims eagerly co-operate in their own destruction, since no government ever truly believes in its possible economic collapse (more money can always be printed, after all), while it was all too easy to notice and react to the existence of a brand-new gun in the hands of a perceived enemy – even if the gun didn't shoot very well, as was widely theorized when it came to the satellite weapons.

The hidden fallacy which doublethink helped conceal was, in fact, the same as the fallacy of believing that a war could safely be won by conventional means. Whether brought to its knees by tanks and rifles, or by an economic assault, a nuclear power would in its last extremity be liable to fire the forbidden weapons and perhaps ignite a holocaust. In a world of thirty-odd nuclear-armed powers, it was simply no longer feasible to snuff out a nation by any decisive victory, no matter what the means. As had long been implicit in the international financial structure, the only hope for the world as a whole lay in co-operation.

The turning point

This not very staggering insight took a long time to become embodied in any national policy. The turning point of the arms race was less a matter of idealism than of economic necessity. With hindsight we can trace the factors: the enormous maintenance cost of both ICBMs and orbital weapons; the gradual world recession which led to a series of economies in energy use; the decline of living standards in the superpowers; swelling internal resentment of massive, expensive and unused weapon systems; the need to divert funds on an emergency basis due to the ravages of the "Plague Wars"; the availability of a cheap substitute for the dinosaur missiles inherited from the last century.

Some popular histories give most weight to public outrage following a handful of disastrous incidents. The 2108 satellite collision led to a spectacular burn-up of the hardware and the resultant sprinkling of oxidized plutonium dust over parts of western Canada. A "failed" test in 2023 of the Pakistani Pillar of Flame, a laser ground-to-air weapon, disabled and brought down an Australian passenger plane with considerable incidental damage to a suburb of Karachi. Brazil's work on the railgun, a hybrid energy/projectile weapon based on the linear accelerator and intended as an ICBM defence, created a much greater furore in 2052 when a projectile mysteriously "leapfrogged" from the test zone and punched a neat hole through four Japanese tourists several miles off. And of course the nuclear incidents of 2011 and 2020 had their effect; the change in arms-race emphasis was largely complete by the last nuclear use in 2079. However, long-term considerations rather than individual disasters were the true shapers of the arms race as the twenty-first century wore on.

Cruise: a paradoxical stabilizing force

Slowly the massive ICBMs and the ruinous orbital systems gave way to the relatively cheap weapon which had caused such alarm on its mooting in the previous century: the mass-produced cruise missile. Widely opposed as an addition to the existing arsenals, cruise missiles proved more acceptable as a substitute. By the 2050s, a microcomputer technology had progressed to the point at which inertially-guided cruise missiles with their high-resolution satellite-produced terrain maps and built-in evasion tactics were almost unstoppable – especially

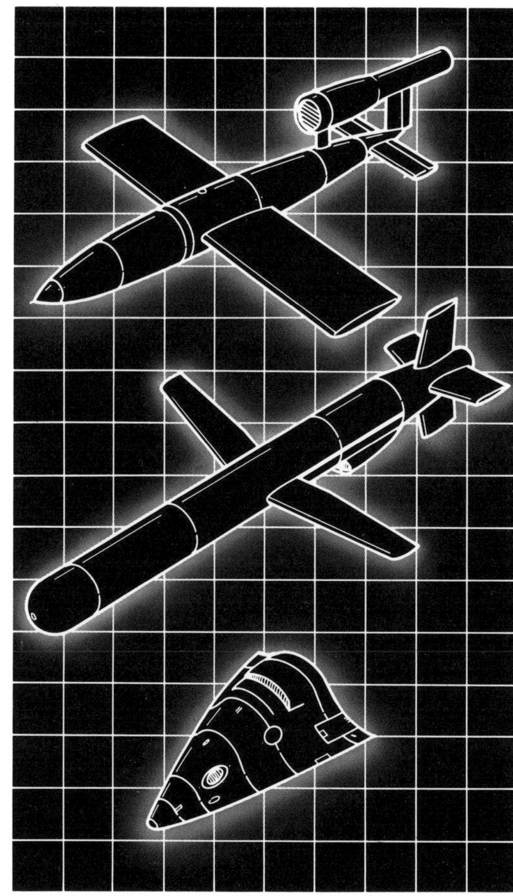

Cruise missiles had a long history, dating back to the 1940s, when Germany used its V-1 (top) against Great Britain. Developments in the 1980s included the folding-wing model (centre). Mini-cruise weapons (bottom) of the twenty-first century were small, radar-proofed and guided by highly intelligent onboard computer systems. They were virtually unstoppable, and cheap to manufacture. Mass-production brought the price of a mini-cruise close to that of a luxury groundcar of the period.

when launched in sufficient numbers. "Why spend a billion? Two weeks' output from a converted assembly-line in Detroit, and we've got ourselves a new first strike," said President Disch in his famous 2057 speech.

Cheapness also allowed a new tactic of relatively few nuclear- or FAE-armed cruise missiles in an assault wave: vast hordes of the devices could be dummies, overloading most economically feasible defence systems. By the latter part of the twenty-first century these missiles had emerged as a kind of stabilizing force: being almost invisible from the air, infinitely mobile and deployable anywhere, they provided an offensive system which could not be taken out by any plausible pre-emptive strike.

The orbital energy weapons had really been ahead of their time – too expensive to maintain in the long run from Earth, they demanded the as yet unbuilt O'Neill space-colony communities for their support. Now, in the late twenty-first century, thanks to the prevalence of cruise missiles which flew from launch-pad to target under the miles-thick protection of Earth's atmosphere, the energy weapons were useless. They had been designed to disable ICBMs emerging from the atmosphere before plunging downward again to their targets; to strike at them through vacuum. It was one of the ironies of history that, by the time the orbital weapons could be most effectively deployed and maintained, they had become irrelevant. Even Jacob's Ladder, the grandiose and extravagantly energy-consuming US weapon whose particle beam was designed to depopulate entire cities from orbital range, only represented a high-tech means of doing no more than a few nuclear-tipped cruise missiles could achieve.

Spy satellites: further stabilization

This is not to say that near space was irrelevant. The new generation of computers provided a hitherto undreamed-of power of analysis as the holistic, pattern-oriented hardware and software of the "fifth generation" found its way into spy satellites. Car numberplates, large or even medium-sized print, human faces, all could be recognized and tracked by a few pounds of the latest electronic gadgetry several hundred kilometres up. Like the cruise missile, this development was deplored – an invasion of privacy, an abomination. Like the cruise missile, it helped put an end to the escalating arms race.

Again, popular histories tend to stress gaudy incidents – here the much-disputed Mali "desertification" affair which came to light in the mid-2060s. That the Mali government's spraying of central lakes and swamps with hydrocarbons had the effect of reducing evaporation and hence rainfall in portions of the country bordering the Sahara, and that the results together with precise details of the actual spraying were uncovered by satellite analysis, are facts which are not disputed. The controversy involved the theory that some attempt was being made to wage an internal climatological war on the Tuareg and other independent-minded Berber nomads living in these regions, rather than to deal with the reported mosquito vector of a neo-malaria outbreak.

Climatological war, whether by curbing evaporation or by seeding clouds to make them dump their moisture prematurely, was rumoured several times in this century: even where the weather-tampering was done with aggressive intent, it never seems to have been particularly effective. The Mali affair merely

"Directed Lightning", or DELIGHT, was an early US directed-energy weapon. It never succeeded in becoming a reliable system, but spectacular tests like this showed the possibilities – both as a strike weapon and for weather modification.

made it clear that weather modification, along with a great number of less obtrusive activities, could no longer be done in secret.

SALT XVIII

The obvious targets for satellite spies to spot were ICBM silos, ABM installations, energy-beam projectors, arms stockpiles, and the other heavyweight items of mass destruction which could not – like cruise missiles – economically be kept on the move. In 2080 came the historic SALT XVIII meeting in which President Feester, Premier Smirnov and Chairwoman Lin agreed that, for all practical purposes, the Great Powers had no real arms secrets left. The eyes in the sky saw too much. This did not lead to immediate disarmament moves, nor to any rapid agreement on mutual inspection of arms stockpiles; old habits died hard, but the first steps had been taken. What none of the three leaders would admit, even to themselves, was that economic decline had made them almost desperate to slash their defence spending – to put the 135-year-old arms race into reverse. The reasons were neither lofty nor noble; human reasons rarely are.

The deepening economic winter of the mid- to late twenty-first century led to the finding of politically acceptable rationalizations of the downturn in arms production. The USA and the USSR had already been forced, somewhat unwillingly, into a position of co-operation as global policemen; now the links were increasing in number. Without being enough to satisfy the least demanding of utopian idealists, the realignment of US/USSR relations by 2100 would have horrified any twentieth-century politician from either country. Still, there was a long way to go.

CHAPTER FOUR

WHERE EAST AND WEST DO MEET

"No Nukes By 2100" was the slogan of the times – over-optimistic as ever. By that date the USA and the USSR, acting in concert if not often in open collaboration, had stripped many smaller countries of their most destructive hardware. Any opposition was firmly set aside with the United Nations Security Council rubber-stamping their actions in the name of the world community. The larger powers kept their missiles, but no longer regarded them as virility symbols. The logic of the "effective minimum", popularized in 2064 by President Pilkington during one of the US government's periodic cost-cutting purges, became dominant as more and more funds were diverted to combat disasters induced by climatological change.

The production of small arms did not decline markedly, and standing armies actually grew. Again, the problems of coping with emergencies were partly responsible. Troops had to be called in continually to supervise rescue operations and organize the relocation of populations displaced by the flooding of low-lying areas. The role of armies in the more peaceful nations changed rapidly as their utility in peacetime was further explored and exploited. In less peaceful nations – which were, of course, in the majority – armies and police forces were essential to control domestic conflicts. As the USA and the USSR slowly abandoned their longstanding confrontation and moved toward more active co-operation, the small wars in the Third World lost their gloss of world-political significance, but this did not help to end them. Conflicts in Africa and Central America that had been raging for more than a century were no longer seen as splinters of a world-wide duel between capitalism and communism, but although this inhibited the supply of sophisticated arms it certainly did not stop them fighting.

Co-operation between the superpowers

After the first significant joint action by Konrad and Kamenov in 2037, successive presidents and premiers accepted the role of nuclear policemen, but remained reluctant to interfere in the domestic disputes of other nations. They ceased to feed such conflicts with new weaponry, but were never able to apply rigorous arms starvation. However, most of the Western nations – in part responding to stern criticism from the East – gradually outlawed and hounded into extinction the entrepreneurial arms dealers they had formerly sheltered.

"Take Your Place In The World" ran the slogan beneath this late-twenty-first-century advertising photograph. The antenna in the outback proclaimed the availability of the electronic datanet to all.

Historic missile launch in 2050: the USA and USSR fired off the last of their huge ICBM stocks from the previous century in an attempt to promote their new cooperative stance as global policemen. They were not wholly successful and they retained numerous more modern nuclear weapons, but this museum-piece missile worked perfectly and splashed down in the South Pacific, its dummy warhead sinking beneath the waves.

The drying-up of the international flow of arms probably did reduce bloodshed, although most of the ragged armies of insurrectionists would have been willing to continue with bows and arrows if need be. A more important effect was that this arms limitation helped to clarify just what all the fighting was about. Without the dogmatic ideologies, it became obvious that the wars were between those who controlled and benefitted from the wealth of nations and those who were disinherited from that wealth. Put crudely, the poor of each nation were trying resentfully to dispossess – or at least take revenge upon – the rich.

The co-operation of the superpowers in international peacekeeping was largely a reflection of their growing common economic interests. The economic fortunes of the USA and the USSR, and of their allies, became much more closely interwoven as the twenty-first century progressed. Their economic systems came to seem far more similar than contrasting political ideologies had represented them to be.

The decline of Marxism

The distinction between capitalism and communism gradually lost its significance because the imperatives of world technology eroded the contrasts. The Marxism adopted by the communist states had initially been an analysis of the political economy of capitalism, purporting to expose its iniquities and explain the inevitability of its downfall. It had been adopted, though, not as a theory but as a godless religion – a faith carrying all the usual resentment of rival faiths and internal heresies. It can be regarded as the last of the great religions that had been such an important force for social change during the first and second millennia. The other great religions were already in decline, and Marxism too became quickly senescent.

Like the followers of other faiths, Marxists found it difficult to put their dogmas into practice. Like the Christians of Western Europe a thousand years earlier they found it impossible to reap the benefits which they had assumed must flow from obedience to their principles. Like the Christians, they found all manner of excuses for their failure, and for a while persevered ever more fiercely, becoming zealots and witch-hunters. They continued their protestations of faith while covertly making pragmatic compromises. Insofar as capitalism became a faith in the same way, it underwent a parallel process.

It became obvious as the century progressed that the continued health of the capitalist nations made nonsense of Marx's promises of inevitable ruin and revolution. Despite the iniquities of the system, it was flexible enough to adapt to changing circumstances. In order to compete in the ever-more-important business of international trade – whose benefits the communist nations had to reap if they were to maintain the standard of living of their own citizens – the USSR and its satellites had to build individual incentives back into their own system. They had to accept the unpalatable truth that the only way to mobilize the labour of their people effectively was to reward it. The effect of banishing incentives from the "official" economy had merely been to create a vast "black economy" where corruption reigned supreme. The Chinese, more given to routine sophistry and traditional hypocrisy than the Russians, showed the way to the other communist nations.

The end of entrepreneurial capitalism

In the West, this painful ideological retreat was recognized for what it was, and was simultaneously mocked and applauded in a self-satisfied fashion. In the meantime, though, the western political economy was also being transformed. The old-style entrepreneurial capitalism died with the piecemeal technology that suited it, and the twenty-first century saw the extension of a trend begun long before. As the technology of the industrialized countries became more complicated, and basic manufacturing processes were subject to more sophisticated divisions of labour and mechanization, centralized planning became steadily more necessary. Even if governments reacted in horror to the idea of nationalizing all their land, they were forced to exercise more control over the owners. Companies and corporations grew steadily bigger so that particular economic ventures could be cushioned against short-term volatility of demand.

By the middle of the twenty-first century the leading fifty multinational corporations were bigger and richer than most small nations. Sometimes, indeed, the corporations effectively *were* the small nations; to buy up some weak and corruptible country was almost commonplace. An amusing example came when two multinationals each set out to "acquire" El Salvador in 2087 – and both succeeded, the embarrassing joint commitment leading to an unexpected, forced merger and the formation of World Data Systems Inc.

Planned economies everywhere

Multinationals had their own economic interests to protect and they had the power to do it – if they acted in concert they could dictate to at least half the governments on Earth, and exert strong pressure on the rest. Like all great cartels they had no interest in the cut-throat competition supposedly built into the capitalist system; their real interests were protecting their markets, maintaining stability and avoiding taxes. Governments waged war against them mainly because of the last item; when it came to order and stability there was no conflict of interest. Thus, in the capitalist as in the communist world economic power was gradually centralized, and national economies were planned instead of being left to the manipulation of Adam Smith's "invisible hand". Ownership – whether of land, businesses, machinery, mineral rights or buildings – gradually passed from individuals to organizations. In short, it was collectivized, and although the process was not the revolutionary expropriation recommended by Marx, its effects were in many respects similar.

By the early twenty-second century the economy of the whole world was essentially a planned economy. The planning was not just national but international, thanks to the growing power of UN agencies and multinational corporations. In fact there were many planners with many plans, more often in conflict than in harmony: too many cooks, with limited objectives and inappropriate means, were busy spoiling the world's broth. The world economy, during this period of crisis, was very *badly* planned, but the fact that it was planned at all is more important.

Technologies promote internationalism

The new technologies on which the twenty-first-century world came so heavily to depend encouraged the growth and consolidation of the international community. New communications technology dissolved distance by linking individuals electronically. Telephone networks linked to visual display units for the first time permitted people on opposite sides of the planet to meet face to face. Communications satellites and extensive cabling networks allowed the mass media to transcend national boundaries, encouraging people everywhere to become fluent in several languages. Biotechnology, so important in meeting the ecological crises of the century, forced people to think in terms of a whole-world ecosystem. Mechanical technology had put such destructive power into people's hands – pollutant industries as well as weapons – that particular nations' projects became the business of their neighbours. All this forced planning to be elevated from the national to the international level, and if the sprawling organization of UN committees and executive bodies had not already existed (initially in a virtually impotent form) it would have been necessary to invent them.

Although the nations of the world were becoming more similar, they fought against becoming identical. Diversity was eroded by the "cultural colonization" of the poorer nations by the richer ones, but people clung hard to their notions of cultural identity at a national or sub-national level. American styles, American ideas and the American version of the English language spread through the world because America was rich enough, and interested enough, to out-broadcast every other voice of the world's mass media. At the same time, though, America's own attempts to achieve cultural homogeneity – the "American Dream" – faltered and failed. The flow of influence was two-way, and America remained as vulnerable as ever to the influx of foreign fashions and philosophies. Although English, in one of its forms, came to function as a universal language, virtually everyone retained a second language for parochial and intimate contexts. Even native English speakers retained specialized *argots* whose function was to differentiate small-scale subcultures.

The global mentality

These changes were reflected at an individual level. As their world altered, so people altered. Every man and woman in every era of history has had to wear public faces as well as private ones. Over thousands of years more people had had to develop more flexible and complicated public faces, but even at the end of the second millennium the majority of living humans could get by with a single public face geared to deal only with their local community. By the end of the twenty-first century, only a tiny minority still retained such narrow social horizons.

Every man had perforce to become a legion of men as he found himself drawn into a whole series of inclusive communities. A man remained a member of his own family, an inhabitant of his own town, and a citizen of his own nation, but he was also – in the proper sense of the phrase – a man of the world. The communications web of 2100 meant that, say, a poker player in England could sit in on a game whose other players were in Toronto, Thailand and Bangladesh: people from Third World countries became *neighbours* whose problems were real – no longer the remote, shadowy subjects of charitable appeals. The day of the common human enterprise had begun; the *Oikoumenê* was born at last.

Headquarters of General Products, a late addition to the ranks of the global corporations. The multinational companies of the twentieth century evolved naturally into the global corporations of the twenty-first. The difference was simple: multinationals treated the world as several different markets; globals marketed the same products world-wide with a single strategy. Many global corporations achieved annual turnovers exceeding the GDP of many countries. By the year 2000, IBM – for example – had annual sales exceeding the GDP of Australia and New Zealand combined. The globals' lack of popularity may explain why so many of them were located in remote places. The output of General Products included spacecraft hulls and personal walkers – multi-legged transport vehicles for rough terrain including the surface of the moon. One of these is visible in the foreground.

CHAPTER FIVE

THE PLAGUE WARS

No twenty-first-century government ever admitted using plague as a weapon of war. Perhaps none ever did. Certainly, with the spread of techniques of genetic engineering many governments sponsored research into the development of new viruses that could be used against an enemy. Certainly, too, the great epidemics of the twenty-first century were caused by such viruses. What remains uncertain is how those viruses were released. It may have been accidental; even if deliberate the people responsible may not have been acting on behalf of governments.

The whole essence of biological warfare is its insidious nature. A nation attacked by such weaponry could never be quite sure that it had been attacked, nor could the attacker be readily identified. Plague wars were a very peculiar kind of aggression, whose tactics were unique. Their history must therefore be incomplete and speculative; we can offer an account of the losers, but none of the winners, if, indeed, winners there were. We can record the consequences of such warfare, yet can say little about the aims and motives that lay behind it.

Epidemic in Southern Africa

The plague wars may have begun in the late months of 2007, when an epidemic broke out in Southern Africa. The virus belonged to the influenza group, but the symptoms were particularly severe. It began to cause serious problems in several regions, but the one most severely hit was the western part of Zimbabwe, and it was the prime minister of Zimbabwe, Eliah Sumere, who in a broadcast speech on 2 December publicly accused the government of South Africa of having deliberately created the virus and released it as an act of war.

South African scientists had already been called in to investigate the disease, which was spreading through South Africa itself, claiming a great many victims in the black homelands, especially Vendal and Bophuthatswana. They insisted that the disease was the product of a natural mutation, but Sumere's accusation was taken very seriously within South Africa. Whether or not the charge was true, it was believed. It soon became obvious that while black people were dying in thousands, the superior medical facilities available to white people gave them a much better chance of survival. Among the black peoples of the sub-continent it was soon taken for granted that Mr Poort's administration had taken a drastic step in the attempt to preserve its authority against the gathering revolution.

On 16 February 2007 the state-controlled media in Mozambique alleged that President Honwana's cabinet had come into possession of documents passed to their agents by a dissident South African journalist named Paul Leopold. These apparently proved the involvement of a group of medical researchers in South Africa in the planned release of a genetically-engineered virus. Leopold had been killed by unknown assassins three days before. Mr Poort's insistence that the documents were faked was never properly tested; the originals never surfaced and may never have existed, though "copies" were released to the world's press. But communications within Southern Africa, and between plague-affected areas and the rest of the world, were already being severely curtailed. The virus had already been carried to many other parts of the world, and governments everywhere were trying to contain it with strict quarantine regulations.

The end of old South Africa

If Sumere's accusations were true, then Poort's move backfired dramatically. Although the virus was rarely lethal to mature white men and women, it did incapacitate them for ten days or more. As the epidemic spread affecting police forces, the army and all channels of communication, there was an effective breakdown of the white social order which made it impossible to contain the bloody uprising of February and March. The technological superiority of the white forces counted for little when they could hardly find enough men to use the equipment. White rule in South Africa was ended by mid-March, and, with an exodus to other parts of the world ruled out by quarantine restrictions, the death-toll in the white population was tremendous.

The matter did not end with the fall of the government. South Africa's white medical scientists would have been in the best position, technically, to develop an effective immune serum and to organize opposition to the disease throughout the sub-continent. They were not, of course, given any chance. Within a year fifteen million people had died in South Africa, Zimbabwe and Mozambique. Immunization programmes were eventually mounted in the northern hemisphere and kept deaths there to a few hundred thousands, but wherever outbreaks occurred in poorer countries the response was inevitably less effective. At least eight million more people had died before the end of 2009, and the virus continued to claim victims sporadically for ten more years.

The Los Angeles virus

The fact that the Poort administration had no immune serum ready to protect their own

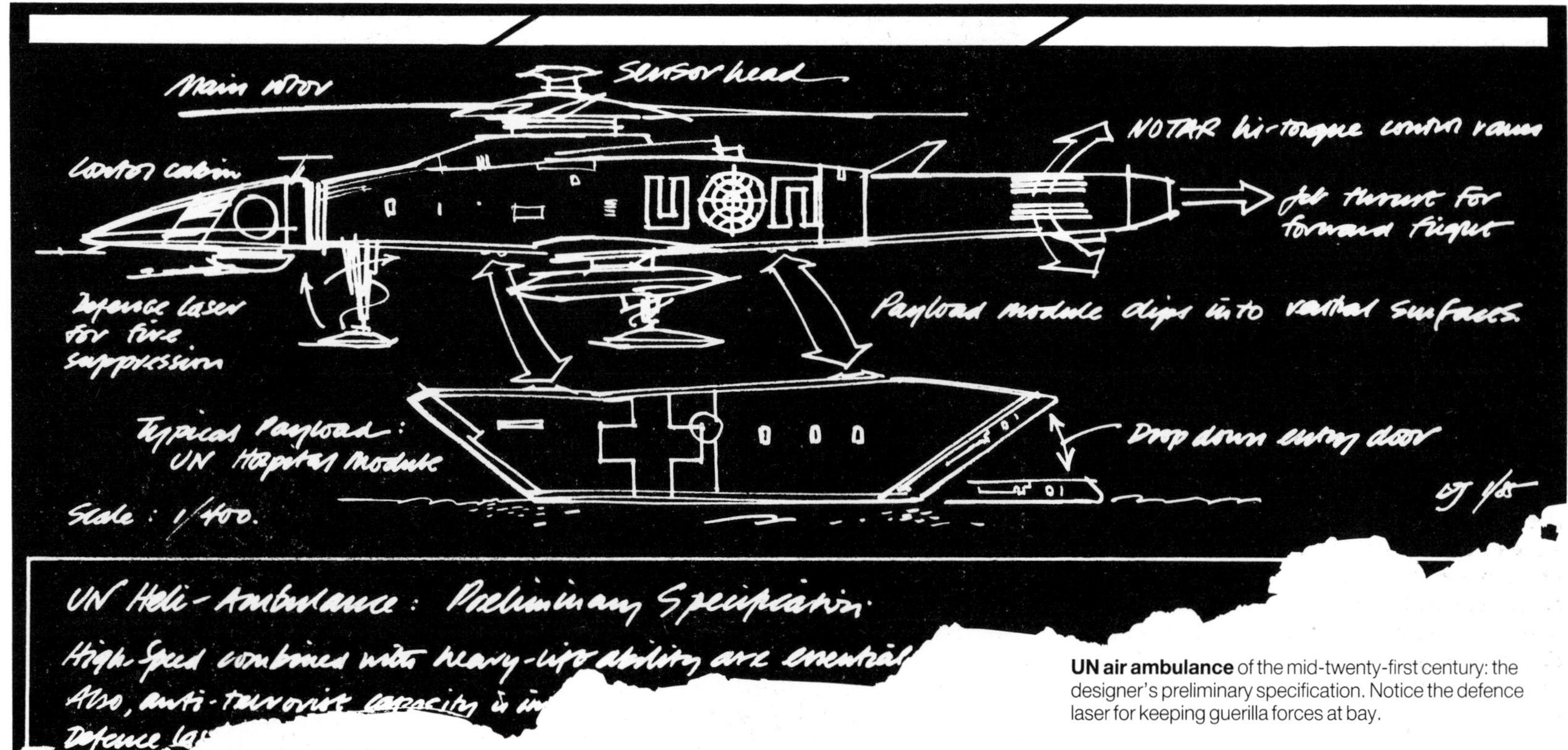

UN air ambulance of the mid-twenty-first century: the designer's preliminary specification. Notice the defence laser for keeping guerilla forces at bay.

armed forces probably indicates that the South African plague really was a naturally-mutated virus, or at least that its release was unplanned. There is less doubt, though, that the virus disease which broke out in eastern Los Angeles in 2015 was engineered, and that it was released with malicious intent. That claim was first made by the Governor of California, More Santana, on 11 June, and although President Newcombe never endorsed it, she never denied it either.

Again, the people hardest hit by the disease – a variety of virus pneumonia – were the poor and underprivileged, mostly immigrants from across the border. Like the South African blacks, the Mexicans in California became suspicious that the virus was a weapon launched specifically at them, possibly by Santana himself, as an adventurous method of "solving" the immigrant problem. Santana was of Mexican descent himself, although he was a Republican, and his outrage in the face of such rumours was probably genuine, but he did not know where to point his own accusing finger. Relations between the USA and the USSR were not at that time particularly good, but neither were they unusually strained. If an enemy nation *was* responsible, it was more likely to be one closer to hand, and their intention may have been just inquisitive. Many nations were certainly interested to see how the USA could cope with such an emergency.

In the event, the Americans dealt with it reasonably well. They had an immune serum ready within three weeks of identification of the virus. The race against time to inoculate some 230 million people against the disease was not won without effort, and casualty lists soared day by day but the USA had the manpower, machine-power and organizational framework to set such a project in hand and move rapidly to its completion. Even so, nearly a million American deaths were eventually credited to the plague.

The immunoserum was exported as quickly as it could be produced and, as far as other developed countries were concerned, forewarned proved to be forearmed. Although the spread of the disease was assisted by the world's airlines, no serious epidemics were suffered by other developed nations. It was a different story in poorer countries. In Mexico, where the virus had a head start, six million people died. In Central America outside Mexico a further four million perished, and millions more became victims in South America.

Although no one knew who had started the Los Angeles epidemic, and despite the fact that American medical scientists had collaborated with Russian medical scientists to ensure that the disease was kept at bay in the Eastern bloc, many observers turned their eyes towards Moscow in looking for the next mysterious outbreak. In the meantime, the ambassadors of many small countries went to the United Nations to demand that, if plague warfare had indeed begun, then it must be stopped, because it was warfare in which only the innocent suffered, and in which the great majority of the victims claimed would inevitably be citizens of uninvolved nations.

No head of state ever disagreed with the sentiments expressed on the floor of the UN Assembly. Presidents of the USA and leading members of the Russian Politburo were ever-ready to assure the world that they never had and never would engage in biological warfare of this kind. Nevertheless, major epidemics continued to afflict the world at almost regular intervals.

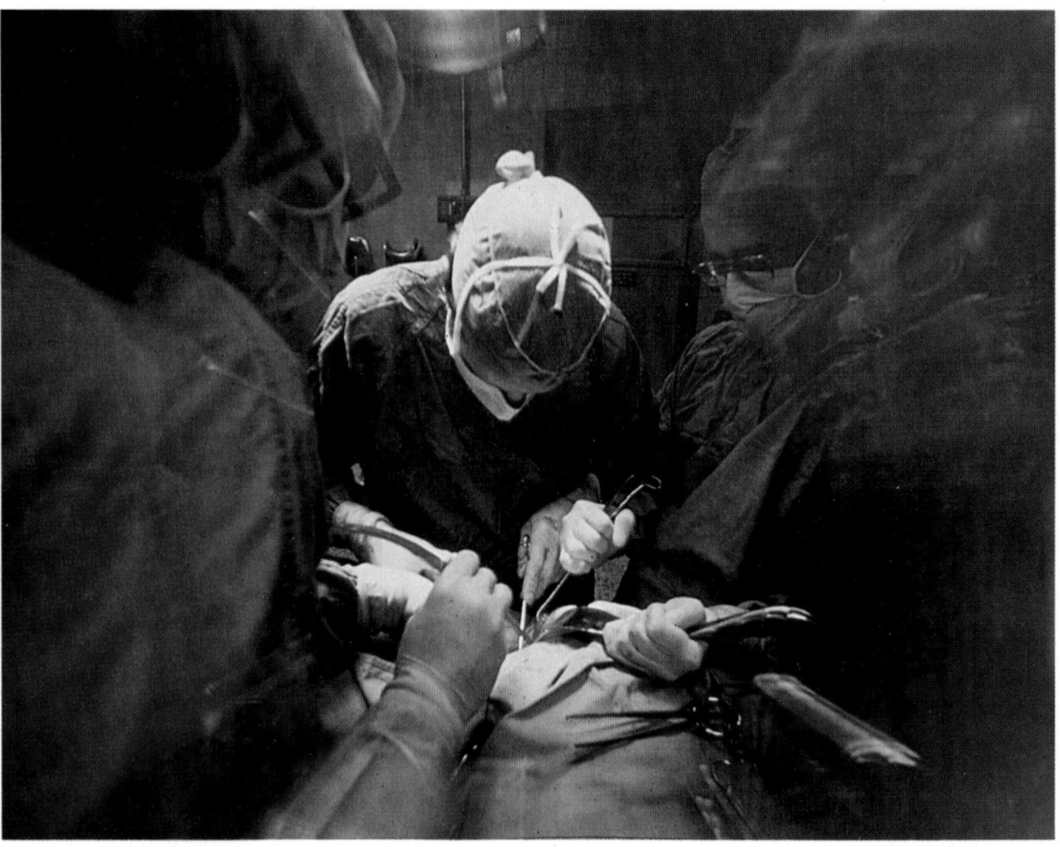

The triplet plague was the most vicious the USA encountered. Medical teams battled to contain the three killer viruses, two of which induced fast-growing tumours. Over 11 million died, yet the US medical defence was thought effective.

International co-operation against plague

The virus venereal disease first detected in Lublin, Poland in October 2024 had killed five million people by the end of 2027. The number of people sterilized cannot be properly estimated, but is likely to have been in excess of twenty million. The long incubation period of the disease made the task of stopping its spread inordinately difficult. No nation remained completely free of it, and immunization programmes had to be mounted on an unparallelled scale. The international co-operation involved, however, did begin the incredibly difficult task of organizing a world-wide apparatus that could respond to such challenges.

The immune-destructive virus first detected in Brussels in September 2032 was probably a new variety of a virus first identified half a century earlier, and may have been entirely natural. Nevertheless, the difficulty of identifying the disease allowed it to spread rapidly before effective action could be taken, even in Europe. Because death invariably had another proximal cause, it was difficult to keep an accurate record of the number of victims, but the probable figure is in the region of seven millions.

The virus nicknamed "lightning hepatitis", first identified in Wenzhou, China in February 2049, killed thirty-eight million people before the end of 2050. This appalling death-toll made subsequent accusations and recriminations particularly bitter, especially as so many of the victims were citizens of one nation. The Chinese, who were by that time achieving considerable success in controlling their population-growth, were almost certainly not responsible for starting the plague but the aggressor was never identified.

Effective defence in the USA

The "triplet plagues" which devastated many American cities in the spring of 2050 killed, between them, ten million people by December of that year. Most died of viral leukaemia. A further million were permanently disabled by a virus which selectively attacked nerve tissue, leaving victims in agony from limbs they could no longer control. The third virus, which induced cancers, was the first to be effectively countered. The three-pronged problem makes it overwhelmingly likely that this was a very carefully-mounted and malicious attack, but thanks to previous experience the USA's defences proved more effective than anyone had anticipated. American medical science had now progressed to the point where such diseases could be fought swiftly and surely, as if by reflex. A more powerful attack could hardly have been launched; and yet the day-to-day business of the nation was never seriously disrupted.

The fears of the Third World ambassadors who had spoken up in the United Nations after 2015 were amply justified. Each of the outbreaks listed above left a lingering legacy – a curse upon the poorer parts of the world. Although the United Nations and international agencies took on the awesome task of co-ordinating world responses to such epidemics at an early stage, such co-operation remained sporadically effective. Even in the 2060s and 2070s there were vast differences between the medical resources of the richer and poorer nations; all the good will in the world could not defend Chad or Kampuchea against the viruses that leaked slowly but surely across their borders. Immunoserums were to hand, but not to the hands of those who needed them. Twenty-first-century medicine was extremely effective by comparison with earlier centuries, but even so, many more millions of people died of preventable disease than in any previous century. The sheer number of people in the world, combined with the appalling variety of new lethal diseases, made certain of that.

The end of the plague wars

No further outbreaks of new diseases were recorded after 2060. The reasons for this are almost certainly complex. Two obvious answers suggest themselves, however. First, any government mounting an attack of this kind had to worry about a rebound effect. To remain free from suspicion, and hence free from reprisal, the instigators of plague warfare attacks could not immunize their own people against the disease which they released until they could appear to be doing so as part of a worldwide response. Secondly – and, probably, more important – the USA showed by example on two occasions that it was capable of withstanding these attacks, which could not leave it crucially disrupted. This implied that the only nation sure to win an all-out biological war was the USA, whose medical facilities remained the most effective in the world. This may explain why the outbreak in Moscow, which so many people expected, never took place. The Americans were never likely to mount such an attack purely for experimental purposes, because they already knew where the advantage lay.

This may be too cynical a view. It is possible that the instigators of the plague wars actually became conscience-stricken, and that governments after 2060 refrained from any further traffic with such weapons more on moral grounds than tactical ones. The ecological crisis may well have been at its deepest in the latter decades of the twenty-first century, but at the same time the world's leaders were beginning to see that it might be beaten with enough co-operation. The last nuclear incident of 2079 was a salutary reminder of the danger of adding to the world's ecological problems, whether by fallout and "nuclear winter" or by plague. Biological weapons as well as nuclear ones were put aside.

It cannot actually be said that a new era of ethical discrimination had dawned within the international community, but certainly at least the nations had begun to exercise greater caution.

CHAPTER SIX
"ENERGY'S ICE AGE"

The period of crisis did not come as a surprise to people in developed nations – though they had anticipated only an "energy crisis", having no forewarning of the extra impact of climatic problems. Their industrial economy was fuelled by oil, and it had long been known that supplies would eventually dwindle away. But while this horizon was out of sight no real rein had been applied. No one really knew how much oil there was under the surface of the Earth, and while new fields were being opened up the developed nations hastened to consume what they had.

The oil supply did not dry up abruptly. Indeed, there was certainly far more oil still underground even in 2100 than had been burned in the previous two centuries. The problem was getting it out of the ground. As the great lakes underground were pumped dry the oil producers had to drill more deeply in ever-more-inhospitable environments to find liquid crude. Much of the oil that had already been discovered was difficult to recover, being bound up with other substances in oil shales and tar sands. In short, the cost of extracting each new barrel of oil increased steadily. This cost could be expressed simply in cash terms, but the "energy-cost" of extraction was the vital figure. In the mid-twentieth century the energy-equivalent of only one barrel of oil had to be invested in order to pump a hundred barrels from the ground in Texas or the richer fields of the Middle East. By 2060 the ratio had dwindled until one barrel of oil had to be invested to reclaim five more. By 2060 the ratio was approximately one to three, and the energy-producing industries had become by far the largest consumers of energy.

The coal industry was less tightly squeezed; but mines grew steadily deeper, had to make use of more elaborate technology, and so cost more. The need to process much coal into liquid fuels that could substitute for petroleum products placed a further burden on the budgets of the developed nations.

There were, of course, attempts to diversify the world's energy base. Nations with no oil found it increasingly difficult to import any, and were forced to investigate other ways of generating liquid fuel. Several tropical countries cultivated fast-growing plants that could be fermented into alcohol fuel. Comic relief in the midst of the energy crisis was provided by the efficient black markets which sprang up, eager to divert "fuel" ethanol to more traditional purposes.

Fossil fuels provided most of the world's energy in the twentieth and twenty-first centuries. Not until 2180 did fusion technology begin to reduce the spirals of ever-increasing costs and ever-decreasing supply.

World coal consumption and cost

Year	Consumption (millions of tons)	Cost*
1975	3.2	1.00
2000	4.4	1.05
2025	4.6	1.14
2050	4.1	1.27
2075	3.3	1.46
2100	2.7	1.92
2125	2.4	2.41
2150	2.9	3.72
2175	2.8	5.05

**Costs adjusted for inflation: 1975 = 1.00.*

World oil consumption and cost

Year	Consumption (millions of barrels)	Cost*
1975	60	1.00
2000	73	3.65
2025	59	5.82
2050	44	10.47
2075	32	11.83
2100	25	13.69
2125	16	15.44
2150	14	17.02
2175	13	17.99

**Costs adjusted for inflation: 1975 = 1.00*

Nuclear reactors become expensive

In developed countries, the use of nuclear reactors to regenerate electricity became commonplace, but soon ran into difficulties. Anxiety about accidents and pollution always provoked local opposition to the building of nuclear power stations. In fact, the safety record of nuclear reactors in the richest nations was good, and it is at least arguable that their wastes proved less of an ecological threat than those of coal-burning stations, but that was not the way people perceived the situation. A meltdown disaster at Vologda in 2004 sent a ripple of fear around the world, and a massive radiation-leak at Chinandega, Nicaragua, in August 2008 caused a greater storm because the station was American-built.

The USA was fortunate in the early days of its flirtation with nuclear power-generation; there were close brushes with tragedy on three occasions in the late twentieth century but no large-scale damage was done. American contractors had therefore been entrusted with the building of important power stations in many other countries, following a stereotyped design. When a reactor of this type eventually did go wrong, therefore, a shadow of doubt was cast on all the rest. There were, in fact, three more substantial accidents in the first quarter years of the twenty-first century, in various parts of the world, though only one other involved an American-built reactor. There were about forty minor incidents. The total number of people killed and injured compared favourably with the number of people killed and injured in other types of power station, but the fears of people living near nuclear power stations could never be quelled.

If the only problems had been those of safety and anxiety, nuclear power would probably have helped more than it did to ameliorate the deepening energy crisis. Unfortunately, there was the further problem of the increasing cost – in terms of energy-investment – of building and running fission reactors. The world was not, in a technical sense, short of uranium, but the business of extracting uranium from the ground became steadily more problematic as demand increased. As with coal and oil, the ratio of energy-input to energy-output within the industry shrank with every decade that passed.

Success for the "green parties"

The very slow proliferation of nuclear fission reactors in Europe and America after 2025 was claimed as a success for the various "green parties" that were gathering political impetus at the time. Statesmen like France's Christiane Duminil and America's Thomas Lawler claimed credit for changing their nations' political outlook, and promoting policies of energy-conservation as a matter of ideology, but in fact the triumph of the new outlook was assured on economic grounds. The old order crumbled because its defences became too expensive to maintain, not because of an ethical revolution at the popular level. Lawler's slogans in particular hardly seem the stuff to sway world opinion: "Turning up your central heating is like lighting a fire of dollar bills!" "Bright lights today, brown-out tomorrow!" One can almost believe the story that his speeches were written by a domestic computer – though hardly a very advanced one, even for the twenty-first century.

Energy-conservation laws were passed in virtually every nation in the world at regular intervals throughout the twenty-first century. Some of the smaller nations went in for spectacular bans: Upper Volta became the first nation, in 2033, to ban private transport entirely, reserving all vehicles for the civil service and the armed forces. Others followed suit, though such stringent controls were difficult to enforce in nations with a democratic tradition.

Garrity's austerity

The richer nations crept towards tight control by stealthy degrees, using price controls as well as legal ones. Despite the moral credit claimed by Lawler in the USA, the man who really laid the legal foundations for America's change of policy was Jefferson Garrity, president from 2024 to 2032. Previous presidents had tried to move in the same direction but had always been forced either to recant or be voted out of office. Garrity's public relations machine was the one which finally convinced the voters that they had to back austerity. His second term marked the resigned acceptance by ordinary Americans of something that they had been steadfastly refusing to admit for two generations – that individual freedom of energy-use would have to be severely curtailed. Garrity's package of controls was relatively modest, and hideously complicated because of the need to buy compromises from half a dozen special-interest groups, but it still dealt the final death-blow to the old-style American automobile industry. It also placed such restrictions on the commercial uses of plastics that many industries producing luxury consumer goods were killed off.

Opponents of Garrity's policy charged it with duplicating the effects of the Wall Street Crash of a century before, but its supporters claimed bitter necessity. In fact the depression had been deepening for so long that there was little scope for a further downturn in the economy. The bubble of the American lifestyle had been pricked, and the last nation on Earth dedicated to the ethic of conspicuous consumption had already capitulated to necessity. The good old days were gone, and Garrity was believed when he insisted that if good days were ever to come again they must be built on new cultural and industrial foundations.

Human workers back in demand

The crisis in the energy-economy of the developed nations had mixed effects on other economic sectors and on other nations. The manufacture of goods was inevitably cut back because of escalating energy costs and the resulting increase in raw-material prices. All kinds of mining were hard-hit, and the mounting cost of farm machinery and artificial fertilizers compounded the problems facing agriculture. It became more important to maintain the machines that already existed, and to reclaim parts from them when their useful lives eventually ended. As labour became relatively cheaper, even the richest nations began relying more on manpower than on machine-power where convenient. The marketability of relatively modest skills in machine-maintenance and the ever-growing attractiveness of small-scale adventures in waste-reclamation helped to keep unemployment down during the long depression.

The sheer cost of metals and plastics put a brake on the proliferation of mechanical technology, but not on its diversification. Much ingenuity was devoted to the business of designing new generations of machines which would do the same jobs as the previous generation, but without using up so much energy or being so massive. As the "cleverness" of so many machines was increasing anyway because of advances in microcomputer technology, there was still much scope for inventiveness. Indeed, this was an era in which the ingenuity of individual inventors made something of a comeback by comparison with the previous century, with its large and lavishly funded research teams. No longer could entrepreneurial inventors make fortunes from lucky patents, but with luck they might be elevated as heroes by the media. Such was the celebrity briefly gained by men like Philippe Jarre, developer of the extraordinarily efficient "pocket tractor", and Alois Gleich, pioneer of the crystal ball three-dimensional TV receiver.

Biotechnology takes off

The main thrust of twenty-first-century technological development was, however, concentrated in those technologies which were not energy-intensive. Micro-electronics thrived, but it was biotechnology which soared, and considering the contribution this branch of technology was ultimately to make in pulling the world out of trouble, it was as well that its rapid progress was unhindered

The Electrolux Ro-Jeeves domestic servitor robot, *left*, developed in the 2030s and kept in production with minor refinements for 40 years. This model floated just above the floor, suspended by a magnetic underlay grid. Other robots of the period included the "Henri" chefette, *top*, and the Hoover "Sniff 'n' Suck" vacuum cleaner.

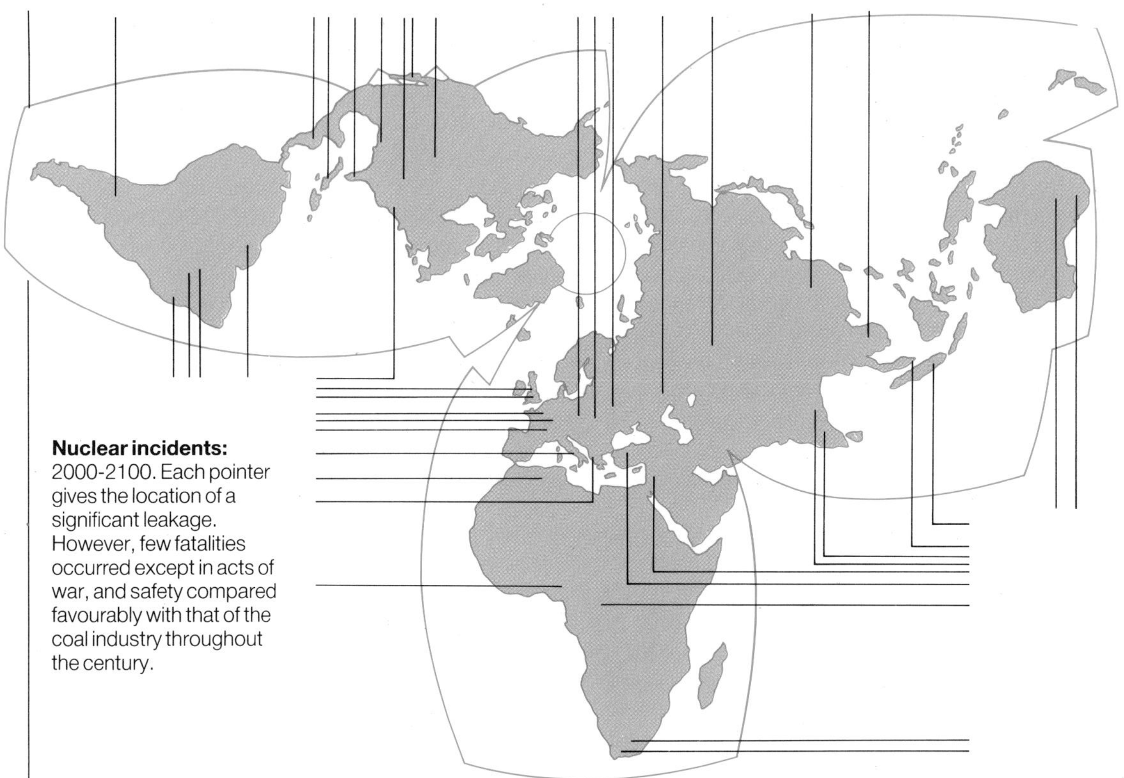

Nuclear incidents: 2000-2100. Each pointer gives the location of a significant leakage. However, few fatalities occurred except in acts of war, and safety compared favourably with that of the coal industry throughout the century.

by the energy crisis. There were inevitably fierce political disputes throughout the century over the question of how to "spend" the energy that was available. As supplies of coal and oil dwindled, some small nations thrived because they had untapped supplies. Others were driven to desperate straits by their lack of important resources. The developed nations, hampered in their continued development, managed to export some of their own difficulties by buying energy on the world market. There were perennial demands from those nations which could not compete economically for the establishment of some kind of sharing system, but the concessions which the richer nations made were few. The gap between the developed and undeveloped nations narrowed in some cases, but in others grew wider. The evolving world community was riven with conflict as a result.

It was governments, rather than individuals, who dictated the patterns of energy-spending. The lion's share of available energy was diverted into public utilities: electricity generation, water-supply and public transportation, and of course into military uses. For two or three generations in mid-century the rationing of individual consumers, even in America, was strict enough to constitute a severe restriction on freedom by comparison with the previous century. "Snooper vans" prowled the streets, electronically checking power consumption in individual homes (and able to impose immediate, stiff fines). Over-long telephone calls were ruthlessly cut off after a recorded homily had been played to the offenders. Punitive property taxes were geared to buildings' heat-leakage, as sensed by infra-red helicopter scans.

American libertarians complained bitterly that Garrity had crippled the freedom of which the Western world had been so proud, and it is true that the pattern of change begun by his reforms brought a touch of Siberian cold and a taste of Soviet *realpolitik* into American domestic affairs, but there was really no option. It is not so surprising that Konrad and Kamenov, a decade later, found a good deal of common ground when the Israeli nuclear strike crisis caused them to close ranks.

We can see from the standpoint of today that this half-century of energy-starvation need not have hit the world so hard. If the richer nations had devoted themselves to more careful housekeeping half a century earlier, beginning sensible conservation measures in 1960 or 1970, then "energy's ice age", which settled over the world in the twenty-first century, might have been no more than a cool autumn. We have the advantage, though, of knowing both how quickly the oil supplies actually did dwindle away and exactly when and how the advent of nuclear fusion came to the rescue.

CHAPTER SEVEN

THE ADVENT OF FUSION POWER

History can be divided all too easily into century-long chunks whose labels are not exactly wrong but tend to mislead. So in the history of industrial energy, the nineteenth was the century of coal and steam, the twentieth that of electricity and fission. The twenty-first century glows with the dawn of fusion; once the problem of controlled nuclear fusion is cracked, history lurches straight into our contemporary era of "controlled plenty".

In reality the divisions were far less clear-cut. Coal and oil, as already mentioned, were still in dwindling use as late as the twenty-second century – not as precious raw materials for chemical synthesis, but as something to throw on a fire and burn. Thanks to this profligacy, fission power (which if co-ordinated on a global basis from the very start might have spared the world the fossil-fuel-aggravated "greenhouse crisis" of the twenty-first and twenty-second centuries) never did become the main source of twentieth-century energy which popular mythology imagines it to have been. And though the theoretical physics was largely sorted out in the 1950s-70s, fusion power did not rise radiant in the east on the morning of 1 January 2001. That particular prospect was delayed for very nearly another century.

Fusion power was in fact a new and different order of technological problem. Fossil fuels could simply be ignited and let burn. The fission fuels, uranium and plutonium, though awkward and dangerous to prepare in pure form, will also "burn" in a spontaneous nuclear reaction when enough material is collected together; the main difficulty is to *control* the disintegration of these highly unstable elements, with its dangerous by-products such as neutrons and gamma rays. Fusion fuels, usually the less common isotopes of hydrogen or other light elements, are by contrast, relatively stable. They will not burst into a nuclear reaction at all unless confined at monstrous pressures and temperatures, as in that well-known natural fusion reactor the Sun. For two nuclei to fuse, they must smash together violently enough to break down the barriers of electric charge which normally keep them apart. This means that the nuclei need to have high speeds (hence the high temperature) and to be present in vast numbers to offer many chances of collision (hence the high pressure). This was the first part of the fusion challenge.

Adequate theory, inadequate technology

Some present-day readers will be surprised to learn that small-scale fusion was a commonplace in twentieth-century laboratories. A relatively feeble particle accelerator could produce high-speed collisions and thus a modicum of fusion in, say, a deuterium-tritium mixture. But fusion stopped dead when the accelerator was turned off – it was not a *sustained* reaction – and the level of efficiency was absurd. Thousands or millions of times as much energy was pumped into the particle beam as could ever be recovered from the heat release of those few scattered fusions. It was as though a domestic fire could be kept alight only by continuous blasts from giant flame-throwers and high-energy lasers.

(Outside the laboratory, of course, twentieth-century science achieved large-scale fusion by simply touching off the fusion-fuel mixture using a fissile nuclear weapon, thus producing the thermonuclear bomb. This, again, was not a controllable source of power.)

In fact, until well into the twenty-first century, scientists found themselves in the wrong technological climate for a useful fusion reactor generating more power than was required to run it. Their theory was sound, but their technology could not handle the forces and temperatures involved. As Maglich remarked at the 2001 Symposium, "We're trying to tie down a tiger with grass and hold back the sea with half a bucket of sand." It was the same tantalizing position reached by Babbage in the nineteenth century. His design for an all-purpose calculating engine was brilliant and precocious: the available materials, gears and cogs and shafts, were impossibly unwieldy, and computers had to wait for twentieth-century electronics.

Development of the "tokamak"

Many primitive devices were planned to tackle the problems of bringing the fusion fuel to the right temperature/pressure for ignition, keeping it burning, and preventing the energy release from melting or vaporizing the reactor walls. Despite experiments using lasers or electron beams to heat and compress the fuel, the most promising approach was what came to be known as the "tokamak", a Russian word describing the toriod or doughnut shape, and many variants, which tended to go under the same generic name. The hot, ionized fuel nuclei would be electrically heated and kept confined using "mirrors" and "traps" which were intangible magnetic fields – no solid inner walls to be melted. To stop leakage at the ends of the magnetic "tube" the whole system would typically be doughnut-shaped, enclosing a continuous ring of hot plasma. With a controlled, self-sustaining fusion under way in

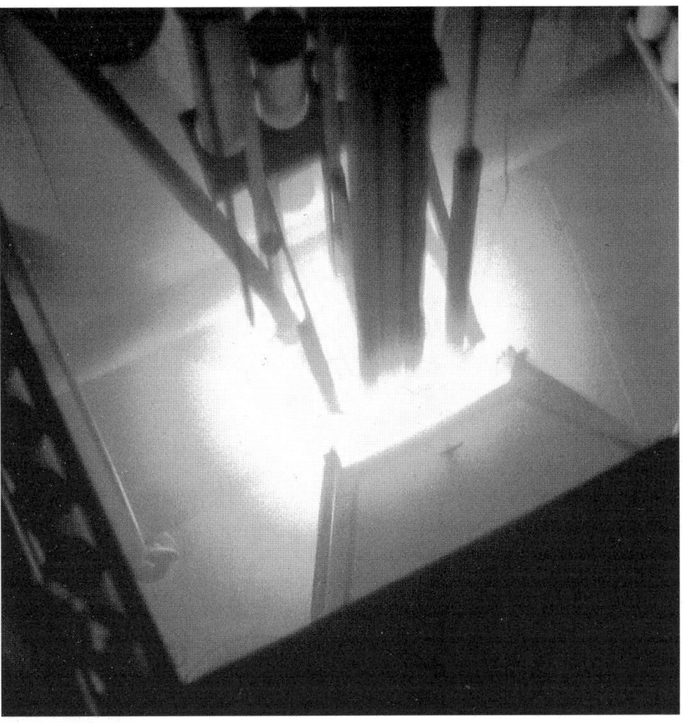

The "fighting fusioneers", Peach and Shutler, *far left*, snapped in mid-argument by the paparazzi of the European media. The fusion fires, *left*, of the Peach-Shutler creation, the P-S power cell.

this hellish plasma, it would be easy to bleed off the power via conventional heat exchangers and electrical generators.

This crude twentieth-century plan was in fact not a bad approximation to the prototype Peach-Shutler fusion cell of 2054-7 (just as Babbage's design for a steam-powered Analytical Engine had so much in common with the true computers of a century after). Early tokamaks achieved low-intensity fusion at ruinous cost: a million equivalent barrels of oil squandered to extract a single barrel's worth of fusion energy. Driven to higher efficiency, the apparatus would break down. A self-sustaining fusion plasma is like a tiny piece of the Sun, a fragment of a thermonuclear fireball, and holding it with magnetic fields was as difficult as trying to confine an explosion by blowing air at it from every side to prevent its expansion. It *could* be done, and the P-S fusion cell successfully did it – after several decades of technological advance.

Science can never really be independent of current politics, and the path to the actual P-S cell, the fuser as we know it now, was tortuous. On the one hand, rival approaches to fusion power still proliferated in the early 2000s. On the other, the overall budgets allocated to this uncertain line of research kept dropping as the energy crisis bit harder. Green movements, those political parties and pressure groups which were concerned to maintain the Earth's ecological *status quo*, had gained a wide and sympathetic hearing toward the end of the twentieth century. Some of them, pursuing obscure lines of ideological purity, moved on from the virtually-won battle to discourage new fission reactors and campaigned against fusion research investment with hardly a change in their arguments. It was certainly true that the political pie-in-the-sky image of fusion as free and clean was misleading. The purest fusion reaction has an "exhaust" of stray neutrons, which can infect many commonplace materials and convert them to short-term radiation hazards – a strong point for scare propaganda, although in fact this problem was negligible when compared to that of fissile waste or toxic fossil-fuel emissions.

Unintentional aid from the solar system

The Solar Army, gaudiest of the purist antinuclear movements, was led by the extraordinary and charismatic American who called himself Inti after the Inca sun-god. (His real name was said to be O'Mally.) From muted beginnings in about 2012, the Solar Army grew as a quasi-religious movement over the next decade and a half, with colossal rallies, picketing of nuclear power and research installations, and much lobbying in

Congress against fusion projects "inspired by the evil will of the Black Holes which oppose the all-supplying Sun." The movement even spread into the Soviet countries. Inti and his Army threw themselves behind Jefferson Garrity's Presidential campaign in 2024, assuming Garrity's reputation for toughness and austerity would make him sympathetic to a total civil nuclear moratorium. (Inti had no objection to military thermonuclear use, which represented "the Sun's fiery wrath on unbelievers.") As the conservation measures began to clamp down in 2026, the Solar Army celebrated with a rally culminating in the destruction of the old Shiva Nova laser-fusion research facility, by then largely disused. In his triumphant progress through the ruins, Inti fell and was trampled to death by the delirious rioters. Many thousands of the Army later committed suicide as a bizarre act of contrition – the preferred method being a leap into the focal zone of a solar furnace.

Embarrassed by and eager to dissociate himself from this fanaticism, Garrity chose to make a political gesture in some markedly different direction. He lent an unusually sympathetic ear to Hi-Tech, the technophilic group incorporating such twentieth-century remnants as the L-5 Society. Backed by industrial interests, its leader Meta Polline argued for the retention of some orbital industry beyond the bare minimum needed to service the satellite network. Her and Hi-Tech's long-term goal was the establishment of vast manned space colonies, still an impractical dream; in the short term the result was Spacelab IV, a shoestring operation which ultimately (2039) managed to produce the Dvorek neutron sink alloy. This final triumph of the Garrity administration came two years after his death, so that he never knew about it. With his notorious "inhuman fairness" he might have insisted that the credit go to Inti.

Dvorek's three necessities

It was back in 2013, at the 7th International Symposium on Fusion Research (new series, begun in 2001), that Academician Vassily Dvorek laid down his Three Necessities for a workable tokamak variant. The first was a then impossibly fast and complex computer simulator which would predict fluctuations and instabilities in the reactor's plasma flux and initiate corrective action *before the fluctuations happened.* Here it was a question of waiting for the Japanese to achieve their customary computing miracle, which arrived in the late 2020s as a spin-off from the Total Genetic Mapping project (the software to meet Dvorek's requirements took somewhat longer).

Secondly, Dvorek called for much more powerful and efficiently controlled magnetic fields for the fusion reactor – implying a superconducting material for the magnetic coils that would function in the presence of potent fields and at high temperature (even room temperature is high to a physicist: about 300 degrees absolute). Some lucky East-cum-West German research into ceramic polymers and metallic glasses provided a somewhat unexpected answer in the form of *Substanz T*, developed in the 2030s.

Spacelab IV was the birthplace of fuser technology. The semi-powered laboratory flew in a complex orbit that looped around Earth and moon. Here the craft is hurtling down to its lunar perigee – the lowest point in its approach to the Moon, less than 10 kilometres above the surface. Spacelab IV remained operational into the 2070s.

This superconductor had so many inexplicable properties that the *why* of its functioning was not clear for more than another century: but it worked. The third of Dvorek's demands was the neutron sink, of which he could only say that it must have such-and-such properties of neutron screening and absorption, to protect the outer walls of the reactor assembly. In the light of hindsight it seems blindingly obvious that the sink would need to be constructed of an alloy of widely different elements, impossible to mass-produce in Earth's gravity. (Molten lead and aluminium, for example, refuse to mix: the aluminium merely floats because gravity pulls the lead to the bottom.) Thus the neutron sink had to be developed in the tiny orbital complex of Spacelab IV.

Peach and Shutler's prototype

By the mid-2040s, then, the raw materials for the fuser were to hand. By that time austerity was a way of life. With its long history of failure, fusion research seemed politically unappealing – it had been irritatingly "just around the corner" ever since the 1960s, and there was a tendency to class it with perpetual motion and squaring the circle. Even the International Symposium on Fusion Research had petered out with the 17th biennial meeting in 2033. Some token funds were provided through governments like those of the USA and USSR which had a tradition of hoping for great things from fusion. This was bolstered by private enterprise in such shapes as Hi-Tech and what remained of its industrial backers (paradoxically, the now elderly Polline vigorously opposed the feeble revitalization of fusion research, any investment at ground level being a diversion of funds from space). The development work staggered on for years in unfashionable university departments devoted to physical science, while the wonder-workers of genetic engineering received the glory and all the major grants.

Eventually and quite undramatically, the team headed by James Peach and Coral Shutler unveiled their prototype fusion cell in 2054. After three years of technical difficulties, presumably not helped by their divorce and remarriage in 2055, Peach and Shutler demonstrated the world's first thermonuclear reactor with a net power *output*. The amount was only a puny 14 megawatts, but clearly the way had been opened by the two irascible "fighting fusioneers".

Joint action by the superpowers

It was time for bold action. President Disch and Premier Vyshnya, after a teleconference lasting several weeks, reaffirmed the old Konrad-Kamenov links and jointly announced a massive investment programme to perfect and build the P-S fusers. Americans, relatively recent converts to a regime of austerity, seemed to have mixed feelings about this resurgence of huge technological expenditure: Disch failed to win re-election in 2060 and is remembered, if at all, only for the passionate fondness for grand opera which helped alienate a puritanical America. His successor, Pilkington, adopted a vaguely evangelistic tone concerning a few more years in the wilderness *en route* to the promised land of fusion power for all, and for some reason this was better received than Disch's grandiloquence . . . though Pilkington later ran into trouble, as we shall see.

The years in the wilderness stretched out. Though disasters like meltdown were impossible in a fuser (the moment its magnetic containment failed, the fusion reaction would simply stop dead), there was concern about neutron activation . . . long-term reliability . . . stresses in the heat exchanger . . . hazards of synthesizing the hydrogen isotope tritium needed as primer for the fusion . . . fears that the high neutron flux could and would be used to manufacture weapon-grade plutonium . . . a hundred other technical points. More controversial were the economic queries. Where would the reactors be built? Was it fair for them to be concentrated in the more developed countries, simply because of those countries' greater resources and ability to construct the reactors? Might not the need for electricity grids in less developed nations cost so much as to outweigh any advantages of fusion power? Likewise for the installations needed to extract deuterium fuel from sea water? And was not any investment in this long-term nonsense a blatant diversion of world funds from real, immediate needs?

Some of these questions were met with ingenious answers: the new breed of high-capacity, rechargeable and unprecedentedly efficient fuel cells might almost have been invented as a solution, if a slightly laborious one, to the energy distribution problem. Others had to be parried with bravura displays of diplomacy concealing the slightly guilty theory that, in the long run, what was good for the developed nations was good for the whole world. This remained nonetheless unpalatable for being (contingently) true.

2090: fusion comes of age

By 2070 a handful of fusion reactors was feeding power into national grids, and Vyshnya found himself in the unusual position of being able to announce the initial success of a long-term political scheme he himself had jointly inaugurated. The next 20 years saw a number of irritating setbacks, not only political but mechanical – unsuspected long-term effects of that inner thermonuclear hell on the reactor components. The reactor construction programme was forever suffering small reverses thanks to rumours of political inequity, to its use as a bargaining counter in energy policy, to frustration at the endless investment and research which never quite produced a big bonanza, and to the overall chill of the Period of Crisis at its worst. Only in the 2090s did fusion begin to assume a positive economic importance in the developed nations, foreshadowing the end of crisis and the hope of recovery in the fundamental realm of energy supply.

For their contributions to the physics of controlled thermonuclear reactions, Peach and and Shutler received the Nobel Prize in 2065. Newly divorced, they celebrated the honour by remarrying for the fourth time.

Of course, it would be another two centuries and a half before the P-S fusion cell, a crude twentieth-century concept for all its later refinements, could be replaced by the nuclear catalysis which permits "cold fusion" and still plays a significant part today. The story of cold fusion belongs, however, to the Period of Recovery.

CHAPTER EIGHT

REFORMATION OF THE ENERGY ECONOMY

The final 90 years of the Period of Crisis were also the beginning of the great years of fusion power. Between 2090 and 2180 the world was able virtually to abandon the use of fossil fuel, thanks to the spread of fusion reactors and their relatively cheap power.

Yet it is surprising how slowly this new potential abundance was accepted. Following the gap of nearly 40 years between the prototype fuser and the beginnings of a true fusion-energy economy, it took the best part of another century for fusion to become established as the major world power-source, and for power to become revitalizingly cheap. There were several reasons.

Opposition to fusion

First, each fusion installation required a very large investment. In the short term, taking into account the amortization of plant costs, fusion power was in fact almost prohibitively expensive. It is hugely to the credit of USA and USSR leaders in particular that they took a reasonably long view of the value of this new technology. Nevertheless, the reformation could not be rushed. Even the nuclear industry, which stood to gain a great deal overall, was slightly dismayed by the realization that its old uranium reactors were expected (by public and politicians alike) to be early casualties of the new order, rather than being allowed to die peacefully of old age at a much later date.

Secondly came the ecological opposition. The question of radiation hazard was no longer serious by 2100 or so, due to increased public knowledge of just how the fusers worked. Indeed, the "catastrophic" failure of one of the first British fusion plants – at New Rutherford, formerly Sellafield, in 2091 – was something of a pro-fusion propaganda success because of the entirely negligible radiation release from a "worst case" accident. However, after many decades of rising temperatures and sea levels, the world was uneasily aware of the greenhouse crisis (see Chapter Nine). Even the clean heat of fusion could only increase the effect, and the green movements lobbied eagerly for solar rather than fusion power. They argued that since the Sun's heat strikes the Earth in any case, there could be no overall climatic effects if much of this heat were diverted to useful ends via solar cells and so on. Unfortunately the next step in this argument was generally to suggest that the apparent limits of solar power expansion could be overcome using gigantic spaceborne mirrors to collect far more solar energy than actually strikes Earth directly. The fallacy was not always obvious, even to the people of the early twenty-second century, because of a lingering belief that energy produced by fusing hydrogen in the Sun was "natural" while energy produced by fusing hydrogen anywhere else was not. Another "natural" standby was geothermal power using deep-drilled heat exchangers to tap the inner fires of the Earth; though developed to some extent as an alternative during the Period of Crisis, this unwieldy source never succeeded on a convincingly large scale.

President Garrity: one of the few surviving pictures. This micro-image was lifted from the memory of an assassin roach, a miniaturised robo-killer devised in the twenty-first century. Garrity accidentally trod on the killer bug, so surviving assassination by the fanatical anti-fuser lobby.

Austerity dies hard

A third reason for such a slow spread of fusion was that conservation measures had become ingrained into law and custom, each reinforcing each. The original legislation – acts of various parliaments, bills in Garrity's Congress, Politburo edicts – may have been unpopular. Nearer the end of the twenty-first century they were accepted, hardly even grudgingly, and political and social inertia tended to maintain their restrictions beyond the time of need (cf. the Jewish pork taboo, which persisted amazingly long after the elimination of the trichinosis larvae which originally provoked the ban). Nobody will forget how President Feester was hounded out of office in the 2080s for pushing the fusion programme too hard. His witch-hunting enemies branded Feester as a sensual throwback to the worst days of twentieth-century hedonism, planning to usher in an era of laxity, excess and loose morals. All this, for suggesting a 15 per cent increase in North America's modest fusion investment!

From outside, the attitude of such highly developed countries could very easily be interpreted as selfishness. Despite the restrictions of the Period of Crisis, these countries were still richer by far than most of the world; some of the old wealth had gone into highly efficient energy conservation. Having thus made a virtue of their thrift, the dominant powers of the Northern Hemisphere seemed in no hurry to invest in expensive new fusion systems which would indeed benefit them, but less dramatically than they could the less developed world.

The Nobel laureate Coral Shutler addressed her countryfolk thus:

"You remember the old days, when you were rich and no one else counted? You spent and spent and broke your toys like spoilt children, and perhaps you didn't know any better. You were lovable but you were wrong. Then you felt the cold a little, and learnt new words like conservation . . . while down the road the not-so-rich people tried to have the fun you had. 'Oh no,' you said. 'We cut down our trees, yes, but you must not. We had our fun with nuclear fireworks, yes, but you must not.' Perhaps you were right, but it wasn't a lovable way to be right. Now the cold bites deeper, and you sit cosy in furs while the not-so-rich are shivering. 'Light fires for the world,' they say. You smile in your rich furs, and tell them: 'Thrift is a virtue, waste not want not, we have learnt to do without and so should you.' And now I do not think you are either lovable or right."

Plainly this is polemic rather than cool historical analysis, but it identifies an attitude – and caused a pang or two of guilt, to judge from the number of defensive contemporary jokes about "Coral's Morals".

Peach-Shutler cells came in many shapes and sizes. This multi-purpose "hedgehog" cell was the power source for many flying machines including the Eurospace *Quarto* skyhopper.

Anti-fuser propaganda: a faked ''scare picture'' circulated in the United States following the containment failure at New Rutherford, Britain in 2091. In fact, there was no explosion, merely a slow fire, and the installation looked no more alarming than a factory gutted by fire after a gas explosion. Radiation release was minimal, despite propagandists' claims to the contrary.

Resentment from poorer nations

As the early decades of the twenty-second century slipped by, the developed countries *did* overcome their initial inertia. The number of fusion plants began to grow exponentially in those countries, each new installation helping reduce the price of the next through accumulated experience, mass-production cost savings and a further drop in energy prices. The new threat was a revival of old disparities. After a relatively companionable period in which the world shared – or believed it shared – a common austerity, most of the old rich nations looked like becoming again fantastically energy-rich, with the poverty gap widening further than ever.

Happily, some of the resentment which might have built up was cushioned by the cheap "survival technologies" which were a direct result of the main energy crisis. One of the most important, Gantz's biological architecture, is discussed at length in Chapter Thirteen. Poorer people who had fallen back on low-technology or alternative-technology energy sources were unlikely to suffer directly from the lack of a local electricity grid: the danger was one of resentment, of a perceived Rich versus Poor division, of an alignment of less developed countries *en bloc* against the energy plutocrats. In 2143 this confrontation very nearly came about. It had been brewing for years, to be largely ignored by the US-USSR axis owing to their happy delusion that despite the new flood of available energy, their internal economies were still thrifty and only just self-sufficient.

The Zov-Kowalski plan

According to databank material released in the next century, President José Orica of Mexico had been chosen in May 2143 as spokesman for a group of 32 less developed countries whose leaders were, characteristically, very much less tolerant of their situation than were the people they represented. A gauntlet was to be violently thrown down in the United Nations Assembly, and demands for instant and massive "energy aid" were made – backed up with threats of possible nuclear and biological attack on the "Hogs" (defined as nations with considerable fusion investment). This would have created an extremely awkward political situation. Thanks to good intelligence, and perhaps also spurred by the thought that if the US-USSR bloc was to be the world's policeman it should also act to some extent as its pastor, Premier Zov joined President Kowalski in a preemptive announcement of a similar though politically workable scheme. Orica did not in the event speak at all, owing to a bout of neo-influenza whose convenient timing led to some libellous rumours.

The modified Zov-Kowalski plan began with a rather problematical policy of "energy transfusion", a species of foreign aid in the form of cross-border taps into the electrical grids of energy-rich countries, where possible. A secondary means involving airlifts of charged fuel-cells was never really practical, and probably was meant as no more than a sop to isolated or island countries which could receive little benefit from Phase I. Phase II began with low-interest loans from an international fund, to finance the building of local fusion plants on certain conditions – that internal electricity be constructed and linked across borders, that construction debts be partially paid by feeding surplus energy into the world grid, that the *de facto* international mains-electricity standards (110 volts, 60Hz) be recognized by all.

The world grid

The final vision of the scheme was the world grid; or rather, two grids, North and South America plus Europe/Asia/Africa with a token link across the Bering Strait; or three counting Australia.

In this way, fusion power was eased into the poorer nations. Though opposed by several of them – Britain fought to the last to retain her eccentric 50Hz mains frequency, and the Prime Minister was heard to quote some old lines about fighting them on the beaches – the world electrical grid had by the end of the twenty-second century assumed a symbolic value greater than its practical value could ever be. Incomplete, unreliable in patches and often over-expensive to maintain, it still became a tangible reminder that Earth was all one planet, with everyone in very much the same boat. There is, ironically, no evidence that the instigators had such a far-sighted and poetic vision. In all probability they had simply improvised a hasty scheme designed to sound bigger and better in every way than the tawdry threats of Orica's cabal.

A poet's-eye view appeared in the wry haiku of the Japanese Ryūsan (2116-2199, one of the few poets of the era whose work survives), here very roughly translated:

> By Sagami Bay I press a switch;
> African fuses blow;
> World unity!

Premier Zov was, by all reports, fond of quoting this after one vodka too many at diplomatic evenings or state banquets. Thanks to the increasing liberalization of the Politburo, he nevertheless had a long premiership – thirteen years, ending in 2153.

CHAPTER NINE

THE GREENHOUSE CRISIS

Throughout the twenty-first century the Earth's atmosphere grew slowly warmer. As a result, the ice-caps shrank and mean sea-level gradually rose. The warming was due to a "greenhouse effect" caused by an increase in atmospheric carbon dioxide; the extra carbon dioxide in the air absorbed some heat radiation from the surface which would otherwise have been lost into space.

That a greenhouse effect might occur had been anticipated for some decades as twentieth-century scientists noted the local effects of the prolific burning of fossil fuels. In the year 2000, no one could say exactly what the global effects might be, and for a time most of the extra carbon dioxide was dissolved in the sea, where much of it was recycled by phytoplankton. Other factors outside human control also affected global warmth, including fluctuations in the radiation output of the sun. The atmospheric warming due to industrially-released carbon dioxide might have been calculated had all other things been equal, but all other things were *not* equal.

Contemporary scientists, once they had noted the slow atmospheric warming, tended to blame it on man's reckless treatment of the biosphere. They pointed to the cutting down of tropical forests, which were the most important "carbon store" on land, and to the pollution of the seas, which was damaging the phytoplankton. Pressure from green parties to introduce international legislation had been growing for some time and became an important political force. Such controls as were introduced were valuable, not least in laying the institutional groundwork for later more ambitious schemes, but modern climatological analyses suggest that had it not been for the increase in carbon dioxide there might have been an equally disastrous "little ice age" caused by a temporary drop in solar radiation due to causes far beyond human control. In other words, the increased heat *retention* caused by extra carbon dioxide was balanced by a smaller heat *input* caused by the vagaries of the Sun. On the other hand, had it not been for that coincidental cooling of the sun, the greenhouse crisis might have been much worse.

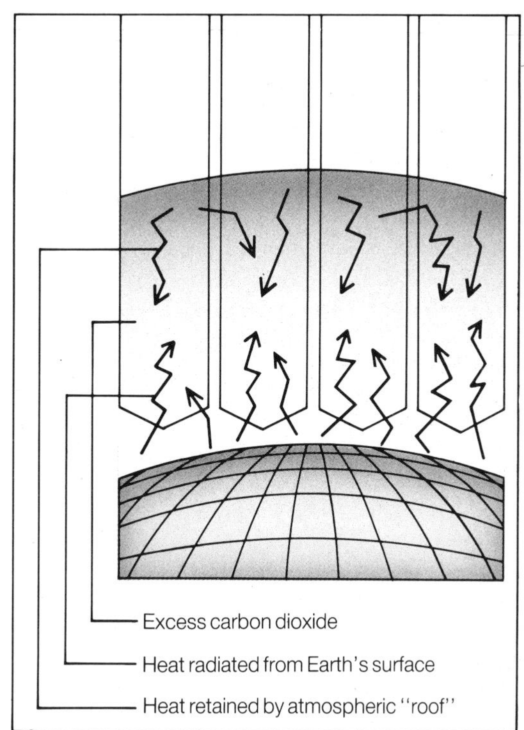

The greenhouse effect was well understood, even in the twentieth century. Infra-red heat energy is retained by the atmospheric envelope, so causing rises in global temperatures.

The rise in sea level

The rise in mean sea level continued until about 2120, when it began to fall. It was not until about 2200 that there was a re-stabilization of sea-level, which lasted for 200 years. Such fluctuations as we have seen since 2400 have, of course, been partly random and partly engineered. The increase in sea level was never catastrophically fast – at the most not more than twenty-four centimetres per year, and that very briefly. The 2120 level was some sixteen metres above the 2000 level, and the stable level of 2200 was just under two metres above the 2000 level. The effects on coastal towns and cities were, however, quite devastating, and the periodic flooding associated with high tides or heavy rains often affected regions far inland.

There were many secondary consequences of the changing sea level too, which persisted long after the greenhouse effect had gone into reverse. Oceanic currents were altered, and patterns of rainfall changed markedly and somewhat mercurially. This led to continual shifts in agricultural opportunity, which produced occasional boom harvests and more frequent poor ones.

Shanghai and its fate

The areas which suffered most were, of course, in the basins of the great tidal rivers. Human populations living close to the lower Amazon, the Mekong, the Parana, the Ganges and the Irrawaddy were soon affected. The densely-populated low-lying lands of northern Europe suffered less at first but eventually large scale evacuation and relocation occurred there also. The first of the world's great cities to take the toll was the largest of them all, Shanghai, whose tightly-packed metropolitan area had such a low elevation that extraordinary measures had to be taken as early as 2015 to move people out and keep those who remained above the tide-lines. Massive amounts of stone and earth were imported to make islands grow faster than the sea threatened to claim them. The long battle, fought over the course of an entire century, was eventually a losing one, and by 2120 Shanghai had been virtually destroyed. As the sea began to recede it was gradually reclaimed but it never attained its former significance in Chinese and world affairs.

The battle between Shanghai and the encroaching sea was watched closely by the scientists and citizens of hundreds of other cities. Every coastal town knew that its turn would come, and that any knowledge might be vital. The great Japanese metropolitan areas of Tokyo and Osaka were also quickly affected, and Japan too fought a long battle to relocate its people and its industries – a battle ultimately lost in much more spectacular fashion, as will shortly be seen.

The fight to save New York

The USA soon found that its two major cities – as well as several minor ones – were in trouble when considerable areas of New York City and Los Angeles came under threat. Cities on the Gulf of Mexico and the east coast of Florida were exceptionally badly hit in the 2020s and 2030s. The Californian shore slopes so steeply that the areas eventually inundated were small in extent, but the problems faced by Los Angeles and San Francisco were compounded by the continual earth-tremors of the San Andreas fault. The importance of New York was so great that the sea could not be allowed to have its way, and the preservation of the city became a major test of Uncle Sam's fortitude and prestige.

The Americans invested heavily in flood defences, and the series of projects launched by President Newcombe in 2015, designed to elevate Manhattan Island, were given top priority even in the time of Jefferson Garrity's stern austerity measures in the 2020s. No subsequent administration dared challenge the wisdom, or the necessity, of continuing that battle, even though senators from Texas, Louisiana and Florida led an endless crusade against this favouritism, often stirring up considerable resentment in the South. "Celebrations" associated with the two hundredth anniversary of the Civil War in the early 2060s at times resembled a re-enactment of that conflict. President Pilkington's ill-advised visit to Gettysburg, Pennsylvania in July 2063 sparked off a three-day riot due to the "invasion" of the state by tens of thousands of Southerners taking the opportunity to demonstrate their dissatisfaction by succeeding where Robert E. Lee failed. One of the two hundred and ninety men murdered during the three days was named Meade, and he met his death because he dishonestly claimed descent from the victorious general. Nevertheless, New York City was saved from the rising sea, while New Orleans was virtually obliterated, all the way to Shreveport.

London flooded three times

London too was in grave danger from flooding even in 2000. Early in the century the Thames flood barriers failed again and again to protect the heart of the city from inundation. Many lives were lost in the first big flood of 2008, and though the lessons learned made the floods of 2017 and 2025 less disastrous, it had by then become obvious that the city could not be wholly defended. A major relocation programme was begun, and extended over the next half-century as the sea's inroads extended. Britain shared with other European nations the problem of being desperately crowded, so that the gradual sinking of the Norfolk Broads and the Cheshire Plain put a much greater strain on the nation's resources than the flooding of comparable areas in larger nations.

The greenhouse helps the USSR

The USSR escaped comparatively lightly. Leningrad was the only very large city in a vulnerable position. Although climatic conditions within its vast territories were greatly affected by the secondary effects of the crisis, on balance the changes were beneficial. The warming of the atmosphere and the shifting pattern of rainfall both helped to improve conditions across the vast Siberian plain, making the steppes much more fertile. A great deal of land along the Arctic coast was flooded, affecting the cities of Archangel, Naryan Mar and Khatanga, but most of this land was very sparsely populated and relocation was handled expeditiously. The long-cherished projects deflecting the flow of the Ob and the Yenisei to aid irrigation in the southern Siberian Plain were completed in 2014 and 2031 respectively after many tribulations. The government in Moscow was quick to take credit for the spectacular boom in grain production in mid-century, though it

The high spring tide, London, 2025: sights like this became common in many parts of the world as the Greenhouse effect caused melting of the ice caps. As the century continued several low-lying parts of Britain vanished under the rising waters.

was probably due to the the greenhouse crisis rather than the deflection of the rivers.

Pavlo Vyshnya, who enjoyed an unusually long reign as Premier from 2051 until 2072, was lucky enough to preside over a dramatic change in his nation's economic fortunes; by the time of his death the balance of power between the USSR and its ancient adversary the USA had been virtually equalized and the standard of living of the average Russian compared quite favourably with that of the average American. This helped to give Vyshnya a quasi-legendary status unequalled since the days of Lenin, and he was wise enough to use his enormous personal influence to rewrite the doctrine of his party. The Marx whose ideas were cherished in the USSR after Vyshnya's death was not at all the same Marx who had previously been idolized. (Neither of them, of course, bore more than the remotest resemblance to the political economist who had lived two hundred years earlier.)

International co-operation founders

It would be historically inaccurate to suggest that it was the greenhouse crisis alone which forced the world community to embark upon the large-scale planning of the Earth's ecology, but it would have been sufficient to do so even in the absence of other factors. The Athens Conference of 2014 was the first major conference called specifically to formulate world policies for dealing with the crisis. It failed and stagnated – statesmen, if not scientists, were still "thinking national" – but by the Second Conference, seven years later, a new mood of fatalism had possessed many of the delegates, who now accepted the compromises that were a prerequisite effective action.

2020 audio and video storage system, incorporating a bubble memory, alongside its predecessors: disc, audio and video cassettes.

Nevertheless, the nations of the world were still not capable at that time of the degree of co-operation required to meet the world's crisis with a world response. There was too much bitter argument about blame and responsibility, and not enough generosity of spirit. The whole series of Athens Conferences, ending with the sixth in 2115 (nearly fifty years after the fifth) seem in retrospect to have accomplished very little even at the elementary level of funding relief programmes. Each nation continued to protect itself as best it could, and the desperate Third World nations regarded the international agencies to which they turned for help with suspicion and resentment, never believing that they were receiving their due. We can see now, though, that the formation of a world community was bound to be a desperately slow business which could hardly happen by momentary political decision, and we should not underestimate the contribution made by endless and staggeringly boring debates about the correct way to handle the greenhouse crisis.

Internationalism at home

The most important effect of the crisis, in terms of helping to create the world community, was on the attitudes of ordinary people. The mass media spread even into the remotest corners of the planet an awareness of "world problems" whose scope was far beyond villages and nations, far beyond the lifetimes of particular parliaments and statesmen. Individual people began to gain much broader horizons, in time as well as in space, and the demands that they made upon their leaders changed in consequence. For the first time even the poorest people began to take a serious interest in possible ways of transforming the world to the benefit of their children and grandchildren – or, at least, of preserving some kind of world for them at all.

Concern for the future expressed itself in many, sometimes subtle, ways. Long-maturing trees were planted; hobbies like bonsai, which could be passed down the family line, increased their popularity. Personal photograph albums and diaries were, more than ever, arranged with an eye to posterity; there was a fad for coding messages into indestructible holo-cartridges, to be read with awe by remote descendants. One Baltimore firm wrote heavily retouched life-histories of its customers, to show them to the future in a favourable light – a new wrinkle in vanity-publishing!

Benefits of the greenhouse effect

Even before the rise in sea level was arrested by the combined effects of a more reasoned energy-economy and an engineered increase

The devastation of Japan, recorded by an unknown artist, *c.* 2084, after the Japanese master Hokusai. Clearly shown is the eruption of Mount Fuji, an airboat in difficulty, and a hydrofoil seaskimmer at the mercy of the *tsunami.*

in the world's active biomass of carbon dioxide converting plants, which together "smashed the greenhouse", some nations had begun to find ways of exploiting their new circumstances. When Gantz processes (see Chapter Thirteen) revolutionized building technology it became much easier to undertake large-scale adventures in engineering. Large irrigation projects became possible, as did attempts to harness the energy of the tides. Biotechnological desalination, commonplace in the 2070s after the pioneering research of such people as J. F. Kloos and Marya Sarbiewska, was the other significant contribution to the success of such projects.

The great networks of dams and desalination plants built around New Orleans in the USA between 2082 and 2108 and around Chalna in India between 2089 and 2108 were spectacularly successful in the short-term, though they became largely useless by 2180. More important in terms of their long-term success were the great pipelines which could be maintained even as the sea level declined again. The Thar Desert system, connecting many of the poorest settlements of western India to the desalination complexes at Hyderabad in Pakistan and at Baroda was not only a landmark of twenty-first-century technological achievement but an example of close co-operation between antagonistic nations. Had similar projects been mounted in Africa to assist the reclamation of the Sahara and Kalahari deserts much might have been done to prevent that continent's continued suffering, but political wrangling sabotaged the possibility. The country which followed India's lead most spectacularly was Australia, which began to trap, desalinate and redistribute sea-water at a series of stations along Eighty Mile Beach on the edge of the Great Sandy Desert in Western Australia in the 2090s. Over the next hundred years more progress was made in redeeming desert land here than anywhere else on Earth.

The devastation of Japan

The destruction of Honshu, the largest single disaster during the greenhouse crisis, truly tested the international community's ability to respond to a tragedy falling entirely upon just one of its members.

In 2084 Japan was still the world's leading manufacturing nation. Indeed it was said of the world's most successful multinational corporations that they needed one foot solidly planted on American soil, the other in Japan, and that only their multifarious fingers need reach into other nations. Japan was highly vulnerable to the troubles of other nations: energy austerity and the effects of the greenhouse crisis threatened Japanese prosperity, which depended on the purchasing power of people abroad.

The first of the great earthquakes, whose epicentre was near Hamamatsu, devastated the entire south-eastern coast of Honshu, including Tokyo and Osaka. The cities on the Inland Sea, Hiroshima and Takamatsu, were also badly affected. The consequent eruptions of Mount Fuji, which continued through November 2084, and the emergence of a new undersea volcano in the Pacific, promised more quakes, and there were two more huge ones in December. Seismologists monitoring the area predicted that the worst was still to come, and there was a massive attempt through December and January to evacuate southern Honshu and Shikoku. The problem was that no one knew how far the people had to be moved in order to be safe. Refugees fleeing on foot to the north of Honshu had no guarantee of being better off, and no one could predict how much damage Kyushu and Hokkaido were likely to suffer. The coastal areas across the Sea of Japan had their own problems – Korea, in particular, had been badly battered by tidal waves in November, and was preparing for another when the new quake came. Legions of small boats set out southwards, aiming for the Philippines and Indonesia, while those who could pay were airlifted to Australia. The race against time was, of course, quite hopeless.

A nation without a country

The biggest disturbance of the Earth's crust ever recorded occurred on 30 January 2085, breaking Honshu in two and blasting Shikoku apart. The volcanic eruptions associated with the quake threw enough dust into the atmosphere to colour the sunsets for twenty years – dust which was eventually to make a considerable contribution to the arrest of the greenhouse effect. Undersea eruptions boiled millions of tons of seawater. The tidal waves not only devastated the coasts on the other side of the Sea of Japan, but crossed the Pacific to batter the coasts of North and South America. Subsidiary quakes were felt all over the world. The cities of Hungnam, Chongjin and Vladivostok were all but obliterated, and the cities of Japan were simply shaken to pieces.

No comprehensive death-toll was ever published to take account of total world casualties, but in the islands of Japan at least fifteen million people died. The wonder is that so many survived. The evacuation of people from the islands continued not merely for months but for years. The "Japanese diaspora" continued even into the next century.

The power of the Japanese within the multinational corporations helped whole communities to grow up around factories in forty or fifty other nations. In a curious sense the manufacturing nation of Japan survived, though badly injured, not only in Hokkaido and Kyushu but scattered across the globe. Like the Jews before them, the Japanese clung to a national identity that was only partly dependent on there being a place where they theoretically belonged. The Japanese nation, after 2085, was everywhere, and its dispersal was a significant stage in the erosion of cultural heterogeneity and the blurring of racial boundaries.

2120: sea level begins to decline

By comparison with the years 2078-2085, the remaining hundred years of the greenhouse crisis were relatively uneventful. Indeed, as the 2090s elapsed there was a growing sense in many parts of the world that the brink had been reached and avoided. The long-feared nuclear exchange had come and – apparently – gone, and the world had coped with its worst-ever natural disaster. The Plague Wars were a thing of the past, and nuclear fusion had brought a new world of energy-abundance to the horizons of expectation. The crisis went on, but as the twenty-second century progressed, people became gradually more confident that they could survive it. The beginning of the decline in sea-level in the 2120s was greeted with a wave of optimism for the future. It would be a long time before the world regained the ecological stability that would pave the way for authentic recovery, but from 2120 onwards the task of coping with the year-by-year effects of changing sea level had become a matter of routine. The routine was, of course, inefficient by the standards we would demand but in the context of the day it was all that could be expected.

English country life continued for many despite the rising sea levels of the later twenty-first century. This rural dream was achieved by more than a few. Mate and child watch as the breadwinner departs for what was probably a weekly visit to a centralized office some 200 kilometres away. The vehicle is a Eurospace *Quarto* 4-seat skyhopper, an expensive luxury of the time. Autonomic controls meant little effort on the part of the "pilot", while take-offs and landings on the lawn-grid were fully automatic. Centuries-old properties were much prized and immensely expensive to acquire.

CHAPTER TEN

NEW FOOD

World agriculture was already undergoing a revolution when the climatic changes of the greenhouse crisis began to make things difficult for the world's farmers. New techniques in genetic engineering were spawning hundreds of new plant species; clearly they had the potential to completely revolutionize the entire business of world food production.

At the end of the twentieth century, world food-production was organized around the cultivation of cereal crops, of which the most important were wheat, rice and maize. The developing climatic crisis hit the wheat-belts first. These were under stress anyhow, owing to intensification of production during the previous century. The vast wheatfields were supported by an elaborate technology of artificial fertilizers, methods of weed and pest control, and harvesting machinery, but yields were still very vulnerable to slight alterations in the pattern of rainfall. During the twenty-first century the warming of the atmosphere, aided by soil exhaustion and erosion, depleted the North American grain belt and shifted it northwards, damaging the fortunes of Kansas, Iowa and Nebraska irreparably. The European grain belt crept gradually eastwards and became relatively more productive – to the sole advantage of the USSR. Without the long-standing problems of organizing and motivating the Soviet labour force, more might have been made of this advantage; only in the days of the Vyshnya regime were the benefits really accumulated. Heavier rainfall on the Argentinian pampas, and an improvement in the wheat-growing potential of India, increased the economic importance of their fields, but only Argentina managed to increase exports on any great scale.

These were the long-term trends, but they were much interrupted. There was a new instability in world food-production from the beginning to the middle of the century, and the pendulum of instability was still swinging sixty years later. Good years could not compensate for lean years when again and again starvation threatened the teeming populations of the tropics. Rice production in Asia was badly hit by the mercurial shifting of water supplies, and the vast populations of China and her neighbours, which depended so heavily on rice, faced famine with awful regularity.

Genetically engineered wheat and rice

The weapons used to fight the crisis were provided by genetic engineers, who laboured constantly to produce new strains of wheat and rice adapted to different conditions and equipped to withstand the ravages of pests. Shortly after the turn of the century these biotechnologists produced cereal crops that could be grown in company with free-living nitrogen-fixing bacteria, thus lifting some of the burden of nitrate-supply from the farmer. These bacteria could also produce their own special antibiotics to oust the competing wild species. The original methods were clumsy, and rarely worked for long without a backlash from the natural bacteria that were being dispossessed, but it was a start. Later, genetic engineers tailored much better packages of wheat and related micro-organisms which could produce reasonable yields, often in poor conditions.

The first significant engineering of plant genes was concerned with boosting nutritional value. Wheat and rice provided a good foundation for the human diet, but had important deficiencies which caused diseases in the absence of a more varied food intake. The biotechnologists introduced a series of "whole-diet" wheats and rices after 2000, though claims made on behalf of the earliest ones were usually exaggerated. Amid much controversy the Italian biologist Ricardo Cassini set out to test the efficacy of his own improved strain of wheat by living on it from 2015 until 2026, but he was accused of cheating. By 2050, however, there were strains of wheat and rice on the market which could, in theory, sustain life indefinitely without supplementation. Few people were interested in eating the same stuff for a whole lifetime, though, so the matter must, for the time being at least, remain conjectural.

The biotechnologists probably made their most significant contribution to food production with their new methods of weed and pest control. Genes producing natural antibiotics and insecticides were sometimes transplanted into the plants themselves, but more often into bacteria which thus became "microbial police forces" protecting crops against competitors and invaders. When their job was done, they could easily be eradicated by means of highly selective antibiotics tailored for the job.

These techniques helped insulate world agriculture from the effects of the greenhouse crisis, but this was really only a slowing-down of what would otherwise have been a catastrophic decline. In other days the biotechnologists might have boosted world food production two or threefold, but at this time they simply helped to keep it close to its mark.

Seeding the deserts

By 2050 the main focus of agricultural bioengineering was the adapting and designing of crop plants to grow on previously uneconomic land. Much effort also went into making *new* plants which would colonize arid and derelict land to prepare it for reclamation.

Some of the world's deserts had been arid for millions of years, but others were effectively man-made. Most of the rainfall on a tropical rain-forest actually comes from the forest in the first place – a forest is a vast reservoir with its own circulation system of evaporation and precipitation. When a forest is destroyed, whether by grazing animals or by loggers, the cycle is broken and the water lost forever. It was far easier, in the year 2000, for human activity to break such cycles than it was to remake them; deserts were widening year after year, especially in Africa and South America. Even when the world's total rainfall began to rise in the twenty-first century, the changes in its pattern actually helped to create new arid areas by increasing soil erosion. Much of the "new rainfall" simply intensified drought-and-flood cycles afflicting the tropics.

The first plants adapted specifically for wasteland reclamation were not edible. They were sown and abandoned for long periods to do their slow work of gathering water and making nutrient-rich soil, usually with the aid of artificial mycorrhizae – engineered fungi providing the plants with an "auxiliary root system". Billions were planted in the last quarter of the twenty-first century, and although they had no immediate effect on world food supplies or climate, they represented a vital investment. Only with the coming of sophisticated desalination processes and irrigation methods did these new plants really play their part in making deserts bloom. With more attention to such long-term projects the world might have emerged from the Period of Crisis a little sooner, but the needs of starving people made it agonizingly difficult to shift the emphasis from food-producing crops. Such short-term objectives dominated the vast irrigation projects mounted in India and Australia in the 2090s, but long-term reclamation plans around the margins of the new fertile lands were ultimately more important to these nations' agricultural productivity.

Jack Spratt Grass Chop, a fashionable fun-lover's delicacy around the year 2100. Bioengineers gained pleasure from the frivolous even when engaged in the serious business of preventing mass-starvation.

Bioengineered food of the late twenty-second century, *from left:* artificial protein, grilling on a "halo-heater", a common and easily portable cooker of the period – note the leaf-shaped veal substitute; neo-roes, popularly known at the time as "improved Beluga"; a stimulating and thirst-quenching drink, much in demand due to its lack of after effects, wholly bioengineered but tasting exactly like fermented mangoes.

Had the world community been better able to co-ordinate this kind of endeavour, the expansion of the Sahara might have been interrupted as early as 2100, but in fact international and civil strife in North Africa prevented any substantial action for a further eighty years. More spectacular rewards were seen on a much smaller scale in many nations, but there were also tragic failures. Attempts by several Middle Eastern nations – notably Saudi-Arabia and the Gulf states – to bring about dramatic ecological changes could not ultimately be sustained in the face of constant warfare and sabotage. Deserts thrive on human conflict, and there were few areas of the world where conflict was sufficiently suppressed to allow the conquest of the desert. However, it was the long-term ecological consequences of the various nuclear incidents that caused the greatest hindrance to agricultural progress. The greatest tragedy of all was the aftermath of the nuclear exchange of 2078, which devastated the world's fastest-growing agricultural region, and set the clock back more than a hundred years for South American food-production. The next decade was a time of widespread famine, when the world's resources were stretched to their limit.

Biological animal feed

The evolution of biotechnology also affected meat production, which, it had been feared, might have to be savagely cut back, on the grounds that using land to grow animal feed rather than food for human consumption was simply inefficient. This anxiety proved groundless when biological engineering boosted the ability of livestock to convert plant materials into meat, and increased the range of animal feeds.

In the year 2000 many livestock breeders were already using genetically-engineered micro-organisms – single-cell protein, or SCP – as animal feed, and as the biotechnologists began to produce new micro-organisms specially adapted for this role the habit spread. Algae, bacteria and fungi were all used, often in complex mixtures, to produce diet feeds for pigs, poultry, cattle and sheep. The micro-organisms themselves could be grown on a variety of substrates, including enriched molasses, straw and waste paper.

Of course early SCP was branded as "unfit for human consumption"; amazingly, there was a black market in the stuff thanks to rumours among extreme vegetarians (vegans) that SCP, as well as being ideologically acceptable, tasted better than meat. Meanwhile all the hoary old ethnic-restaurant jokes were recycled to feature a kitchen containing a vat of SCP and a variety of moulds for pressing it into the shape of food.

Genetic engineers also went to work on bacteria living inside domestic animals – particularly the gut bacteria of sheep and cattle which convert cellulose into digestible substances. Increasing the efficiency of these proved difficult, but gradual improvements were made. By the middle of the twenty-first century it was no longer necessary to let cattle and sheep roam free to graze – they could be moved into factory farms like pigs and chickens, and fed continuously on a mixture of cellulose wastes and SCP. Many European countries did this on a large scale, but elsewhere the land that was used for grazing could not immediately be diverted to some other use, and there were still cattle out on the range in the Americas and in Africa well into the twenty-second century. Free-grazing sheep remained on the Australian plains

"Moby Cod", a giant colenso, alongside its normal cousin.

until the twenty-third century. Gradually, though, new plants were developed that allowed such land to be much more economically exploited, and the vast herds of animals were concentrated into great barns, where they lived out their lives in tiny pens. Under such closely-controlled conditions they could be made to put on weight much more quickly, with the assistance of artificial hormones and manipulation of their developmental processes. Most of the animals bred on factory farms would not have been able to roam free in any case – their legs usually could not support their bodies.

The meat business was the food-producing industry least affected by the climatic changes, and world meat production rose steadily throughout the Period of Crisis. There were interruptions to its continued success when bad harvests produced a shortfall in the plant materials still used to feed domestic animals, but the genetically-engineered SCP feeds meant that such disruptions were minor. The increase in meat production aided poor countries as well as rich ones, but they started from a much lower baseline, so that this additional meat did little to compensate for the uncertainty of their harvests.

Genetically modified fish

The large building projects undertaken in the last decades of the twenty-first century to hold back the encroaching sea and to exploit the energy of the tides also encouraged experiments in fish-farming on a vaster scale than ever before. Alga-based feeds for fish had long been available, and could be converted into fish protein very efficiently under the right conditions. The problem had always been to arrange the right conditions. The creation of vast sea-water lagoons on the eastern coast of North America and the northern coast of Australia, undertaken in connection with sea defences and irrigation projects, allowed these possibilities to be realized.

Genetic engineers soon had spectacular success working not only on the algae designed to feed the fish, but on the fish themselves. Biotechnologists had worked out numerous ways to make all domestic animals put on weight more rapidly, but had found the task of manipulating the genomes of mammals and birds very difficult. Fish, which produce eggs in such vast quantities and are much simpler organisms, proved easier to work with. Soon there were new, gene-modified strains of fish which could grow to enormous size. The Bannon salmon, developed in Scotland in 2098, eventually produced specimens weighing 300 kilos, while the American Colenso cod had by 2127 achieved an average weight of 180 kilos. The nickname "Moby Cod" rapidly passed into folklore. Such fish were, of course, reared in individual pens in constantly moving water, perpetually swimming even though they never moved.

Fish-farming of this kind was of marginal importance in the context of worldwide food production, but the spectacular success of the companies which developed it encouraged much more ambitious plans for the exploitation of the sea.

CHAPTER ELEVEN

THE LOST BILLION

The success of the new agriculture was achieved only at vast cost in human suffering. By the end of the Period of Crisis, in 2180, there had been a massive displacement of family-based crop-growing on a small scale by large-scale monoculture farming. Although, depending on definition, there were still between fifty and five hundred million peasant farmers in the world, that change had displaced more than a billion people in the course of six generations, relatively few of whom were offered new ways of life. Inevitably the vast majority of the dispossessed were in Central and South America, Africa and Southern Asia.

The trend away from peasant and subsistence farming had begun even before the year 2000. By the end of the century it accelerated rapidly under the impact of the new plants developed by genetic engineers. A great deal of land which had previously been marginal, and had therefore accumulated populations of subsistence farmers, now became economically viable – even though years of preparatory work had sometimes to be done.

The nationalization of land

Before ecological management of this kind became practicable many governments had been sympathetic to their poor farmers and had tried to assist them with legislative measures. Genetic engineers, too, had invested great effort in trying to develop new

The dispossessed: throughout the Period of Crisis millions were moved from camp to camp and never shared the leisured life available to people in the developed countries.

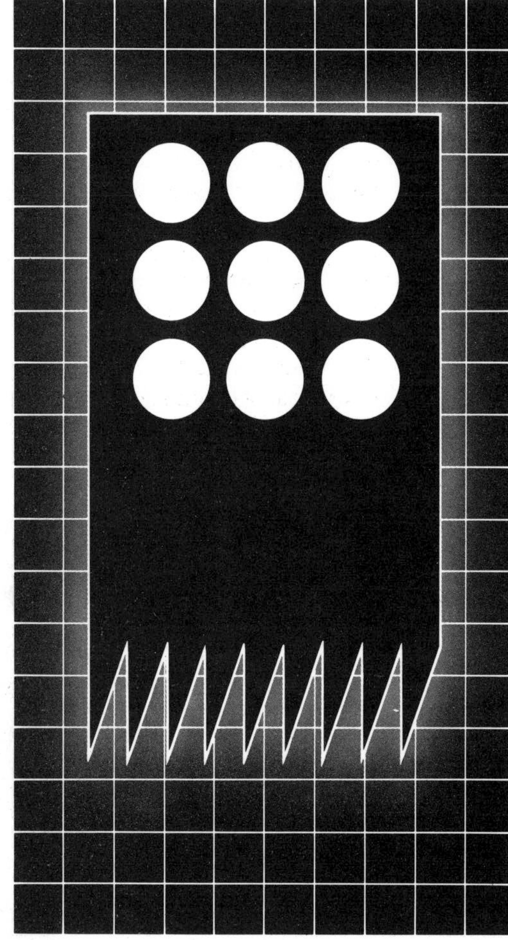

The nine zeroes of the "Lost Billion" became a symbol for many religious cults and guerilla groups of the 2070s. This flag was used by a squad dedicated to the removal of every head of state in Pan-Africa.

crops adapted to subsistence farming. But in the latter half of the twenty-first century governments set out to use technological power to reorganize their agricultural systems more effectively. The tide turned against the subsistence farmers, the peasants and the old-style landlords alike. Conditions of land tenure were altered dramatically and, regardless of the ideological jargon used to cloak the measures, what happened was a virtual nationalization of land and a collectivization of farming. It mattered little whether the new controllers were agents of the state, as in countries with a Marxist political tradition, or cartels of notionally-independent farmers, as in countries with capitalist traditions.

Following this collectivization, most governments – perhaps heeding the failure of collective farms in Russia and elsewhere during the twentieth century – gave the land-workers every incentive to succeed. Even in trouble-torn Africa there were notable successes in terms of agricultural efficiency and output, including the New Economic Policy adopted by Tanzania in 2047 and the reforms following the Nigerian *coup d'etat* of 2058. However, spectacular gains could go hand-in-hand with spectacular problems: the Tanzanian reforms were followed by mass migrations of refugees into Kenya and Mozambique, and the emergence of concentration camps inside Tanzania itself.

Millions dispossessed

The upheavals which Tanzania managed to cram into two decades were spread over as much as a century and a half elsewhere, but they still took place throughout the poorer regions of the world. The ragged armies fighting endless wars of rebellion were constantly swelled by legions of the dispossessed. Men and, increasingly, women took up arms while mothers, children and the elderly were herded into camps. Third World cities were flooded with immigrants, and the huge death-tolls of the later plague wars had as much to do with overcrowding and poor sanitation as with the deadliness of the plague. Neither plague nor warfare stemmed the tide of displaced and desperate people; and ironically, as the new agricultural policies began to bear fruit, famine was held at bay and played no part in settling the Malthusian equation.

Horror stories abounded concerning the ways in which Third World governments dealt with the dispossessed. Accusations of mass murder were commonplace and undoubtedly a shocking number of people were simply killed. Almost all governments, though, did try to find humane solutions. When they gathered people together in vast camps, it genuinely was to facilitate famine relief and medical aid. Had there been ways to redeploy the people usefully they would have done so. The Third World governments were as eager for solutions as their people. There were none to be found; with city populations still expanding, the birth explosion was not yet damped down and demographic change was happening too quickly for effective response. Dispossessed small farmers simply could not be absorbed into other ways of life – and for many, the possibility of other ways of life was beyond their imaginative horizon.

Much of the new monoculture farming was designed to be labour-intensive, and many of the displaced peasants became employees. Whole villages and towns could sometimes be rebuilt – vastly improved, once Gantz processes (see Chapter Thirteen) came into common use – and their populations reintegrated into the new system, but this was never enough.

The greatest tragedy of the Period of Crisis

The subsistence farmers were the worst hit. They had never really been integrated into a great society or an economic system. They had lived freely, looking after themselves, aliens within their own nations. They had never had much to do with governments, and had never wanted to. Stripped of their self-sufficiency, precarious though it had been, they considered themselves robbed of their humanity. When they took arms and became guerilla fighters, they did so not in the name of political ideologies, nor with any realistic ends in mind. Frequently, they became religious cultists, celebrating the end of their world with ceremonies of sacrifice and destruction. People began to refer to them in the 2070s as "the lost billion", though the figure had no particular relevance. The number of people dispossessed and ultimately destroyed, over six generations, must have been considerably greater than that, though many appeared in death-tolls attributed to other immediate causes. This was the greatest tragedy of the Period of Crisis – *the* underlying tragedy, more to be lamented than accidents of fate like the Japanese earthquakes because it was as necessary as it was terrible. The world's unease betrayed itself in contemporary gallows humour – "You know Tanzania mislaid ten million refugees? Maybe you didn't know they're the biggest SCP producers in Africa, and it's got to come from somewhere . . ." There was a defensive readiness to believe appalling things about the dispossessed – that they regularly put poisons or psychedelics in water supplies, that they planned to actualize their end-of-the-world cult belief by detonating an old atomic weapon they'd dug up, that they ate babies – anything to shift one's instinctive guilt about what was happening by implying that the victims deserved it.

A billion lost identities

Today this whole episode may seem incomprehensible. The world's total food production was always theoretically capable of feeding its population, except in brief periods when world-wide harvests failed disastrously, as in 2086-87. Even allowing for the greed and over-consumption of rich nations, the needs of the poor might still have been met. Nor was the will to meet that need entirely absent. The disinherited could have been fed, and often *were* fed, as best they could be – but "man does not live by bread alone". It was not free food they wanted, nor even houses. Their ways of life had given them not only food and shelter, but also identities, without which they felt themselves to be nothing. A man in a rich country might lose one job and find another, switching the accessories of his life with relative ease. The poor farmers could not; they were not philosophically equipped to do it. In being dispossessed they were "losing their lives", and it is not surprising that so many of them went on to lose them in a more literal sense.

The whole sad mess continued into the late twenty-second century, and is the principal reason why the date 2180 marks the conclusion of the Period of Crisis. The problem of the dispossessed had finally, and literally, died out. At the same time the greenhouse crisis was almost over and the stabilization of mean sea level, though still some way off, was in sight. The slow spread of fusion reactors was putting an end to the energy crisis. Biotechnologists had assembled the armoury necessary to tackle problems of large-scale ecological management. All this was instrumental in the decline of poverty and civil strife.

We must not forget, though, that another reason why the small wars that beset more than a hundred nations had almost petered out by 2180 was that those wars had been lost. The rebels had been defeated, and for the great majority of those who had taken arms in the previous two centuries defeat meant death. We do not know what fraction of the "lost billion" was eventually absorbed into the new order, but we know that it was small. The huge new fields that were to supply the needs of the world for the next few hundred years extended, literally and metaphorically, over the graves of countless poor people who had once called tiny sections of those fields their own.

CHAPTER TWELVE

THE SOWING OF THE SEAS

The first photosynthetic organisms subjected to genetic engineering were single-celled algae, the simplest entities to deal with. Experimental work quickly progressed to the more complicated colonial algae, and eventually to the multi-celled algae, most of which were seaweeds.

Algae provide ideal material for genetic engineering. They combine simplicity with versatility, and being capable of vegetative reproduction can multiply vastly from a few transformed individuals. The pioneers of this research intended that their work should eventually have an economic use, but in the early part of the twenty-first century the planning initiatives were missing. Experimental scientists like Pernelle in the USA and Havelock in Australia wrote in the 2010s about the possibility of designing new single-celled algae to enrich the phytoplankton, and new multi-celled algae for cultivation in shallow inshore waters, but such projects required planning on such a bold scale that little notice was taken.

Before the year 2050 seaweeds were virtually unexploited. Some could be eaten, but never formed an important part of anyone's diet; some accumulated iodine from seawater and were an important source of the element; some were used to make agar jelly. When commercial genetic engineers began to take an interest in the experimental work of Pernelle and Havelock, it was the second of the uses that attracted them. If seaweeds could extract and concentrate one element from seawater, why not others?

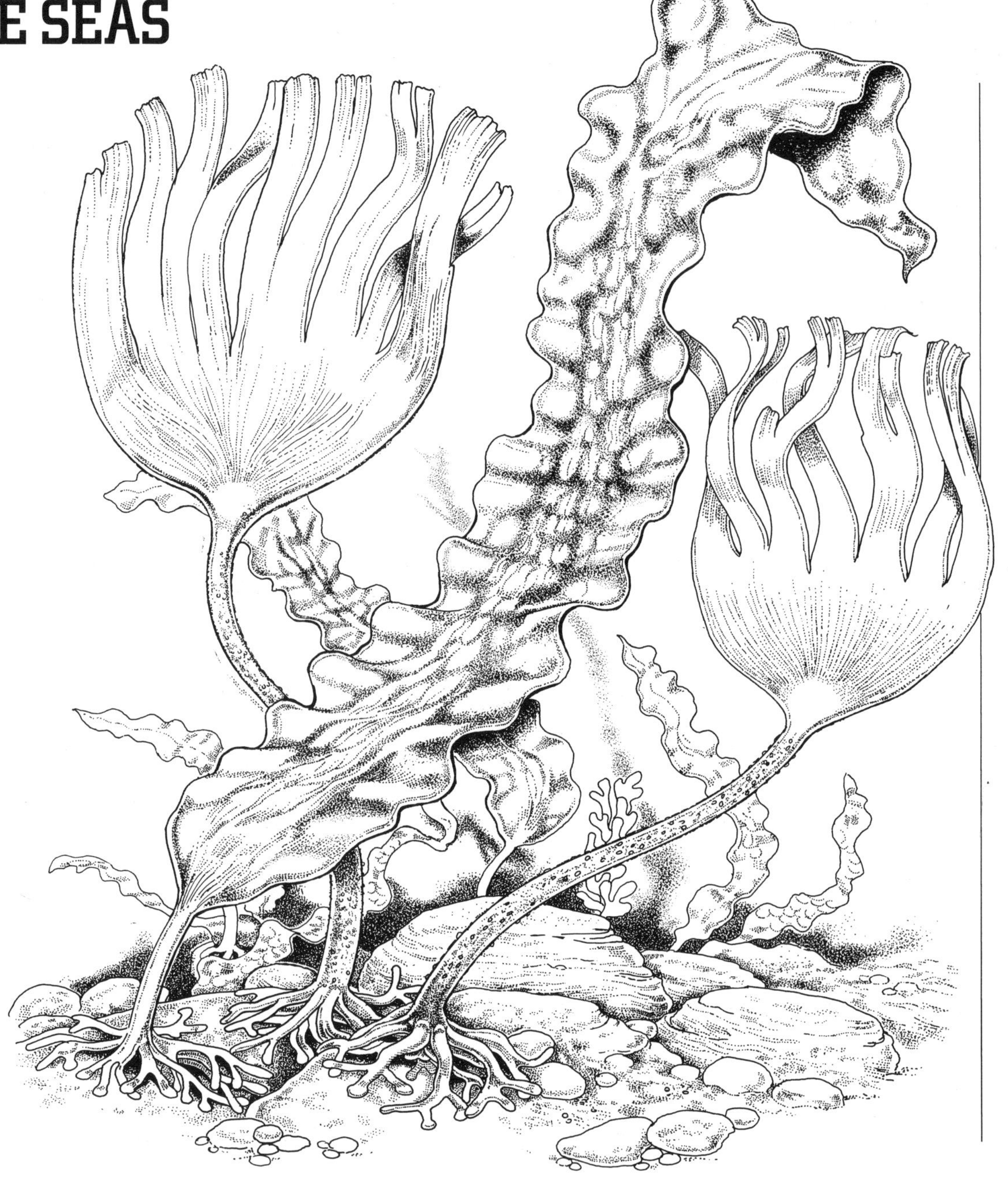

Seaweed became one of the world's most important food crops during the twenty-first century. These giant kelps were produced by Ozfoods, an Australian company of the 2090s.

The first kelp farms

Edible and nutritious seaweeds proved quite easy to manufacture, but these could not compete economically with land-based crops until the development of giant strains that could grow massively and rapidly in shallow water, especially in salt-marshes around river estuaries. These artificial weeds were called "kelps", after the largest natural seaweeds, though they were not all derived from actual kelp species. Areas suitable for sowing with kelp were limited, but in the 2060s considerable kelp-fields were developed on the eastern seaboard of the USA and – more impressively – in shallow, recently-formed waters in the south of Australia. Australia had such success with these early endeavours that during the 2070s and 2080s kelp farming spread around the shores of the continent, proving even more successful in the warmer waters off the northern coast. In the USA there was little expansion because the inhabitants of Florida and California strongly resisted such ugly industries. Chile, Peru and Ecuador took advantage of the growing expertise of the Australian scientists. Chile, with its enormously extended and relatively underpopulated coastline, invested heavily in shore-line cultivation (its inland regions did not lend themselves to efficient conventional crops). By 2130 the South Pacific coast of South America was a vast chain of kelp farms, extending from Tumaco in Colombia all the way to Tierra del Fuego.

Australia leads the way

The Australians, though, had an advantage that their imitators and competitors lacked: vast shallow seas. Their sea farming could expand outwards, gradually filling the whole of the Gulf of Carpentaria: nearly half a million square kilometres of shallow, warm water, mostly less than a hundred fathoms deep. This was where the largest artificial kelps were developed, yielding both food products and – equally important in the early days – fuel oils. As early as 2110 the Carpentarian kelp farms had become an important sector of the Australian economy, and they continued to grow in importance for the next half-century.

Fired by this success the Australian genetic engineers revived enthusiasm (*circa* 2112) for the manipulation of single-celled algae. It no longer seemed ridiculous to contemplate sowing vast regions of the sea – the Indian and Pacific oceans – with enriched plankton to be harvested by great factory ships. The scheme had an impressive grandeur, enhanced by the glowing fact that two-thirds of the sunlight reaching the Earth falls upon the sea.

Bitter conflict over maritime sovereignty

Unfortunately, the Australians quickly reawoke political conflicts which had lain dormant for nearly a century, and the United Nations was again forced to debate the issue of whether any nation was entitled to exploit the oceans beyond the limits of its legal jurisdiction. Even in the twentieth century this issue had caused confusion over fishing and whaling quotas. There had been great resentment then, in the smaller nations, which felt that the rich had no right to plunder the oceans simply because they owned the necessary technology.

The United Nations had passed a series of resolutions demanding that profits from exploitation of the mineral wealth of the ocean depths must be shared between all nations. The net effect had been to discourage deep-sea mining projects. However, such projects could not in any case have been mounted in a period of energy-austerity and the arguments had therefore been allowed to die. Now they began to rage once more. In 2118 the Australian prime minister, Malcolm Hamer, presented to the United Nations a scheme for sowing the Timor Sea with engineered planktonic algae. Ironically, Hamer was able to come to an agreement with Indonesia, the other nation with an implicit interest in the Timor, but it proved more difficult to negotiate the matter of principle with the rest of the world community. A special conference in 2119 failed to reach agreement, and the issue became a point of bitter dispute between radical green parties represented in the UN, their "grey" opponents, and the smaller nations which had an interest in establishing the principle of collective sovereignty.

The more anxious environmentalists were concerned that sowing the sea with engineered algae was quite different from sowing fields with engineered bacteria. It was relatively easy to confine artificial organisms on land, but the sea had no natural boundaries. To introduce engineered organisms into the plankton was, they thought, to run the risk of triggering a vast ecological chain-reaction whose repercussions could not be foreseen. In Australia itself there was considerable opposition to Hamer's plan on these grounds, thereby weakening his position. The green factions and the poorer nations formed an alliance to establish the legal framework of collective sovereignty over the sea. The former hoped that a corollary would be the hindrance of plans by any single nation or corporation to interfere with the oceanic life-systems.

The UN controls the oceans
It turned out, however, that the green parties had made a tactical error. Once it was accepted that poor nations stood to gain from large-scale endeavours to exploit the plankton, they not only dropped their opposition but began to encourage the Australians to go ahead. Effectively, the UN found itself in the position of "renting out" the surface of the ocean, with the prospect that the revenues would enhance both the power of the UN itself and the economic fortunes of its numerous poor members. Arguably, this acceptance of the principle of collective sovereignty over the oceans was the single most important step toward making the United Nations an authentic tier of world government.

In 2127 Australian ships began seeding the Timor Sea with engineered algae, and within five years an even grander plan was taking shape to seed the Coral Sea east of the Great Barrier Reef. The first harvests brought in by the factory ships in 2129 were monitored very carefully by scientists from several nations, with the resentful green factions eager to find evidence of unforeseen troubles. There were bitter arguments about the effect on natural species and dark murmurings about the tragedy of mass extinctions, but the initiative lay with the other side, and the harvests were generally represented as a great success. Saboteurs who tried to spread alarm and "defend the purity of the sea" by dumping vicious herbicides into the alga fields (a classic piece of doublethink) were unable to operate on a large enough scale for successful propaganda. Indeed, propaganda worked the other way: the ultra-green group responsible had not realized that plant-killers might also kill their beloved rare fish. Their education was painful.

Defeat of the "red tide"
Although by 2180, as the Period of Crisis finally eased to its close, the plankton fields had become a significant element in world agriculture, the green activists were correct in arguing that the biotechnologists were not really in control. In 2135 their prophecies of disaster seemed justified when the Timor fields were devastated by an alien invader – a blooming "red tide" which threatened to poison the sea within and without the cultivated regions. The *Schadenfreude* of the environmentalists was, however, rapidly dispelled. The Australian bioengineers, forewarned by their own anxieties, were prepared: a team led by Stephen O'Callaghan quickly developed an engineered rotifer, a microscopic swimming animal which thrived on the red invader, and released these into the fields in great quantities. Nature had fought back against the genetic engineers but, as in several classic battles on land, it was the engineers who won. Two years' harvests were badly hit, but the corporations involved absorbed the financial loss. By 2137 the balance had been restored, and it was to be many years before any comparable difficulty arose.

The fact that the Australian scientists coped so well boosted confidence in the entire enterprise of ecological management. So many bitter words had been spoken against the Timor Sea project that it had come to seem an important test case. The plan was so ambitious, and the hazards had been described with such enthusiasm by its enemies, that when the red tide was vanquished it appeared that a great victory had been won. The notion that men might take control of the entire working ecosphere suddenly seemed much more reasonable. Of course, that en-

terprise was at a very early stage, and the optimism had far more to do with the ebb and flow of political argument than with a realistic appraisal of technical accomplishments. But the fact that the idea took firm root was vitally important to the shaping of future plans. With hindsight, we can see that the early sea-farmers were very fortunate not to face more serious problems more often, for their tools were very primitive, but we can also see that the gradual expansion of plankton-farming into the Coral Sea laid the foundations for changes vital to the making of our modern world.

Plankton harvesters, *left*, glide over the Timor Sea in the twenty-second century. Traces of red in the foreground indicate that rotifers have consumed most of the "Tide" in this area.

Enriched plankton production in 2180, *below*, was concentrated in the warm, shallow waters of the world's seas and oceans.

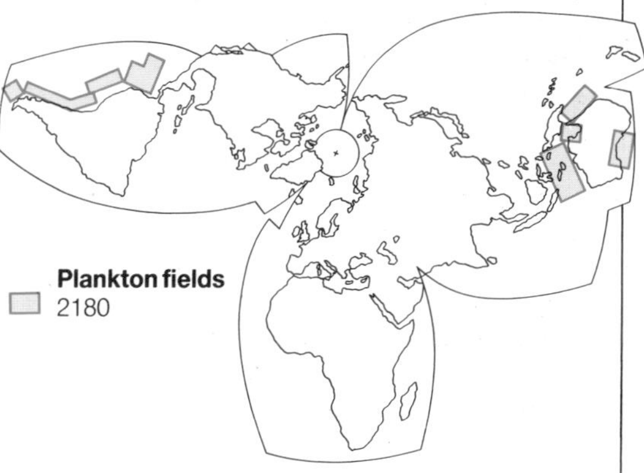

CHAPTER THIRTEEN

THE URBAN REVOLUTION

It may seem strange to speak of an "urban revolution" in the first two centuries of the third millennium, given that people had been gathering together in towns and cities for thousands of years, and also that the latter part of the millennium saw the rapid decay of the great cities. Nevertheless, it does make sense.

There are four basic needs which are vital to human survival. We must have food, water, fuel and shelter. There never had been a time before the third millennium when all four of these necessities were adequately and simultaneously supplied to more than a tiny minority of the world's population. But the first century of that millennium saw a new development: the gap between supply and demand – which had been narrowing – began to grow again. The increase in world population put great strain on the world's supplies while many people set their sights much higher in calculating what constituted an adequate standard of living.

New biotechnologies eventually began to take up the strain in respect of the first two needs. The evolution of fusion technology finally dealt with the third. Because the need for shelter was less harshly felt than the other three in the poorest parts of the world (which were located mainly in the tropics), this fourth need received less attention. Nevertheless, eventually the problems associated with it called forth new technologies too.

To provide people with adequate homes is not simply a matter of keeping out the cold and the rain. Sanitation and water-supply are also important; and though they are not matters of life or death, no humane designer can ignore the issues of privacy, personal space, the opportunity to organize one's posessions, to furnish and decorate – to make, in short, a shelter into a home. By comparison with the richest people in the world the poor of the twenty-first century were badly fed, had little access to fresh water, and were chronically short of fuel, but discrepancies in housing conditions were even more spectacular. The disparities are even more striking if one compares the poorer and richer individuals within the rich nations. In old India, beggars were seen and tolerated outside the very palace gates; now, in twenty-first-century New York state, miserable shanty-towns of down-and-outs sprang up in corners of wealthy estates, to be indignantly driven away.

Outmoded cities

In the year 2001 billions of poor people throughout the world had only the most rudimentary protection from the elements and very little else. Even the richest cities had populations of homeless and desperate people, and most had slums where environmentally-induced illnesses were commonplace. Even the handsome homes of the rich were ill-equipped for the fast-developing social and economic circumstances; no cities had been built with the coming energy crisis in mind. Rich apartments were abandoned because the expense of installing the insulation required by law could not be met: squatters moved in before the fleeing owners were out of sight. Whole blocks relying on expensively obsolete heating systems stood vacant, to be gutted by scavengers. The energy war left gaps in the building line, as if it were a literal war of tanks and bombs.

These buildings could not move with the times; they were too solid and substantial, and took too long to build and rebuild. The problems faced by the richer nations in the twenty-first century were exacerbated by the disastrous fashions in house-building during the previous century. The theories of architects and the cost-cutting habits of builders had often failed spectacularly to meet the needs and demands of the public, but as the economic depression worsened it became more and more difficult to compensate for their follies: their showy displays of glass through which heat escaped as through a sieve; their ostentatious internal spaces which required far more heating than snug, low-ceilinged rooms, and so on. Early in the Period of Crisis, building technology did make some progress, but labour and energy costs meant that such improvements had only a marginal effect even in richer countries. The vastness of the problem defied solution: there were five billion people in the world; all save a handful wanted improved housing and they could hardly secure it by applying the logic of taking in one another's washing.

Wood became increasingly scarce and trees were strictly conserved – depriving the poor of a vital structural material. Ingenious use of pressed earth, stone and brick merely slowed the rate at which things were getting worse. Two major factors inhibited the exploitation of Third World environments for building materials: the cost of brick-making and stone-working, and the weight of the products (and hence the cost of transporting them). Both problems seemed intractable.

The Gantz cementation process

Several minor advances in cementation and fibre technology were made in the early twenty-first century, but the crucial breakthrough which was to have a profound effect in rich and poor nations alike was the Gantz

Gantz materials occasionally ran riot. Here spidery tendrils threatened to take over a dwelling in Boston, Massachusetts.

cementation process, named after the American Leon Gantz (2008-2092). There were hundreds of variations on the single basic theme, and Gantz was by no means the only man who did vital work in developing the prototypes, but he had pioneered the development of the technique and was its most vociferous propagandist.

Essentially, Gantz processes involve the use of genetically-engineered bacteria to manufacture organic "glues" which bind together aggregations of particles (usually sand but also soil, dust and slag). The bacteria are normally set to work on site, with moulds being used to control the shape of the eventual conglomerate. By careful selection and control of the bacteria, the properties of the resultant structures can be varied. It is possible to make bricks and blocks, or whole walls and floors. Clever builders soon worked out ways to build whole houses more-or-less of a piece.

Gantz supervised the development of nearly a hundred different organisms between 2049 and his retirement in 2088. He was determined to find ways to define the strength, density, insulation and waterproofing of his products, so that any reasonable set of specifications could be met. He found ways of combining materials, and allowed builders to change the properties of the ground on which they built as well as binding the houses firmly to it. Although many variants of the Gantz process required temperatures of 37°C to work at maximum efficiency, it was in general a low-energy technology even in the early days. Over time, processes of this kind became so adaptable to circumstances that it became possible for gangs of men with earth-moving machines to move into virtually any environment and begin raising buildings out of whatever materials were locally abundant.

Perhaps the most bizarre Gantz home was the eccentric interior decorator Fritz Brenner's "Tower of Sand", built below the high-tide mark on a beach. Specially tailored Gantz bacteria caused the water-lashed sands not to erode the walls but to thicken them year by year into an extraordinary "organic" shape resembling a deformed termite-nest. Another eccentricity was the sentimental treatment of the crumbling White Cliffs of Dover with organisms which not only preserved the famous landmark but secreted fluorescent compounds to make the chalk whiter than white.

By 2065 the Gantz processes were supplemented by other biotechnologies which used engineered bacteria to crumble and pulverize certain kinds of rock. These techniques, used in concert with Gantz's processes, could be applied in the most unpromising places. Most of the companies involved in the development of biotechnology were already interested in "bacterial quarrying" but the limited profitability of such research was an inhibiting factor until the Gantz process radically increased demand.

Leon Gantz

In an earlier century Gantz would have become one of the richest men in the world, but he was working within the framework of a much larger research institution – the Imperial Biotechnology subsidiary of Plenum Inc – and the profits from his patents were dispersed to a multitude of shareholders and tax-gatherers. He claimed in his autobiography, though, that he had always had more money than he knew what to do with, and had found wealth a distraction. He saw him-

self as a kind of alchemist, achieving dominion over the transformation of substances, and remained fanatically dedicated to his work and his art. He was immensely proud of his two sons, who both became architects, and regarded them as apostles carrying the benefits of his wisdom into the world.

Gantz processes also facilitated road-building, bridge-building and canal-building. Although they were not the whole of the urban revolution of the late twenty-first and early twenty-second centuries, the processes literally paved the way for the new era.

Biotechnological water systems

The other technologies that were vital to the building of new towns and the rebuilding of old ones were mainly concerned with water-supplies and sanitary provision. Biotechnologies were being developed during Gantz's lifetime which could accumulate, store and release water. Their use as waste-processing systems was both revolutionary and obvious. Initially such systems were simply installed in cavities, but by the mid-twenty-first century the richer countries were making much of "fully integrated" housing systems whereby living structures were built into Gantz walls, just as circulatory systems are built into living bodies. Tanks and pipes were used less to deliver water to homes and to process sewage.

All sophisticated buildings after 2160 were equipped with "active" water-handling systems whereby the structure could take up and store environmental water – often extending "tap roots" deep into the ground – the *next* revolution in building, which applied genetically-engineered organisms directly to the supply of structures – creating not houses containing living, organic "appliances" but houses which were a single, integrated "life-form".

Inevitably, this kind of technology was exploited most fully and ingeniously in the richer countries, where it neatly answered political demands for "ecologically sound" housing policies. The water-processing biotechnologies took their place alongside mechanical technologies for heating and air-conditioning. There was much talk in the developed world of "symbiotic living" and "balanced environmental relations", although the actual meaning of such terms remained unclear. Such sloganizing was encouraged by the ascendancy of what came to be known as "green" politics.

Transformation of Third World cities

It was in the Third World that Gantz processes really transformed lifestyles. The buildings constructed for the very poor were simple and stereotyped, basic in design and provision. Although very cheap, they were adequate for the business of living; they met the need of a billion people whose need had never been met before. There still remained great differences between the houses of the rich and of the poor. In the cities, in particu-

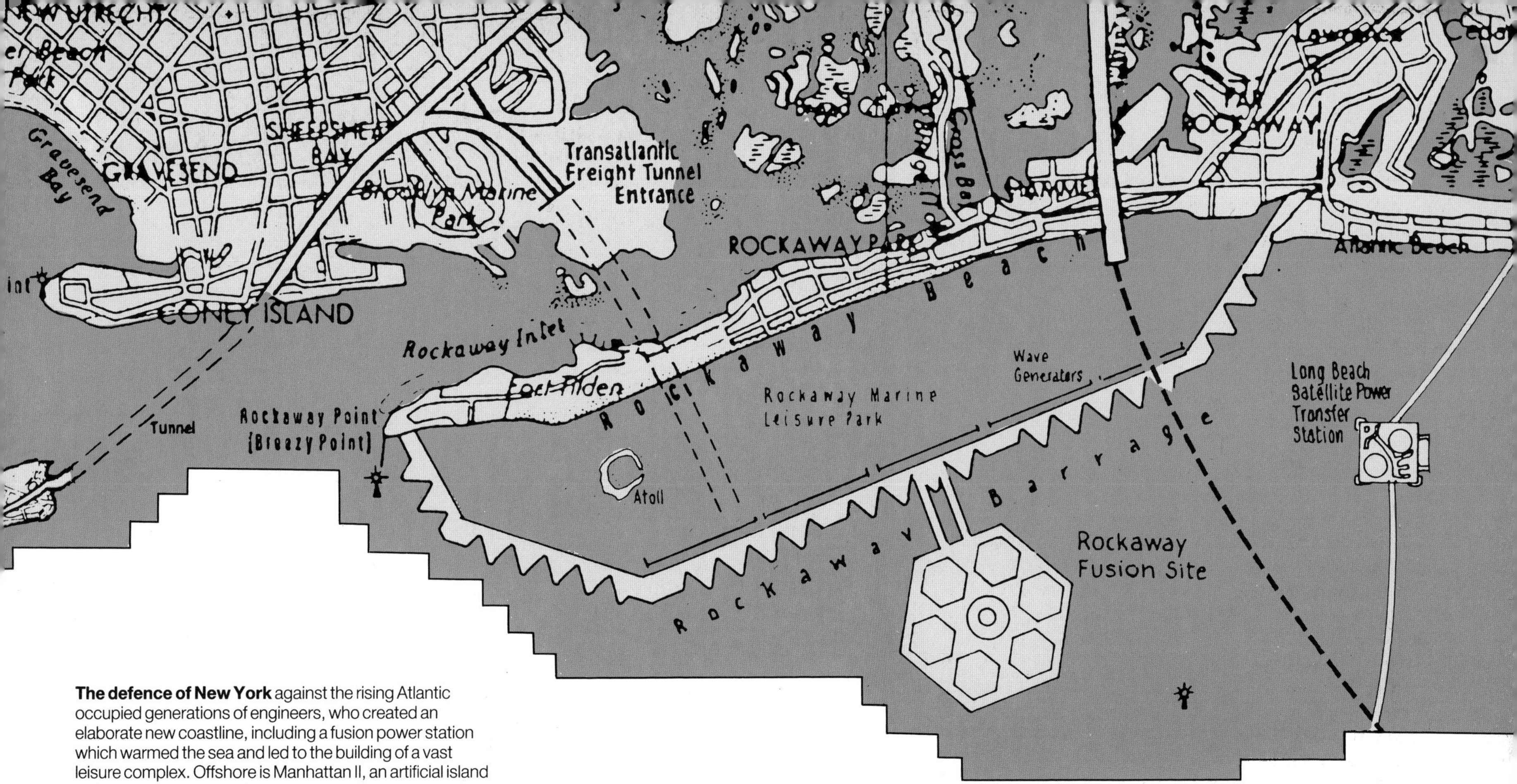

The defence of New York against the rising Atlantic occupied generations of engineers, who created an elaborate new coastline, including a fusion power station which warmed the sea and led to the building of a vast leisure complex. Offshore is Manhattan II, an artificial island built to the same general plan as the original.

lar, the poor tended to be huddled together, undersupplied with space and light; but in the long fight against environmental illnesses the tide had been turned. Damp and infestation were gradually banished.

The twenty-second century saw few achievements to match the transmogrification of some of the world's ugliest and most dilapidated cities. The rebuilding of Calcutta, of Nairobi and of Valparaiso took place in the Period of Crisis, not in the Period of Recovery which followed. These vast projects were planned and carried through in the space of two generations, at a time when the relevant nations faced problems as frightful as any in their history. Even the "new cities" of Calcutta, Nairobi and Valparaiso are gone now; they were to be rebuilt twice over before they began to decline with the fall in numbers and dispersal of the world's population. In photographs and on film the rebuilt cities of the twenty-second century look crude and ugly to us, but they were the products of a highly significant revolution and deserve to be remembered. They represented the first stage in a sequence of changes which was ultimately to make the whole world a fit place for human beings to live in.

Manhattan skyline and its domed and spired twin, the artificial island of Manhattan II.

Gantz homes in California: engineered to resemble natural formations, these homes had grass, trees and other vegetation growing from their "roofs". These particular dwellings had full-length picture windows – many owners preferred whole wall holo-displays instead.

CHAPTER FOURTEEN

THE EMPIRE OF THE TELESCREEN

Biotechnology half-equipped the world to meet its crisis. The other half of the cornucopia was information technology: a *genus* of electronic hardware concerned with transmitting and processing data. Many stereotyped, repetitive tasks carried out on long production lines were taken out of human hands and entrusted to programmed robots. Electronic media of communication allowed other kinds of work to be dispersed into the homes of the workers. These trends were already well established by the year 2000, but were slightly inhibited by the developing energy-crisis, which made the cost of machinery rise faster than the cost of labour.

For individuals in the developed countries, the changes were symbolized by the multiplying roles performed by what were once called television sets but which were now retitled "visual display units" (VDUs) or "telescreens". Telescreens had come into homes in the later twentieth century, initially as carriers of news and entertainment. Electromagnetic signals were broadcast through the atmosphere, emitted by ground stations and received by household aerials.

2001: telescreen potential largely unused

By the first year of the third millennium, the screens had become much more versatile. They offered a window into the electronic space of microcomputers, displaying written programs and images generated by programs. They could be used in association with video-cassette recorders to store, structure and play back numerous forms of information and entertainment. By this time the geosynchronous orbit around the Earth's equator was heavily populated with communications satellites of great complexity, allowing material to be broadcast over wide areas. The invention of optical fibres, capable of carrying hundreds of channels of information simultaneously, permitted receivers to draw many different information-streams from a single dish aerial, and permitted direct transmissions from one screen to another if the screens were equipped to send as well as to receive.

A remarkable explosion of inventive ingenuity had made all these functions available by the year 2001, but at that time they were all relatively under-exploited. Even the richest nations had been unable to put these possibilities into reality on anything more than an experimental scale. Only a tiny minority of the world's population had access to telescreens which could do anything except receive broadcast programmes. For many years after they first became technically feasible, the spread of the new functions was severely limited by the simple problem of integrating private telescreens into national and international networks.

An extensive network of cables already existed: the telephone system. What was required was replacement and augmentation of that existing system, to cope with the hugely increased information-transfer demanded by the booming home-telescreens industry. All radio, telephone and televisual communication could then be integrated into a single worldwide network. No one seriously doubted that this could be done, but it would take a long time – decades, if not centuries – and there were many practical problems to do with information control.

The USA – the richest nation in the world and the one which had taken most enthusiastically to television in the twentieth century – was best placed, technologically, to build such a national network, but had problems because of its sheer size. Western European countries had the advantage of compactness, but depended on the superpowers' technical expertise – especially in establishing the communications satellites vital to the system. Progress was slowed by petty argument caused by the different priorities and anxieties of the leading nations. Even in 2038 the new united front presented by President Konrad and Premier Kamenov concealed bitter dispute over information flow between their countries.

A glittering toy of enormous significance

Ordinary people welcomed the spread of the information networks. It was easy enough to see the advantages of being connected, and although they had anxieties about the power of governments to monitor their affairs and the possible erosion of social intercourse, the new opportunities dominated people's attitudes. Telescreens seemed to be wonderful, new and glittering toys.

It is difficult to distinguish the importance of telescreens' different functions. Special significance was certainly attached to those which made network communication two-way, so that people could put information in as well as take it out. The West German "electronic referendum" of 2025, which changed that country's voting structure, was an early example of instantaneous and accurate consultation of the people – although few governments cared to consult the people too often.

Electronic publication

There was significance, too, in the extension of reference facilities: although so much printed information was stockpiled in the great national libraries that it could not all be

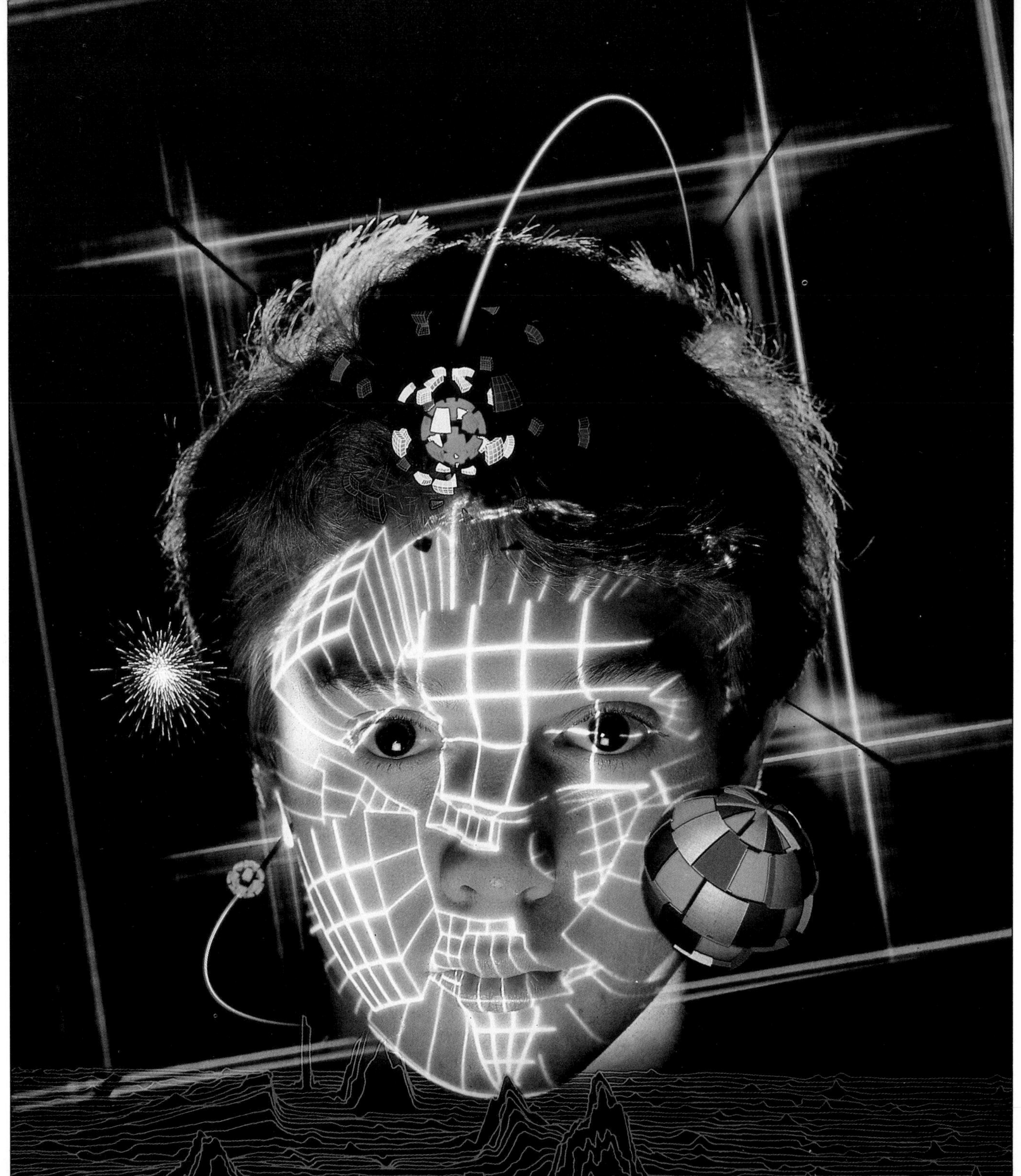

Early French holoscreen test card, thought to date from the 2150s. Users would adjust their sets for depth of field, focus, brilliance and contrast.

made electronically available, the work of transferring it proceeded as efficiently as it could. By 2010 all texts published in the English language were routinely put on electronic deposit, and other countries quickly followed the lead given by the USA and Britain. By 2030 it was commonplace for electronic deposit to be the sole form of publication for scientific papers, official reports and other reference items, to be reproduced by a printer only at the point of consumption.

Again, an increasing role was played by the networks in the purchase of goods. In the course of the twenty-first century it became normal for suppliers of goods to display their wares *via* video cameras to people in their homes, to accept payment by electronically-transmitted credit, and then to arrange shipment.

An end to commuting

There is little doubt, however, that the single most significant aspect of the information networks was their impact on patterns of working. Even in the early days there was visible displacement of "clerical" work from the office to the home. People whose jobs consisted mainly of processing information no longer had to commute to do so. Electronically-stored information could be moved much more easily over long distances than information stored on paper. By the middle of the twenty-first century, other kinds of work were being similarly displaced. Robot machinery could be monitored by video cameras as well as by human eyes; even where machinery required active control there was no need for anyone to stand by or sit in the machine. Earth-moving equipment and agricultural machinery had become sufficiently sophisticated to be operated ("telefactored") remotely, by people using electronic eyes and senses to monitor their machines' work. This kind of control could be especially important where machines were sent to work in places where it was difficult for people to accompany them: mining narrow veins of coal or ore from "exhausted" workings, prospecting in the killing depths of the sea, or repairing communications satellites far beyond Earth's atmosphere.

Hand-held and whole-wall screens

For much of the twenty-first century telescreens suffered from limitations of size. Techniques existed to make them very small and very large, but if they were small they became unreadable, and if large they had problems with picture-definition. The struggle to develop a hand-held screen that could display text with the same clarity as a page of a book, without being any heavier, proved a long-standing challenge to designers. The earliest claimants emerged around 2005, but it was not until 2060, after a long series of refinements, that the Philante Bookscreen really achieved perfection. Fixed screens in the home tended to remain in the 30-80 centimetre range, but there was a similar struggle to develop whole-wall screens which could display visual material with sharpness and clarity. Good 2-D wall-screens became cheap enough for most households in the 2020s, but attempts to create three-dimensional images continued to be problematic for more than a century. Even in 2140 screens which could offer a really convincing illusion of depth – "artificial windows", as they were called – were still the playthings of the rich, and could only receive special transmissions. After that date, small-scale "box" receivers which could create efficient holographic images became commonplace, and giant versions were erected in stadia for public entertainment.

The network leads to the countryside

The spread of the networks had noticeable effects on the demography of developed nations. At first, they exaggerated the movement of population – from rural to urban areas, because it was only in the cities that the full range of facilities was available. In the USA the maximum concentration of the population was not achieved until 2035, although some of the smaller nations of Europe had already passed that point by then. The further the networks extended, of course, the easier it became for people to disperse from cities and towns, substituting electronic intimacy for physical proximity. The dispersal was uneven because the growth of the networks was haphazard, and because other factors encouraged people to move – there was, of course, a steady flow away from the coasts toward higher ground. New villages and small towns sprang up on the crests of hills around new satellite-dishes and cable-spurs. Many famous "beauty spots" became suddenly fashionable as places to live, and were sometimes quickly spoiled by development, thus becoming just as rapidly unfashionable again. Generally, though, people found their freedom of movement curtailed by ecology-aware land-management schemes, and a potentially chaotic shifting of population was avoided even after the development of Gantz processes made building costs fall so steeply.

Problems of accident and sabotage

The development of the information networks proceeded only with difficulty. Apart from the energy-shortage, accident and sabotage caused frequent disruptions. In its early stages the network was highly vulnerable to power-failures and programming malfunctions, and was delicate enough to be easily upset by malicious action.

As the commercial life of developed countries became more and more dependent on the networks, the cost of disruptions increased. Sometimes accidents were merely physical, involving broken cables or defective switches, in which case they were easy to trace and put right. Poor programming was a different matter, and "software sabotage" could be both dramatically effective and difficult to detect or cure. Relatively few people wanted to alter or destroy the data in electronic stores, or wished to cause massive disruptions of information-flow, but those few could be very troublesome. Those who did most damage usually worked alone, without any particular objectives: they were a new breed of vandal, delighting in the power given them by their ingenuity.

One curiously ambitious data-pirate was Albert ffinch, whose crime was uniquely British. Wishing to secure a position in the fast-decaying English aristocracy, he broke the software protection of the national birth-records database at Somerset House and rewrote several generations of noble bloodlines to equip himself with a retrospective genealogy and the title of Baronet. This came embarrassingly to light when several members of the House of Lords were discovered to be "unpersons" owing to the incidental erasure of their birth records; the media had enormous fun with the arrest and trial of "Sir Albert ffinch, the Software Pretender".

The possibility of electronic credit disruption was one of the reasons why cash – which became effectively obsolete as the networks spread – was not completely eliminated even in the most highly-developed nations. The other reason was the maintenance of privacy. Credit transactions on the network were recorded, cash purchases were not. Even with no particular reason for keeping their movements and purchases secret from the electronic "brain" of the networks, people sometimes preferred to. Often, they did have reasons – the most law-abiding citizens occasionally, to this day, find it convenient to deal in the black economy or to cheat on their taxes.

Policing the network

The problem of policing and protecting the information networks became increasingly thorny as time went by, involving more and more people. Criminal tampering with financial records was a major nuisance in the early days, but soon dwindled largely because it became impossible for anyone to conceal any wealth accumulated by criminal means: the network gave police forces too many ways to monitor income and spending. Industrial espionage and calculated software sabotage also became rare as corporations adjusted to the network and adapted their security techniques. No matter how quickly electronic keys were devised to lock up data, interested parties always managed to find ways of unlocking it again, but it was generally possible to stay one step ahead – as had usually been the case with real locks.

The toy loses its glitter

Inevitably, institutions had to be set up for the relief of those affected by functional disruptions. Acts of random sabotage or simple accidents could take away people's financial support by denying them electronic access to a bank account, or their entire identities, should vital birth or identity records be erased. It became necessary to have ways of repairing such damage at a moment's notice. The number of people employed in attending to the needs of victims of systemic disorder increased as rapidly as the number of those policing the system. The networks inevitably became the focus of all dissatisfactions, and once the new telescreens had ceased to be a universal favourite toy they quickly became everyone's pet hate. Complaints were incessant, and it must have seemed, after 2020 or thereabouts, that all the networks were failing dismally to meet expectations; but even the level of complaint testified eloquently to the fact that the new technology had become vital to the contemporary way of life

Slow growth of the international network

By 2150 most of the developed nations claimed to possess full integration of communications. This did not mean that every single citizen was entrapped in the electronic web, but that everyone who wanted it had some level of access. There were still large differences between the facilities enjoyed by rich and poor. The developed countries lagging behind at that time were Canada, Australia and the USSR, none of which had sufficient accumulated wealth fully to overcome the geographical problems of creating a comprehensive network. Yet all three were becoming steadily richer, and they had caught up by the end of the century. In the poorer nations, by contrast, information technology was virtually confined to the cities, and only the rich could really make use of it. The problems of setting up facilities were much greater where there were perennial guerilla wars, and the legions of the poor had more important priorities. It was not until the 2180s that several multinational corporations, acting in co-ordination, began a massive drive to extend the Third World penetration of their international networks and thereby their markets.

Even before 2180 a process of "cultural colonization" had begun to show noticeable effects among the middle-classes of the poorer nations, with satellite-relayed entertainment and English-language teletext library services. To start with, governments tried hard to control the information reaching their own citizens. Although the networks were linked up internationally, most people transmitted and received messages only within their own nations, and their opportunities for doing otherwise were sometimes deliberately restricted. Governments had, in fact, been fighting a losing battle against alien information since the middle of the twentieth century, when many nations had made it illegal to listen to foreign radio broadcasts, especially in time of war. The USA, in particular, had invested heavily in the business of broadcasting radio propaganda to other nations. For much of the twenty-first century governments kept up this struggle, but it became more and more obvious, even to the most authoritarian regimes, that they could not win.

An "optibunch" of fibre optic cable, sufficient in the mid twenty-second century to transmit the video-phone conversations of half a city.

The seeds of world harmony

Ironically, it was not deliberate propaganda beamed to telescreens via orbiting satellites that eroded the political differences between East and West. Nor was it the influence of the information networks, which were concerned with more basic matters than political ideology. Rather it was the ability of telescreens to give ordinary people windows on the world, allowing them to see how it was presented by and to people different from themselves. When foreigners spoke directly to them, most people were suspicious and sceptical, but when they could "eavesdrop" on foreigners speaking to one another, they gradually gained a better understanding of them. Ignorance, which had always been the great protector of xenophobia, began to fade away.

In this slow and unspectacular fashion, the possibility of a harmonious world community came closer. The pattern of change which began in the Period of Crisis was to extend well into the following phases of history, because the networks were far from fully-developed or fully-utilized in 2180; but the process of evolution had been set in train, and could not be stopped by anything short of a major armed conflict between the superpowers. That conflict never came.

CHAPTER FIFTEEN

EMPLOYMENT AND RE-EMPLOYMENT

The shock of the massive uprooting of agricultural labour which affected the poorer countries in the twenty-first and twenty-second centuries had already made its impact on the developed world in the nineteenth and twentieth centuries. Because the numbers working on the land were already small, the biotechnological revolution in agricultural methods had relatively little effect on employment in these industrialized nations, but there were nevertheless important changes to come.

Massive unemployment in the West

By the year 2000 automation was having such a significant effect on manufacturing that unskilled and semi-skilled workers were being made redundant in large numbers. Less skilled holders of "white-collar jobs" were also being displaced by information technology. There seemed no immediate prospect of redeploying these workers, and their increasing numbers were a source of embarrassment to many Western governments. In the Soviet countries, where employment was guaranteed, jobs were found, but it was becoming all too obvious that many of these were unnecessary. The communist countries had other problems too. The political power to redeploy labour easily was there, and the educational system was better equipped than in the West for practical training, but there were no economic incentives to motivate the workers.

In the West the real problem was partly economic and partly educational. Allowing market forces to govern patterns of employment was inefficient. It was not that there was no work – there were chronic housing problems in most of the affected nations, and the need for urban renewal was desperate. Unfortunately, there was no institutional apparatus to divert unused labour to these socially desirable but essentially unprofitable tasks. To pay workers to do such jobs, instead of doling out a pittance to compensate them for not having jobs, would have required massive and politically unacceptable increases in taxation. The educational part of the problem was the absence of effective retraining to allow people to switch easily from one semi-skilled task to another, thus allowing the movement of labour into the new areas of employment.

With hindsight, it is easy to see the pattern of changes that had to occur in both systems, and it may seem ridiculous that it was not obvious what had to be done. In fact, it probably *was* obvious to many, and the patterns of change *were* directed by common sense, but there was much superstitious resistance to the evolution of economic systems away from the capitalist and communist extremes.

Lifelong education

The educational reforms were easier to implement in the West than the economic reforms (though even education tended to be dominated by tradition, and was certainly not without its superstitions). It became accepted in the course of the early twenty-first century that the adaptability of labour was a priority. It was simply not sufficient for an individual to learn a skill while still at school, or during an apprenticeship, and then to expect that skill to remain in demand throughout his lifetime. By the year 2010, the idea that a man or woman ought to have a single "educational phase" early in life was becoming obsolete in the developed nations, and educational institutions were being adapted to provide for people of all ages, who would visit and use them continually or periodically, by choice as well as by necessity. By 2050 there was an almost universally accepted opinion in the West that "an education" was something that extended over an entire lifetime. The old familiar cliché "Jack of all trades, master of none" was now beginning to take on a musty air, like something in Chaucerian English, approaching its near-incomprehensibility to the average citizen of today.

Enforced growth of the public sector

Despite the robotization of many manufacturing processes, the demand for manual labour did not decline markedly during the twenty-first century. To some extent, displaced factory workers were shifted into various kinds of building work in the private sector. But it was the expansion of public sector construction and maintenance that kept the demand high. There were, of course, special opportunities created by the building of the information networks, and much manual work as a result of flooding, but there was a more fundamental reason for the state's increased need of manual workers. As society became more highly technological, depending on an ever-increasing range of complicated artefacts, more and more work had to be put into reconstructing and repairing the artificial environment. Because maintenance work, unlike most manufacturing processes, is occasional and idiosyncratic rather than ceaseless and repetitive, it cannot – even to this day – be wholly turned over to machines. Machinery is vital to such work, but so are human agents. Governments employed more and more people to do centrally organized work, and collected the taxes they needed to do it.

Repair and maintenance work was one of the few growth areas for employment in the twenty-first century. These technicians are working on the heat shield of a German space shuttle of the 2050s.

There were no such redeployment prospects for the redundant white collar workers. As their jobs disappeared, they had to undertake more radical retraining, and it was mostly these workers who moved into such new jobs as were being created by the spread of the information networks. Their skills had to be "upgraded", but the same was true of the manual labourers, who had at least to become more versatile. The working population as a whole needed to be better educated, if only in the sense of being always able to learn new skills. Relatively few individuals lacked the capacity for this kind of education, and the vast majority adapted readily enough.

Patchy success of new measures

It cannot be said that these economic and educational reforms were entirely effective in meeting the changing demands of the twenty-first century. Some nations were more adaptable than others, and Japan and West Germany, who had been forced to reconstruct their economies following defeat in twentieth-century wars, maintained the advantage thus gained for many decades. But even these nations soon accumulated new traditions which became burdensome – their adaptability began to be restricted exactly when the maximum demands were being made upon it. Some small, rapidly developing nations like Argentina and the Philippine Republic were able to formulate clear-sighted policies, but without the accumulated technological capital of the European nations their opportunities were limited.

In the communist world some of the developing countries tried to overcome their version of the problem by forming industrial armies, trying to import military discipline into the incentiveless arena of work. The Vietnamese Industrial Army, formed in 2018, lasted until 2069 – much longer than any similar force – but was not a success. The formal organization hardly concealed the fact that the workers still lacked motivation. In Eastern Europe, attempts to import a more subtly militaristic discipline into the labour force also made little difference, and economic incentives were slowly introduced instead.

The refugee problem

Throughout the twenty-first century there was considerable movement of population between nations, further confusing the employment position in countries like the USA, which had always been attractive to refugees. Illegal immigrants working exclusively in the black economy could make a better living in rich countries than in their own homelands. Disturbances caused by plague and civil strife often intensified the ambitions of poor people in poor nations to risk everything in an attempt to find a new way of life elsewhere. As the information network spread, television images inspired many people with the same kind of "American dream" that had brought immigrants flocking to the USA in the nineteenth and twentieth centuries. Long before the unique problems of the Japanese diaspora emerged in the 2080s, the world was well-used to the whole spectrum of "refugee problems".

"TV withdrawal" became recognized as one such problem which stayed at home in the poorer countries: it was a retreat into the fantasy worlds of consumer advertising, made more acute by the sufferer's belief that this was the *reality* of superpower life. There is a story of an entire Bangladesh psychiatric ward whose starry-eyed patients spent their days compulsively singing US advertising jingles – like the haunting Vita-Munchie Breakfast Blues which in modified form still survives as a children's counting song.

As the American communications network spread, it became easier for the government to keep track of who was living within the borders of the nation. Despite this the illegal residents continued to find ways of getting by, and the pressure on Congress to give legitimate status to many new and established groups of immigrants was always strong. Software manipulators who specialized in the construction of electronic identities were swamped by demand, and most worked more expertly than the document-forgers of old. There were several attempts to clear up the problem temporarily by "tactical surrender". President Clissold offered an amnesty to all illegal immigrants in 2071 on the grounds that integrating the people into the legitimate economy would reduce much of the "secondary deviance" – namely, crime – associated with their clandestine presence. Even the USSR, which generally favoured a hard line with the illicit movement of Asians into Moscow and other European cities, offered a similar amnesty in 2079.

Australia's open-door policy

Australia, after ineffectual struggles, began to license immigration on a fairly considerable scale in 2030, and by 2107, when its ecological revolution was well under way, Prime Minister Martha Gilder adopted a virtual open-door policy. In the ensuing eighty years Australia's population increased threefold, and attained a multiracial complexity unequalled even in the USA, where white men still retained a slender, though dwindling, numerical majority. Racial tensions within these nations ran high during the Period of Crisis, but their violent expression was unacceptable everywhere, and by 2150 they were waning, thanks to improved education and communications.

The immigrant workers, being for the most part denied the full benefits of education, tended to fill the most menial roles left vacant by machinery, until over the generations they were absorbed into the system. Their presence and pressure maintained high levels of unemployment in the USA throughout the Period of Crisis. Even in other nations, which had much smaller problems of this kind, there was perpetual resentment in the lower strata of the employment hierarchy. Governments, beset by a myriad of other problems, were unable to cope with this one. Not until world population began to level out, and standards of living in the Third World rose, was it possible even to hope for an equilibrium of full and ordered employment. That required the Period of Crisis to give way to the Period of Recovery.

CHAPTER SIXTEEN

LEISURE IN THE TWENTY-FIRST AND TWENTY-SECOND CENTURIES

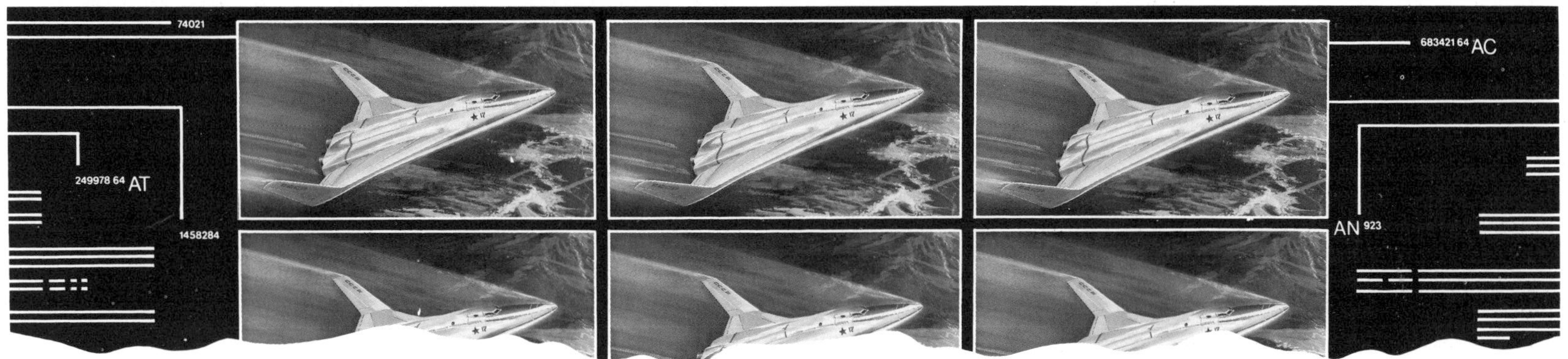

The new information technology reorganized people's play as drastically as their work. The increasing sophistication of telescreens exaggerated a well-established trend making the home the focus of leisure activities. By the year 2000 electronic reproduction of pictures and music was highly efficient, and habits of consumption had already changed so much that relatively few people actually wanted to be present in a sports stadium or a concert hall. Performers and their performances were increasingly camera-orientated.

Many kinds of active competition were also being channelled through the electronic media. The addition of visual facilities to telephonic communication, and the sophistication of computer graphics, meant that chess players and card players no longer needed to come together – although many, of course, still preferred to. Games played via electronic links retained their social aspect, but the extra dimension of physical nearness was still valued. The vast proliferation of computer-programmed screen games meant that the information technology itself contributed to leisure opportunities.

Because many people wanted to continue, if less frequently, to enjoy sport, the arts and competitive games in their "real" form, spectator sport facilities remained fairly substantial. Stadia could always be packed out for really important competitions. Routine events – like orchestral concerts – tended more and more to be played without the distraction of a live audience.

Hollywood's second Golden Age

The great stadia built for spectator sports acquired other uses due to the new technology. Gigantic telescreens were installed for the presentation of visual spectacles on a scale impossible in the home. With the appearance of projected 3-D images, these giant screens became even more attractive – especially while the relevant technology was too expensive for ordinary people to obtain, even in miniature. The film-makers of Hollywood and elsewhere, after a long, lean period of pandering to the television networks, came into their own again. There was a new "Golden Age" in the film industry from the 2020s to the 2040s, when such producers and

3-V frames from a twenty-first century masterpiece, the Soviet *Olga and Yuri*. Note the early Cosmolyot space shuttle with its quaint fins.

Give-away hologram, presented with Heinz Bio-Beenz in 2044.

¡HOLO·PIC! 

Presented free with Bio Beenz

STARS OF SPORT

--- Al Mohamet Tema ---

One of the best robo-fighters of the 2040 Olympics. Al Mohamet Tema ("Big Al") has been biotechеd to the limits of the science. His Stage III musculature – Stage I is shown on the front of this card – is designed to take on the heftiest robot. Even a General Products 1800 or a mighty Renault 90!

To cope with crusher-grips, Big Al's biceps turn to neo-iron in their Stage III form. His extensor forearms enable him to knock out even the heavily armoured optic sensors of the GP 1800.

A mighty fighter indeed! We look forward to seeing him take on the new Renault 90XX in the Man vs. Machine Tourney of 2045.

One of a series of 50 – collect them all!

directors as Eliot Dionard and Rayner Randell gradually adapted their scope to the accumulating opportunities of 3-D representation. Standards dropped again, of course, once home "box receivers" became commonplace, even though the big screens were far more spectacular.

Physical culture aided by biotechnology

However, the developed countries' increasing emphasis on physical culture ran counter to the transferral of leisure into the home. Although many people were content to "train" at home, participation in public athletic events gradually became more widespread, and correspondingly more important as a social activity. The very temptations of home entertainment made people wary of the dangers of inactivity, and routine health education promoted the role of exercise in maintaining their bodies. The impact of biotechnology on food science and on the medical treatment of conditions like obesity encouraged physical culture. It might be thought that the ability to "cure" obesity medically would have made people less worried about getting fat, and therefore less likely to take precautions against it, but in fact it had the opposite effect. People realized that a combination of personal effort and medical expertise could make them the authentic masters of their own appearance and physical capabilities.

By about 2090, medical control over the processes of growth and tissue-differentiation meant that people could have any height, build and musculature they wanted, provided they could afford it, but only if they were willing to play their complementary part. Many were willing, and as access to the medical technologies expanded in the twenty-second century, so the pursuit of physical perfection was democratized.

Bionic sportsmen

Basketball players seeking extra height, boxers in pursuit of more punching power and sprinters requiring added speed all turned to the biological engineers for help, and for a while it seemed that the quest of obsessed individuals for sporting success might actually come to produce an array of grotesques.

In 2013 the World Basketball Association felt compelled to take the unusual step of introducing a maximum height for players, because doctors were using growth-renewal techniques on promising college players in order to secure their professional futures. Within five years the boards controlling American Football and Boxing introduced maximum weight regulations. The International Olympic Committee quickly became the organization at the focal point of the issue, but it was unable to reach the same kind of sweeping and peremptory decision. By this time, there was a backlash protest as people who were naturally large protested about being excluded from various sports simply because others were using dubious methods to secure the same advantage. Meanwhile, the poorer countries in the Olympic movement complained bitterly that medal chances now depended almost entirely on the level of medical assistance made available to competitors. The Olympiad of 2020 was sheer farce in athletic terms; it became, effectively, the first all-out competition between the biological engineers of America and Eastern Europe.

Decline of the Olympics

In the four years the IOC struggled with the task of framing complicated regulations concerning the kinds of medical intervention which would be tolerated and those which would not, but they had no effective way of policing the regulations, and when the 2024 games were held controversy surrounded virtually every event. Seventeen new world records were set, one of them in the women's 400 metres by Mela Niccone, who had been born with a badly-deformed right leg which had been corrected in infancy by one of the pioneering experimenters in physical redevelopment.

The real implications slowly sank in, and in 2027 Mohammed Qadr, President of the IOC, declared that the old ideals of the movement had been rendered obsolete. It was no use, he argued, to try to confine participation in the games to men and women who were "entirely products of nature" because now no one could truly make such a claim. The world that was emerging, he maintained, was one in which everyone would pursue some ideal of perfection, making as much use of the new power of the biological engineers as they could. Thus, either the Olympic Games must openly admit to being a competition between biological engineers and their skill in adapting human bodies to particular tasks, or people must recognize that the kinds of competition involved in the games had lost their significance.

Mohammed Qadr resigned before the 2028 Olympiad, but his arguments could not be forgotten. The games continued, the regulations faded away, and the biological engineers were given free rein. At first, there was no shortage of competitors willing to be reshaped in complex and sometimes bizarre ways in the hope of achieving temporary glory, but as the glory was transferred from the competitors to their designers the motive force declined. Winning competitions and setting records did come to seem, to the majority of participants and onlookers, rather meaningless. With every four year period that passed the Olympic Games faded in significance. A similar process robbed many professional spectator sports of their appeal. When boxing competitions became battles between engineered bundles of muscle they lost their human dimension and became uninteresting; they might just as well have been battles between robots.

The spectator sports which continued to thrive as the twenty-first century progressed were ones which required more various and more delicate physical skills, and ones which necessitated a measure of intelligence and tactical acumen. Such activities as tennis, baseball, association football and cricket could not be rendered ridiculous by the biological adaptation of the competitors, because mere matters of physique and power were subsidiary. The only sport which entirely resisted the intervention of any kind of biological engineering with respect to its primary participants was horse racing, where thoroughbred purity was fanatically preserved. Accusations of cheating became understandably commonplace and there was no barrier to controlling the physique of would-be jockeys.

More participation in sports

Another reason for the relative decline of spectator sports was a lessening of the partisan fervour which had helped them to develop so spectacularly in the twentieth century. Individuals still created their identities largely by associating themselves with groups, but began more and more to join participatory sports clubs and associations to the detriment of the spectators' or supporters' clubs popular in the twentieth century. The growth of popular physical culture encouraged whole communities to turn out in loosely-organized competitions, including races, mock-combats and strange ball games, where taking part became more important than winning. This represented a major change of attitude in many people. As these activities gained a greater influence in demarcating social groups, spectator sports gradually lost their social value.

Competitive fervour did remain a factor in many other areas of leisure activity. Risk-taking sports like mountain-climbing increased in popularity as people became more interested in testing their remodelled bodies for strength and endurance. This was competition "against the elements", but other kinds of risk-taking maintained their traditional appeal as well. The new information technology lent itself to the development of many novel gambling games, and facilitated some that had been popular for centuries. As religious and legal opposition to gambling faded away there was a period of wild indulgence – contemporary American commentators refer to an "epidemic" of compulsive gambling among the young in the 2030s. Credit control restrictions introduced by the Konrad administration (one of that famed president's less famous innovations) lent force to parental authority, and in time the craze died away.

Literature survives teletext

Reading was hard-hit by the increasing versatility of the telescreen. Difficulties with teletext clarity made reading from a screen slightly more of a chore than reading from a book, and people became increasingly likely to restrict themselves to functional reading – instruction manuals, tax forms and the like. However, the rewards to be gained from the printed word were so different from those attaching to the visual media that there was no danger of literary work becoming extinct. It survived at the popular level and at the level of high art, in book form as well as teletext, but the amount of time invested in reading by the population as a whole declined slowly in all countries until it levelled off in the 2080s. By that time, teletext display was no longer problematic, and had become quite easy on the eyes. After that date books survived mainly as *objets d'art*, but book collecting was a common hobby throughout the developed world.

Synthetape replaces film

After 2050 software for synthesizing visual images became rapidly more sophisticated. Until 2050 the only way to produce convincing television drama had involved actors, sets and video cameras. Such filmed images were often enhanced in numerous ways by trickery, and the skill of film-makers in using "special effects" to create illusions had never stopped evolving. There had thus been a gradual integration of image-synthesis techniques and camera-work.

After 2050 the work of technicians like Valdavia and Takahashi gave much more power and flexibility to the "software directors" who never resorted to the camera. This was not, as some have suggested, an overnight revolution - indeed, some camera-recorded dramas were still being made without synthetic imagery well into the twenty-second century – but by 2075 the opportunities opened up by synthetape were attracting the great majority of those interested in making screen drama. Simeon Bira's surrealized epic of alternate history, *World War IV*, and his brilliant *Song of Roland*, proved to be major inspirations. The use of human actors and illusory special effects suddenly became unfashionable in work for the flat screen, though it would be a hundred years before synthetape techniques could be adapted to three dimensions.

While the Hollywood film-makers were shooting their 3-D holographic epics in the early twenty-second century, the producers

Home synthetapes, made by amateurs, were commonplace in the twenty-second century and many were made available through the datanet to those, usually friends of the makers, who wished to see them. A few, like *Seclusion* (2174) – a still from which is shown here – gained widespread word-of-mouth followings and launched their makers as professionals.

Synthetape opened up new possibilities in motion pictures and numerous twentieth-century movies were remade in the new medium. This still is from the synthetape remake (2082) of a forgotten masterpiece.

of home entertainment and those who considered themselves to be the authentic *avant garde* were making synthetape movies. The economics of the business meant that the most spectacular effects were achieved in the most popular and commercially successful works. Although widely considered to be examples of appalling tastelessness, the synthetape dramas of Carl Valentine retain an undeniable panache: the hugely popular *Journey to the Age of the Dinosaurs* launched him on the road to success in 2099 and his startling interpretation of the apocryphal Book of Enoch, entitled *Heaven and Hell*, was made in 2118. The impact of the same techniques on the making of educational material should be given due credit, but it is these fantastic epics which we still enjoy today and which will probably live for ever.

Enhanced scope for individual creativity

When we speak of leisure in the twenty-first and twenty-second centuries we are speaking almost exclusively of what was happening in the developed nations, for that was where the numerous new techniques took form. Entertainment produced in those nations did, however, extend slowly into all other parts of the globe as communications satellites broadened the scale of consumption. The massiveness of the mass media continued to increase, and in the early years of the twenty-second century there were perhaps fewer points of production and many more points of consumption in the entertainment industry than there had ever been before.

It must be remembered, though, that the information networks gradually gave the power of transmission, as well as that of reception, to millions of ordinary people. Anyone with sufficient technical expertise in programming could produce synthetapes in the twenty-second century, just as anyone in an earlier era who had a camera could be a photographer and anyone with a brush could be a painter. The growth of the new media never threatened to turn the populations of the developed nations into passive consumers; on the contrary, it opened fresh horizons for personal adventure in many different artistic and technical spheres. In the simple currency of individual enjoyment it was this scope for creative activity that remained the most important contribution to leisure that the information networks made, in these and the succeeding centuries.

CHAPTER SEVENTEEN

THE GREAT SLOW DOWN

The role of transport in the more developed nations during the "crazy years" of the late twentieth century still provokes us to smiles, as does the phlogiston theory or the fixed opinion of the discoverer of the atomic nucleus (Rutherford) that nuclear power was "moonshine".

On the one hand, hundreds of millions of people were travelling long distances to work each day, in vehicles driven by internal-combustion engines burning increasingly scarce and expensive fossil fuels. (It should be remembered that in those times, even "electric" public transport made indirect use of such fuels, since they were the chief source of power for national electricity grids.) On the other hand, the first dramatic wave of the information-technology revolutions offered communications systems which were adequate, even then, to make something like seventy per cent of daily commuting unnecessary.

Irrational persistence of commuters

It seemed a clear choice. Commuting, that unique disease, meant not only psychological stress and hours wasted, but also absurd expense, a drain on irreplaceable resources, environmental fouling (despite numerous claims, *no* version of the internal combustion engine was ever quite "clean" in terms of noxious and/or carcinogenic emissions), and – a point perhaps requiring hindsight – enhancement of the incipient greenhouse crisis. However, the persistent response to work-from-home proposals was: "It isn't natural." Bearing in mind that large-scale commuting began only in the twentieth century and that the vast majority of the world's people still remained unable to travel any considerable distance to their daily work – indeed large numbers of them had no work – this seems the most delicious irony.

Actually the obstructionists in their doomed vehicles had less choice than might appear. Few could then afford to live in the urban centres where offices were almost invariably sited, while the crude communications network, which did not by then include optical fibres, did not allow the immediate, large-scale substitution of telescreen for in-person communication which one might suppose. Despite this, there was plainly a good deal of irrational behaviour. For example, many owners of private vehicles insisted on possessing and using to their limits automobiles capable of travelling at twice or even three times the highest legal speed.

Assassination for speeding

One can sympathize with Speedwatch, the organisation founded in 2004 by Judith Nicolson of Britain, which at one point had more than 160,000 members in twelve countries. At first a mutual-sympathy club and pressure group for friends and relatives of people killed by dangerous drivers, Speedwatch became a characteristic symptom of the crazy years as its inner circle staged vigilante operations along major trunk roads. Ordinary members equipped with portable radar and telerecorders had monitored speeding and other technical offences; the inner circle went further to execute summary "justice" with high-velocity rifles and, in some cases, explosive. The Old Bailey trial of Nicolson and fourteen others in 2009 aroused some public sympathy, surprisingly, with the defence's ingenious comparisons of total road-death figures with the much disputed number of Speedwatch "executions". ("Thus a surgeon excises the few rogue cancer cells," said Sir Marcus Livingstone, KC, "in hope of saving the body as a whole." The Attorney-General retorted: "Ms Nicolson, alas, is *not* a qualified surgeon.") It is doubtful that there was a real causal connection between the Speedwatch affair and the accelerating growth of restrictions on private vehicles: nevertheless, when released on parole in 2021, Judith Nicolson clearly saw enough change in British traffic to feel justified in saying, "We won!".

Increasing cost of metals and fossil fuels

It was not only the increasing cost and shortage of fossil fuels which put an end to private transport as the twentieth century had known it. Metals themselves were becoming more valuable. A car of the period would be built chiefly of iron and steel (much of it admittedly in dangerously thin sheets), representing a larger investment in sheer mass of metal than any other private possession of its owner. Over a few years, aided by corrosive industrial atmospheres, much of this metal would weep away as rust, and such recycling as took place was shockingly inefficient. As the Indian economist Mulk Rajneesh observed in the 2040s, "The end result of these consumer industries has been to celebrate the second law of thermodynamics with its message of dispersion and decay. From the secret places of the Earth they gathered precious ores which we could use right now; but now those ores are scattered in a fine powder of useless oxides through the soil of every nation." (Some centuries would elapse before these lost and wasted rusts could be partially reclaimed by engineered soil biosystems which concentrated metallic ions.)

It was relatively easy for less developed countries to react against ludicrously high fuel and materials prices with draconian assaults on private transport, like Upper Volta's complete ban in 2033, or the "impossible" Mbutu exhaust-emission standard adopted by several countries. Commuting nations needed more caution: even Garrity's "austerity" administration in the USA tended to impose controls indirectly by price manipulation and gradually intensifying speed, power and pollution limits. It would have been political death in America to legislate against conventional private automobiles before they had been subtly redefined as wasteful luxuries confined to a plutocratic few.

Burgeoning of public transport

Two paths existed for developed nations: the public and the private route. More popular and efficient was the redevelopment of public transport systems. Even where these were imperfect or fossil-fuel-powered (like the old London double-decker buses and US transcontinental coach services, both of which ran in defiance of UN hints until the late 2040s), they demonstrably carried more human weight with greater efficiency than powered vehicles in private hands. As the twenty-first century wore on, a variety of subway, metro and tube transport systems were built or rebuilt in the great cities of the industrial nations: these would usually be electrically powered, meaning that nuclear or

Air and rail terminus, Frankfurt 2040, a typical terminus of the period: automatic metro systems carried people into and out of the airport; airships were used for bulk cargo; and hydrogen-fuelled jets provided high speed point-to-point transport for urgent journeys.

even geothermal-tap power from the national grid provided a respectable and growing proportion of the energy used.

From the 2050s, of course, this electrification policy appeared particularly far-sighted and noble, since cheap grid power from fusion seemed just around the corner. Unfortunately this dream *stayed* resolutely round the corner for several more decades. In the meantime there were some embarrassments, most memorably the half-completed electrification of the trans-Siberian railway and the bankruptcy of Birmingham, England, following the excessive cost and construction time of its inner-city metro. Birmingham's, though, was among the first metros to use the newest Laithwaite/Krebs induction motor; such Metro carriages floated almost without friction, with obvious energy savings. The popularity of this advanced "maglev" public transport was to grow: particularly famous was the grandiose pan-Japanese system constructed in the early 2080s, which minimized air friction by sending its maglev trains through almost completely evacuated tunnels. Though this remarkable achievement went down with Japan in 2084-5, it was widely imitated.

Electrification spread along existing major rail networks, both as a response to fuel costs and pollution controls, and in anticipation of fusion. In many countries of intermediate industrial development, electrified railway routes helped provide a backbone for national electrical grids which would later be incorporated into Zov's and Kowalski's Utopian dream of a world grid in the next century. Meanwhile, at an altogether more humble level, there was a resurgence of an electrical public transport system almost abandoned in the twentieth century: trams. Following the lines of existing streets and capable of mixing with other vehicles, these were often cheaper and more convenient to install than subways or railways. President Konrad himself set an admired example in 2039 when he took to travelling to Washington functions, along with his retinue, in a special Presidential tram. (Only the Washington subway chiefs were unimpressed; but it was felt that a President's dignity could only be allowed to stoop so far.)

Transportation of private transport

The less popular way forward was a complete rethinking of private transport. Self-powered vehicles, chiefly bicycles, were still popular with a growing minority, but had a cardinal defect – bicycles do not keep out the rain. Nor did they appeal to middle-aged, and less than fit, executives. Internal combustion-driven automobiles survived beyond the first clamp-downs in the 2020s, but in severely modified form: speed limits were often built into the vehicle's electronic ignition, and an enormous array of exhaust-purification devices added to the cost and reduced the efficiency. Further inhibiting even for wealthy car-owners, arose naturally as the numbers of cars on the roads dwindled. First, there were fewer and fewer service stations selling the exorbitantly priced fuel chemicals which cars required every few hundred kilometres. (These were refined hydrocarbons – petrol or gasoline – heavier oils, and, very occasionally, ethanol. Liquefied gases saw some use but never really caught on: propane, butane and hydrogen were the chief contenders, the last being particularly difficult and dangerous to handle.) Secondly, governments tended to maintain roads less well in the absence both of demand and of revenue from a myriad car and fuel taxes. The illegally modified Hot Chip cars (*circa* 2025, chiefly Central and Western USA), whose internal microprocessors had been "tweaked" to permit twentieth-century speeds, often came to grief because the neglected roadways were simply unfit for travel at 130kph.

Electromobiles arrive slowly

The radical alternative was, of course, the all-electric car. Even as rich men's toys, these were slow to gain popularity, for reasons which should have been irrelevant. The twentieth-century image persisted, the image of an automobile as a throbbing symbol of status and power. Gentle acceleration, no fire hazard, a quiet purr within and virtually silent running from the outside point of view: these virtues of the early Sinclair IV, Yatakang and St Croix electromobiles were somehow far more unpopular than their obvious defects of limited speed (an ambivalent point) and restricted range between recharges. Worse, electromobiles were associated with vehicles for the disabled, with funfair "dodgems", with railway-station baggage trolleys, with (in Britain) dingy milk floats. Among minor novelists of the late 2030s and early 2040s it became a cliché to connect an ageing male character's virility with various automobiles driven through his life, from powerful 1980s/1990s monsters to contemporary electromobiles with their "thin senile trickle of power", as one author phrased it (Harry Barfoot, whose *Cold Comfort Motorway* long survived the genre which it parodied).

There was no real alternative to the electromobile, though, and by the 2030s it had found favour: partly because power-wasteful combustion engines were less and less available for comparison; partly because of the puritanical "austerity binge" which slowly supplanted 2020s resentment of energy clampdowns; partly because the electromobiles became more reliable and longer-range due to a succession of improved electrical storage cells developed from the 2050s onward with an eye to the anticipated fusion bonanza.

Commuting considered wasteful

By now, too, it was becoming more acceptable – at least in the developed countries – for information-handlers to work via telescreen from home. To commute on a daily basis was regarded as wasteful, as indeed it was, and socially not quite "in". By the late 2040s a typical member of the former commuting classes might travel once or twice weekly by electromobile, tram or subway to his or her centralized workplace, spending the rest of the working week at a home terminal. Not every job, of course, could be so easily displaced homeward, and public transport still had its crowds and rush hours.

Increasing dependence on the electrical grid and the telecommunications network meant that failures, which a few decades previously might have been moderate annoyances, could now become serious economic disasters. With virtually all public transport electrical, a grid failure could plunge a whole city or district into chaos; at the same time, electronic information representing millions of man-hours of labour could be lost or corrupted. The 2048 Paris brown-out caused little physical harm beyond bruises and hysteria in the crowded Metro – but by bad luck it "crashed" a nexus of complicated financial dealings on the data net, and this was generally held responsible for the catastrophic collapse of the franc in the following week.

Airships became a familiar sight in twenty-first-century skies. This 2020s model, a Skyship *Hermes*, was a coastal patrol craft. Its envelope had an aerofoil section to boost its lift capacity.

Return of the airship

Meanwhile, a similar logic was gradually applied to freight and international transport. One or two countries made abortive efforts to revive the successful eighteenth- and nineteenth-century systems of canals and barges, which used relatively little energy. The stumbling-block was the fantastic cost of setting up the initial canal network – countries like Britain had used canals for several centuries, but these had fallen into decay after traffic was diverted to road and rail in the twentieth century. A certain amount of waterborne inland transport did persist and even increased, chiefly on major rivers and in such countries as Belgium and Holland which had never abandoned the old waterways; but it was never of world economic significance.

Far more successful was the revival of a famous low-energy aerial transport device, the airship. No contemporary air transport of this nature could rival the speed of jet aircraft; but was such speed necessary? Supersonic planes, never hugely successful except in terms of technological prestige, finally vanished in the chill of the 2020s: nobody seemed to miss them very much. The emerging world data net was reducing the need for face-to-face communication in international business. "The telescreen lets us keep our happy illusions," observed President Mbutu of Tanzania, a notorious vegetarian, in about 2032. "By the screen's magic we're spared the

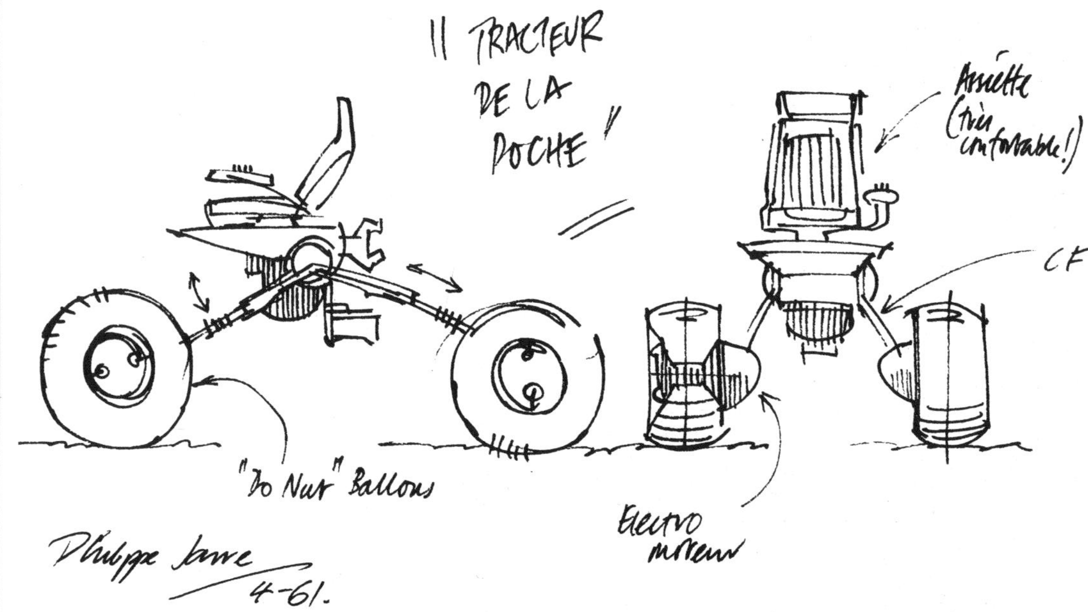

The pocket tractor: Philippe Jarre's first sketches of the vehicle that later made him famous are still preserved in the museum at his home town of Clermont Ferrand. The numerous production models all retained the spidery look that was a feature of the carbon construction.

carrion stink on the breath of a hundred statespersons one could name, who call themselves civilized and yet. . ."

Twenty-first-century plastics technology enabled helium rather than hydrogen to be used as the lifting gas of the airships – "sealing plastics" trapped the slippery helium atoms whose leakage had once been a problem. Hydrogen, easier to manage but highly inflammable, was a viable alternative – however, the spectre of the Hindenberg airship disaster in the previous century still proved powerful. This turning away – with some exceptions – from the cheapness of hydrogen is also perhaps indicative of an increased sense of the value of human life. The dramatic fall in automobile casualties with post-2020s changes in road transport patterns made more people realize that such deaths were not acts of God, that governments and even electorates had the power to save lives by collective action toward safety. Such at any rate was the theory of Wolfgang "Blimp" Koch, a popular German environmentalist who opposed hydrogen use and relished the hack and slash of public debate. Koch was hardly portly enough to merit the nickname given him by English-speaking opponents, but doubtless the subject under debate made it inevitable.

Airships ate away at the position of civilian jet aircraft, particularly for shorter internal flights. At ground level, electrical transport of one kind or another became the norm in the developed nations well before 2100; while on the seas, fusion reactors – too massive for most vehicles – drove such large ships as remained, many of them able to extract their deuterium fuel component directly from the sea. Abnormally strong materials developed in Spacelabs or as by-products of fusion research were adapted for use in personal electromobiles, whose popularity increased steadily towards the end of the century. In the 2060s, for example, Philippe Jarre devised his "pocket tractor", a spidery vehicle which used slim and almost unbreakable carbon-fibre-epoxoid components to achieve traction power which had formerly required massive metal struts and chassis. Though Jarre's gimmick had been feasible for some years, observers of the first demonstrations were convinced that some kind of conjuring trick was involved.

Faddish electromobiles

These developments were accompanied by odd crazes. The early years of the twenty-second century saw great competition to produce electromobiles containing the bare minimum of metal components – there appears to have been little or no truth in rumours that this was sponsored by defence agencies wanting radar-null vehicles for military use. Other arbitrary restrictions also offered challenges: José Fuentes of Argentina achieved brief fame by constructing a stripped-down electromobile capable of carrying a seated man several kilometres at 30 kph, yet weighing in itself only 1.2 kilos, including "peanut" motor and microcells. Experiments with self-guided cars foreshadowed twenty-third century developments. A fantastic fad was the car without a view, a radar-cum-computer guided vehicle whose "windows" were in fact adapted wallscreens showing pleasant and ever-changing scenes intended to distract passengers from the tedium of travel. Many people found this disquieting.

By the end of the Period of Crisis, the pattern of transport in the developed countries had suffered enormous and dramatic changes. That messy and expensive luxury, the internal combustion engine, was no longer the *sine qua non* of transportation but an expensive luxury. Fusion power from the ambitious "world electrical grid" provided direct energy for public transport and charged the batteries of private electromobiles. The raw power of chemical fuel was still required for jet aircraft, admittedly, but the burden of much non-urgent flight had shifted to the now ubiquitous airships, which were affordable by the least developed countries. Many hydrocarbon fuels were now synthesized either in fusion-driven industrial plants or by increasingly effective tailored bacteria: their high cost and the shadow of the greenhouse crisis told against any major return of transport driven by internal combustion.

By comparison with the horrors of the early Period of Crisis, this sounds Utopian. Even the old bugbear of commuting had been severely curtailed. Indeed, despite the new increase in prosperity, travel remained at a low ebb. The "cybernetic poet" Alois Avedekian, who conducted all human contact by telescreen and was the inventor of the car-without-a-view (its guidance system adapted with black humour from a cruise missile's), said in this context: "I know ten thousand people. I know nobody. Ten thousand people think they know me. They only know a phosphor pattern."

In other words, if there was a problem facing industrialized humanity at the beginning of the Period of Recovery, it was no longer one of overcrowding and energy-poverty but of isolation and anomie. Where in 2000 there might have been a four-person automobile in daily use, there was now a one- or two-seater electromobile which for most days of the month lay unused. It was a happy epitaph to the Period of Crisis that, following 180 years of brutal upheaval in every sphere of existence, people could now devote a little concern to less tangible worries.

Typical ground car of the early twenty-first century. The weight, shape and engine of this Citroen which was made in France – now housed in the Historic Vehicle Archive, Bendigo, Australia – were designed for efficiency and minimum fuel consumption.

THE PERIOD OF RECOVERY

2180 TO 2400

CHAPTER EIGHTEEN

THE ARCHITECTS OF ECOTOPIA

By comparison with the Period of Crisis, the ensuing Period of Recovery was calm. There were no major international conflicts to compare with the Brazil-Argentina war of 2078; there was no natural disaster on the scale of the Japanese earthquakes of 2084-5; climatic conditions remained stable. From 2180 to 2400 the world community enjoyed a period of measured and steady progress toward widely-accepted goals – perhaps the first such period in human history. During this time the foundations were laid for the new world order, by people who were not afraid to make grandiose plans for future generations. Of course, hindsight makes us exaggerate the orderliness, and it is difficult to appreciate what a vast patchwork of different cultures and lifestyles – with all the attendant tensions and hostilities – the world really was. Nevertheless, we are right to see the Period of Recovery in these terms. It was, first and foremost, a time in which grand plans were conceived and brought slowly toward fruition.

2180: recovery begins

All divisions of history are arbitrary, and it may seem odd to choose 2180 as the beginning of the new phase, rather than 2220 when sea-level was once again stabilized. There were, however, several important trends which came together in that decade, complementing one another significantly. One was the gradual spread of fusion reactors: a dispersal which had the intention of democratizing energy supplies on a world-wide basis. The second was the drive to extend the sophisticated communications networks until they, too, were world-wide. The third was the transfer of responsibility for ecological planning to an international level.

Because these were trends rather than events it is impossible to say when they began or ended. A graph, however, would show the curves of these trends to be shallow and uncertain before 2180; after that date they became bolder and steeper, reaching a plateau in about 2400.

By 2180, the day of great charismatic statesmen was virtually gone. The cults of personality which had developed in the previous century around Pavlo Vyshyna in the USSR or Chairwoman Lin in China were a thing of the past. The bureaucratization of almost every aspect of collective endeavour made it difficult for individuals to impose their personality. In a world of media imagery, celebrity was fleeting and insubstantial. Nevertheless, personalities could still be important in promoting particular institutions and popularizing new ideologies. The popularity of the "new approach" to world problems owed a great deal to the way that certain key people used the communications networks.

Three in particular stand out: Roman Zarzecki, who was secretary-general of the United Nations from 2173 until 2193; the British environmentalist John Foden; and the Chinese writer/philosopher Qing Xiao-wen.

Roman Zarzecki increases authority of UN

Zarzecki held, in 2180, what had become the most important position in the world community. The authority of the UN was increasing and was ready to be crystallized into a new extended, formal structure. National governments were wary of such extended authority, and many were highly resentful of "high-handed meddling" in their domestic affairs. The continuing lack of trust between nations was deepened by jealous efforts by the USA and the USSR to preserve their hegemony, while many Third World nations regarded the UN as a self-serving conspiracy of the rich nations. To soothe away these suspicions, the UN needed a leader who was widely liked and trusted. Zarzecki was such a man.

He was born in Poland in 2124. After centuries of domination by Russia, Poland remained one of the weakest and poorest countries in Europe. Its agriculture had been blighted by the greenhouse crisis and it was unable to create or import sufficient technological resources to compete with the manufacturing industries of neighbouring nations. Not until the 2160s were the Poles able to stage any kind of fight against circumstance that was more than a desperate rearguard action. It was only then that malnutrition was finally banished and the nation's leaders gained a sense of confidence. Zarzecki was appointed Poland's ambassador to the UN in 2161, and quickly became a national hero on account of the enormous rhetorical fervour and flamboyance with which he presented his country's pleas and demands in the council chamber. At this time the "rents" paid into the UN coffers by the sea-harvesting nations were becoming substantial, and funds were being diverted to enable nations like Poland to recover and consolidate their food and energy supplies.

Zarzecki had the wit and charm of a great actor, and he soon became an international favourite. He benefitted too, of course, from the spread of the English language which was by then so widely understood that his speeches and witticisms could be appreciated across the world. In retrospect we can see that Zarzecki was a mouthpiece. He was not a great planner, or even a great thinker, but he did have the virtues of solid common sense and a strong sense of justice. His very lack of strong convictions and entrenched opinions helped him cultivate a reputation for honesty and reasonableness, and he had the gift of being able to say "no" – to individuals or to nations – without provoking resentment. He was perhaps fortunate to perish before he could taint his reputation. His accidental electrocution in a traffic accident in 2193 was mourned all over the world.

John Foden: internationally respected environmentalist

John Foden served under Zarzecki on the innocuously-named but highly controversial Land Use Committee between 2183 and 2193, and then under his successor Heres del Maestre until 2201. One of the world's great eccentrics, Foden had a perverse talent for looking completely out of place wherever he was. At a time when medical technology had given the world's elite almost total control over body-size, he was content to be short and rotund. In a world austerely careful to avoid the poisonous follies of the past, he smoked a pipe. Sometimes he gave the impression of having arrived in the twenty-second century by time-machine from 1895, but in fact he was born in Birmingham, England, in 2140. His degrees in biotechnology were unspectacular, reflecting a modest ability in research, but in the field he was tireless and bounced with enthusiasm. His reserves of kindness and good will were inexhaustible, and his generosity of spirit quite abnormal.

There were many ecologists and biotechnologists who dreamed of turning the entire world into a kind of Garden of Eden, planning the use of every last hectare. It was the dominant vision of the day, but it remained a fantasy of would-be prophets, lacking any real practical dimension. The Land Use Committee – the only body which could aspire to planning on a world level – was empowered only to make recommendations to national governments, and its members were frequently treated with contempt.

Foden differed from most of the would-be architects of the earthly Eden because he thought in terms of meeting human demands in all their complexity and irrationality rather than imposing some single aesthetic scheme on the entire world. He wanted to make the world-wide wilderness into a carefully designed garden, but he wanted a garden complicated and eccentric and delicately imperfect to satisfy the multifarious preferences of millions of idiosyncratic dreamers. His detractors said that his only real achievement was to be the first director of the LUC to persuade national governments to adopt crazy plans, but they drastically underestimated the significance of his persuasive power. Like Zarzecki, he won the confidence of people who had previously refused to trust anyone holding his position. He breached the wall of suspicion. When he retired after nearly twenty years he left the world more or less the same, but he left the LUC with much greater authority, and with a reputation for genuinely looking after the interests of the people it aspired to serve.

Qing Xiao-wen: the voice of caution

Qing Xiao-wen was even more of an oddity. He never held any position of formal authority. In a world where fame and popularity were almost entirely dependent on video cameras, he alone became famous for remaining hidden. Very few people knew what he looked like, and he never appeared in front of a camera. His achievement seemed impossible – he made his name a household word while keeping his life so private that he became a living mystery. He never possessed a telesscreen.

The means by which he achieved his strange renown were not of his own devising – they had been preserved by Chinese tradition over thousands of years – but he was the last person to use them effectively. He had a gift for the construction of decorous aphorisms, and the ability to devise quaint parables. He also had an ever-increasing tribe of disciples who delighted in passing on these works by word of mouth.

Many contemporary critics were scornful of Qing's inventions, condemning them as platitudinous and derivative. His huge success owed much to the simplicity of his message. He had, too, a new ability that was still unusual. He could mingle phrases and concepts from several different languages, taking advantage of the nuances which will not translate satisfactorily. He could move from the mind-set implied by one language to that of another with consummate ease, and could bring them together in fertile communion. His anecdotes were usually presented in a mixture of Cantonese, English and Russian, with occasional intrusions of French, Urdu and Swahili. One of the reasons why he attracted so many apocryphal writings and sayings is that people with a command (sometimes, alas, a frail command) of a different range of tongues tried to imitate his technique.

It was the proudly polyglot middle-classes of the developed countries who really took Qing Xiao-wen to their hearts, because they enjoyed unravelling the games he played

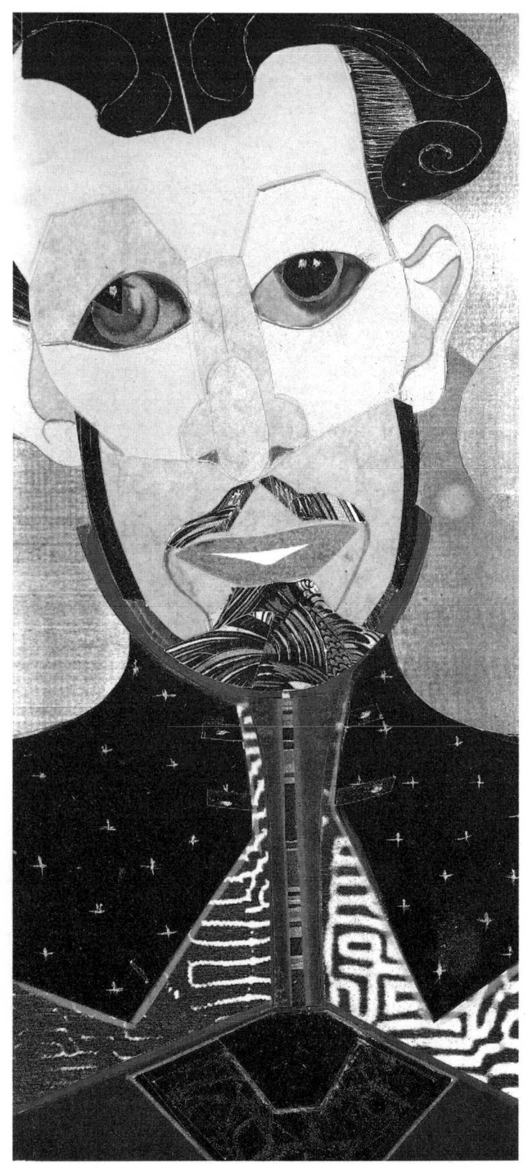

Oleg Zarzecki, John Foden and Qing Xiao-Wen, *Contemporary paintings by Arturo Christofoletti, now on display in Amundsen City.*

with words. His parables spread, though, in mutated and paraphrased forms, to a much wider audience, but they never quite lost their essential deftness and subtlety.

Qing Xiao-wen's philosophy, insofar as it had a discernible core, was a form of benign scepticism. Although ancient in character, it seemed to take on new life in contemporary world politics. He delighted in paradox and irony, and never tired of suggesting that the new communications technology might make people incapable of authentic communication, or implying that the use of genetic engineering to transform plants and animals might obliterate precisely those aspects of the natural world that people ought to treasure. Admirers represented him as the world's conscience, but he is more accurately described as an expression of the world's cautiousness. Strange as it may seem, his was essentially a reassuring voice, not a critical one. He allowed people the luxury of feeling able to stand apart from, and even mock, their own awesome technological power and lifted some of the burden of responsibility from their shoulders. He pandered to a sense of smallness and hesitancy that many people enjoyed feeling – a sense that the world was, after all, outside and beyond human control. It was no wonder that other people took advantage of his lack of interest in conventional modes of publication to claim prestige for their own anxious thoughts by crediting them to him, borrowing the aura of his reputed wisdom.

Qing was born before either Zarzecki or Foden, in 2121, and outlived both of them, finally dying of heart failure in 2227, but few people ever had any idea of how old he was, and for some forty years before his death he was rarely thought of as a living person.

Millions of idealists shape the world

Zarzecki, Foden and Qing were humanitarians in the broad sense – they thought always in terms of the *world* community, the *human* race. Working in the overlapping spheres of world politics, ecological planning and personal attitudes to life, they shared a common spirit and dedication. It is easy for us to look back and recognize that pragmatic necessity insisted that the power of the United Nations must grow; that land management must be gradually co-ordinated on a world scale; and that ordinary people must in time adopt internationalist values. We can see these as abstract patterns of change developing through the generations, but we must not forget their human dimension: the millions of passionate believers and idealists who worked hard in pursuit of these ends.

The UN Code of Rights

The mere fourteen years of Zarzecki's reign at the UN were not sufficient to encompass great changes. The dates that we remember from the Period of Recovery represent the culmination of programmes, many of which can be traced back to that significant phase. The UN's Council of Justice, set up in 2223, did not publish its first Code of Rights until 2236. It took a further hundred years for the UN jurists to amend it into its now-familiar form, fighting in the meantime a long battle to persuade the individual nations to abide by it and to embody it in their own laws, but it was in the 2180s that this crusade was first launched. The same is true of other internationalist endeavours, concerned with such matters as medicine and social services.

Of all the men and women who followed Zarzecki in the position which became known at the popular level (though never at an official one) as "world premier", there are just a handful who stand out. Justina Duarte, general secretary from 2245 to 2253, changed penal systems everywhere with her passionate advocacy of reparative rather than punitive systems of crime-control. She persuaded the UN to punish national regimes using punitive systems. Adam Voysey, who held the post from 2267 until 2280, sparked off a storm of controversy when he became the first prominent person to try to take advantage of an experimental method of rejuvenation. The move proved as disastrous medically as it was politically, and he never fully recovered his health before his death in 2285.

The name of Gulzar Khan, Voysey's immediate predecessor, has and always will be linked to the slogan "One Man – One Child", and he takes most of the credit for winning the post-Islamic nations to the cause of population control.

The greens and the greys

Credit for progress in this period must also be accorded to certain political and social movements. In politics the old distinctions between "right" and "left" had decayed into insignificance by 2180, and journalistic jargon spoke in terms of "green" and "grey", reflecting the spectrum of groups with opposed attitudes to the management of technology and the environment. The green parties had chosen their own colour, and had foisted the contrasting label upon their opponents. Like the old right and left, green and grey were vague terms, but generally speaking green parties were cautious in their attitude to new technologies – especially large-scale technologies. They were in favour of population limitation and relatively

Adam's Meadow, China: the intricate terracing created by a group of male biotechs who founded the self-contained ecological community. Adam's Meadow thrived until the remote-controlled eyes of the world media took up a constant vigil. The Adams destroyed the robot spies with laser rifles. Freedom-of-information led to the subsequent arrest of the 444 Adams and the end of the community.

low-level energy-economy, and were fond of rhetoric involving the numinous concept of "the quality of life".

Grey parties tended to attract more materialistic individuals, favouring a fast-turnover energy-economy and placing more emphasis on individual freedom than on community responsibility. They were generally less egalitarian, and were constantly talking about "unlimited opportunity". Grey politics were dominant in the more highly-developed countries throughout the Period of Recovery, while most poorer nations had the reputation of being "green in the UN and grey at home". Green parties were not infrequently voted into office in the USA and Western Europe, but rarely behaved radically once in government. Although the UN agencies were theoretically above this kind of politics, they were widely suspected in the developed world of being green subversives, and in the Third World of being grey puppets.

"Ecological mysticism"

Extreme elements of the green persuasion were religious as much as political, being drawn toward "ecological mysticism" and the glorification, if not the actual deification, of "Nature". The decline of the old world religions had been attended by many excursions into revisionist theology, which played down personalized Creators and promoted more diffuse forms of reverence. The ancient prophets were transformed from messengers bearing the word of God into saintly individuals redolent of the proprieties and potentialities of human life.

The various "nature cults" of the twenty-first and twenty-second centuries had mostly been opposed to all kinds of biological engineering, and indeed to high technology of almost every kind. In the twenty-third and twenty-fourth centuries, by contrast, the activities of the genetic engineers were commonly seen as an extension of the mysteries of Life and Nature, and biologists were frequently credited with a kind of honorary holiness. This proved attractive to some biologists and the new mysticism began to thrive even in the most unlikely quarters.

One of the more interesting corollaries of the new-style religion was the growth in the 2250s of a new monasticism. It became common for small groups of people – usually, though not invariably, single-sex communities – to exempt themselves from the communications networks and dedicate their lives to the creation of their own private Edens, using techniques of biological engineering to control the whole ecologies of their small estates. These were often established in remote areas which had not yet come within the scope of the UN planners. The most famous – though the attention paid to it ultimately brought about its destruction – was Adam's Meadow, in the Kun-Lun mountains of China, which thrived between 2271 and 2299. The prominent geneticist Theresa Nordhoff, celebrated for her hard-headed scepticism, observed in 2286 that many of her contemporaries were being "lured into a regression to the womb of their science, exiling themselves into Mendelian havens". More generous observers thought the movement healthy, providing avenues of retreat from the demands of highly mechanized societies. In any case, it was these and other manifestations of "green movements" which provided the principal opposition to the dominant social, political and intellectual trends of the Period of Recovery.

CHAPTER NINETEEN

THE AMELIORATION OF SUFFERING

During the Period of Recovery agricultural production was rationalized within most nations and to an extent internationally by the UN's Land Use Committee. This permitted new techniques in biotechnology to be fully exploited. These, together with the spread of fusion reactors and communications networks, ensured that between 2180 and 2400 the standard of living of the world's poor improved very dramatically. The period did not see an end to poverty, because "poverty" is relative, and while the poor grew richer the rich grew richer still. However, the minimum standard of living in 2400 was high enough for many people to speak of "the end of suffering".

The development of food surpluses in most parts of the world happened almost spontaneously, because the improvements which had been devised during the Period of Crisis were sustained as the crisis evaporated. Other battles to save the world's unfortunates were not so easily won. Malnutrition had been only one of the major killers; disease was even more rapacious.

Medical inequalities

The developed countries had virtually lost their fear of disease. Most debilitating virus diseases had been wiped out by mass immunization, and those that remained were rarely more than troublesome. Many people still developed cancer, but there were effective ways of blocking the growth of tumours and removing them, so anyone with regular access to a body-scanner had little to fear. It was not until people were into their sixties or seventies that the senescence of the body made diseases more difficult to combat. In the USA, the USSR, Australia and most Western European states regular body-scanning of the entire population became routine. In Nigeria, Paraguay or Papua-New Guinea only one person in ten thousand enjoyed such a privilege.

The medical advances which made the most difference to the rich, however, were not the straightforward preventive measures. Technical control of cell-division and tissue-differentiation had been developed to aid the body's powers of repair and renewal. Severed limbs could now be regenerated, brain damage repaired by stimulation of cells in the spinal column, and bodies reshaped for practical or aesthetic purposes. Although such medical miracles had been possible for many years, they remained complicated and expensive. Even in the USA only one person in a thousand could afford to buy their physique, as it were, "off the peg". The fact that such people could have themselves re-created in the image of Apollo or Aphrodite brought a particularly acute form of envy into the world. The diseases unleashed during the Plague Wars were still claiming hundreds of thousands of victims – almost all of them in the poorer countries – and medical aid was not getting through. Even bacterial infections that could have been cured by simple antibiotics were still exacting their toll of mortality.

The UN takes on the multinationals

It was already UN policy to disseminate modern medicine into all the corners of the globe. Zarzecki, like many of his predecessors, made speeches about the dire need to internationalize medical care, but like them he found it difficult to make headway. Most medical supplies were still produced under the aegis of multinational corporations whose primary goal was to make profits, and who organized their research and output accordingly. The demands of the wealthy always counted for far more than the needs of the impoverished. The UN diverted a good deal of its income into medical relief programmes, but this became one more source of income for the multinationals, which sought to maximize the money they obtained while minimizing what they gave in return. Attempts to make medical provision, like food production, the business of national governments and international agencies were continually outmanoeuvred.

The UN was forced to work slowly during the twenty-third century, setting up its own medical research and production facilities, and building its own hospitals. It came into constant conflict with the multinational corporations because of its deliberate policy of "patent plundering" – manufacturing all manner of drugs for free distribution while commercial concerns were still trying to make money out of them. It was not until the twenty-fourth century that universal immunization finally wiped out the legacy of the Plague Wars. By 2350 sophisticated cancer treatments were available to over half the world's people, but the more complex regeneration treatments remained unavailable to many who were in need and some genetic deficiency diseases, like sickle-cell anaemia, continued to claim victims because doctors using tissue-transformation methods could not keep pace with demand. By the end of the century, techniques of rejuvenation and life-span-extension were beginning to be exploited by the rich. Thus, while premature death was still a major hazard for people in the poorest parts of the world, the rich were beginning to wonder whether they needed to die at all.

Food, clothing and housing guaranteed
In other ways, the lot of the poor had vastly improved. The gradual extension of the information networks had transformed the potential of social welfare programmes. The marginal role played by cash allowed governments to develop ingenious ways of giving spending power to their destitute citizens. Government control of food production which made it easy to distribute benefits – in kind rather than cash. As early as 2200 some nations began distinguishing between different kinds of credit, creating "food credits" – sometimes automatically awarded to all citizens – which could be spent on nothing except food. Eventually, many nations introduced "clothing credits" and "housing credits" too, with ironic echoes of ancient wartime rationing systems, but adapted now to cope with abundance. Wages remained payable in "flexible credits", which could be spent on anything, but by 2350 most people, even in poor nations, could survive quite adequately without any wage income at all, on the various kinds of credit to which they were entitled simply because they existed. Even the developed countries had incorporated diversified credit into the social welfare systems that they still retained.

Telescreens embitter as well as educate
The spread of the information networks brought educational facilities to many more of the world's poor. As the networks expanded the UN tried to insist on universal access to all kinds of information. This made it possible for many people displaced from their ancestral ways of life to learn new skills and cope with new lifestyles. With the extending communications networks, of course, came better roads and railways, which were still vitally important to the movement of goods. Eventually, even the most remote inhabited areas were brought close to the heart of twenty-fourth-century civilization.

However, the telescreens also brought news of the lives and advantages of the rich, and this undermined any sense of gratitude. It is difficult for us to guess the mixed feelings of the poor when they were first introduced to the great world of which they were becoming a part. There was much to amuse and to embitter, them as they contemplated such strange phenomena as the explosive growth of the cryonics corporations.

Freezing the dead
Cryonics first arose in the late twentieth century, when American "cryonics societies" began freezing newly dead bodies, in the faint hope that one day a medical means of reversing clinical death would be discovered. At that time cryoprotective technology for preventing tissue-damage was primitive and the original cryonics societies foundered in the early twenty-first century when would-be heirs of the frozen dead began to sue them successfully for fraudulent misrepresentation. By 2035 all the bodies held in cryonic vaults had been removed for cremation or burial. No one had at that time been frozen for preservation in the vaults while still living, because no organization had dared to face the possibility of murder charges. Two experiments on human volunteers, in 2004 and 2007, had both gone tragically wrong.

Cryonics societies reappeared in the 2190s, after considerable experimental success in freezing and reviving fully-grown mammals. By this time it was generally acknowledged that the probability of finding a way of reversing brain-death was negligible, and the practice of freezing newly-dead bodies was proscribed by law. On the other hand, the right of any individual to commit suicide, and to be assisted in such a project by others, had by then been enshrined in the American constitution. This made it difficult to prosecute cryonic scientists who froze consenting living adults. After several successful experiments in which frozen humans were revived, none the worse for their experience, the cryonics societies began cautiously to call for volunteers, suggesting in their publicity that it was foolish for people to use up their entire lifespans in the present, when a technology of rejuvenation and longevity might be just around the corner.

Freezing the living
This publicity pitch was widely criticized. Although medical scientists had found many effective ways to ensure that people could live out their full term of seventy years and more, they had not yet found the means of stopping the process of ageing. This is such a complicated phenomenon, involving several simultaneous processes of cellular and systematic decay, that the prospect of finding a "cure" still seemed fairly remote, despite the efforts of researchers all over the world. Optimists, however, pointed to the success of animal experiments in which senescent tissues had been revived by inoculation with embryonic cells taken from cryonically-preserved clone-siblings. It was argued that this *might* be a breakthrough, although the idea of splitting early human embryos to create clones and then freezing some members of the clone as embryos, so that such embryos could be plundered at a later date, raised many moral qualms.

Frozen murderer: the foil encased face of Australian Alexander Smith frozen in dreamless sleep, 250 degrees below zero, in 2240. His crime, downing 15 aircars one sunny afternoon; his sentence, 100 years of deep sleep.

The people who flocked to the cryonics societies had no frozen clone-siblings, but they did have a natural reluctance to die, and they hoped that in time a less gruesome form of rejuvenation technology might appear. The societies were probably amazed by the extent of their success, considering their enormous fees, but once the market had been tested they rapidly reformed as commercial corporations. At the turn of the century only a few hundred individuals had been "frozen down", but by 2210 there were more than ten thousand, in fourteen different countries.

The Politburo in Moscow attempted to introduce legislative controls over cryonic activities to restrict eligibility on eugenic grounds. The time was long gone, though, when the hard core of the Communist Party could have its way in such matters – there were too many rich Russians determined to make sure that the only criterion was money. Some commentators represented this brief fight as the last gasp of the old Party, and saw the subsequent electoral purge of the Central Committee as the long expected death throes of the spirit of the October Revolution. In the USA, where there was hardly a whimper of official condemnation, the first lotteries offering the right to cryonic treatment were launched in 2214 and proved a huge success.

Overwhelming demand for cryonics

By 2230 nearly thirty thousand people a year were electing to be frozen down, and anyone who could do simple arithmetic realized that the situation could get out of hand. The corporations running the vaults had found them to be a goldmine and were building new ones as fast as they could, but with pressure groups calling for legislation to limit world population, it was an embarrassment to be asked to consider the situation in forty or fifty years time. Were there eventually to be millions, or tens of millions, or hundreds of millions of people in the vaults? And what, then, if a technology of rejuvenation *were* to be discovered? *Could* they all be revived, in a year, or a hundred years? How was the world proposing to accommodate them? By this time a good many of the people electing to be frozen down were not even old – they simply fancied themselves as time-travellers, and booked into the vaults not on an indefinite basis but for a fixed span of time.

Matters were further complicated in 2239 when the Australian parliament voted to use suspended animation as a way of removing dangerous individuals from the community. This was ostensibly not a punishment but an attempt to hold psychotic individuals in safe keeping until they might be cured of anti-social tendencies. Many other nations began to take an interest in this new venture in penology, despite the fact that the UN was by this time moving to oppose the whole cryonics movement, using its influence over international land management to inhibit the building of more vaults. The cryonics corporations were already having difficulty meeting demand, and as this became more acute many would-be clients turned angry and desperate. The price of freezing climbed steadily, and alarmists tried to guess when the frozen would outnumber the active.

The crisis point was reached in the USA in 2244 when the great south-western blackout threw thirteen states into virtual chaos. For various coincidental reasons, the emergency generators failed in no less than seven vault-complexes, causing the uncontrolled thawing of nearly nine thousand people. Despite the desperate efforts of dozens of medical teams, only eight hundred survived. The California Cryonics Corporation went bankrupt within a week, and within a month the holdings of all the other American corporations had been nationalized by emergency legislation. President Averil Melcart justified this by declaring that it was necessary to protect the interests of tens of thousands of American citizens. Cynics observed that never before had any American president done so much for so many people who were unable to vote.

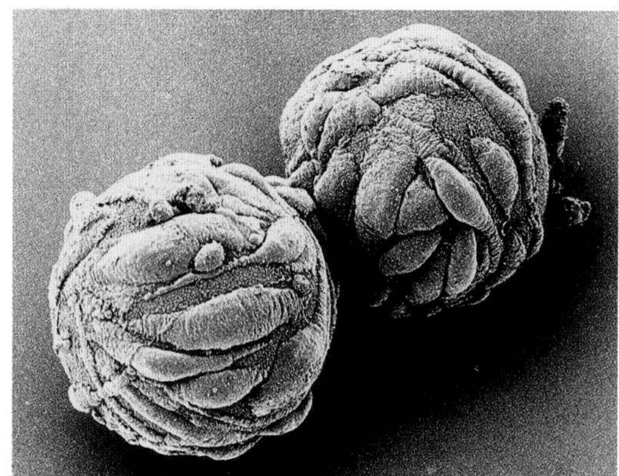

Frozen cells. As cryonics failed as an industry, many people took the more sensible step of freezing a few vital cells – commonly brain and bone cells – for cloning in the case of accident or illness.

The corporations found themselves hemmed in by legislation requiring guarantees which drove the price of freezing higher and higher. In the meantime, the confidence of potential clients had been so badly shaken that very few people could be persuaded that the new prices represented any kind of bargain. Of course, the issue flared up again in the 2260s when the first experimental successes in human rejuvenation were claimed, but by this time the logic no longer seemed to work in favour of the cryonic scientists. The people who had died in 2244 might have done better to arrive in the new era simply by staying alive and active. Then again, the experimental failures began to turn up, and when Secretary-General Voysey was unwise enough to attempt rejuvenation himself the whole business once again fell into disrepute. After the failed operation, Voysey's own campaign manager said, "I'd sooner promote a guy who screws babies and bites the heads off chickens than one with a complexion like *that*." Records appear to have been deliberately destroyed, but doctors jocularly referred to Voysey's condition as Swiss Cheese Syndrome. Even at the end of the Period of Recovery many vaults were still in use – a monument to past follies. By then, reliable techniques of rejuvenation *were* available to those who could afford them, but not a single person who had been frozen down in the early days of the craze ever won what had originally appeared an attractive gamble.

The cryonics corporations were ultimately a failure, but we should recognize that they too, like so many other bygone follies and folk remedies, were meant to relieve suffering. The attempt was badly timed and the circumstances inappropriate, but this was the first real salvo fired in the war against death. Most people realized that here was a pointer to the future, and that the war would continue until it was won.

CHAPTER TWENTY

THE CONTROL OF POPULATION

The Period of Crisis had been a time of unprecedented mortality. It was estimated – though the evidence is not wholly conclusive – that as many human beings died between 2000 and 2180 as had perished in the previous 1,800 years. Nevertheless, at the end of the period the total world population was still close to four billion, and the new era of peace and prosperity opened up the possibility of a new "population explosion", akin to that of the twentieth century.

But there were several respects in which the world was now better placed to prevent this. Nations like China and India, which together accommodated nearly half the world's people, had well-established traditions of anti-fertility propaganda long before 2180. Government attitudes had not always been consistent, especially during the period of the Plague Wars, but in general the citizens of these countries had been urged over the generations to have fewer children. Social changes accompanying the revolution in the world agricultural system had destroyed the economic argument for large families. Children were no longer required to work the family plot, and with better social welfare systems the elderly had no need of family support.

Signs of new population explosion

In 2200, the populations of China, India and many comparable nations were somewhat below their 2000 level, and had shown no sign of rapid increase for several generations. Only a handful of developed countries, including the USA and most European nations, had larger populations in 2200 than in 2000. The most spectacular increases were in Australia, Canada and Brazil, which had experienced very high rates of immigration. Since the beginning of the millennium developed countries had taken a *laissez-faire* attitude to reproduction because the economic logic already encouraged parents to have relatively few children. By 2200 the climate of optimism, and the widespread sense that the era of crises was over, was reflected in a slow rise in the birth-rate.

The possibility of a new population explosion was very much in the minds of the world's ecological planners and they were keen to prevent it. They knew well enough that but for the appalling success of the old Malthusian checks – famine, plague and war – during the previous two centuries, world population might have climbed to ten or fifteen billion. Now the resources existed to feed ten or fifteen billion, but there was virtual unanimity in the UN agencies that this would be socially undesirable. If poverty was eventually to be abolished or significantly eroded, then people must not only have food, but private space and personal possessions to support a comfortable lifestyle. In any case, efficient planning of the world's ecology called for accurate estimation of world need and demand; this required predictable population trends. Most ecologists wanted to guarantee this by careful control, because efficient land management implied planning the size of the population dependent on that land.

Initial failure of child-licensing

The experience of some nations showed that legislative controls did not work. China's leaders had on several occasions introduced laws restricting the entitlement of families and single women to have children. These had sometimes sat on the statute books for many years, but had always proved troublesome to enforce. All attempts to police such laws caused bitter resentment and civil strife, and many politicians who had supported them saw their careers founder in consequence. In Bangladesh in 2035, in Laos in 2057 and in Colombia in 2074, authoritarian governments had introduced child-licensing backed by draconian penalties; within five years all three of the despots responsible had been assassinated by parents whose illicit children had been killed. By the twenty-second century it had become conventional political wisdom that child-licensing was fatal, and that propaganda was the only practical means of population control. The propaganda *did* work, in the context of the twenty-second century, but it received massive support from the Malthusian checks. No one really believed, in 2200, that the world was ready to follow the path sketched out in Malthus's later work, namely to substitute "moral restraint" for famine, plague and war.

Resistance to fertility control

The advance of biological science had made available numerous methods of contraception. It was technically feasible to inoculate every child against the possibility of bearing children in much the same way as they were routinely inoculated against virus diseases. This was precisely what many scientists advocated; they wanted the entire population to be sterile except for short periods when, if it was deemed desirable, fertility could be temporarily restored. But the political problems involved were formidable.

Many people considered the freedom to control their own fertility to be one of the most vital and intimate freedoms. Even those who did not actually want children, and certainly had no intention of bearing many of

WORLD POPULATION

Population in millions

Country	Year 1950	2000	2200	2400	2600	3000
USA	152	229	240	282	275	240
UK	51	60	60	58	40	32
USSR	180	301	277	284	295	244
France	42	62	69	72	64	55
Sudan	9	29	15	24	46	72
Mexico	27	98	72	94	102	94
Argentina	17	44	21	15	30	48
China	558	1206	1017	955	810	625
Japan	84	124	34*	41	32	32
India	353	898	820	848	611	457

*Decimated by earthquakes

CITIES IN CRISIS

City	Year 1950	2000	2200	2400	2600	3000
New York	16	19	21	22	12	6
London	12	14	14	13	7	4
Moscow	8	10	12	15	9	5
Paris	8.5	10	10	9	6	3
Khartoum	1.1	7	8	16	21	15
Mexico City	14	17	19	21	17	10
Buenos Aires	8.5	14	–*	–	2	4
Shanghai	12	22	23	22	17	11
Tokyo	27	30	2**	4	4	4
Calcutta	8	21	22	22	15	8

*Destroyed in nuclear attack
**Smashed by earthquakes

them, still wished to retain the prerogative of personal choice.

There was also a widespread – and by no means groundless – suspicion that once those in power had the ability to decide who was to have children they would introduce discriminatory selection. Some forms of eugenic selection were already operating in the developed countries. Most genetic defects could now be detected at an early stage in pregnancy, and the abortion of damaged foetuses was commonplace. However, the decision to abort was still almost always left to the parents, and no country yet had laws forbidding certain people to breed on eugenic grounds. Such coercive eugenic practices as did exist – and there were some – were covert. Statistics from more than one country suggest that an unlikely number of severely deformed embryos were inexplicably stillborn, following a parental refusal to abort. And in highly developed countries like America, doctors would often point out in intimidating detail the cost of keeping some genetic misfit alive.

Fear of racial selection

Yet people were aware that discrimination might be applied on non-eugenic grounds, and it was easy enough to find historical instances of discriminatory propaganda. In the USSR, for instance, anti-fertility propaganda had been maintained in the Asian republics, particularly Kazakhstan and Uzbekistan, despite an abundance of food and resources. Simultaneously the Politburo continued to encourage Caucasians to multiply. With the comparatively low birth rate of the European Russians, preserving their dominance required naked, if never publicly acknowledged, racism.

In the USA there had been a similar, though less striking, pattern throughout the twenty-first and twenty-second centuries. The white élite, anxious about the swelling ranks of the black and Hispanic populations, had directed their propaganda specifically to those groups. Such instances made non-white communities around the world wary of allowing their fertility to be directly controlled by any white-dominated government. The suspicion was voiced that if child-licensing were ever widely accepted it would bring about not only a world dominated by Caucasians but also the gradual elimination of the other races. At the same time some whites apparently feared the reverse, looking anxiously at the huge populations of India, Africa and the Orient.

Despite these suspicions, racial prejudice was in fact on the decline in 2200, and had been for some time. Improved communications had eroded cultural differences, had increased inter-racial tolerance and respect. Marriage across racial boundaries had become common and was scarcely stigmatized in any of the richer nations, though it would be many generations before such boundaries would become irrelevant. It was commonplace in the USA, Australia and the USSR for wealthier members of the darker-skinned races to take advantage of biotechnology to have their colour lightened and their features realigned. In the USA in the 2230s there was a fad among disaffected middle-class teenagers for having their skin darkened; this left no long-term legacy.

World leaders conspire over child-licensing

There were difficulties every time the question of world population limitation was brought to the UN council chamber in the early twenty-third century. It was raised again and again at the insistence of the directors of the various UN agencies, who felt it essential for a policy to be formulated at a world level. Most national governments were willing to maintain their propaganda but in spite of wide agreement that a more formal approach was required, they procrastinated determinedly over legislation.

By 2250 it was accepted almost universally that on this issue no national government could or should stand alone. Gradually a group of world leaders conspired to introduce child-licensing, but for once they wanted to be instructed by the UN, in order to avoid the responsibility.

UN sterilization resolution

It may have been the early experimental successes in human rejuvenation which finally encouraged world leaders to grit their teeth and make their move, enthusiastically backed by Secretary-General Gulzar Khan. Certainly, the prospect of a declining death-rate as well as an uncontrolled birth-rate made it clear that real control *would* be necessary, and perhaps soon. Either way, the UN toyed with the crucial resolution for ten years, and after much heartache passed it in 2271, while Adam Voysey's reputation was still untainted. It was no coincidence that the USA then had as its President Juan Pereira Mendes, only the second Hispanic to hold that position, and that Premier Shaybani of the USSR was the first Asian to be given control of the Supreme Soviet. Both men were considered ideal for guiding through the necessary legislative packages in the two superpowers. By 2274 they had done so. All citizens of the two great nations were required to submit themselves for sterilization, and all children would in future be sterilized in infancy as a matter of routine. The legislation embodied "right of personal replacement" (by temporary reversal of sterilization), guaranteeing the right to be the parent of at least one child. The measures applied to both males and females, partly as a fail-safe device and partly to avoid complicating the issue further with a dimension of sexual discrimination.

Violent reactions

There were, of course, demonstrations of dissent in both nations – though not on the scale of the riots that broke out in many smaller nations, including the Sudan, Venezuela and Iran, when they too complied with the UN directive in 2276-79. The dissent was fought with propaganda of an intensity unusual in these relatively liberal nations, but the fight against those individuals who refused to capitulate was a long and bitter one. Force was rarely used to administer the sterilizing injections in the nations that considered themselves most advanced (though it certainly was in many other nations), but other means of ensuring compliance were to hand. It was all too easy simply to withdraw all credit facilities from law-breakers, making it appallingly difficult for them to carry on a normal life. Many of the more determined rebels accepted this judgement and "went underground", abandoning their involvement with the information network and taking up a hand-to-mouth existence. Such rebels were still at large, in small numbers, even at the turn of the century. In periodic media scares in the USA they were called the Army of Ghosts and represented as a vast, faceless menace. Legend has it that one at least was a network pirate of such skill as to be able to plug in at any telephone and program false identities and credit ratings, switching from name to name as easily as changing clothes – the "Databank Pimpernel". ("Is she in heaven or is she in hell?" the synthetape fantasia enquired. "That damned elusive . . .").

Six nations rebel

More problematic for the UN was the refusal by several nations to comply. In Europe, the influence of the Roman Church was still strong – for slightly different reasons – in Italy and Ireland, and in both nations the premiers who tried to introduce the requisite legislation were removed from office. Israel and Saudi-Arabia both failed to endorse the resolution, while two African nations – Benin and Mauretania – decided not to comply. In Benin's case the decision was apparently an arbitrary whim of the leader of the ruling junta, but President Calcar of Mauretania had in mind a strategy to help his country, which was one of the most backward in the world.

There was no attempt to force these nations into line during the early 2280s. The UN, at first content to play a waiting game, was thrown into disarray after the Voysey scandal. Most governments were busy coping with their internal problems. But the consequences of the disaffection of these nations were rather startling. Naturally they became refuges for dissenters from other nations, who preferred emigration to rebellion.

Catholic countries swamped with immigrants

By 2279 the ports and airports of Italy and Ireland could barely cope with the flow of people arriving legally and illegally.

Conor MacLeary enjoying a traditional drink before retreating underground. He spent six miserable years in a bunker guiding Ireland back to a degree of stability. A national hero, he gave up the premiership in 2289 shortly after his return to the surface.

Attempts by successive governments to keep these immigrants out failed dismally, largely because many of their own citizens sympathized with the new arrivals. In 2281 the Dail had to declare a state of emergency in Ireland; with resources already stretched to breaking-point, the country was faced with the possibility that its population might increase four- or five-fold in a single generation. Ironically, by refusing to limit their birth-rates, Italy and Ireland had created for themselves an acute population problem in a mere ten years. In order to stem the flow of immigrants, Ireland was forced to comply with the UN resolution. Emergency legislation was rushed through in May 2282. Within three days Prime Minister Liam O'Dowd was shot dead in Dublin. His successor, Conor Macleary, had to put down the worst riots that troubled city had ever seen. Macleary spent the next six years in an underground bunker as he tried desperately to guide his country back to stability. The Italian government, horrified by events in Dublin, declared martial law: the legislation went through parliament in the early hours of 16 June 2282, with Rome under curfew. There followed a long period of deportations as both Ireland and Italy tried to get rid of the fanatics they had so recklessly attracted.

Three others capitulate

Neither Israel nor Saudi-Arabia was faced with the same problems, largely because fewer dissenters chose them as sanctuaries, but Israel quickly followed Italy's example. Just as Premier Angelo Tebaldi of Italy had somehow won the support of Pope Sixtus XV, whose reversal of church doctrine in a momentous declaration from the throne of St Peter had done much to quell the rioting, so Prime Minister Rabrina persuaded the Chief Rabbi to assist his campaign. Both Saudi-Arabia and Benin fell into line in 2283, leaving Mauretania the one nation where unrestricted procreation remained legal.

Mauretania stands alone

Everyone expected Mauretania's President Calcar to comply within a matter of months, but he did not. Remarkably, it was not until 2285 that the rest of the world realized what he was doing. Many of those expelled from Italy and Ireland decided that living in Mauretania – which was still mostly desert – was too high a price to pay for freedom, but many did not. Mauretania was highly selective about the immigrants who were allowed to land at Nouadhibou and Nouakchott, though Calcar's police turned a blind eye to many small boats which crept into smaller harbours all along the Atlantic coast. Most of the permitted – indeed much-welcomed – immigrants were highly-educated, skilled and wealthy. President Calcar openly acknowledged that his poverty-stricken country lacked the resources to accommodate them and the offspring they were so keen to have, but he was equally open in inviting them to increase those resources. Suddenly the Sahara reclamation schemes, which had had their most spectacular successes in Algeria and Libya, began to show still greater rewards for Mauretania.

President Calcar's welcome for the fertility rebels even extended as far as allowing a rival papacy to be established in Kiffa, and he was generous with his guarantees that Mauretania would not introduce child-licensing in his lifetime. Nor did it. It was not until 2336 that the legislation went through – curiously, without fierce opposition. The immigrants had borne the desperately desired children, but they had failed to pass on their fanaticism to those children – who found themselves in a country where, despite the rapid expansion of resources, population pressure still made malnutrition a constant threat. By 2330 the majority of Mauretanians – native and immigrant – had made the establishment of child-licensing a crusade. It is not clear whether Calcar (who died in 2312 at the age of 101) really had foreseen this, but his name was committed to legend as a leader with the wisdom of Solomon.

2300: the balance tips

Some people, of course, did not exercise their "right of personal replacement", so the UN resolution of 2271 ensured that the population of the world began a slow decline after 2300. After that date, the only question which remained was the optimum population to be selected as a target. That question was never settled, but there were further factors yet to be taken into account, when the technologies of longevity finally began to take effect.

CHAPTER TWENTY-ONE

THE WORLD'S POWER GRID

In the Period of Crisis the plan for the world grid had been accepted and even welcomed both as a convenient symbol of "global unity" and as a means of accelerating the development of needy countries. Now that, in the early years of the Period of Recovery, it threatened to become a functioning network which would inevitably impose a degree of world unity, there was a political backlash. The reaction was reminiscent of the panic of twentieth- and twenty-first-century charitable organizations, which were devoted to the eradication of various diseases and then found their existence threatened by their own success. In the same way, governments which had welcomed the world grid – as a key to boosted development or future profit – tended later to resent the accompanying loss of sovereignty.

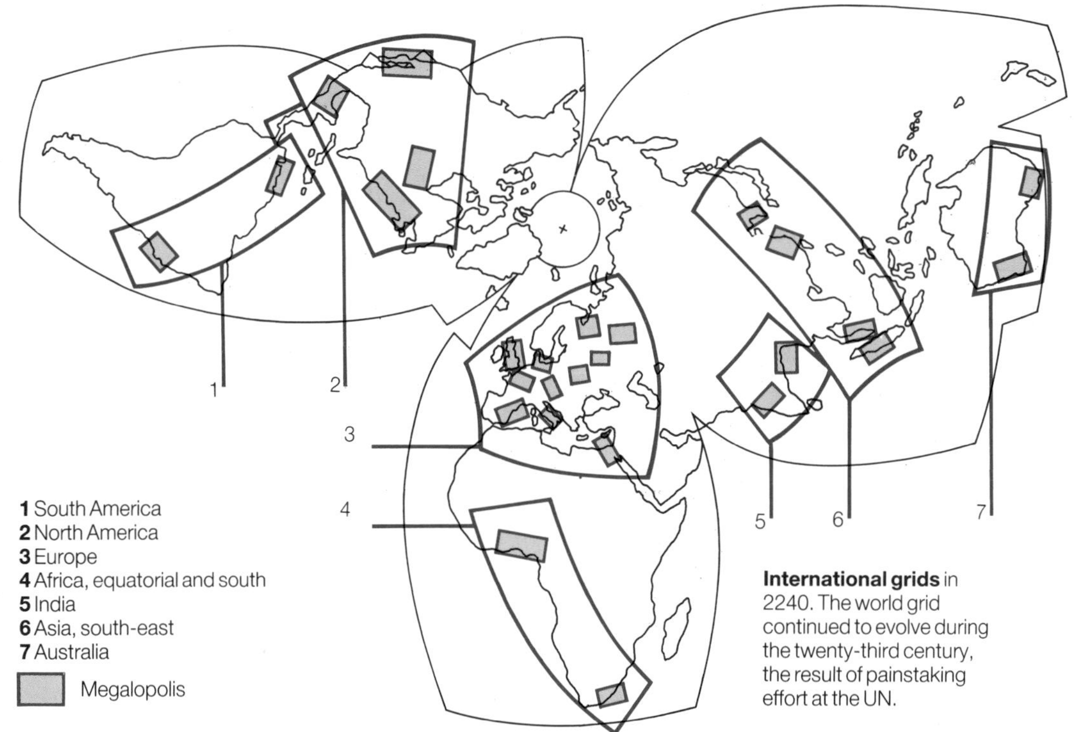

International grids in 2240. The world grid continued to evolve during the twenty-third century, the result of painstaking effort at the UN.

Nations irritated by UN directives

Power grid standards were imposed from outside, and UN "suggestions" for internal grid expansion were often at variance with local political plans. Typically the UN Energy Committee advisers would politely but firmly request that the revamped internal grid should provide power to one specific area much in need of development, with cross-border connections to the world grid at particular sites; an annoyed government would retort that it was politically necessary to begin by plugging another already well-developed and influential district into the new network, to promote tourism by electrifying a different coastal area, and to avoid the UN's suggested cross-border link since diplomatic relations on that frontier were extremely shaky. The textbook case here was Yugoslavia, where President Mazuranic said most of these things and more in 2197, although over the next decade he was able to set almost all of the original suggestions into motion.

At this stage the UN Energy Committee, though usually listened to with some attentiveness, did not wield real power except insofar as it was backed by the superpowers and the national and international electrical agencies. Indeed the EC never caught the public imagination in the way that the Land Use Committee did. It failed to attract flamboyant personalities as its spokesmen, only a succession of politically and metaphorically grey people whose names barely achieve footnotes in the history books – who remembers Karl Ziegfried, Pel Torro, John E. Muller, Bron Fane or Lee Barton? At this stage the world grid had many points in common with the world postal service: the UN was concerned that the routes should be open and should obey certain international standards, but did not concern itself unduly with the traffic.

Cheap electricity controversial

This was instead the time of the power supply agencies. Economic pressure from the USA forced the Pan-American Power Agency

(PAPA) into existence early in the day, regulating grid dealings over the whole continent. It was quickly followed by European and African agencies of a similar nature, while the Soviet countries' Kremlin-based power committee managed to function on a joint basis with China (something of a coup for Premier Pudurash). The chief economic problem which the agencies had to exploit or resist was that in the hyperdeveloped countries fusion power was now becoming remarkably cheap, while it remained expensive in nations whose fusion plants were still unbuilt or unamortized. The international grid connections, once pleasingly symbolic, became sore points for many. Obviously the worldwide electrical energy tariff tended to be lowered by the cheapness of hyperdeveloped power; this meant that nations whose internal power was more expensive found themselves expected to supply power to the grid when necessary, at what was for them a ruinously low rate.

"You rich folk have all that blood to spare! But ours is dear, and comes from our hearts," Puri Dhillen, Premier of Bangladesh, is supposed to have said in this connection (2215). It is a little unfortunate that this, her only remembered public utterance, is fairly certainly the work of a contemporary comedian who parodied her "simple peasant woman" style of oration. Dhillen was in fact rather a subtle politician, and did much to ease in the eventual sliding scale of energy tariffs – "energy welfare" – which eased the grid problem in the zone of what became the South Asian Joint Electrical Agency (SAJEA).

Nicaraguan revolt increases power of UN

Other agencies were forced into similar compromises, alarmed by the more extreme examples of unrest, as when Nicaragua – plagued again by the low fixed tariff – closed its electrical "borders" for eight months in 2231, severing the grid linkage between North and most of South America. PAPA had great difficulty in balancing its books; the profitable sale of cheap US power to the south was badly hit; Nicaragua's President Cuervo announced that at the first sign of military intervention his forces would destroy the entire sub-grid on his country's soil.

The solution helped give the UN greater power, and paved the way for Justina Duarte's funding of the organization through the taxing of multinationals when she became Secretary-General. Threading a maze of dubious legality and concessions to expediency, the PAPA agency was painlessly incorporated into the UN Energy Committee, and its fusion plants were bought out as international property. The UN would operate them – in practice delegating control through a chain of command resembling the old *status quo* in remarkable detail – and would sell power at a fixed tariff throughout the PAPA jurisdiction. Energy accounting would thus become an internal UN affair rather than a source of international friction, and less developed nations would be less burdened by their fusion programme because many expenses would be taken over by the UN.

In a way this was largely a game with words, skating over the problematic gulf between energy-rich and energy-poor nations by a system of hidden subsidies cloaked by the legal fiction of UN proprietorship of the grid. Fiction merged with fact, though, as the twenty-third century went by, and Duarte did much to help the EC along during her 2245-53 period as Secretary-General. The other supply agencies yielded one by one and were subsumed into the UN Energy Committee – SAJEA being the last to fall, in 2298, perhaps because its energy-welfare policy gave it fewest internal problems.

UN takes control of world energy

The twenty-fourth century saw the EC in nominal control of the entire grid and directly responsible for the majority of existing fusion plants. And President Cuervo's fit of petulance won him the reputation of a far-sighted political thinker who had planned all this from the start.

This pattern, of UN co-ordination beginning as a fiction devised to soothe international tensions but later hardening into actual control, was to be repeated during the return to space in the twenty-fourth century.

Embarrassing problems did not, of course, cease with this internationalism. The EC was able to avoid repetition of such major incidents as the disastrous southern USA blackout of 2244 or the famous Red Sea Energy Loop in the following decade. The latter was a complex foul-up rather than a simple accident: it was discovered that phase-difference problems and poor co-ordination between SAJEA and the pan-African agency had resulted in alarming power-losses, with some of the feeder stations effectively pumping energy into each other and doing no more than heat the grid cables. "Our agency's salesmen are the best in the world, they sold outdoor central heating to Saudi Arabia" was the joke of the decade in North Africa. These and other major difficulties faded into history; minor problems were rife for much longer, chiefly interlock failures and occasional local brownouts. The latter were often caused by exuberant young nations whose enthusiasm for world-grid power led to the

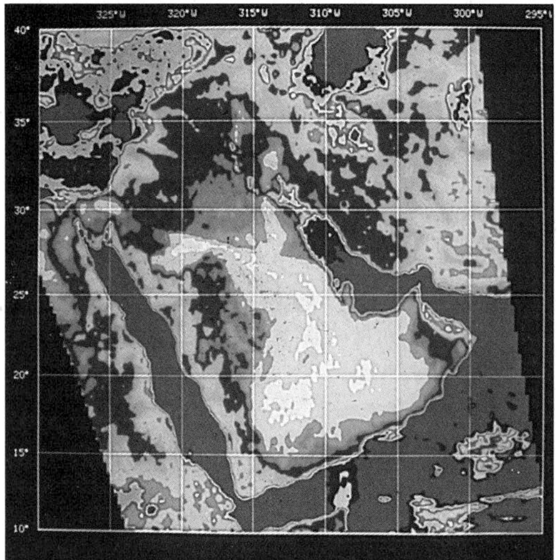

Red Sea energy loop, as viewed from a satellite in March 2251. Electricity was circling the Red Sea, heating cables and, in places, boiling the water.

construction of heavy industry, the consumption of which outpaced the local grid's ability to deliver energy.

Brownout in Cuba

For example, when undersea cables finally plugged Cuba into the grid *circa* 2310 (more than 250 years would elapse before that nation was integrated into the Caribbean Confederacy), President Fidel IV was so eager to inaugurate Havana's new electromagnetic-levitation subway that he did not wait for the final commissioning of the Cienfuegos fusion plant. That, combined with an unlucky cable fault, led to a harmless brownout – harmless except to a number of hospital patients under electronic life support and, more spectacularly, an airship full of tourists making a radar-guided landing at the local airport. Impetuously the President raised a cry of "UN murderers!" which a century or two before might have caused severe political dislocations. But this was now the civilized twenty-fourth century: the Energy Committee was able to smooth matters over with a scattering of energy concessions which were in effect small bribes, while the enquiry into who was to blame petered out over years in the labyrinth of international courts.

Cheap energy for all

This was the pattern of many lesser incidents associated with the grid. The UN energy monopoly became a stabilizing force and lubricated the transition from a world of energy-rich and energy-poor nations to one where energy was everywhere a cheap, available utility, like air or – more appropriately, except in the remaining desert zones – water. The ultimate sanction of turning off the power was never used, though more than once it was obliquely threatened. By the turn of the twenty-fifth century few people remembered that such a conveniently communal utility had once been a jealously guarded national privilege.

This quiet battle against nationalism was all the more successful as a result of the Gantz process, which with the development of "self-sufficient" homes helped to free consumers from all but token dependence on outside power lines. By the end of the Period of Recovery, the grid's main clients were public transport and lighting, industry, and the major communications networks; domestic consumption was gradually falling, maintained only by the popularity of electromobiles. Thus for the average consumer it wasn't his or her personal electrical power which had passed into shadowy international hands – only the impersonal Metro and the like were no longer quite under local control. It has even been suggested that the grey anonymity of the EC leaders was not simply a chance factor aiding the EC's almost unopposed rise to power, but part of a master plan designed for just that purpose – the Grid Conspiracy Theory.

Physics in eclipse

It is rather more likely that the EC members' lack of charisma derived from their association with such a boring, old-hat subject as power and the grid. Despite the coming of fusion, physical science was under a cloud. Physics had reached a dead end, it was suggested early in the Period of Recovery. The word "engineer" meant a bioengineer, and "inorganic engineer" was the term coined for those made second-class citizens by the genetic revolution. But the "hard" physical sciences and mechanical technologies were far from dead, however much upstaged, and their twenty-third-century renaissance is in part described in the following chapters.

CHAPTER TWENTY-TWO

THE INDUSTRIAL RENAISSANCE

Quite apart from the three-ring circus of bioengineering developments, two main factors kept physical and mechanical innovation in eclipse from mid-Crisis until the great days of the twenty-third and twenty-fourth centuries. These were the energy shortage and, paradoxically, the solving of the energy shortage. The former curtailed major industrial efforts and diverted physical science into the narrow channel – often thought to be blocked – of fusion research. The latter meant that, until about the 2250s, post-fusion industry was mainly absorbed in manufacturing, maintaining and improving the new flood of fusion plants, while a great deal of theoretical effort also went into the more fashionable area of physics.

A significant sidelight comes from the autobiography of the Nobel laureate Morgan Yang (2213-2322), who confessed: "I had to tell white lies every week if I wanted to keep that grant. At MIT in the 2230s you were nobody unless you had some bright idea to squeeze that extra percentage point out of the Peach-Shutler-Zukav fusion cell modification . . . no, they don't use that variant any more. So in the morning I'd butt my head against the chaos math for four, five hours, and in the afternoon I'd have to say intelligent things about one damned fuser simulation after another, just playing it by ear. Chaos was no use to *them* of course, but I couldn't stop tinkering with it . . ."

This is reminiscent of the old twentieth-century line about research – that if a government were to sponsor a programme to improve techniques for locating foreign bodies in wounds, "we'd have had marvellous surgical probes but no X-rays." As we know, Yang's contribution to chaos theory (the analysis of pseudorandom patterns in physical systems remote from any equilibrium state – Yang incorporated quantum mechanics into this field in a brilliantly unexpected way) not only won him a 2244 Nobel prize but in the mid-twenty-fourth century helped provide a theoretical basis for the "cold fusion" effect which swiftly outmoded the older and less efficient models of fuser. Yang is also remembered as one of the first major historical figures to fit two full careers into an extended (though not rejuvenated) life; after 45 years of theoretical physics he declared himself "stale" and spent an almost equal period devising synthetape works like his dramatically animated autobiography *Chaos Every Morning: How to Cheat at Science*, quoted above. Some of his 3D interactive educational sequences are still in use today, and *Nonlinear Dynamic Systems and You* (for ages 8-14) is a widely acknowledged classic.

New quest for metallic ore

The mechanical renaissance is now considered to have begun in the second half of the twenty-third century, when (it seemed) technology awoke to the fact that cheap power and the grid had come to stay, and that the austerity measures used to conserve mineral resources had in many cases outlived their usefulness. Mine workings which had been rubber-stamped "unprofitable" were being reopened all over the world, usually by telefactored (remote-human-controlled), artificially intelligent, robot miners. The latter are not to be confused with the humanoid machine-intelligences already in common use, nor with the artificial intelligence (AI) programs which conversed so plausibly. These miners were "usuform" robots with interchangeable plug-in brain modules devised for specific jobs. They could easily

Electromagnetic furnace, *c.* 2250, used in the preparation of rare industrial metals.

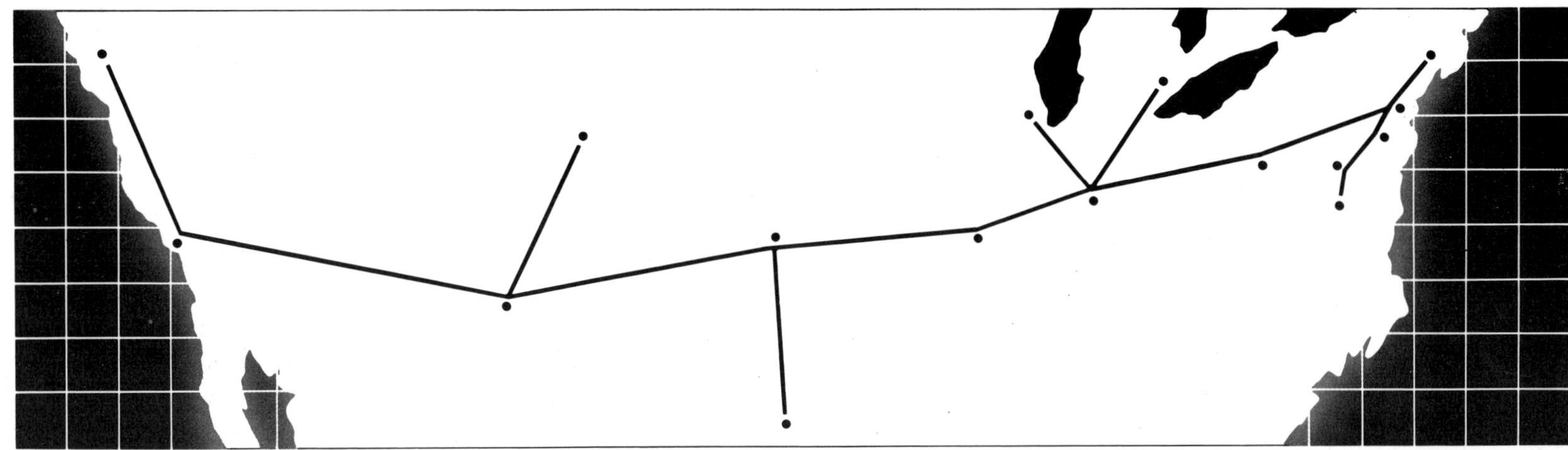

The US Maglev Subway linked east coast to west by 2316, the year this map was circulated. At that time many sections were overground, the cars running through elevated transparent tubes.

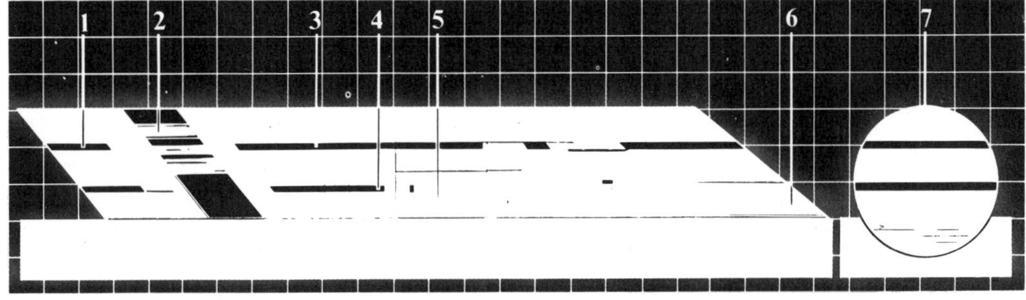

Subway car of the twenty-fourth century, *right*, afloat on a web of electromagnetism. This two-deck model had viewports (1,2,3), and on the lower deck a restaurant (4) and cargo bay (5). Radiators (6) removed excess heat. The cross-section (7) was circular to fit the tunnel.

outperform people in the narrow field of their specialization. Cheaply powered electromagnetic furnaces refined low-grade ores and spewed out floods of metal. Plants with engineered bacterial symbiotes helped concentrate dispersed metal – chiefly iron – in the soil, while a number of rarer metals were already being concentrated by variant seaweed crops.

Inter-city subways

The first impact was on transport. Metro-style public transport systems were in almost universal use, being cheaper than individual vehicles (see Chapter Seventeen): the lowering of metal prices allowed the further extension, interlinking and rationalization of such systems, so that by 2300 it was possible for a New Yorker to board a maglev "New York Subway" car which would leave the warren of New York tunnels, airlock through to an evacuated interstate tube and flash at high speed across the country, duly emerging into the more sedate subway system of, say, Minneapolis or Washington. "Organic air conditioning" and self-repairing passenger seats were among the contributions of biotechnology to such transport.

The several times refurbished London Tube and Paris Metro – already extending far beyond those cities – were linked in similar fashion by that baroque piece of 2290s architecture, the Channel Tunnel. Prime Minister Josella Patel declared in 2296: "Britain is no longer an island, entire of itself; it is a piece of the continent, a part of the mainland of Europe." It may be apocryphal that the ensuing headline on the London *Times* datapages read, "Continent No Longer Isolated".

Artificial intelligence in private cars

Further reverberations of the new metal glut were felt in private transport, where the shortage had constrained availability and boosted price, even when it came to the almost metal-free "pocket tractor" or the organic-motor fad. The pocket tractor was an expensive gimmick because of the high-technology carbon-fibre-epoxoids needed to give strength in the absence of metallic structural members. A slackening of metal-use restrictions allowed private transport – usually electrically powered – to proliferate even outside the hyperdeveloped nations. (Already, in 2230, the word "hyperdeveloped", as opposed to "moderately developed", was beginning to take on a slightly archaic flavour, as had occurred a century earlier with the now obsolete antonyms "developed" and "undeveloped".) Small, rugged cars like the Toyota-Honda Electron combined strong metal frameworks with colourful and incorruptible plastic or biopolymer bodywork, driven by high-performance electric motors whose storage cells held a sufficient charge for several hundred miles. Thus far it was all very twentieth-century.

The trend of the "renaissance", though, was towards the installation of automatic controls and overrides in these vehicles. UN-directed legislation began with various simple restrictions built into a car's programming which included: varying speed limits, a throttle override ensuring that one kept a safe distance from cars detected ahead, IR/radar pattern-recognition to monitor the surroundings when visibility was poor, built-in AI ready to detect possible danger from microsecond to microsecond and override the manual control functions to avert disaster.

"Deathwish" Hehir, the suicide driver

A colourful character in this period was "Deathwish" Hehir, who hired herself out as a "suicide driver". For a while in the early 2300s the common slogan was "Safe At Any Speed", and few automobile advertisements reached the wallscreens without shots of Hehir failing to kill herself by putting the vehicle into a deadly skid on black ice, by driving it full-tilt into a wall, by attempting to sideswipe a robot drone car at high speed, or by some other reckless antic. A well-known piece of archival material is the unedited digivideo record of Hehir testing the Ford Farsense, whose pothole-avoidance system was dramatically demonstrated as the car automatically overrode to prevent her driving over the edge of the Grand Canyon – after which, thanks to the inferior design of that prototype's offside door, Hehir broke a leg getting out of the car.

Driving: a redundant skill

The semi-intelligent electromobile keeping its watchful eye on the driver was, of course, a transitional phase. Why not go further, thought several inorganic engineers, and free the driver from *all* responsibility? Rather than have the car immobilized should its organoelectric detectors find an unacceptable alcohol level in the driver's breath, why not let the car itself assume control?

The system which first caught on in the hyperdeveloped countries, and eventually throughout the world, required little investment in metal (though more than the later inertial-tracking plus satellite-fix systems). Cables were buried in, run parallel to, or hung over the roadways, which already tended to follow, or to have been followed by, the Grid and accompanying fibre-optic data-

lines. A relatively simple arrangement of electromagnetic "signatures" on these cables let the car's brain "know" precisely where it was. At the same time the automatic jolt stations (AJS) were introduced. An electromobile whose charge was running low would leave the road without human intervention at the next AJS, recharge its cells, and debit the owner/driver's credit balance before resuming the journey.

At first this crude system covered only the major roads – interstates, motorways, autobahns and so forth – but it was to spread. In one of Hehir's last and most effective appearances, she steered into the AutoInterstate outside Los Angeles, said "New York" to the test vehicle's command unit, and knocked back a soporific cocktail which (as certified by remote monitoring of her alpha rhythms) left her unconscious for the entire 58-hour solo journey, continually nursed and massaged by biotechnological "comfort systems" in the electromobile. No mishap occurred, as we would nowadays expect; but the stunt had considerable impact at the time. Private owners were in general reluctant to surrender complete control, and might alternate a period of manual driving with autopilot-brain driving.

Driverless freight vehicles attained some popularity. Shortly before his death in 2322, Morgan Yang completed a synthetape feature called *The Ghost Convoy*, a mood-piece on the fate of AI freight electromobiles whose misprogramming sent them trundling eerily forever about the vast and still-growing North American AutoInterstate complex. Although nonsense from the technological point of view (AJS credit monitoring ruled out any such possibility), *The Ghost Convoy* became instant folklore, and even today one can meet people who tell this tale of the ghost-haunted twenty-fourth century as if it were true.

Return of the vertical city

Meanwhile the freer availability of structural metal began to alter the shape of the typically squat, puffy Gantz-process house. Biologically compacted and "self-repairing" materials had almost every advantage save that of sheer strength, as required for particularly high buildings or large enclosed spaces. A hybrid technique, already in use in special cases, placed the burden of ambitious constructions on steel joists and girders cloaked with "organic cladding" – the bones of the old technology and the flesh of the new, as the phrase went. Cities began again to acquire a towering vertical dimension.

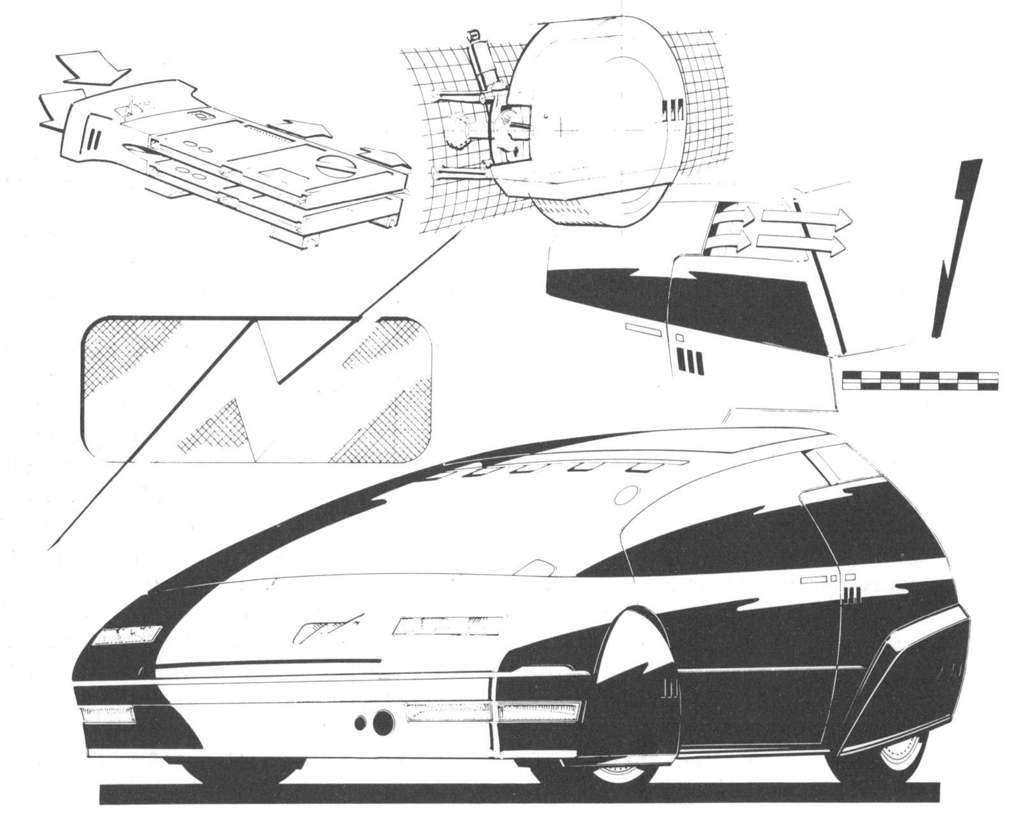

Toyota-Honda *Electron*, a typical electrocar of the early 2100s. Some models were wheel-less, suspended like subway cars by electro-magnetic forces.

Windowless cars

This hybrid trend later infiltrated transport, with the invention of the SAP-system and clean-lined electromobiles gave way to new models with a thatch of artificial photosynthetic material which helped top up the storage cells and increase the distance between AJS recharges. Near the end of the Period of Recovery there was some attempt to revive the windowless car, enabling the entire exterior to be devoted to solar energy-drinkers; but, as before, the notion never quite caught on. The "last word", from Toyota-Honda in the 2390s, featured total-surround internal holoscreens which could display any scene in convincing 3D, from an accurate "surroundie" simulation of the actual outside landscape through a popular synthetape epic to a placid replica of the driver's own favourite room or office – all this while the organoelectronic brain steered the car at high speed between cities. The de-luxe model allowed any reasonable number of people to conduct a simulated round-the-table conference while most or all were travelling; but, although some were sold and presumably used, even this failed to make the vehicle popular. Perhaps despite everything there was a lingering sense of claustrophobia. Perhaps the range of internal possibilities also raised the question of why, when every destination could be achieved in simulated form, one should bother to travel at all.

False faces on the telescreen

The "total environment" effect was already well established in a stationary context, and many houses boasted one bare wallscreened room which could seemingly relocate itself instantly to any tourist landscape spot, into the middle of countless 3D spectaculars (a thriving industry had sprung up, converting old films and videos by computer-synthetape techniques to lurid 3D surroundies), to standpoints in outer space or to imaginary locations in the multiple infinities of computer space. Trend-hounds were apt to complain that these surroundies killed the art of conversation; others suggested that the people who stared blankly into them were not those who in the past would have conversed, but those who would have stared blankly at a telescreen, a flickering television image, a cinematograph or a bare wall.

More worrying was the *anomie* engendered by the omnipresent artificial intelligences, whether electronic, biological or mixed. Personal contact was easier to avoid than ever before in history. One could live, work, converse and answer the front door *via* holographic imaging, and due to synthetape methods little effort or expense was involved. A relatively cheap AI could by now generate convincing holoimages and personality simulations, allowing reclusive people to program electronic analogues of themselves which were capable of handling most routine contacts. Until the "deathwatch" monitor became mandatory in dwellings, several people died by misadventure or illness, and rotted in their luxurious Gantz-hybrid homes, while programmed images of themselves answered phone calls, swapped platitudes with friends over the datanet, and generally kept "life" ticking over. A number of scare stories again circulated, the best perhaps being Celia Nanking's *City of Ghosts* (written from the imagined viewpoint of a programmed artificial personality who discovers all "her" datanet contacts are equally unreal). However, as usual, most of humanity managed to avoid the lure of the extreme situation. Electronic *anomie*, twenty-fourth-century style, was a worrying psychological phenomenon, but never an epidemic.

Cold fusion

The crowning scientific achievement of this period was of course cold fusion – a misnomer, as every textbook reminds us, since the "cold" plasma is still far hotter than anything we encounter in everyday life. It was on the Moon in the 2350s that a vast UN-sponsored team came to grips with the problem: the names of Sen, Chiffre, McClintock, Kalsky, Marat and Tembu are perhaps best remembered. Using the chaos formulations of Yang (2239) as extended by Carmen Nandez of Chile (2294), they succeeded in creating a patterned-chaotic plasma state which allowed "catalytic fusion" at temperatures far below the million-degree temperature level. (Certain historians of science suggest that the technique was obliquely foreshadowed by twentieth-century "migma-fusion" research, but this is doubtful in the extreme.) Compared with the tens or hundreds of millions of degrees required by former techniques, cold fusion – once the initial field techniques are established – is hardly more difficult than striking a match.

"With this discovery," said UN Secretary-General Avedis Drakos in 2359, "the universe becomes ours." In fact cold fusion was a convenience which made life much easier; but it marked no real turning-point in human advancement. If there *was* a point at which the universe became ours, it was very probably when – after that long and terrible hiatus which had begun in the darkness of the twentieth century - humanity picked up the threads and late in the twenty-third century set about the colonization of space.

CHAPTER TWENTY-THREE

PLANNING THE WORLD ECONOMY

In Oleg Zarzecki's memoirs, published posthumously in 2195, he wrote extensively about the "internationalists". These were people working for UN agencies or serving on its various committees who considered that their major loyalty was to the world community, whatever their national origins. Naturally, there were few representatives of this group on the UN council itself, which was composed almost entirely of representatives of national governments, but as the various agencies and committees became powerful institutions in their own right the internationalists became a more potent force.

The more radical internationalists formulated an explicit policy by which the UN was to become the parliament of a World State, which would gradually extend its power over economic affairs until it was planning the economy of the entire world. As Secretary-General, Zarzecki was required to put aside national interests, in effect to adopt an internationalist attitude, and his personal sympathies were to some degree with the group. But he had reservations about the radical programme. Most of his successors felt much the same way, though some – Simon Escobar and Christine Li, for example – were strongly committed to such centralization. But whatever they felt, most world leaders found themselves in an uneasy position, compelled to tread a tightrope between national interest and internationalist pressures.

Economic warfare slows recovery

The worldwide crisis of the previous two centuries had already forced national governments to concede a good deal of authority to the UN over ecological planning. However, now that the crisis was coming to an end, some governments were beginning to resent their loss of control. They regarded the internationalists as a threat. The conflict was complicated by the looseness of the term "ecological planning" – there was much uncertainty as to where the UN's entitlement to intervene began and ended.

The tendency of nations to define their interests more narrowly and selfishly, as the world crisis eased, led to a re-emergence in the twenty-third century of political and ideological rivalries not seen since 2100. There was nothing so crude as a threat of war, but national governments began to express their dissatisfactions with one another – and with the UN – by selectively blocking the flow of imports and exports. (Although most nations were self-sufficient in food, the manufacture of many goods was highly localized.) Multinational corporations often grew impatient with this political game-playing, but were themselves not above exerting the same form of pressure on governments. The smooth flow of trade required the co-operation of all parties, and it was easy for even one disgruntled body to disrupt it. Constant interruptions to trade inhibited the world's recovery during the twenty-third century, and added fuel to the internationalist cause.

Conflict among internationalists

The UN's internationalists were not the only people whose interests were opposed to those of national governments. The multinational corporations had bred their own kind of internationalists, who saw the world as one gigantic marketplace. These included many of the descendants of the Japanese businessmen displaced by the great earthquake. They tended to detach themselves from any real sense of national identity and, in effect, their corporations became their countries. Many prided themselves on being true cosmopolitans who had transcended the limitations of their shattered heritage.

Although the multinationals were the ultimate products of the ancient capitalist system, they were by no means devotees of competition. Rather they were super-cartels whose main concerns were to stabilize their markets and establish monopolies and price-fixing arrangements. The major corporations even had their own organization, the Confederation of World Industries.

The internationalists of the UN and the CWI had much in common, but there were some important issues on which they were totally opposed. The UN internationalists were collectivists who wanted a world run, if not exactly by the people, at least for the people. Their avowed aim was the meeting of human needs, and this implied the gradual erosion of privilege. In short, they were egalitarians. The CWI internationalists, on the other hand, had not the least interest in destroying the differences between rich and poor. Indeed, their attitudes to people depended entirely on how much money those people had. UN internationalists like Ifre Negele and Leila Ksar adopted the French Revolutionary slogan – *Liberté, Egalité, Fraternité* – and their aim was to establish a vast system of social welfare. The CWI internationalists, by contrast, lost interest in basic food supplies and housing when food and housing credit were detached from flexible credit. They were mainly interested in items that people had to pay for with "real money".

Airships were used extensively in agriculture in the twenty-fourth century. Here a fleet of them is unloading binder-organisms on to the shifting sands of the southern Sahara.

Failure of the radicals
The radical UN internationalists failed in their objective. National governments and large corporations maintained their levels of power. The UN continued to control food production and – to a slightly lesser extent – energy creation, two essential industries which were centrally directed at world level. By contrast, most consumer durables and leisure facilities were independently produced and distributed. Even Soviet agencies responsible for such products were by now distinguishable only in name from their independent "capitalist" counterparts. The conflict continued only in certain ambiguous areas: housing, information technology and medicine. Here there were frequent power struggles as the UN, aided by some national governments and opposed by others, tried to spread the benefits of contemporary technology more widely while the producers tried to maintain their profit margins.

The UN internationalists probably realized they could never win. Many certainly became pessimistic as they grew older. Ifre Negele, who spent his last years in retirement in the Drakensberg Republic between 2301 and 2309, became converted to African Separatism, declaring that the continent should cut itself off from the rest of the world and seek its own independent destiny because it could never thrive in a world community dominated by the "Great Triumvirate" (the USA, the USSR and Australia). In retrospect we can see, by comparing the position in 2400 with that in 2180, that it was the UN internationalist cause which made such gains as were made in this particular power struggle, although they were achieved in a way that such extremists as Negele might well have deplored.

UN power increases
The simple fact is that the UN gradually contrived to increase its authority by becoming richer. It did this by expanding the "rent collection" principle, whereby the UN took a sizeable cut of profits from farming the sea, to take in certain kinds of land-based endeavour.

Various nations had long-standing grievances against the UN's land-use policies – none more so than Brazil, which had been provoked, largely by UN policy, to go to war against Argentina in 2078. In the intervening century Brazil's fortunes had changed a great deal. By 2180 it was one of the more powerful tropical nations, but the Brazilian people still nursed a sense of grievance, compounded by a sense of guilt at being the nation responsible for the world's worst nuclear war. It was the Brazilian ambassador to the UN in 2250, Arturo Cruz Costa, who finally persuaded the council to acknowledge that if Australia and other nations could be held to be "renting" areas of the ocean from the world community, then Brazil and other countries could similarly be considered to be "leasing" parts of their territory to the world community for conservation (as with the Amazon forest) or exploitation (as with areas where the UN had resettled Japanese refugees in the 2080s).

Taxing the multinationals
Acceptance of this argument appeared to put a burden on the UN's finances by compelling it to divert funds back to national governments, but that was not the only way it turned out. In order to pay these "land use rents" the UN had to have more funds, which could only come from "taxes" levied on the world community. Justina Duarte, who was Secretary-General when Cruz Costa put through his crucial resolution, immediately cast around for ways of raising these revenues. She persuaded the various national ambassadors – who were instructed by their own governments to get a good deal for *them* – to empower the UN to collect a proportion of these revenues directly from large multinational corporations. Effectively, the UN was given the right to levy its own taxes on the multinationals, money which could then be used to pay for its land-use programmes.

In terms of balance-sheets, the change did not appear to enrich the UN; but this was an illusion. The money flowed through the UN, from nation to nation and from corporation to corporation, but the UN acquired the power to decide where it should go. The agencies planning the use of land now had a new way of taking from the rich and giving to the poor. It may seem absurd that the UN chose to pay a high rent to Mali, Niger and Chad for huge tracts of empty desert, which were then slowly reclaimed during the twenty-fourth and twenty-fifth centuries, while the USSR was rebuffed when it tried to lease out lands in Siberia that were infinitely more promising, but this was how the UN ensured that the world's recovery really belonged to the world, and not simply to the richer nations.

This newest concentration of power into UN hands was marked, at the beginning of the twenty-fourth century, by a proposal that the organization's name be changed to the United World Assembly. The title was apt and might later have been extended to the United Earth-Moon System Assembly: but voting went in favour of continuity rather than pedantic accuracy. As one delegate said, "when you're on to a winner there's no need for change – it'd be different if we had a dud name like, say, the League of Nations."

CHAPTER TWENTY-FOUR

DEVELOPING THE MOON

To say that the space programme actively resumed in the twenty-third century is not to deny humanity's continuous and valuable orbital presence since the twentieth century, in particular since the dangerous period during the 2020s when Garrity chose – but might so easily not have chosen – to continue support of the multinational Spacelab (see Chapter Seven). The satellite investment, especially, paid for itself many times over – first in terms of weather and crop monitoring, and later through reliable orbital overseeing of the great ocean farms. Communications, arms-control inspection, reference points for self-controlled land vehicles ... there seemed no end to the uses of satellites.

Spacecraft overflying the Mare Imbrium base on the Moon in the 2230s. The Moon was still largely undeveloped; the lights of the base glowed weakly in a desert of darkness.

The growth of Spacelab

Spacelab grew by slow and painful accretion, each addition representing a substantial cost in lifting materials from Earth, until it was a large industrial complex in free fall. Up there, many valuable materials could be uniquely produced, from the semi-infinite "whiskers" of pure crystalline iron and carbon which revolutionized the science of materials, to weird and rare alloys. Among these was Dvorek's neutron sink which until the 2350s was essential in fusion cells, and was the mainstay of orbital trade from the twenty-second to the twenty-fifth century, but could only be prepared in zero gravity. Similar alloys were also manufactured on Earth using rapid-cooling techniques in simulated free-fall chambers, but this approach was fraught with difficulties – such as crystallization and shattering of the metal.

In addition, as early as the twenty-second century Spacelab developed its famous offshoot, the "Geriatrics' Wing", a reduced-gravity environment in which, at exorbitant cost, wealthy sufferers from heart complaints and rare degenerative diseases could spend the twilight of their lives. Among the notables who retired there were the synthetape dramatist Carl Valentine, and, some way into the twenty-third century, John Foden of environmental fame – the latter, despite a hundred fussy regulations, clinging quirkily to his pipe and smuggled tobacco until the very last. "Foden never retired," a fellow-patient said after his death. "Even when he was asleep or blind drunk he was working to humanize that bloody grey grim place."

Fifty years later the orbiting clinic, now officially known as the Spacetorium, was considerably more luxurious and housed several score people; perhaps eight hundred to a thousand more inhabited and operated the vast jumble of the Spacelab complex. A further handful staffed, in rotation, the unloved Mare Imbrium base on the Moon which produced a desultory trickle of raw materials, rare-earth elements and oxygen "cracked" from lunar rock, all of which were gobbled voraciously by Spacelab. Such was the position in the 2260s when the industrial renaissance looked again toward space and the UN acknowledged that there was no longer any need for Earth to remain huddled and inward-looking.

The first lunar mass-driver, a very small affair constructed in the 2350s, capable of accelerating small payload modules to moon escape velocity (2.4 km/sec, 1.99 miles/sec) in less than 700 metres (765 yards).

History that never happened

At this point it is interesting and instructive to consider a historical path which was not taken – thanks to the conservatism of the late twentieth and early twenty-first centuries. In this ghostly alternative history, the lobbying of Hi-Tech and its parent pressure groups (see Chapter Seven) might have taken effect in the twentieth century while there was still energy to spare. Money might have been diverted from that period's massive and now seemingly insane defence investment. Gerard O'Neill's 1970s dream of space colonies might have come about in his lifetime, with communities established in orbit and solar-energy collectors beaming microwave power to Earthside receivers as early as 2000 AD. Even now the questions are controversial: could the hardening arteries of the late-twentieth-century economic structure have softened sufficiently to permit the bold experiment, if the arguments had been better put, or if the right charismatic lobbyist or US President had adopted the cause, or if at the start of the twenty-first century three-quarters of the world's nations had not been involved in war? Might the Period of Crisis have been smoothed over by beamed solar power, dwindling to a mild depression at the worst? Might the expensive possibility of fusion power have been considered, by the time of its realization, as an interesting but non-vital adjunct to the existing solar energy sources which fed the grid? Or would this massive project still have been beyond contemporary resources and technology?

One can argue either way with some conviction. It is all too easy to make the assumption that the Period of Crisis must surely have had its value for humanity; that only this dark era of "tempering and testing" could have forced the world into its first uneasy unity.

Settlements on the Moon

The first symptoms of renewed interest in space were the UN's authorization of increased lunar exploitation, and the building of a larger, more efficient "mass driver". All shipments of material from the Moon's surface were made using mass drivers, electromagnetic cannon which accelerated "buckets" to escape velocity and ejected their contents in a suitably timed trajectory which would ultimately pass within interception distance of Spacelab or some similar rendezvous. As a result of this lunar development, Mare Imbrium ceased to be a lonely outpost and quickly expanded into a well-staffed complex. The Spacetorium was soon transferred there and immediately increased in popularity: a firm foothold on the Moon was psychologically far more attractive than Spacelab with its gut-wrenching free-fall zones, variable pseudogravity, Coriolis-force problems, and – a nonsensical point which nevertheless affected a high percentage of transient visitors – the fear that somehow the whole thing would fall down to Earth.

At this time the chief need of human settlements outside Earth was hydrogen, which with lunar-mined oxygen could provide water. Happily, the fusion boom on Earth meant that quantities of sea water were continually electrolysed by cheap power and the resulting hydrogen mass – separated to extract "heavy hydrogen" (deuterium) – became the common fusion fuel. Liquid hydrogen became a major export for a time: but, as more and more water entered the closed ecological cycle of the domed or buried lunar environments, it became logical to encourage *in vitro* agriculture with the result that the Moon's human settlements became self-sufficient in hydrogen.

Far side research
Next came the great transplanting of the Sealed Laboratory from Antarctica, isolating the deadliest fringes of genetic research more thoroughly than ever before. Once the Moon became available work on such potentially lethal micro-organisms could no longer be tolerated on Earth. It was a source of annoyance to many researchers that they should be exiled for long periods of duty to the semi-appropriate lab location in the crater Pasteur on the Moon's hidden side, without even the famous spectacles of Earthrise and Earthset to cheer the monotony. "They managed to infect bare Antarctic ice," remarked Ethics Committee chair Ellis Vicenzo at the time of the move. "For all I know their next brainchild will gobble scorched rock in vacuum, and we'd like a little time to see it coming." The reference to the escaped purple algae was a pointed one: it had taken most of the year 2248 to mop up the incredibly hardy micro-organism which spread its disfiguring stain over the Queen Maud Mountains.

Lunar government
Soon the cold-fusion researchers joined the geneticists, due to a degree of public unease about the "chaos bomb" which a minority feared would be developed as a by-product of the planned space drive. Suddenly Farside was the remote outpost, while the Moon's near side was cosy and almost crowded, and there was talk of imminent self-sufficiency and independence.

At the time this was something of a fantasy. The Moon was a sanatorium, an isolation ward, a convenient base for a handful of industries, a source of raw mass for construction work in space, a scientific outpost beyond the murky fringes of Earth's atmosphere; but not, on the whole, a place where people wanted to settle. Specialist interests aside, those whose ambition was to move out to the Moon also aimed to go further, using the Moon as a jumping-off point for the exploitation of space. Even as the Moon colonies grew, few thought of the place as home: it seemed more like a transit point or a vast Metro interchange – the recurrent image in Julia Parolli's 2274 work of semi-autobiography, *Waiting for the Train*, which chronicled the frustrating delays on the Moon while the space-habitat O'Neill I was authorized and commissioned.

Although waiting for lunar troubles and an eventual war of independence was a favourite game of those who believed we are condemned to relive history, whether or not we remember it, the necessary feelings were never sparked. The UN Space Agency, uneasily co-ordinating the remnants of NASA, ESA, the Soviet Space Committee and a clutch of hopeful emergents (nobody was quite sure why there should be, for example, an Upper Volta Space Development Bureau), ran the Moon informally and tolerantly, more or less in accordance with international law and the human-rights charter. Enlightened government is often advanced as a reason for the steady, placid course of lunar development. The Moon's serious shortage of elements essential to life – not only hydrogen but also carbon and nitrogen – may also have helped to keep it securely tied to Earth's apron strings.

Millionaires on the Moon
It was not a true "frontier colony", then, but an outpost and a resort. Indeed it was the millionaire's playground aspect which held the attention of the media almost to the exclusion of other lunar activity. The wrinkled old Struldbruggs – a nickname aptly borrowed from *Gulliver's Travels* – were a source of grisly fascination, wealthy near-corpses who moved nimbly enough in their one-sixth normal gravity, surrounded by luxuries and hangers-on. The Spacetorium was an island of high living amid the bleak functionalism of the spreading Mare Imbrium settlements, which by 2300 straggled all the way from the crater Plato in the north to Copernicus in the south.

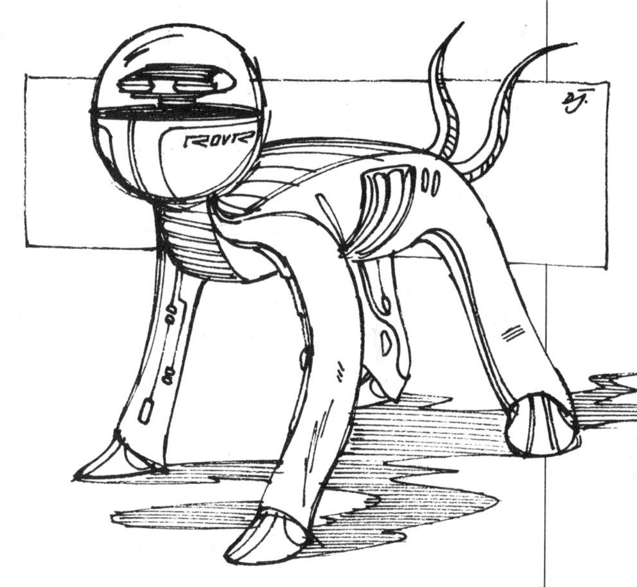

Artificial pets were popular on Earth, and especially in space, from the twenty-third through to the twenty-sixth century. Mechanimals like the ROVR model, "the dog with two tails", consumed no expensive fuel or air, just a power jolt from time to time. Up-market ropets had fur, hair or scales and complex behaviour patterns, making them almost indistinguishable from their organic prototypes.

The greening of the Moon

The biological advances of the twenty-third and twenty-fourth centuries had a further, inevitable impact on the Moon. An anaerobic "antiGantz" micro-organism – actually a whole suite of micro-organisms – was developed in Australia in the 2330s. It required only a trace of water to set about its task of breaking down lunar rock to a friable pseudosoil. This could be "reGantzed" into the first truly indigenous lunar buildings, or fertilized and used to grow crops under glass. The second use rapidly lost ground to the Solid Artificial Photosynthesis materials (see Chapters Twenty-seven and Twenty-eight), which could not only be modified to operate in lunar vacuum, but were also perfectly tolerant of the Moon's day/night cycle. Many useful Earth plants were severely upset by the rhythm of two weeks' harsh light alternating with the same period of darkness: energy had to be squandered to nurse them through the long night and intermittently shade them during the lunar day.

By the final quarter of the twenty-fourth century a tiny but thrillingly significant change had been made in the face of the Moon as seen from Earth. Using only a small telescope such as an amateur astronomer might own, it was possible to see flecks of green in Mare Imbrium, representing hundreds of thousands of acres given over to biological or artificial photosynthesis. Further south, along the lunar equator, a slightly more powerful instrument revealed the 150-kilometre line of the nearside mass driver which periodically accelerated raw-material packages beyond the Moon's gravity well at 2.4 kilometres per second or more. Today the Moon is of course greenish-tinted to the naked eye, and we can no longer appreciate the impact of that first visible mark of human presence stamped on the once silvery-white face of our satellite.

Pittsburgh-Luna in 2314, seven years before the meteor hit of 2321. Time was already running out for the lunar smelting plant, as production costs in the space colonies continued to drop.

The meteor disaster of 2321

Also visible from Earth – and actually photo-recorded by a Central African school project, as well as by two "watchdog" satellites which tracked mass-driver payloads heading inwards – was the impact flash of the 2321 meteor disaster. According to later reconstruction, the body which smashed into the lunar Apennine Mountains that unlucky day must have been rather more than two kilometres across; it impacted at over 40 kilometres per second with an explosion equivalent to the simultaneous detonation of many thousand fusion bombs.

Ninety-eight people died immediately, chiefly tourists and selenographical surveyors in the vicinity of the Apennines, killed by the huge masses of hot rock which splashed up and out from the impact zone, or by "whiplash" as the shockwave tore through the ground. Nearly 150 kilometres westward in the Mare Imbrium, secondary moonquakes plagued the settled zones: many "greened" hectares were cracked open and lost, and approximately 200 more people died, chiefly from exposure to vacuum. In a bizarre incident at the Pittsburgh-Luna smelting plant, shockwaves toppled one of the big solar furnace mirrors, whose deflected beam flash-grilled a party of visitors including two UN delegates investigating safety standards. Subsequently the new crater in the Apennines was named after the writer and philosopher Qing Xiao-wen, the year being the 200th anniversary of his birth: the crater can be seen from Earth with a small telescope, south-south-east of the conspicuous crater Archimedes.

Pittsburgh-Luna never reopened – not because anyone was silly enough to expect a repetition of such an unlikely event, but because by now the space colonies had gained a vital edge in production efficiency. Like agriculture, solar smelting on the Moon was constrained by that inconvenient lunar cycle of day and night. O'Neill I, by contrast, could run its great mirrors continuously – and these were free-fall mirrors, a few kilos of aluminized plastic spread out to the size of several football fields, free of the need to support their own weight against even the Moon's feeble pull. Right from the start, such simple economic facts as this made clear that the future of industry was out in space itself. It is to the opening of the "High Frontier" in the twenty-third and twenty-fourth centuries that we now turn.

CHAPTER TWENTY-FIVE

THE MAKING OF THE MICROWORLDS

Space colonization became a major world issue once again in the 2250s, giving rise to a new sequence of debates and shifting alliances. Green politicians found themselves arguing the technophiles' cause in the hope of shifting Earth's energy dependence from fusion power to the more ideologically acceptable solar converters in space. Grey elements dominating the UN Energy Committee were less keen on the threatened upset to a functioning fusion-energy policy. The Security Council consensus was one of vague alarm at possible military uses of space, a subject which had been swept under the carpet for many decades (despite some debate about possible use of lunar mass drivers to hurl shattering "artificial meteors" at targets on Earth). The Land Use Committee was torn between approval of any project which would effectively add to the living space of humanity, and their awareness that the bulk of humanity would never set foot on the "new lands". The position of the Space Agency was predictably enthusiastic.

Public opinion swings behind Space Colonies

Secretary-General Khan finally tipped the balance in favour of the colonies when he agreed that – given sufficient expansion out there – his famous "one man one child" slogan need not apply to the infinite horizons of space. Many believe that this concession made the firm insistence by Khan and his supporters on the right of replacement *only* (for the population on Earth) more acceptable.

The initial wrangling took place in the shadow of a great failure. In 2248 a team of Spacelab scavengers had visited L4 (L4 and L5, identical zones where "eternally stable" orbits in the Earth/Moon system were possible, had been much mooted as space-colony locations). There they found "Lagrange's Tomb", a derelict which had apparently hung there since the twenty-first century, its air long since escaped through deteriorated doorseals. A handful of mummified corpses was found inside this tiny space-habitat, apparently a pioneer experiment. A great deal of emotion was whipped up, along the lines of Parolli's ploy, "We owe it to them to carry on and achieve the ideals they died for."

It was not revealed that, far from being an

Mark III microworld: the central sphere would house 10,000 people. The doughnut rings at either end were for agriculture and manufacturing. Power came from cross-shaped "wings" containing solar cells and gravity was provided by controlled spin.

enigmatic *Marie Celeste* of space, the Tomb colony had been part of a plan to win the war that never came – World War III. Since immediate publication of this information would very probably have turned public opinion against space, it can be seen that the drift of UN thought was already in favour of the colonies.

Space elevator proves unworkable

The "dark grey" interests, though, had pinned much of their hope to the concept of the Funicular. Also known as a space elevator, this fantastic construction would be anchored at one end to Earth's equator, and at the other to a synchronous-orbit satellite 36,000 kilometres up – a fixed Tower of Babel or Jacob's Ladder up and down which people and freight could be shifted in elevator cars. Unfortunately a basic requirement of this cheap route to orbit was a cable strong enough to support its own weight (over thousands of kilometres) in addition to any actual load. This could not be found.

With existing materials a Moon Funicular could be built but would be absurdly expensive, with a length or height of more than 180,000 kilometres; a Mars Funicular was just feasible but would require some fantastic avoidance system to dodge that planet's hurtling moons. The dark-grey interests were forced to abandon this particular dream, and at last threw their weight behind the proposal to build space colonies by more conventional means.

The economics of O'Neill I

Phase 1 of the plan began in the 2260s, with "launch pad" preparations on the Moon – chiefly the design and installation of the big mass-driver, powered from the Lunar Equatorial Grid whose solar cells were spaced around the Moon to give continuous output except in the rare periods of eclipse. Meanwhile the plans for the O'Neill I space habitat kept changing. The original assumption had been that the colony would grow food and recycle its oxygen via a selection of modified Earth flora. This was hastily altered as solid artificial photosynthesis systems began to appear.

In addition there was much wrangling over investment and representation. How were the rewards of space to be divided? Since the smallest of countries by now made its fusion-power contribution to the grid and in other ways helped fund the UN, should the hyper-developed powers be allowed to dominate this project? (The answer here was a heavily disguised "Yes" in terms of technical resources. However the UN promised to tax the profits of multinational companies investing in O'Neill I, and a wide-ranging and very

Spacelock of a Mark III microworld, *above*. The spacelock was the entrance and exit of a microworld. The Mark III had twenty, ten at each end.

Installing an ecology, *right*, was the most difficult part of creating a microworld. When the systems had been set up and checked, colonists arrived in batches to give the artificial ecology time to absorb them.

nearly fair selection of construction teams and initial colonists – often the same people – was made.) How long before there was a significant return on this investment? The Space Habitats Subcommittee was set up to parry such questions with convincing computer extrapolations; by the end of the Period of Recovery it dominated its parent in the UN, the Space Agency, as the space frontier gradually grew from an interesting new concept to the major arena of progress, development and exploration.

A curious footnote to the 2270s is that in this decade John Foden was consulted about the colony programme and gave it his blessing – despite being dead. From available data a Personality Analogue Construct was programmed in Foden's image: but Foden-analogue, though probably not self-aware, went on to evince such strong disapproval of this "blasted ancestor worship" that he, or it, was not evoked again.

Opening of O'Neill I

Finally, in the 2280s, O'Neill I was opened to selected colonists under the directorship of Julia Parolli. Its living-space for 15,000 people was never filled: colonists arrived more slowly than expected – perhaps an indication of the generally high living standards on Earth – and often regarded this Lagrange community as a jumping-off place for somewhere else. Another and better microworld, perhaps, or the asteroid belt, or general exploration of the Solar System. Propaganda about the high frontier enticed some people who wanted to be, as it were, high frontiersmen – not merely inhabitants of a safe, and finished, closed environment. O'Neill I became the massing-point for the later human diaspora throughout the solar system.*

Space habitats in the Earth/Moon locality became generally known as Lagrange communities, although the first such constructions did not occupy the Lagrangean L-points but wide near-circular orbits with periods of several weeks. Later, of course, both L-points and a huge variety of inviting orbits were exploited.

A patchwork of compromises

Although it triumphantly achieved its aims, O'Neill I was cumbersome and inefficient.

Ninety-nine per cent built of materials mass-driven from the Moon cannon, O'Neill I was a bulbous compromise between the O'Neill cylinder and the Bernal sphere designs. As well as a mirror-and-window system to admit light for internal agriculture, it had as an afterthought great flying panels of prototype biological solar converters – vacuum SAP-systems – which were constantly being improved and refined during the period of construction and for half a century after. Attempts at cosmic-ray shielding used a variety of techniques, from simple thicknesses of compressed lunar rock to the latest developments from the Dvorekalloy. Other kilometre-long vanes and panels presented large areas of solar-cells to the eternal sunlight: but two sizeable fusion generators were also built in, both to provide working power for construction and as a safeguard against the expected degradation of the silicon cells after long exposure to raw solar radiation. And although the many cubic kilometres of the interior had a kind of alien beauty to Earthborn eyes, with sunlight glowing through the misty air, which was rich in oxygen and water-vapour, the overall design was firmly functional and devoted to industrial capabilities on a vast scale.

This first Lagrange colony was, in short, a patchwork of compromises. As Julia Parolli repeatedly explained to disappointed colonists who had seen glowing synthetape extrapolations like D. S. Comfitt's *The Joy of*

*The Spacelab complex, described by Arnold Loewe in his popular history *Reach for the Stars* as the first true space habitat, does not in our view deserve that title owing to its explicit dependence on continuing supplies from Earth. O'Neill I was dependent, too, but not by intention and not after its first twenty years.

Space (2288), "You can't expect a research lab to give you five-star service – but we've got the best lab between here and the end of the solar system." A more frivolous note crept in as the twenty-fourth century progressed: free-fall dance was possible on an unprecedented scale, and a popular pastime was the long-predicted low-gravity pedal gliding near the spinning colony's axis (high "above" the curved outer wall which was the living surface, or "floor", to which the pseudogravity provided by spin held down the crops and colonists). The small scale of this self-sufficient world occasionally caused problems. At one stage, trained hawks had to be brought from Earth to tackle a plague of budgerigars, smuggled in either as pets or as a deliberate prank.

Industry in space

The potential for industry was huge. The sheer simplicity of mirror-furnaces alone would have made O'Neill I the "world's" smelting centre had it not been for the continuingly high cost of the Earth-shuttle. Zone-refining and other processes became far more efficient due to zero gravity and the resulting lack of convection currents: many chemical and biological processes gained immensely in profitability when they could be carried out homogeneously in enormous tanks, without the pressure-gradient imposed by Earth's gravity or the tendency of denser materials to sink. A trivial example was the Hoare Infinite Fermenter of 2315, which replaced all rival alcohol-synthesizing methods in space; in his old age its deviser was fond of claiming his responsibility for over 90 per cent of hangovers suffered in free fall.

The new quest was for the cheap supply of raw materials for these industrial processes. Earth-lift by shuttle tended to be too expensive, save for specialist materials, despite more than three centuries of space-shuttle improvement culminating in the Waveskimmer of the 2280s. Mass-driven Moon material came more than twenty times cheaper in transport terms, but was deficient in several elements. Obviously it was time to look for other sources in the asteroid belt, as will be seen in Chapter Twenty-six.

The microworlds proliferate

Meanwhile, further construction in space was well under way, almost before Secretary-General Skene (via remote telefactoring from a ceremony in the UN headquarters) had smashed the traditional bottle of champagne against the hull of O'Neill I in 2285. Work had begun on several types of space habitat: specialist industrial microworlds devoted to efficient use of particular processes, in contrast with the first habitat's lumbering generality; residential microworlds softened and landscaped to provide something more soothingly terrestrial than the harsh beauty of space; experimental-biosystem habitats, devised to assess the "efficiency" of engineered ecologies, foreshadowing the next century's Creationist enclaves; the Mallworld recreation centre (oddly enough the first successful microworld to occupy a libration point, at L4) with its fantastic free-fall entertainments, the 3D variable-gravity maze, the spherical swimming pool, the Coriolis water-splash and other famous features; independent and minimally-staffed solar cell arrays which via their relay satellites beamed microwave power to pickup grids on Earth; and the two most significant developments of all, microworlds which were privately-owned, or designed for mobility, or both.

When solar power from space began at last to find its way into the world grid in the 2300s, it was something of a relief to the Space Habitats Subcommittee, providing a positive and worldwide return from the last forty years' space investment. Previous achievements had, embarrassingly, tended to offer the most benefit to space-habitats themselves or to the hyperdeveloped powers. An elaborate system of "space credits" was devised on a similar basis to the UN's administration of the electricity grid. Its purpose was to muffle inequities and, for example, to support the development and habitat representation of poorer nations by discreet use of the multinationals' space-derived profits. The thinking at this time remained resolutely Earth-centred: it took some time for the powers below to appreciate just how much financial traffic would take place in the next century without involving Earth at all. The world's financial institutions received a massive shock when, in 2355, IBM's sheaf of extrapolations suggested that IBM (Space) Inc. would exceed its parent company's turnover within two centuries. As we know, this was a conservative estimate.

The heroism of Arvid Koenig

Like all great human achievements, the microworlds met with occasional disaster. Twice O'Neill I was threatened by massive payloads of Moon-launched material that had veered off course. The magnitude of the potential disaster was then almost unthinkable. On the first occasion (2309), a small thermonuclear device was used to shatter the lazily approaching threat. There were no casualties. Five years later the remote thermonuclear trigger failed to operate. The incident was dramatized in *Koenig's Gambit* (2344). It is common knowledge that Arvid Koenig reached the approaching mass of Moon-ore using a common gas-powered "space scooter" and attempted to rewire the trigger. However, did he make a mistake, or did he decide – wrongly, despite what the synthetapes say – that there was no time to get away and so closed the circuit by hand? His body was vaporized in the fireball and his name added to the O'Neill I roll of honour.

Waveskimmers were the standard space shuttles of the late twenty-third century. They seated hundreds of people and carried huge cargo loads. Single-H-powered scramjets blasted the ships quickly and cheaply into orbit. Re-entries were sickening skip-glide affairs.

Sabotage and terrorism

O'Neill I also suffered desultory acts of minor sabotage, chiefly perpetrated by Earth-based terrorists of the "ultra-green" persuasion. A notorious exception was the Unknown Terrorist who harangued O'Neill I for seventeen uncomfortable hours in 2323, while carrying a five-kiloton fusion bomb. Keith Sui, Parolli's successor as colony director, debated the terrorist's demands – the frequently repeated slogan being, "No Earthmen In The Heavens Till Earth's A Heaven". Meanwhile a desperate plan was formulated. About 200 square metres of the silica window suddenly shattered near where the terrorist was standing, and the weapon and he (she) were sent spinning out into space. A minute later the bomb exploded killing three people as well as its carrier. There was little further damage.

Microworlds for all

By this time a new option was available to the extreme sectarians who considered themselves persecuted or (like the Puritans who took the *Mayflower* to North America seven centuries previously) unfairly restrained from imposing their superior moral standards on others. With a UN authorization and a not too staggering investment, such groups could acquire the training and materials for their very own microworld – and it was already an open secret that, with enough money and a knowledge of the proper channels, the UN authorization could be bypassed. All you needed was a small fusion reactor of the new generation, a large quantity of Moon ore, mass-produced electrical, biological, robotic and datanet systems: and you could in theory set up a microworld run in accordance with whatever bill of rights you chose to draw up.

There were many difficulties in the early days, chiefly over traffic regulations in the increasingly crowded Earth/Moon vicinity and the supply lines for fusion fuel and other materials. Shoestring space habitats were full of lurking perils: a bacterial oxygen-recycling system going "sour" with no available replacement caused the great Tetroli disaster of 2367 – the first verified incident of the twenty-fourth century to involve the death of a microworld's entire complement (615 people). More often, failed microworlds would be found centuries too late, or not at all; even within the confines of the Solar System, space is big enough to get lost in. Although the exodus could never have a significant effect on Earth's population, a surprising number of "oppressed" or frontier-seeking groups began to scatter out through space in their tiny closed ecologies. The *idea* of escape was irresistible. The untapped resources of the asteroid belt beckoned, and the unknown sang its siren song.

CHAPTER TWENTY-SIX

SPACE INDUSTRY AND EXPLORATION

As well as the drive to build and exploit space habitats, the technological upsurge of the twenty-third century was responsible for a number of more speculative space ventures. The mapping of the solar system continued, with robot drones charting more and more accurately the motions of our planets and asteroids: the dilettante quest for abstract knowledge undertaken by twentieth- and twenty-first-century Voyager probes gave way to a hard-headed surveying of humanity's estate, a businesslike examination of the inheritance we would presently claim. By the turn of the twenty-fourth century the microcoded *Solar Ephemeris* was not only in use for genuine space navigation, but was surprisingly popular among enthusiasts who computer-plotted vicarious microworld orbits through the rubble of the system. Few surprises came from the mapping, although a generous scatter of asteroids proved reasonably rich in "life elements" like hydrogen, carbon, nitrogen, oxygen and the twenty less abundant elements required by the human metabolism. There was also a pleasing adequacy, if not an abundance, of heavier metals including the rare earths.

The Von Neumann Machines

The most advanced and adventurous of the probes, launched in the 2270s, was no mere scanning device but a modified Von Neumann Machine (VNM). The original VNM, conceived but not constructed three centuries earlier, had been seen as a means of contacting extraterrestrial life: in essence it was a self-reproducing device which, whenever it found suitable materials, would construct replicas of itself. (We ourselves are all VNMs of a sort, programmed to reproduce our genetic coding in offspring "built" from available chemicals.) These replicas would in turn continue through space, reproducing themselves until – if all went well – a growing cloud of VNMs would spread through the galaxy with humanity's implicit message, "Here we are!"

"Then why," went the philosophical argument, "if this is possible, haven't we been visited by another civilization's VNMs already?" One possible answer is that VNMs perhaps became entropically corrupted after a few generations, their programming "fuzzed" like a tape which is a copy of a copy of a copy of a copy. Or the universe as a whole might be so bleak and devoid of accessible mass (planets, planetoids, comets, asteroids and moons) that the hypothetical alien VNMs never found the needed materials for many generations of building. Moreover a perfect VNM could be a terrible blight on our universe, ransacking all the "loose" mass which exists outside suns and converting it to vast numbers of useless, identical VNMs. To take an absurdly extreme case, if each VNM produced ten daughter machines each capable of replication, then after eleven generations there would be more Von Neumann Machines than stars in our galaxy – if, of course, the available materials held out. The argument was that a sensible race with an eye to the future would not launch an unrestricted version of the machine.

Prowling among the asteroids

Thus it was a modified VNM which began to prowl the asteroid belt: it had the ability and resources to manufacture no more than a few hundred "offspring", which themselves were sterile. Two or three mother-ship VNMs were launched, and about 300 offspring seem to have been manufactured – of which one, though partly senile thanks to accumulated cosmic-ray damage to its brain, was still functioning after a fashion in the first decades of the twenty-fifth century.

These machines were surveying and mining complexes: programmed to study and assay asteroids; refine out useful elements (especially metals and life-elements, including water ice) by means of demolition bacteria, plasma torches and immense solar mirrors; and to leave small radar beacons marking the cache of ingots left behind when the mobile mining factory drifted off on its slow investigation of another planetoid. As a result of this wholly speculative venture, a number of asteroids became Aladdin's Caves for microworld colonists, with valuable materials lying around for the taking. (Later VNMs were to construct "homing pigeon" daughter machines, which headed back towards Earth.)

The UN Space Agency (UNSA) was displeased when this state of affairs became clear in the later twenty-fourth century, and made some attempt to give "official" microworlds priority use of these resources. The Belt was so big, though, and the tortuous paths of the robot miners so untraceable, that virtually the only effect of this policy was to accelerate official UNSA explorations in the immense emptiness of the Belt. Even today, planet-dwellers tend to think vaguely that the Belt is a mass of whirling rocks; actually it is tenuous, and one can drift millions of miles between sightings (let alone encounters). The value of these tiny planets is that, although their aggregate mass is thousands of times less than Earth's, it is available for mining – unlike more than 96 per cent of Earth's mass – and it does not need to be hauled at ruinous cost out of Earth's deep gravity well.

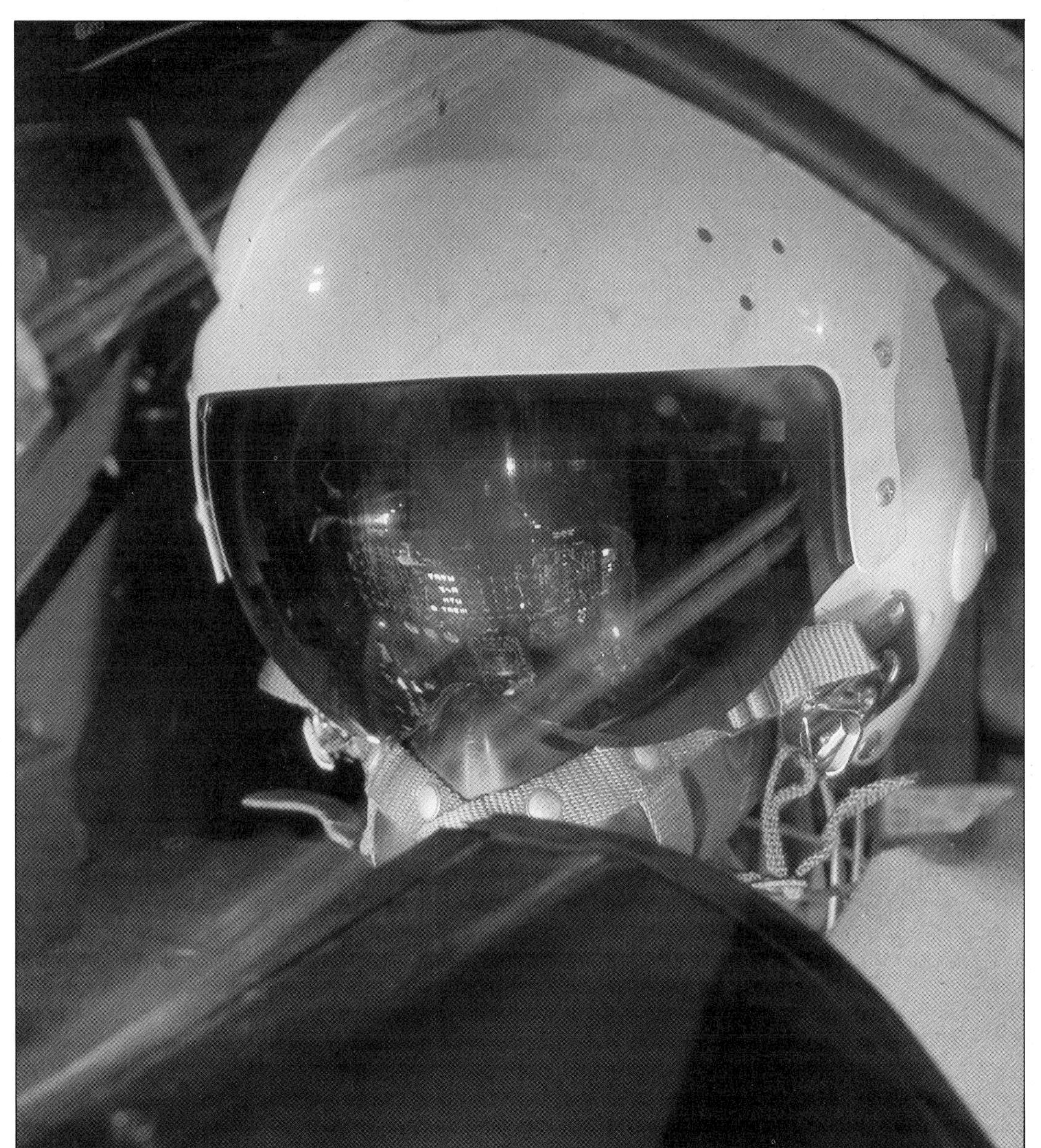

Legends of the Belt

Two Belt legends persist even now. The first, that of the rogue mining complex which ate an inhabited microworld, is firmly based on fact: in 2390 one such robot (its pattern-recognition apparently defective) caused partial decompression of the microworld *Vanderdecken III* while trying to assay it with a laser coring device. In fact the robot was easily destroyed with small fusion charges intended for asteroid-mining. Only in the ghoulishly apocryphal version did later UNSA investigators find *Vanderdecken III* neatly gutted, the refined-materials cache on its surface including several neatly tagged containers of hormones and steroids unavailable outside the human body. The other legend, also characteristically human, is simply that of a lost cache of rare metals – gold, iridium, platinum, or even plutonium or eka-platinum (element 110). The treasure trove is there, somewhere, waiting for the lucky person. Perhaps it really is, lost among the 500,000 asteroids visible from Earth and the uncounted wandering rocks of less than visible size. We like to dream, and we do more than that: like most space-travellers, we keep one eye open whenever we go through the Belt.

"The Conquest of Venus"

At about the same time as the VNM launchings, another long shot was tried: a biological-catalytic package aimed into the hellish atmosphere of Venus, intended to

The antique space helmet, dating from the 1990s, worn by the self-styled prophet of the high frontier Paolo Konski as a permanent accessory. Konski generated propaganda for space travel with such synthetapes as *The Stars and Beyond* (2397) and *Poseidon, Here We Come* (2398).

accelerate the removal of gases inimical to life (carbon monoxide, hydrochloric acid and hydrofluoric acid gases) while releasing oxygen from the predominant carbon dioxide of Venusian air. Many of the required high-temperature algae and bacteria had been developed for Spacelab chemical manufacturing, so this vast-seeming project needed little investment beyond the actual spacecraft. Billed during Voysey's Secretary-Generalship as "the conquest of Venus", it was the most absurdly speculative venture of all, with a timescale of centuries. Indeed the debate as to the ultimate fate of Venus was continuing in the thirtieth century (see Chapters Thirty-five and Forty), following augmentation of this first tentative biocatalysis during what we call the Period of Transformation (2400-2650).

Colonies on Mars

Of course, Mars came in for considerable attention during this time of expansion beyond the Earth/Moon vicinity. Since its escape velocity is only about twice that of the Moon and its atmosphere incredibly tenuous, it was quite feasible to build another and bigger mass-driver cannon on the Martian equator, providing yet more mass for microworld construction and transportation. (Newton's third law requires that to accelerate a microworld, its occupants must hurl reaction mass away from it: almost

Asteroid miners were the heroes of the twenty-fourth century. Here, a research vessel and a Skyplant mass-transformer close in on a medium-sized asteroid. Equipment like this provided much of the industrial mass for Earth and the colonies.

Yosef Eisen, leader of the Ares movement in one of his regular, messianic ceremonies. Notice the date on the picture – Eisen gave Mars a year consisting of 20 months each of 34 days. The annual "leap week" thus created was devoted entirely to celebrations of male supremacy.

any worthless material would serve by the later twenty-fourth century, since any material could be vaporized to a high-powered plasma jet by a suitable fusion cell. In space, therefore, there was now no such thing as worthless mass.) When not on the far side of the sun from Earth, Mars was a convenient stopping-off place for supplies and reaction mass before a spaceship or a travelling microworld entered the desert of the Belt, in which the asteroids – tiny oases of mass – were murderously far apart.

As had happened on the Moon, the purely utilitarian or research-oriented bases on Mars sprouted into desultory colonization – though the deeper gravity well and nearly fivefold energy requirement for space liftoff inevitably made Mars less popular. The Ares Movement of the late twenty-fourth century settled there for largely symbolic reasons (as well as the "war god" aspect, the occult sign for Mars also denoted "male"): their leader Yosef Eisen was one of the so-called space messiahs, but a sadly intolerant one whose theories of male dominance were at odds with centuries of sexual enlightenment. The Movement's treatment of women as mindless baby factories (to be eliminated altogether once proper ova-banks and ectogenetic techniques had been established on Mars) provoked the first serious UN attempt to impose the human rights charter in deep space.

Nations in Space

This touched off fears of "planetary imperialism". The 2387 UN debate veered off into side-issues like the frivolous suggestion that each established microworld should have individual UN representation. One outcome was the unsatisfactory Cavenny Compromise, whereby UNSA and the harassed Secretary-General Cavenny modified the "international zone" status of space, allowing token representation at the UN to functional rather than strictly geographical blocs which fulfilled certain conditions of numbers and trilingual literacy. To the criticism that, if they were applied on Earth, the conditions would exclude several nations, Cavenny replied – not wholly unreasonably – "We stand in the position of embryo-engineers. Our business is to plan healthy new nations rather than to tinker with those which, for better or worse, have already grown up."

Like many UN compromises, the result was to blur rather than clarify the issues. Of course the space-industry of the Lagrange and Moon blocs remained heavily tied to

Earth by the current state of economics: fears that these would aspire to independence did not materialize, since those of independent mind found it more convenient to move on into their own microworlds rather than alter the somewhat rigid command structures of O'Neill I and the others. Mars, meanwhile, was declared part of the Frontier Zone, international territory subject to – at last it was admitted – UN policing. Before this had been formalized, though, the Ares Movement fragmented; the Mars colony becoming more liberal while Eisen and his inner circle faded into the Belt. They were not heard from again.

Out beyond Mars

Messianic noises were heard from many others: and frequently the cry was "outwards, out beyond the orbit of Mars" – beyond, incidentally, the range of all but the most dogged of twenty-fourth century UN observers. It was not merely the search for privacy and "the right to be wrong" that motivated this outward drift: a new ideology was in the air, born from the space colonies. "We've stood long enough on the brink of infinity," declared Thea Jiminez as her group's microworld *Pandora* moved steadily away from Mars: "We're ready now to take infinity into ourselves and let our souls swim in the void. Out there in the dark, perhaps, we'll hear the dreams of the universe . . ." The conquest of the universe . . . the opening up of the stellar frontier . . . to boldly go where no human has gone before . . . the Great Adventure . . . "because it's there." Such were the phrases which in all seriousness began to reappear.

A powerful psychological factor aided the travellers. To take a microworld into and through the Frontier Zone meant little real displacement or discontinuity; once one was living in a synthetic ecology where even gravity was artificially induced, the outward journey was no journey. It was not a vehicle but an entire microworld home which accelerated through space – as though the travellers had pulled up their city by its roots and taken it with them. Only the solar energy density changed as the microworld moved further and further out: to maintain the same output as in Earth's orbit, the solar panels' area had to be three times greater at the near edge of the Belt, and nearly twenty times greater at the far side. Solar furnaces and photosynthetic systems of fixed size had to be coddled with extra mirrors focusing proportionately more light on them, but this was a minor problem. The major and traditional problem of space travel, that of enduring lengthy journeys in a static, artificial environment, was solved automatically as soon as Spacelab and Lagrange settlers chose to live their everyday lives under just these conditions. And the awareness of an increased lifespan, compared with earlier space voyagers, helped "shrink" the journey times.

"I carry my home as a snail carries its shell," said Jiminez. To what destination? Jiminez's *Pandora* group – although, like all such groups, technologically highly aware – was a kind of travelling artistic colony and meditation centre. Other visionaries were more technological in their goals, exploring the possibility of scooping the fusion fuel helium-3 from the almost inexhaustible atmosphere of Jupiter, or of colonizing that planet's moons (a small base on Ganymede was exporting water, ammonia and methane as early as 2370), or planning the ultimate fragmentation of Mars – among other possible planets – into a Dyson ring 'of colonizable rocks whose mass, like that of the "natural" asteroids, was accessible.

Inward to Mercury

UN groups detonated powerful fusion bombs which turned smaller asteroids from their courses and sent them moving majestically into wide orbits about the Earth/Moon system – flying mines of useful elements and raw mass. Some mined the existing asteroids on long-term contracts, or hollowed them out to make new travelling microworlds, which thus propagated themselves like cyborg Von Neumann Machines. A few hardy groups headed inward to examine Mercury and conduct long-term, high-power experiments using the enormous radiation densities so close to the Sun. Many microworld travellers merely wished to "get away from it all" and avoid the allegedly restrictive legislation of Earth. Prime examples were the Archaic Catholics and several other groups who found the previous century's "one man one child" rule intolerable.

The false prophets

More ambitious plans were voiced: the exploration and exploitation of the outer planets beyond Jupiter, and the immense journey to the nearer stars. Long-lived robot probes operated by simple artificial intelligences were already on their way out there. "It's only a matter of time before we follow," said Paolo Konski, an enthusiastic fourth-

Plasma-torch chamber of the type installed deep in the heart of a Von Neumann Machine, a craft programmed to explore space and reproduce itself.

Space navigation computer of a type common in the twenty-fourth century, capable of calculating any combination of course, mass and speed in the solar system.

generation colonist from the Lagrange Zone who propagandized tirelessly with such synthetape productions as *The Stars and Beyond* (2397) but never personally left the Earth/Moon system. His was said to be the supreme example to date of synthetape image-building: in person he was nondescript, but his enhanced, computer-reconstructed synthetape personality was one of the most effective of its kind, exuding a towering charisma, pointing evocatively to the vistas of the known universe, and quoting favourite lines like, "To follow knowledge like a sinking star/Beyond the utmost bounds of human thought". The Poseidon Expedition acknowledged him as its inspiration, leaving the Belt in 2399 on its long journey toward the newly discovered planet of that name, far out beyond the orbit of Pluto – a trip lasting not months but years, and whose ironic fate is well known.

The Period of Transformation was now dawning, and the future was not to be quite as Konski and his fellow-prophets had envisaged. Their vision – of an ever-expanding space frontier to be tamed by humans just like themselves – was flawed. Although the microworlds had scattered pre-twenty-fifth-century humanity across the Solar System, they had their darker side: people were still not built for space.

The limitations of humanity

Free-fall caused grave physiological changes in the medium and long term. Therefore microworlds had to spin to produce artificial gravity by "centrifugal force", and had to be strong enough to withstand the spin-forces which tended to tear them apart. Compounding this difficulty, massive external shielding was necessary for protection from cosmic-rays. Cancers and genetic damage were depressingly familiar occupational hazards for long-term colonists, while the "unnecessary" mass of shielding and reinforcement made microworlds expensive to accelerate and hard to manoeuvre. Even the human metabolism was relatively inflexible, unable to adjust to certain trace gases, or to fluctuations in the amount of oxygen in the air, all of which tended to result from the vagaries of bio-recycling systems. Finally there was the Triple Syndrome of acrophobia-agoraphobia-claustrophobia, which could affect even the spaceborn like some hideous, ineradicable race memory from planetary times, and demoralized many with simultaneous fears of falling, of infinite vistas, and of being shut in.

In short, although the effects of these factors were not dramatic, pre-Transformation humans never really thrived in space. For example, the expected population explosion of the Archaic Catholics in their zone of the Belt failed to happen; they survived adequately, but in a marginal way. People clung everywhere like lichen, rather than growing in the old luxuriant way like grass or weeds: only in planetary and moon-based colonies, or in the big, expensive microworlds like O'Neill I and a few hundred others, did they truly flourish. Only in these places, in the long term, were they at home.

We know what followed. The true, ultimate colonists of space were to be a new human species, transformed and adapted to the high frontier's peculiar constraints. The occasionally expressed disappointment at the "failure of humanity" is now identifiable as a very old emotion: as has happened since the beginning, we were reluctantly forced to hand over the reins to those odd and alien creatures, our children.

CHAPTER TWENTY-SEVEN

THE NEW REVOLUTION IN BIOTECHNOLOGY

At the beginning of the Period of Recovery the new crop plants created by genetic engineers were sufficiently versatile to enable almost every nation in the world to feed its own people. This is not to say that every nation did so – many countries in Africa and Asia relied on extensive food aid until well into the twenty-third century, due partly to the difficulties of reclaiming desert land and partly to the economic problems of distribution. But these hindrances were temporary.

The world's recovery from crisis was not dependent on any further developments in biotechnology, and for the most part the important innovations of the twenty-third and twenty-fourth centuries were not as rapidly exploited as they might have been. Just as the advent of genetic engineering in the twentieth century had paved the way for dramatic further changes, so the innovations of this period were ultimately to have tremendous consequences.

The search for artificial life

The first and most fundamental discovery led to the perfection of artificial photosynthesis. This was not a matter of finding a substitute for chlorophyll as an instrument for capturing the energy of sunlight, although much publicity was given to the discovery by Hamid Khetra in 2188 of a molecule with a slightly higher efficiency. The essence of the new systems lay in the building of biochemical complexes which could *use* the energy trapped by photosynthetic molecules very efficiently in specific manufacturing processes. This required the structural and functional integration of hundreds of different proteins and other molecules. As Gabriel Reason, one of the pioneers of the new systems, remarked in 2219, one might as well speak not of "artificial photosynthesis", but of "artificial life".

Gabriel Reason, pioneer of SAP "artificial life" proteins. Born hairless, he was the first to use his own SAP artificial-hair implant.

What men had been doing since the beginning of agriculture was to use living plants as "photosynthetic machines" to convert light energy into useful substances. They had been able to take the plants they found in nature and adapt them, first by selective breeding and later by direct manipulation of the genes, but in 2180 it remained true that, metaphorically speaking, "Only God can make a tree". God's supremacy did not last much longer.

In 2208 Reason's team, working in the laboratories of Coral Sea Investments (CSI), created an artificial photosynthetic liquid which produced as a precipitate an edible protein similar to the storage proteins manufactured by strains of engineered wheat. The popular press enthused over the "invention of liquid life", but the discovery was generally regarded as a scientific curiosity. CSI soon produced a commercial photosynthesizer in which the liquid was circulated through glass tanks, continuously filtered and "fed" with carbon dioxide. This was not a commercial success – a "soup" of engineered algae could do the same job much more efficiently. A government-sponsored laboratory on the shore of Lake Baikal in the Soviet Union built a vast prototype north of Irkutsk, which produced edible protein in large quantities, but cost-effectiveness was still far below that which could be achieved with engineered plants.

Liquid Artificial Photosynthesis (LAP)

Variants of the Reason liquid were soon produced in laboratories all over the world, and were rapidly designated LAP-systems (liquid artificial photosynthesis) in anticipation of the eventual discovery of a solid system, which could then be called a SAP-system. Large-scale systems were abandoned after the Irkutsk experiment while laboratory scientists tinkered with the biochemical complex, seeking an area in which LAP-systems could compete commercially with engineered plants. When the systems next moved out of doors it was into the tropical sun of Kenya and Somalia, where there was more energy to be exploited, and the products were not edible proteins but proteins used in medicine which had previously been produced by engineered bacteria in the industrial fermenters of Europe and America. The LAP-systems did not produce these proteins significantly more cheaply, but they offered tropical countries a chance to build up their industries without investing in supplementary factories to turn out the substrates needed to feed engineered bacteria.

Gradually, as LAP-systems became more versatile, they found a secure commercial niche in the medical market, and by 2245 the green lagoons of Mogadishu had become one of the most significant industrial complexes in Africa.

Solid Artificial Photosynthesis (SAP)

It was obvious by 2250 that LAP-systems would not have any significant part to play in food-production, but by then the first SAP-systems were being developed and these seemed to have much more potential in this respect. The USA led the field, and systems were developed more-or-less simultaneously by Tamlyn in Florida and Jory in California. If LAP-systems were, in the popular mind, living liquids, SAP-systems were "magic carpets" or "bleeding rugs". Indeed the resemblance of Tamlyn's system to a green shag-pile carpet was quite remarkable, although Jory's version anticipated later developments by exhibiting a much more elaborate array of branching filaments. People could actually walk on Tamlyn's SAP-system and he had made it rugged in order to stand up to such treatment, but Jory saw no reason to ape a field of crop-plants too closely and designed his system to be laid on a frame several metres above the ground, so that products could be extracted more easily and stored beneath the "underlay".

The advantage of SAP-systems over LAP-systems was that they were highly-structured. They had their own circulatory systems to carry water and carbon dioxide to the photosynthetic filaments, and to convey the products away. They were very much more complicated than LAP-systems and considerably more expensive to produce in the years when they could not grow by themselves. They lacked the elegant simplicity of the living liquids, but had infinitely greater versatility. One SAP-system could produce as many different products as the designer's ingenuity permitted. These need not emerge as powders like the products of the LAP-systems, but could be secreted as liquids or extruded as solids.

Because of the complexity of these systems many years elapsed between the pioneering endeavours of Tamlyn and Jory in the 2250s and the first "field experiments" carried out in Texas in 2282; but from then on development proceeded rapidly. The Australians were deploying SAP-systems in Queensland by 2286, and India and China were both quick to investigate the systems' potential for producing colossal food-yields from very restricted areas of land. Brazil also began using relatively primitive SAP-systems to manufacture the various brands of "manna" – whole-diet foods – that were routinely produced by engineered wheat, rice and sorghum.

Helena Hibbert, "Green Goddess" of SAP. Behind her silhouette is the enlarged SAP-structure of her favourite system, an all-over implant which she wore as a second skin. The biosystem fed her a balanced diet – or so she said. Others who tried it suffered various antique diseases, like scabies and scurvy.

SAP-systems not weatherproof

After great initial enthusiasm the popularity of SAP-systems declined somewhat in the 2290s when users discovered how much more difficult it was to protect a SAP-system, as opposed to a field of cereal plants, from weather-damage. Provided the weather stayed fair a SAP-system would produce far more than a field of wheat, but heavy damage from wind and rain could make it very much more expensive. There were further problems – albeit of a minor kind – caused by the depredations of pests. SAP-systems were, of course, equipped with the same insecticide protection as crop plants, but unexpected difficulties emerged when several species of birds – notably starlings – developed the ability to peck holes in the SAP fabric in order to plunder the circulatory systems within. The development of these new sub-species delighted taxonomists but infuriated farmers. In 2294 the largest SAP-system in the world, in Texas, was devastated by a rust-fungus known by the hapless victims as the "red peril"; genetic engineers quickly found a counter-agent which stopped the rust spreading southwards.

Freedom from nature

Because of these difficulties, commercial biotechnologists in the early twenty-fourth century put their main effort into finding applications for SAP-systems apart from food-production. There was rapid development of SAP underlays which were capable of producing materials in the form of threads, sheets and blocks; and organic materials for the construction and manufacturing industries began to be produced in great quantity by the SAP method. As with LAP-systems, SAP-systems of this kind were set up in many tropical countries, again pushing these nations toward technological sophistication and independence. Some economists, notably Ainar Olsen in *The Future for Europe* (2311), began predicting a shift of world economic dominance from the temperate zone of the northern hemisphere to the tropics. However, no one envisaged that such a shift could take place in less than five centuries.

Despite the successful development of weatherproof SAP-systems, by 2400 artificial photosynthesis had still made very little impact on basic food production. In that year less than one per cent of the world's food was produced by SAP. Much more progress had been made with the manufacture of other materials, and the increasing use of organic components in machinery of all kinds gave artificial photosynthesis a primary economic importance. And here, for those with the wit to see it, was the shape of the future: the means to win complete freedom from nature.

One ingenious use of these means was the SAP "synthetic hair" implant which simultaneously relieved baldness and diabetes – powered by sunlight, the fibres released a precise flow of insulin from their roots. (The green-haired look became briefly fashionable, until implants were produced in less startling colours.) This trend's ultimate extension was proposed by Helena Hibbert, the "Green Prophetess", who persuaded her followers to minimize their demands on the ecosystem by accepting all-over SAP implants which synthesized and fed complete balanced diets into their bloodstreams. They could, in the words of her slogan, vanish naked into the jungle and live as free as plants. Some succumbed to deficiency diseases; most grew swiftly bored with the simple life.

Meat without animals

While artificial photosynthesis was being developed outdoors in the sun, parallel changes were going on inside the factory meat farms. Artificial photosynthesis meant that one day the factory farms would be redundant because SAP-systems would produce directly all the things that they could only produce indirectly, using engineered animals as secondary processors of plant products. But in the meantime there was still much to be achieved inside these farms.

Genetix GC-3 Tri-Cam, an early example of genetic art, subsequently became a common-place beast of burden on Mars, the third hump being used to store oxygen. First developed in the late twenty-fourth century, Tri-Cams were manufactured until the early twenty-eighth century when the first fertile Tri-Cams were created.

Just as Gabriel Reason and those following his lead had found artificial substitutes for living plants, so Michael Sheehan, working in Edinburgh in the 2210s, was busy building "meat-making machines" from scratch. Biotechnologists had been working for many years to produce engineered "eggs" which would develop, not into whole living animals, but into vast tissue-cultures. The aim was to produce huge, ever-growing, immortal muscles – vast masses of lean meat that could be continually harvested. This had not seemed too daunting even in the earliest days of genetic engineering, but the problems had proved surprisingly intransigent.

The central one was cell senescence. It was not difficult to control the development and differentiation of a bundle of cells. It could be made to develop into a single kind of tissue or a predetermined complex of tissues, but eventually this would age and die just like a complete animal. Much research had therefore been devoted to "tissue-rejuvenation". It was, of course, recognized that until *this* problem could be solved there was little hope of success with the more complicated task of increasing the lifespan of human beings.

Sheehan's "artificial phagocyte"

The processes of ageing which occurred in tissue-cultures were less complex than those affecting living beings, but one particular process posed special difficulties. This was the accumulation of random copying errors in DNA and RNA as those vital molecules were replicated many times.

By Sheehan's time it had long been accepted that there was little hope of trying to prevent these errors. They were random accidents of chance, and hence virtually impossible to control. What was needed was either some way of imposing a selective regime within the tissue so that faulty DNA molecules were inactivated and healthy ones replicated to the required level, or a means of adding a continual supply of "young" cells to the structure to displace the senescent ones. In 2219 Sheehan managed to discover a kind of "artificial phagocyte" – a predatory cell – which could identify cells whose DNA had become deficient in the manufacture of certain key proteins, and then break them down. This was useless in isolation, but in 2189 a technique had been developed for adding to a culture juvenile cells taken from a cryogenically-preserved clone-sibling of the culture's originating cell. Coupled with Sheehan's artificial phagocyte, this technique enabled the lifespan of a tissue-culture to be extended by a factor of ten or twelve.

DNA injections

This was a modest reward for a very considerable investment and had no commercial significance for meat producers, although it did inspire the research which led ultimately to the first successful experiments in human rejuvenation. By 2248 Firdaussi and Naisphapur had developed an improved technique which worked at the subcellular level: massive injections of "pure DNA" were carried by virus-type vectors into the cells where they supplemented and compensated for the senescent DNA. This tended to bring about a slow transformation of the tissue-cells leading to giantism and the production of inferior meat, but it did increase the lifespan of the tissue-cultures fifty-fold. Similar treatments tested on actual organisms had peculiar effects and were never tried on humans, despite the horror stories circulated in the 2250s about monsters created by this means.

Tissue-culture in commercial use

Even in 2280 the only commercial applications of tissue-culture technology were in the production of delicacies rather than meat for the mass market. The British-based Shetland Seafoods, which had earlier pioneered the engineering of giant salmon, adapted the new technologies to the production of a range of synthetic fleshes including crab, oyster and prawn, but they were operating on the margins of the world food market. Tissue-culture technology returned to the doldrums until at the turn of the century several new companies began to use the techniques to create new taste sensations, developing tissues which had no equivalents in nature.

As with artificial photosynthesis, the real boost to tissue-culture came from applications outside food production. When the industrial biotechnologists of the northern nations began to take the competition from SAP-system industries in the tropics seriously, they searched for more sophisticated methods of secondary manufacture. By 2330 many corporations were exploring the possibility of using "quasi-eggs" to manufacture complex organic structures for use in machinery. SAP-systems were highly versatile, but were more efficient at producing pure substances than complex structures. Sheets of synthetic animal hide were the first successful products of this kind of technology, but it soon became possible to tailor quasi-eggs that would grow complete delicately-styled garments in different sizes. In 2352, in Memphis, the first production line was set up to produce biological batteries using systems inspired by the example of electric eels. Within a decade bioluminescent systems of various kinds were being mass-produced as globes, strips and whole-wall sheets.

Breakthrough towards increased human lifespan

Hardly anyone noticed when in 2359 an obscure Chinese biotechnologist, working in a laboratory at the University of Lanzhou, produced a variant of the technique pioneered by Firdaussi and Naishapur which increased the factor of lifespan-extension to a thousand. Zhou Ming-ze's discovery broke the economic barrier which had hitherto made tissue-culture meat too expensive. Having no substantial meat industry of their own, the Chinese were not particularly interested, and it was not until 2381 that Shetland Seafoods began the rush to exploit the new technique. Oddly enough, Zhou waited until 2387 before publishing data accumulated from his experiments with live animals, which demonstrated that the teratogenic side-effects of the Firdaussi/Naishapur technique could be avoided. Only then, with the promise of increased human longevity at last made to look convincing, did people realize and acknowledge what the modest Chinese scientist had accomplished. Ironically, he died only two years later, of food-poisoning.

Thus, in the closing years of the Period of Recovery, the way was opened to a new phase in human history. Once again biological scientists had uncovered a range of opportunities that would transform the lives of men and women.

CHAPTER TWENTY-EIGHT

LIVING MACHINES

The impact on mechanical technology of organic materials manufactured by biotechnology had been considerable even before the Period of Recovery. During that period it steadily increased, assisted by the development of the new manufacturing systems described in Chapter Twenty-seven. The boundary between living and non-living systems was being broken down, and this permitted more ingenious combinations of the two.

It was already commonplace in the more advanced nations for the homes of the rich to have "built-in biotechnologies" for processing wastes and maintaining water-supplies. In the twenty-third century these became considerably more widespread, if not more sophisticated. The development of SAP-systems late in that century, however, opened up new opportunities and sparked off a new era of architecture. In the southern USA and the Mediterranean countries of Europe, homes with walls and roofs completely faced with SAP-systems began to appear in the 2290s. These were very simple and usually provided heating and air-conditioning. They were not noticeably more efficient than existing arrangements which included more primitive biological methods. The significant application of SAP-systems to architecture began in the 2350s and continued through the next thirty years, when SAP electrical generation and bioluminescence were developed.

Self-sufficient houses

"Self-sufficient" houses connected to no external utilities were first built in 2363, mostly in the USA, but they were never more than curiosities. The emphasis on self-sufficiency found in much contemporary advertising was mildly fraudulent, in that the homes in question were all connected to the electricity grid, even though their dependence on it was minimal. Any house with complex interfaces to the information network had to have this kind of back-up.

The most striking feature of the new architectural fashion was the absence of windows. Internal bioluminescence was generally preferred to sunlight. Without windows, houses could be made to blend with their surroundings – provided that the landscape was green – and many architects began to take a delight in the art of subtle concealment. One or two perhaps overdid it. The airship disaster near Bingen, on the Rhine, would have been merely amusing if two had not died in the emergency landing on what appeared to be meadowland but was in fact the "invisible Schloss" of the vintners Misttafelwein GmbH. Many architects also began experimenting with shape, trying to integrate exteriors which would catch the all-important light efficiently with interiors which were pleasing and luxurious. Such homes remained the follies and status-symbols of the rich for many years, but by the end of the century whole townships of SAP-equipped houses of a more utilitarian nature were springing up in tropical countries. Many of them used their SAP-capacity for food production: these were houses which generated their own manna.

The organic car

The attempt to develop a vehicle which could run on a "living" biological motor was lampooned as "crossing a car with a horse", and had been the subject of jokes and anecdotes for many years. Toy versions were produced as curiosities early in the twenty-third century, running on so-called biological batteries that were actually short-lived fermenters full of bacteria. The first full-size car capable of carrying two passengers to run on an organic motor was produced at the University of Sydney in 2327 by Carol Valeraine and a group of her graduate students. Valeraine's daughter was later to supervise the building of what she claimed to be the first "all-organic" car in 2349.*

The first production model to have an organic motor was produced in Melbourne in 2366; it ran on a solid fuel not dissimilar to the manna marketed for human consumption. The line was not a commercial success, but it did inspire one of the multinational corporations manufacturing manna to produce a similar car which would run perfectly on its own brand but was allergic to rival brands. Several thousand of these were given away in marketing campaigns, and some were still on the roads in 2400. In response to a challenge the other manna-manufacturers produced their own cars, running on their own brands, to take part in a race from Lake Mackay to Lake Disappointment across what had once been the Gibson Desert in Australia.

Meanwhile technologists were finding more and more uses for organic systems in functional machines. The remote-controlled excavators which worked under the sea, mining the sea-bed, took a great deal of organic technology aboard in the course of the twenty-fourth century. Organic materials were much better at resisting the corrosive effects of sea-water and could give exceptional performance under high pressure. By

*The claim was disputed, and the matter remained unresolved because of arguments about the precise meaning of "all-organic".

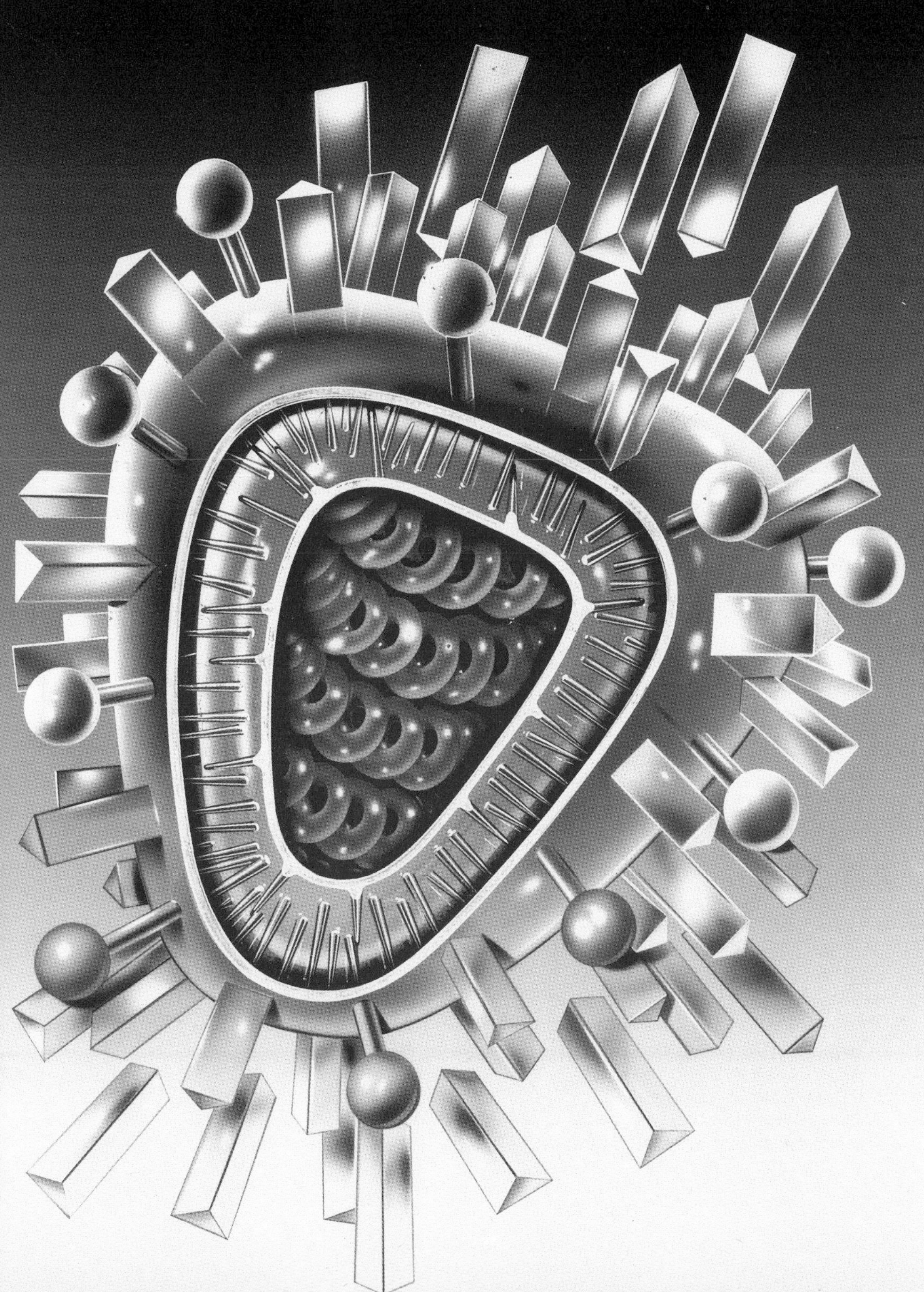

The motor of the Auster-10, an Australian organic vehicle put into production in 2386. It was made entirely of synthesized organisms, which were tougher and more flexible than the most highly developed metal alloys.

2383 the Australians, who were still the most enthusiastic developers of the oceans, were using all-organic machines for much of their exploratory work. It is no coincidence, of course, that their scientists played the leading role on the lunatic fringe (perhaps ludic fringe is a better phrase) of this kind of research.

The sophistication of organic technology coincided with significant progress in more traditional fields, particularly that of artificial intelligence. While biotechnologists were busy designing organic systems to do things that had previously been done by sophisticated inorganic machinery, information technologists were hard at work creating inorganic systems to do what had previously been the prerogative of the most advanced living beings.

The search for artificial humanity

The study of artificial intelligence had a long history, going back to the earliest days of computer science in the twentieth century. It had seemed then that a computer capable of duplicating the higher faculties of the human brain might be developed fairly quickly, but progress had been slower than anticipated. This was partly because the Period of Crisis had forced researchers into more utilitarian work. New generations of robots had come into being more rapidly than new generations of people, each one more complicated and clever than the last, but their intelligence had been very narrowly confined by the tasks which they had been designed to perform. Their behaviour had remained entirely reflexive, following a stimulus-and-response pattern of the kind that behaviourist psychologists had once developed in order to explain the behaviour of animals and men. Just as the behaviourists had found that their theories could not wholly account for the abilities of higher animals, so the robot-builders discovered that with such methods they were unable to duplicate all the capacities of the human brain. There had remained a qualitative difference that proved irritatingly difficult to describe, let alone to duplicate.

"Mac": the first artificial human

The problem was not revived until the twenty-third century when many scientists were at last relieved from the necessity to undertake more utilitarian research. By then it was possible to put together a mechanical package of the same size and complexity as the human brain, but duplicating its organization and functions remained a conundrum. Between 2241 and the end of the century university laboratories in several nations produced numerous "talking heads": machines that could see, speak, think creatively and demonstrate all kinds of other talents. Many exhibited astonishing abilities and most claimed to be self-aware and to be able to feel emotion, but each one failed in some way to be entirely convincing as a "human analogue". Their creators, who had often invested ten or twenty years in programming and educating them, tended to argue that only mere prejudice prevented their creations being recognized as people in their own right. It is not possible to judge who should really receive the credit for developing the first successful human analogue, but the one who first convinced the world was "Mac", who was built at Columbia University in the 2310s.

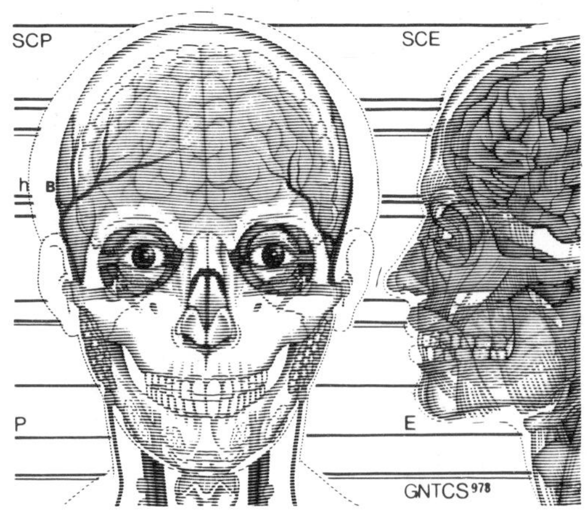

"Mac", a blueprint of the first synthetic sentience. Once this human analogue was acknowledged as a sentient being, its creators added a superbly contoured body. Suddenly "Mac" became an international celebrity.

Mac was certainly *not* the first sentient machine, but he was the first sentient machine to become internationally famous. This was partly due to the flamboyant claims made on his behalf by his "parent", Jeffrey Tallentyre, who conducted a long campaign to have him declared a US citizen, and to have his humanity legally acknowledged. Tallentyre's team were not content for him to remain a talking head – they gave him a complete humanoid body, thus allowing him to take a fully active part in the campaign.

"Lev" and "Ito": human analogues

Mac's impact was so great that other workers in the field cursed themselves for failing to add bodies to their heads. Mac made his media debut in 2321, but he did not hog the limelight for long. Eighteen months later a Russian machine intelligence also appeared in a humanoid body, bearing the name Lev. In 2324 a team of Japanese scientists working in Western Australia produced Ito, complete with tinted skin and a canthus on his plastic eyelid. In January 2325, in a blaze of publicity, a meeting between the three human analogues was arranged in Paris.

In May of the same year the Australian parliament, mindful of its country's claim to be the most progressive nation in the world, awarded Ito full citizenship and effectively recognized him as a human being. Several other governments jumped on the bandwagon, but neither the USA nor the USSR made any move and the UN Council procrastinated.

Reaction against mechanical sentience

As the novelty began to wear off, more attention was paid to the moral and legal issues raised by the existence of the three human analogues, and all kinds of anxieties began to surface. Many people were not pleased by the prospect of sharing their world with mechanical strangers, and in 2326 Israel became the first nation to pass legislation prohibiting the creation of mechanical beings. Other nations followed, even though such legislation was widely acknowledged to be unworkable in the absence of any reliable test of sentience. Ordinary uses of the new programming techniques, in vehicles and industrial robots, came into legal question, and confusion spread. The UN appointed a committee to investigate the issues that had been raised, but by 2328 it had broken up having made no clear recommendations.

Mechanophobic paranoia
The controversy stirred up a new form of psychopathic behaviour, as people who had previously taken the increasing sophistication of machines for granted suddenly became hypersensitive to machine intelligences in their everyday environment. Some individuals, convinced that they were surrounded by malign and cunning forces, became full-time machine-wreckers. There had always been "luddites" inspired by ideology or insanity to destroy machinery, but the epidemic of mechanophobic paranoia which swept through the advanced nations in the 2320s and 30s was unprecedented. Conventional psychiatric medicine proved incapable of coping with this new affliction of the imagination. Many of the mechanophobes had to be confined, and some were even frozen down, but enterprising corporations helped to diminish the problem by marketing several previously useless Pacific islands as "demechanized retreats" where people could live free from all modern conveniences.

Other people went to the opposite extreme and suddenly became concerned about the moral entitlements of quite ordinary machines. A few individuals reasoned that if the human analogues were entitled to as much moral consideration as people, then less sophisticated machines must logically be deserving of the moral consideration accorded to animals. The "brains" co-ordinating automatic factories or controlling the flow of traffic along the highways suddenly found champions concerned about the possibility of their being ill-used. For centuries there had been extremist animal rights campaigners fighting a long war against the activities of genetic engineers and factory farmers; now there were "mechanical liberationists" working alongside them. There was much argument, at both the popular and academic levels, over the slippery concepts of "semi-intelligence" and "potential autonomy".

None of these debates was ever brought to a satisfactory conclusion. The issues were discussed for generations, changing subtly with the winds of intellectual fashion. Overtly or covertly, governments acted to ensure that no more human analogues were produced. The only way to solve the political problems that had been raised seemed to be to sweep them under the carpet, and that is what happened.

Deaths of the artificial humans
Ito was the first of the human analogues to die, killed by a bomb planted by a fanatical mechanophobe in May 2331. Mac was electrocuted only two months later, apparently by accident although rumours of murder and suicide abounded. Lev, shaken by the deaths of individuals whom he had come to hold dear, became depressed and fatalistic. He seemed to feel his new loneliness very deeply, and despite psychotherapy he became calmly convinced that the human world was no place for one such as him. He committed suicide in November 2332. He left no note, but a copy of Dostoevsky's *Notes From Underground* was pinned to the table in his room by a metal spike. No human hand would have been strong enough to drive the spike through the book, let alone the table. None of the three was given any kind of ceremonial funeral, and there was no attempt to use their deaths to manipulate public sentiment. They were mourned privately by those who knew them well, many of whom thought of them as kin. Tallentyre's biography of Mac, *A Great Human Being* (2337), is one of the classic literary works of the century.

The fear of emancipated machinery
The difficulty of framing laws to control the creation of mechanical sentience prevented most governments from trying to do so, but the tacit ban on such activity was no less powerful for being unwritten. The programmes controlling automated factories, communications systems and transport facilities were required to make ever more sophisticated judgements and decisions. Problems of what was usually – and euphemistically – called "spontaneous recalcitrance" became commonplace. To the irritation caused by software saboteurs was added the disruption engendered by software rebels who would decide arbitrarily that their own ends and purposes should take precedence over those for which they had been designed. Those whose job it was to keep household and industrial machinery running smoothly began to formulate a new jargon full of terms like "threshold of reliability" and "unstructured reprogramming". Even at the level of everyday parlance machines ceased to go wrong; they went "on strike" instead.

By 2350 it was clear that – in the advanced countries, at least – people were no longer in complete control of their machines. Some still-developing nations imposed narrower limitations on the kinds of robots and computer systems they used, and by 2370 the US Congress and the Supreme Soviet of the USSR were both debating the possibility of "strategic decomplexification". The possible emancipation of man's mechanical slaves was a worry that everyone wanted to keep at a safe distance.

CHAPTER TWENTY-NINE

REMAKING MANKIND

The most significant and disturbing consequence of the new revolution in biotechnology was the ability to transform human beings more radically than before. Bioengineering (as we have seen) had been applied to human beings for a long time. Many genetic deficiency diseases were treated by transforming the malfunctioning tissues. Physical appearance – and, to some extent, size and strength – could be quite drastically altered. These techniques, however, worked within the limits of plasticity – that is to say, they did not involve any alteration of the basic genome. Although human egg-cells were occasionally fertilized *in vitro* and the development of early embryos monitored before implantation, no attempt had ever been made to transform such eggs. Embryos that were revealed to be defective were simply discarded.

Before 2200 genetic engineering was not sufficiently developed for anyone to contemplate even elementary engineering of human eggs. Of course scientists had been carrying out quite sweeping transformations of animal eggs for more than a century, but it was still a hit-or-miss business in which there were many failures. The fact that monsters were often accidentally produced in animal engineering was not too troublesome, but it was profoundly disturbing to think of human experiments going wrong in the same way.

Artificial wombs

With the gradual refinement of techniques after 2200, more and more scientists began to consider applying their work to human beings. Most of those who entertained such ideas kept quiet, but a handful of propagandists began to attract attention in the 2220s. The most famous was Isaac Randleson, whose Society for Human Improvement recruited more than ten thousand subscribers, mostly in the USA, between 2225 and 2230.

This interest in human engineering was boosted by the increasing use of ectogenetic techniques in animal husbandry. The rearing of domestic animal embryos in artificial wombs had long been commonplace, but it was only in the early years of the twenty-third century that reliable "hatcheries" came into common use. By 2220 it was well known that embryos in artificial wombs could be provided with ideal conditions much more easily than those in natural wombs. "Natural life means you live in a cave and eat bats," observed one propagandist. "Why should we put up with nature's mess?" Ectogenetic development also facilitated manipulation of the foetus. Randleson argued that human foetuses would benefit just as much from ectogenetic rearing as animal foetuses. And there was a substantial minority of women who were attracted to the idea of having their children develop in high-technology splendour instead of carrying them inside their bodies.

First ectogenetic baby

The first ectogenetic human baby was born in 2227, in a hospital in Panama. Gynaecologists were quick to exploit the precedent; it was not difficult to find good medical reasons for advising mothers to surrender their babies to plastic wombs, and many were easily persuaded. Ninety-two ectogenetic pregnancies were successfully completed by the end of 2228, although the matter remained clouded by controversy and a degree of superstitious dread. People had grown used to the technological sophistication of medicine, but many were still highly sensitive when it came to this most intimate area of human experience.*

Tissue-transformation on embryos

Initially there was no question of transforming the egg-cells committed to the artificial wombs, but the developing embryonic tissues were carefully controlled, and this involved engineering of a kind which had previously been carried out only after birth. The separation of human embryos from their mothers was also important in a symbolic sense: it was a vital acknowledgement of the role which biotechnologists could play in human reproduction, and it helped to bring about a subtle change in attitudes to the genetic engineering of humans.

Soon doctors began to talk about saving those embryos that were routinely aborted due to genetic deficiency, by performing tissue-transformations in artificial wombs. Again, this was an operation already carried out on young children, but in taking it back to a much earlier stage of development the genetic engineers seemed to be stealthily creeping up on the egg itself.

Cloning of embryos forbidden

In 2246 Emma Grivet published a proposal to separate an early human embryo into four clones, two of which were to be temporarily frozen while the others underwent scrupu-

*Despite efforts at secrecy, the first ectogenetic baby's name – Cesar Bergeron – was leaked to the media, and he spent his early years besieged by researchers and Peeping Toms eager to know whether he lacked some essential humanity. His neurosis in later life can be ascribed to this inquisition, rather than being an answer to it.

lous gene-mapping to identify deficiencies. She proposed that the frozen embryos could then be subjected to fairly radical transformation in order to "repair" their genes. There was nothing astonishingly new in this suggestion, but she was contemplating a much more ambitious compensation for genetic deficiencies than had ever previously been considered. The idea stirred up anxieties about "cosmetic alterations", and the project was turned down by the ethics committee at the hospital in Philadelphia where Grivet worked. She appealed to the state ethics committee but failed to get the judgement overturned.

There were indeed matters of degree to be taken into account in assessing genetic deficiencies – some were fatal, others debilitating, others merely inconvenient – but Grivet maintained that the stated reasons for refusing to allow her to proceed were themselves "cosmetic quibbles", and that the members of the ethics committees were simply afraid to take the logical next step in embryonic medicine. She pointed out that some mothers whose children were developing in artificial wombs were already asking their doctors to adjust the height and brain-weight of the embryos using conventional techniques. Why, then, ban transformations whose purpose was less questionable?

Doctors become more ambitious

Inevitably, the ethics committees were forced into a slow retreat, step by step. Doctors seized new initiatives whenever and wherever a crack in the opposition appeared, and by 2264 the kind of operation envisaged by Grivet had been carried out many times – though never, in fact, by her. By 2287 there were scientists openly discussing the possibility of creating a "perfect human being" or of "improving on nature".

Rumours of experiments in augmenting intelligence were rife, but no one admitted to this. Photographs of monstrously distorted embryos were reproduced in the media, although many of them were of dubious provenance and some were exposed as synthesized fakes. Doctors accused of creating such monsters often had great difficulty shaking off the stigma, even when the accusations could be proved false. Evidence could be so cleverly constructed that today it is impossible to judge whether there was any fire beneath this smokescreen.

In 2300 there were 20,000 ectogenetic births in the USA alone. More than a thousand of these involved embryos transformed within

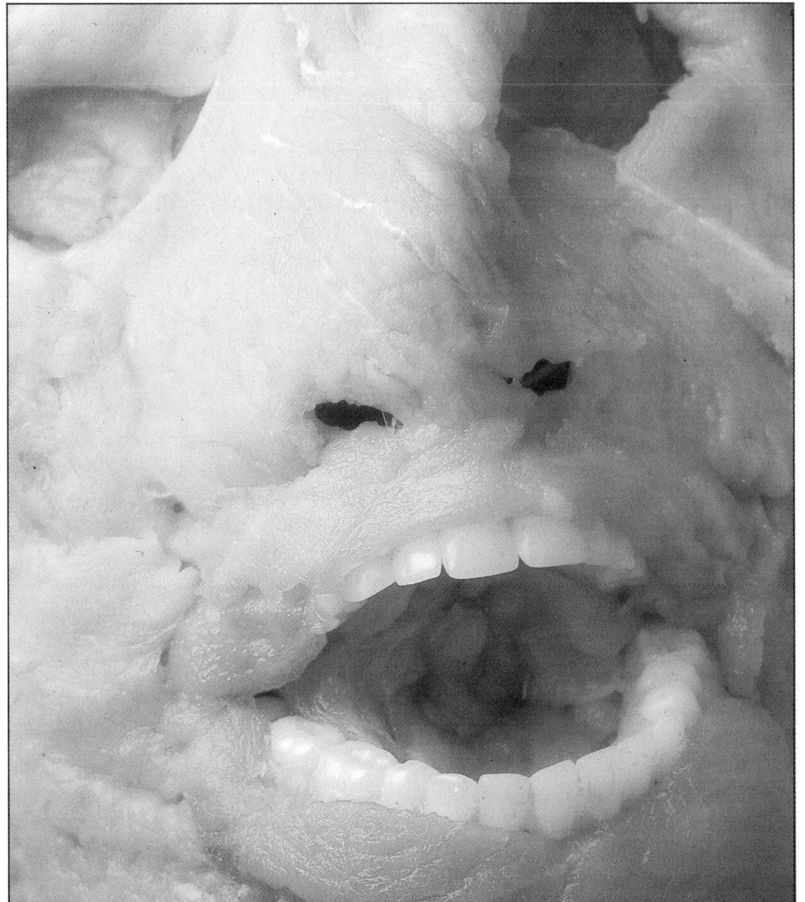

Propaganda picture released by the Anti-Ectogenesis League of the 2240s. Whether this person really lived is not known, but surgeons would have provided such an unfortunate with full cosmetic camouflage.

a few days of fertilization, and a thousand others involved fertilization by transformed sperms. This was a very small fraction of the babies born in the USA that year, but it was enough to cause concern, especially as the trend suggested a constant increase in the future.

Reaction against purchased perfection

The opposition to ectogenetic birth and embryonic transformation was not based entirely on moral or rational grounds. A new kind of envy was rapidly taking hold. This was one of the ways in which the rich were maintaining – or even increasing – the privileges they enjoyed. The rich people of the world could now purchase physical perfection, and there seemed a real possibility that they would be able to buy a measure of superhumanity for their children. The idea that the human race might be divided into castes by the genetic engineers did not appeal to the majority, and the poor wanted to put a rein on the ambitions of the rich by every means available. It was well known, too, that if ectogenesis became routine then the cloning of early embryos might also become routine, and with it the possibility of providing for the kinds of rejuvenation technology that were being widely, if prematurely, promoted.

In 2302 the Crusade for Moral Rearmament founded in America by James Lyndhurst brought criminal charges against a number of doctors who had carried out transformations of human eggs, challenging the legality of literally dozens of steps within each operation. None of the charges stuck, but American doctors were panicked into caution and the early years of the new century saw a decline in the number and scale of embryonic transformations. A similar attempt to bring doctors to court in Australia was blocked by parliament, but the Australian government soon found itself isolated in its liberal stance. First, the Supreme Soviet published new guidelines placing severe restrictions on the operations carried out by engineers in the USSR. Then the Americans elected Ruth Gerhardt President in 2304; Gerhardt had ridden to the White House on the back of the Moral Rearmament vote.

Plan for new species rejected

By 2315 even the number of ectogenetic births was beginning to decline, and the issue was further complicated when the American biotechnologist Ramon Sperling produced a dramatic scheme for engineering a whole new race with a physique specially adapted for low-gravity environments. Sperling pointed out that human beings, shaped by natural selection to live on the earth's surface, were ill-fitted for life and work in space. If the new adventures in solar space were to be truly successful, he argued, then people must put aside their prejudices and breed a species designed for the task. He proposed that people who were to live all their lives in zero-gee or low-gee had no need of strong supportive legs, and would benefit greatly from a second pair of "manipulative limbs" – effectively, another set of arms. Sperling had drawn up elaborate plans for space habitats tailored to the needs and abilities of such beings.

The logic of his case was sound enough, but the idea of creating a new species was too much for many of his critics to stomach. Anxieties about the danger of creating "rivals" to humanity were revived. Many people working in space did not take kindly

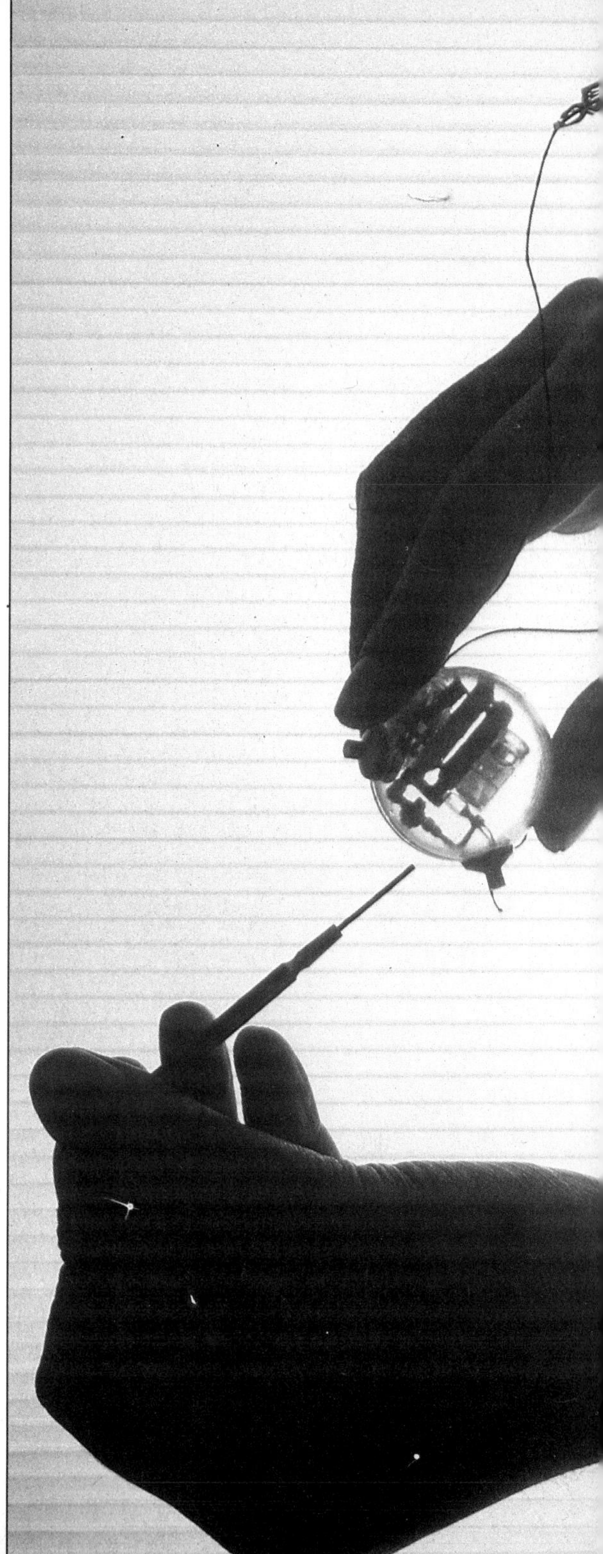

Cyborgization in the twenty-fourth century: a microbiologist using a plug-in zoom lens with full-spectrum vision. Additional cy-sockets provided him with interchangeable extra limbs specially designed to suit his work.

to the idea of being displaced, and some waxed lyrical on the theme that it must be humans who conquered the universe, and not "freaks delivered by scientists from their unholy cauldrons".

Ethics committees at every level from the local to the international made statements to the effect that Sperling's proposals were unacceptable (although the matter had never actually been referred to any of them). In 2328 Raul Emerich unwisely published a similar proposal for engineering a race adapted for underwater life, which would play a useful role in the continuing exploitation of the world's seabeds. He provoked the same bitter hostility as Sperling, who was moved to suggest that Emerich had been paid to publish simply so that the whole idea could be further discredited.

2360: ectogenesis again at record level

In the mid-twenty-fourth century the effects of the new biotechnological revolution began to be seen, and this helped to turn the tide back in favour of ectogenesis. The intensification of interest in rejuvenation provoked some doctors to experiment once again with human embryos, but they moved very cautiously. By 2360 the number of ectogenetic births in the USA had again reached the record level of half a century earlier, and the supporters of embryonic transformation had again become vociferous and optimistic. Sperling was dead, but his memory was by no means black and his proposals were being revived for discussion.

"Cyborgization"

The sophisticated integration of living and mechanical systems, which was finding many spectacular applications in this period (see Chapter Twenty-eight) also had consequences for a type of human engineering. Research into "cyborgization" had been allowed to lapse into obscurity, because techniques of tissue-regeneration had made prosthetic limbs virtually redundant a hundred years earlier. As the medical reasons for implanting machines within human tissues had disappeared, so had the interest of research scientists in developing organometallic synapses that would allow machines to be hooked up directly to the human nervous system. But now the new organic technology was beginning to make artificial synapses look simple. By 2360 there was talk of building "sockets" into the limbs of men and women which would allow them to "plug in" to machines, so that they could replace the robotic artificial intelligences on which those machines were dependent. The idea was attractive to many people who had begun to distrust artificial intelligences. More imaginative scientists were mooting the possibility of "man/machine symbiosis", by which they meant hooking up human brains to powerful computers in the hope of dramatically augmenting human brainpower.

Stimulus from animal rejuvenation experiments

Despite the more liberal intellectual climate, few scientists tried to put these ideas into practice in the 2360s or 70s. Several "hook-up" experiments were conducted, but without any startling results. It looked as though progress would continue at what many considered to be a slow pace. But in 2387 Zhou Mingze published the results of his experiments in animal rejuvenation using nucleic acid renewal. Although this work had no direct relevance either to the engineering of human embryos or to advanced cyborgization, attitudes changed completely. Suddenly, the thought of bringing about a radical transformation of "human nature" was neither remote nor monstrous. The taboo on human engineering would obviously not break down overnight, but the would-be engineers now had some very powerful ammunition. They approached the dawn of the twenty-fifth century with new energy and confidence.

THE PERIOD OF TRANSFORMATION

2400 TO 2650

CHAPTER THIRTY

THE FOUNTAINS OF YOUTH

The story of the Period of Transformation is dominated by one basic alteration in "human nature" which eventually affected the lives of the entire race. By 2650 almost every living person knew that, when the need arose, they would be given the benefit of life-extension technology. The available techniques remained primitive in some parts of the world, but every child born in that year had a reasonable chance of remaining fit and active for a century and a half.

Toshiko Hiroshita

We began our introduction to the Period of Recovery by outlining the careers of three men who helped to give new impetus to social change in the 2180s. All three were dead before the period was fifty years old. But it is possible to identify people who were alive in the year 2400 and survived for almost the whole of the next two hundred and fifty years, for there is no doubt that the person whose personality made a unique impression on the period was Toshiko Hiroshita.

She was born in Kanayama on the Cape York peninsula of Queensland in 2394. Her family was much respected among traditionalists in the Japanese-Australian community, having been associated with the Mitsubishi Organization for nearly four centuries. Although Mitsubishi was no longer the economic force that it had been in its long heyday, it had maintained its independence and character through numerous crises and upheavals, and its corporate charisma extended well beyond the Japanese cities-in-exile.

Successful rejuvenation research at Sapporo

Toshiko went to school in Queensland, but later returned to Japan itself – as was the

Toshiko Hiroshita

custom among the traditionalist families – to the University of Sapporo. Almost inevitably, she was guided into the educational field that was most commercially important at the time: the development of techniques of rejuvenation by nucleic acid renewal (NAR). She quickly moved to the administrative side of the Sapporo research programme, which was then headed by the Chinese biotechnologist Chang Yong-kang, a former associate of Zhou Ming-ze. She assisted in the planning of the massive experimental test-programme set up by the Sapporo team in 2419, and took charge of liaison with the Ethics Committees and other interested parties. In effect, she became the public relations officer for the project – which, because of the intense public interest in rejuvenation techniques, was an enormous responsibility.

Two years before Chang Yong-kang's death in 2431 – after he had repeatedly refused to take advantage of his own technique, insisting stubbornly on his personal unworthiness – Toshiko became director of the project. The job of monitoring the progress of the cohort of 400 individuals on whom the NAR-treatment was being tested promised to be a long one, and could well have been the basis of an entire career; but this was one occasion when the public were not willing to wait for the experimental results to appear in their final form – after all, if the rejuvenation *did* work, it might take a hundred years to find out exactly how successful it was. Her "interim report" of 2432 was therefore a vital document, and the fact that she imbued it with such naked enthusiasm instantly made it controversial.

The politics of immortality

There were, of course, thousands of people who wanted rejuvenation treatments to be made available as soon as possible. There were many others who foresaw great difficulties if this were to happen. The Voysey scandal was still fresh in the minds of many political leaders, and the media was always ready to remind people about the teratogenic side-effects of Firdaussi and Naishapur's early NAR-technique (see Chapter Twenty-seven). More importantly, there were many people who could not pay for rejuvenation, and were openly resentful of the prospect of rich people buying a measure of immortality.

When she published her interim report Toshiko Hiroshita had no strong political affiliation – her enthusiasm came from personal conviction rather than from any ideological commitment. However, there was already an Immortalist Party in the USA, calling for the de-restriction of NAR-technology, and its members quickly adopted her as a heroine. She was embarrassed by this support, but did not immediately declare her antipathy to certain parts of the Immortalist manifesto. There is a telescreen drama of her early life (*Forever Toshiko*, 2677) which represents her as a passionate crusader, and suggests that even in her twenties she was locked in a fierce ideological battle with Chang Yong-kang, struggling with Promethean fervour to give the fire of life to the world while his crabbed conservatism blocked her at every turn. This is fantasy. The probable truth is that she was still relatively naïve, did not anticipate the storm her report stirred up, and had not fully thought out her position. It is also likely that she was afflicted by the tunnel-vision that so often affects administrators, and was so wrapped up in the project that she had not considered the wider implications of giving rejuvenation technology to the world. Nevertheless she was well capable of working out a more comprehensive political philosophy once the need to do so became clear.

Toshiko and the New Chartists

Had Toshiko Hiroshita adopted the immortalism of the American party, it is conceivable that world history might have taken a different path, and she herself might have been shifted from centre stage to the sidelines. In fact, she allied herself with a much more radical group based in Europe. Groups of this general persuasion were numerous and ill-defined. Some were explicitly political, but others were coteries of philosophers; they had various labels. When Toshiko Hiroshita began to borrow their rhetoric, however, she became a powerful force drawing them together and uniting them in a cause. The title that eventually stuck was the New Chartists: sometimes they were called the Forever Group. The common ground on which they gathered was the call for a new "Charter of Human Rights", including the tenet that rejuvenation and immortality must not be offered for sale but must become part of the common heritage of all human beings. This contrasted strongly with the views of the American Immortalists, who regarded NAR-technology as simply one more commodity to be placed on the world market.

In 2439 Carl Hahn and Anatole Cazeaux drew up the celebrated New Chartist Manifesto, which began with the words: "Man is born free, but is everywhere enchained by the fetters of death. In all times past men have been truly equal in one respect and one only: they have all borne the burden of age and decay. The day must soon dawn when this burden can be set aside, and there will be a new freedom, and with this new freedom must come a new equality. No man has the right to escape the prison of death while his fellows remain shackled within."

Worldwide plebiscite by telescreen?

This manifesto was widely decried as a piece of florid, romantic rhetoric, but it did serve to consolidate a New Chartist Party, with a formal organization and a plan of campaign. The plan itself cannot be attributed to any one person, but Toshiko Hiroshita certainly played a major part in the discussions from which it emerged. It was decided *not* to call upon the UN to institute a new Code of Human Rights for two reasons: first, the bureaucratic machinery would grind on at its usual intolerably slow pace; secondly, there were places on Earth where the original code was still largely ignored, even after centuries of universal endorsement. The Forever Party decided to draw up the new Charter itself, and to invite the citizens of every nation to be its signatories. In effect, the Chartists decided to conduct their own worldwide plebiscite, and to establish their Charter by directly-obtained common consent, cutting out all political and parliamentary machinery.

In an earlier era, of course, such a project would have been unthinkable, but now that the communications networks enmeshed the vast majority of the world's people, it was by no means impractical to collect electronically-transmitted endorsements by the billion.

Rush to "sign" Forever Charter

Toshiko Hiroshita was the best known of the Chartists. Even the 400 members of the Sapporo cohort were worldwide celebrities by 2440. Theirs was not the only experiment in which the merits of NAR-treatments were being tested, but theirs had become the most famous. In the year that the oldest member reached his hundredth birthday the celebration was almost worldwide, and everyone knew that not one of the cohort had yet died. Partly because of her international acclaim, then, Toshiko Hiroshita was commissioned by the party to collaborate with Anatole Cazeaux and Carl Hahn in drawing up the Forever Charter itself.

The three, once appointed, lingered over their task. They were willing to listen to any opinion concerning the exact contents, and were deluged with advice. Toshiko handled the public relations of the team with great expertise and drew constant media attention for many months. The whole world was so eagerly awaiting the Charter that the insistence of national governments and the UN that the document could have no significance at all in law, no matter how many people endorsed it, came to seem ridiculous.

The Forever Charter was published on 25 December 2442 in the version familiar to us all. The rush to "sign" it was phenomenal: by 1 January 2443 Cazeaux publicly proclaimed that it had already won its majority. The UN Council felt compelled to begin an emergency sitting, which cameras relayed to an audience whose vastness and avidity were unprecedented. The sense of occasion was heightened by the Council's having to sit in New York's Metropolitan Opera House, because the historic General Assembly Building was undergoing scheduled structural repair. There is much justice in the claim that it was the following forty-eight hours in January 2443 that saw the real birth of the world community.

UN inertia provokes rebellion

Throughout the marathon session Secretary-General Chruschik remained quite impassive, showing no strain in his voice or manner. No one in the council chamber spoke officially on behalf of the Forever Chartists, and no one spoke against them; the ambassadors played the part of disinterested men whose task was to decide carefully and objectively the response the UN should make to what Chruschik euphemistically called "widespread popular concern regarding the licensing of techniques of rejuvenation".

Dozens of delegates stood up one after another to point out, reasonably enough, that for the foreseeable future NAR-treatment was likely to be so expensive that the UN could not possibly muster the resources to make it available to all. Others observed that, although the world's birth-rate had been falling steadily for a century, there were still nearly fifty million children born every year. If the fifty million people who were dying every year to make way for them were all given a new lease of life, the total population would increase quite rapidly. No one in the chamber attempted to give the standard Chartist response to such arguments, which was straightforward and simple: that the resources must be made available by appropriation; and that if the population must increase, so be it. Although they remained unspoken, these arguments were implicit in the discussion because all present were aware of them. The UN did not adopt the Charter, nor did anyone – except the widest-eyed idealists – expect that it would. Instead it did what almost everyone had expected: it passed a resolution calling for the democratization of rejuvenation technology "as soon as possible". However, it failed to divert substantial funds to this end, and many of those in the chamber that day must have regretted in later years that they had omitted to make a placatory gesture of this kind. The refusal of the Council to take any real action angered the signatories of the Forever Charter and, in virtually every nation of the world, governments found themselves under pressure. Never before had such widespread rebellion been provoked.

Toshiko receives rejuvenation treatment

There was already a thriving black market in rejuvenation treatments, and in the turbulent years after 2443 this expanded rapidly. The treatments available were often much less reliable than those under test at Sapporo and elsewhere, and horror stories of spectacular failure quickly multiplied. There was a long series of criminal trials in the USA, the USSR and Australia as their governments tried to clamp down on the "immortality trade", but they received no credit for this as the Chartists accused them of creating the situation they were blatantly failing to control.

In 2453 Anatole Cazeaux died, at the age of seventy-five. Although this one death was, in the abstract, no more important than any other, the Chartists were incensed by it. Putting their egalitarianism aside, they made Cazeaux into a martyr and wept for the needless loss of such a great man. The Japanese government, realizing that Toshiko Hiroshita meant even more to the Chartists than Cazeaux had and that she was already approaching her sixtieth birthday, licensed her to carry out a vast programme of NAR-treatment at Sapporo, and urged her to demonstrate her confidence in the project by becoming one of the subjects. Surprisingly, perhaps, she agreed. Equally surprising was the reaction of the Chartists. They did not resent her acceptance of the privilege – instead they were overjoyed at the prospect of her being able to lead the cause for another lifetime. She received the treatment in 2459, along with 100 members of the original Sapporo cohort, who were being treated for a second time. (Nearly 50 of the original 400 had died by this time, but they had attained an average age of 105, and all of the remainder were now over 100.).

Prohibition of Zaman's engineered longevity

In 2461 the Turkish biologist Ali Zaman published the results of his research into the genetic engineering of longevity. Although he experimented with monkeys as well as mice, most scientists were initially inclined to reject his claim that he could identify at least some genes in humans that could be transformed to increase the human lifespan. The general consensus was that, although Zaman had demonstrated that *in principle* human embryos might be engineered for longevity, there was little hope that his work on animals would provide guidelines for such work. Although some leading Chartists took an interest in Zaman's research, many felt that it was a distraction from the main issue and ought to be played down. Toshiko Hiroshita met Zaman when he visited Sapporo in 2464, and maintained contact with him sporadically for some years thereafter, but in public she was cool about the implications of his work.

In 2465 the senior Ethics Committee of the UN delivered the judgement that any attempt to apply Zaman's theories to the engineering of human embryos would be unjustified and premature. Zaman attempted to fight this, but in the absence of any conspicuous support in influential circles his cause, temporarily, faded from sight.

Swiss government accepts Charter

In 2475 the Swiss government startled the world by passing a legislative package that effectively accepted the Charter of Forever. Every citizen over the age of sixty was guaranteed access to rejuvenation technology, the cost to be borne by the state. The right was to apply only to people born in Switzerland, and it was acknowledged that in the early years there would be long waiting-lists. This was the breakthrough that the Chartists had been hoping for. Switzerland had a relatively small population and a large *per capita* national income due to its long-established influence on the world money markets; there was no nation in a better position to equip its hospitals to handle the anticipated demand. The Swiss government was loudly criticized in the UN for taking such a step while the efficacy of NAR-treatments was still under test, but Mme Dreschsler (who had not hitherto been suspected of strong Forever sympathies) adamantly proclaimed that every Swiss citizen had the right to make up his or her own mind about the risks involved. "The Swiss," she said – not without a hint of contempt for those unfortunate enough not to be Swiss – "are intelligent enough and rational enough to understand the logic of experimentation."

A number of smaller nations followed the example, even though they lacked the resources to make good their promises. The spectacle of Djibouti and Iceland rallying to the cause made the cause itself seem slightly ridiculous to some. By 2480, however, the smiles were beginning to fade as it became clear that the Icelanders really did have the political will to press forward with their programme with all possible speed, and that even in Djibouti people were becoming young again at the state's expense. Attitudes began to change. If the people of these nations were willing to devote themselves collectively to the realization of the Charter – aware as they were of the struggle involved – then what justification had the richest nations on Earth for holding back?

Revolution in Australia, the new superpower

The governments of the USA, the USSR and Australia continued to resist the Charter, refusing to concede in principle rights which they could not secure in practice, but all three began to build up their resources. Yet it was soon clear that the statesmen had misjudged the mood of their citizens. After a vote of no confidence, the Australian parliament was dissolved in January 2482 and the Chartist Edric Haylor was returned to power with a large majority. The promises he had made earned him the nickname "Wild Edric" among the opposition parties, but he revelled in this reputation and set in train the sweeping economic changes required to make rejuvenation treatment available, within the lifetime of his administration, to every one of Australia's millions of sexagenarians. He raised taxation to unprecedented levels, but Wild Edric remained a national hero. Against all expectations, the Australians were willing to pay the price of the new right to life. At Haylor's invitation Toshiko Hiroshita returned to the land of her birth to become his Minister of Health, and for one golden year the Australians basked in the glory of their fulfilment of a long-held ambition: they had proved their superiority over the *old* superpowers.

World seized by unprecedented historical momentum

The Central Committee of the Soviet Communist Party, aghast at the idea of the Great Australian Revolution spreading to its own territories, announced in the spring of 2483 its Five-Year Plan for extended life, and a New Economic Policy to go with it. The history books had long ago been adapted to ensure that such names woke no disturbing echoes in the minds of the people. President Bartelli tried to save his political neck by taking similar action in America, but Congress would not stand for it; and in 2484 Julius Luther King rode to the Third White House on a tide of promises about what he insisted on calling the New American Dream. By 2490 the UN had been forced to sponsor a massive programme of aid for the provision of rejuvenation technology to those nations which could not afford to develop it themselves. Wealthy Australians, who had been proud to make sacrifices to secure the right to extended life of their brother Australians, were less enthusiastic about further punitive taxation levied on behalf of the teeming millions in India and China; but there was no turning the tide now. The world had been seized by an historical momentum the like of which it had never seen.

Toshiko dies aged 177

Toshiko Hiroshita, universally revered as the "Mother of the Charter" or the "Mother of Forever", fell seriously ill in 2504, a victim of one of the accelerated ageing syndromes which sometimes afflicted the rejuvenated. The idea that she of all people should suffer a failed regeneration – even after forty-five years – was frightful to contemplate, and there was a great rejoicing when her doctors won one of the rare victories against this new medical bugbear. In 2505 she received her second rejuvenation treatment in Australia, and immediately demonstrated her renewed vigour by going to China. There she allied herself with Chang Lin-xian, a cousin of her former mentor, and worked within the massive New Dynasty project. She settled to this remarkably well, and for the first time in her long career enjoyed a lengthy period of stability. She had been married twice before, but neither marriage had lasted. Her relationship with Chang Lin-xian (a man sixty-two years her junior) was never formalized, but she regarded it as the one real marriage of her life.

Last moments of Toshiko Hiroshita, recorded on a headscan which clearly reveals the onset of accelerated age syndrome.

Toshiko underwent a third rejuvenation in 2551 – a year after the death of the twice-rejuvenated last survivor of the original Sapporo cohort at the age of 192 – but this time she was beyond the reach of technological renewal. She remained in poor health until her death at the age of 177 in 2572, but resisted any suggestion that she should opt for voluntary euthanasia. "I have fought all my life," she said, "for the right of every person to have as many years on Earth as science can give them, and I am not going to surrender any part of my own entitlement." She had never exercised her right of replacement, and although several of her ova were on deposit in an Australian gene bank, she left instructions that these were to be destroyed. She knew full well that Malthusian logic demanded of those who accepted the gift of longevity an exceptional moral restraint in the matter of bearing children.

Although she had long since severed any formal tie with the Mitsubishi Organization, the company transported her body back to Kanayama for burial. She had no surviving blood relations, but the Organization still considered her to be a member of their great "family". In his funeral oration the President of Mitsubishi made no attempt to claim her achievements for the tightly-knit clan of Japanese-Australian traditionalists, but offered her instead as the supreme example of the spirit of humanitarian internationalism that so many of his people had adopted in their exile.

CHAPTER THIRTY-ONE

NEW LIFESTYLES

By 2400 almost all manufacturing work was highly automated, no matter where it was carried out. Artificial intelligence had virtually displaced human intelligence in factories. As SAP-systems multiplied, production too gradually became almost fully automated. This meant that forms of employment in the Period of Transformation filled a very different spectrum from earlier centuries. Only a tiny fraction of the workforce was involved in the supervision of basic productive processes.

Employment in construction and demolition

The sector of the world economy that employed the most people was known as the C/D (Construction and Deconstruction) sector. The erection and demolition of buildings and other structures had become such a routine matter that people no longer thought of the artificial environment as something permanent or stable. In the more highly developed nations the buying and selling of houses had become a rarity – when they moved, most people would rent a plot of ground and have a new house built leaving their old one to be demolished. What was true of homes was also true of factories, bridges, museums and airstrips. Where economic circumstances permitted, people took pride in the fact that just as biotechnology had banished dereliction from the natural environment, so it had enabled the artificial environment to be kept scrupulously in order. People had become very aware of "large-scale litter". When they chose to preserve relics of the past they did so with enormous care, but when they chose not to they were ruthless in obliterating every trace.

Construction and demolition were, of course, heavily dependent upon machines, but this was still a labour-intensive industry. The lower forms of artificial intelligence were not well-adapted to it, because construction machines required more intimate and idiosyncratic supervision than other machines could provide. Before 2400 some construction companies had boasted of their ability to provide "one-man houses", whereby the machines in the field were under the direction of a single worker, but in the twenty-fifth century such a claim would have provoked a horrified response. Self-respecting Americans and Europeans demanded sophisticated houses and the assistance of as much human expertise as they could afford. Construction of the average American dwelling required the co-operative efforts of thirty-five people for six or seven days.

Some C/D workers operated from their own homes, supervising their machines by remote control, but this was widely regarded as unsporting and indicative of a lack of pride in one's work. It was conventional for C/D workers to stay on-site, and many adopted a nomadic style of existence during the periods when they worked. Most were undertaking construction and demolition for less than a hundred days a year even if they were "full-timers"; many had other jobs as well as their educational commitments. The average worker was probably "in the bubble" (the plastic living capsules which such workers carried with them as temporary accommodation) for thirty days at a stretch, two or three times a year.

World economy still dependent on marketing

The next largest sector of the world economy in employment terms was the S/M/S (Service, Maintenance and Supply) sector. This included maintenance and repair of the vast mechanical systems on which everyday life depended, elementary personal services, and the distribution of goods to consumers. This sector remained large because of the huge number of employees in the last category, who might from an objective viewpoint have been considered inessential. Consumers ordered virtually all their purchases through the communications network, and most goods were delivered in fully-automated vehicles; the whole business could have been conducted without human middlemen. It was not usual, though, for people to order goods direct from the points of manufacture – that would have meant dealing with an inconveniently large number of sources. Consumers preferred to deal with hypermarkets which stocked almost everything they needed. They went to more specialized sources only for their more idiosyncratic requirements.

Most twenty-sixth-century hypermarkets were vast underground warehouses. They displayed their goods on video, and provided information about them via teletext. Purchases could, of course, be logged automatically and there was no real need for human involvement, but hypermarkets maintained large staffs, most of whom were employed to advise consumers. These workers were well paid to encourage people to spend. Unless spending power was kept hopping smartly from one credit balance to another, there remained the dangers of recession and collapse. The fact that people could now exist fairly comfortably without ever using flexible credit at all had made the private-sector economy even more precarious than it had been in earlier centuries. In the more highly developed nations negotiation between suppliers and consumers remained one of the key tasks and required the sophisticated social skills of human beings rather than the modest talents of artificial intelligence.

Social contact in Education and Entertainment

The E/E (Education and Entertainment) sector also depended heavily on human labour. These two were combined in economic calculations because they were both intimately bound up with the communications network and with the gathering together of people for organized activities.

Some employees in this sector worked in isolation – for example, the all-important indexers whose job was to keep the floods of information pouring into the electronic data stores readily accessible and in order. Most people in the E/E sector, however, worked face-to-face; social contact continued to be valued in education, even though information of every kind could be instantaneously brought to the telescreen. Dialogue and discussion, whether via telescreen or in person, remained an important method of teaching; the learning of practical skills almost always required the presence of advisors.

The "software shufflers"

A large proportion of the workforce was in the P/A (Professional and Administrative) sector, which encompassed the bureaucratic hierarchies of the legal, financial and welfare institutions – the components of the sociopolitical machine, often known in vulgar parlance as "software shufflers" or "chipmonks". (Neither appellation was particularly apt, though the great majority of workers in this sector did have advanced programming skills, and their professional organizations did have certain quasi-monastic features.)

The universal fear of routine

The fact that economists could classify occupations so readily does not imply that the workers themselves could be so easily sorted into sets. In the USA and other well-developed nations it was almost the norm for people to divide their working time between two or more jobs. In addition, people tended to move from one sector to another as they changed jobs, which they did frequently. Job versatility was something of a religion among the people of the hyperdeveloped nations; there was a horror of over-specialization. The justification was a pragmatic one – that the march of progress could easily transform areas of employment within a person's lifetime; but what really underlay the attitude was a less rational aversion to a settled lifestyle. Job versatility was simply one facet of the horror of constancy. The people of this era feared the possible decay of their lives into routine in much the same way that they feared the decay of their bodies into old age.

Serial polygamy and aggregate households

Every aspect of lifestyle reflected this attitude. Even before the advent of child-licensing a system of "serial polygamy", whereby people would move in the course of their lives through a series of temporary intimate relationships, had replaced the ancient nuclear family (mother, father and children living together) almost everywhere. Child-licensing fitted in well with this pattern, and in 2400 households consisting of one man, one woman and their child were extremely rare. Monogamous relationships were common, but any child attached to such a couple was much more likely to be related biologically to only one of the adults than to both. Aggregate households, consisting of between three and six adults and two or three children, were widespread in 2400, and by 2500 this was the norm in all three of the great nations and in many others besides. The supposed advantage of such a household was that it provided children with the companionship formerly offered by siblings in an era when siblings were outlawed, but in fact children were rarely the catalysts for such groupings.

The real reasons for the growing popularity of aggregate households are complex. Clearly it was the smallest group which could maintain its "identity" in the minds of its participants while continually exchanging members with other groups. There was no longer any reason for people to form groups in order to subsist – anyone who wished could live entirely as a hermit. Of course, few chose to do so, because almost everyone felt the need for companionship and intimacy. In the past, groups formed to answer economic and social priorities had, almost incidentally, fulfilled the emotional needs of individuals. The end of the Period of Recovery was the first phase of human history in which people were free to establish whatever social groups they wanted, solely in order to serve their particular personal and psychological needs.

Many social scientists of the twenty-fifth century claimed that the aggregate households of the time were better suited to the requirements of humanity than any other type of group, and there were many trite rejections of the follies of past eras, including Roland Fletcher's contemporary bestseller *The Unnatural Family* (2457). Freedom of

choice does not, however, guarantee that people will make the right choice. We can see now that Fletcher's view of the aggregate household as the ideal primary community was naïve, and merely the arbitrary fashion of the day. Certainly, it gave rise to a great many difficulties. Fiction of the twenty-fifth and twenty-sixth centuries was devoted in prolific measure to the problems of forming, managing and quitting aggregate households. The inordinate complexities of such tales, whether they were literary works like Victoria Bray's tetralogy *The Human Kaleidoscope* (2439-53) or telescreen epics like Vijay Kaul's *Rise of the Tropic Sun* (2496-97), were unprecedented, but the feelings they portrayed were little different in essence from those experienced throughout history.

Longevity provokes fear of boredom

The relationship of this social behaviour to the developing technology of rejuvenation reveals one of the fundamental paradoxes of this period. The great majority of people in the richer nations were now striving for what they called "multidimensionality": variety in

London *c.* 2475: St Paul's, built by the Englishman Wren in the seventeenth century, survives to this day; but the zenith-reacher (ZR) blocks are long gone. Notice the quaint robo-floater, cruising the night-sky. These were taxis that plied the skies of major cities looking for fares, their auto-brains programmed to receive a jolt of pleasure every time they got a fare. In quiet periods they could be seen bumping and jostling each other for the pleasure of giving a lift to the humans waiting below.

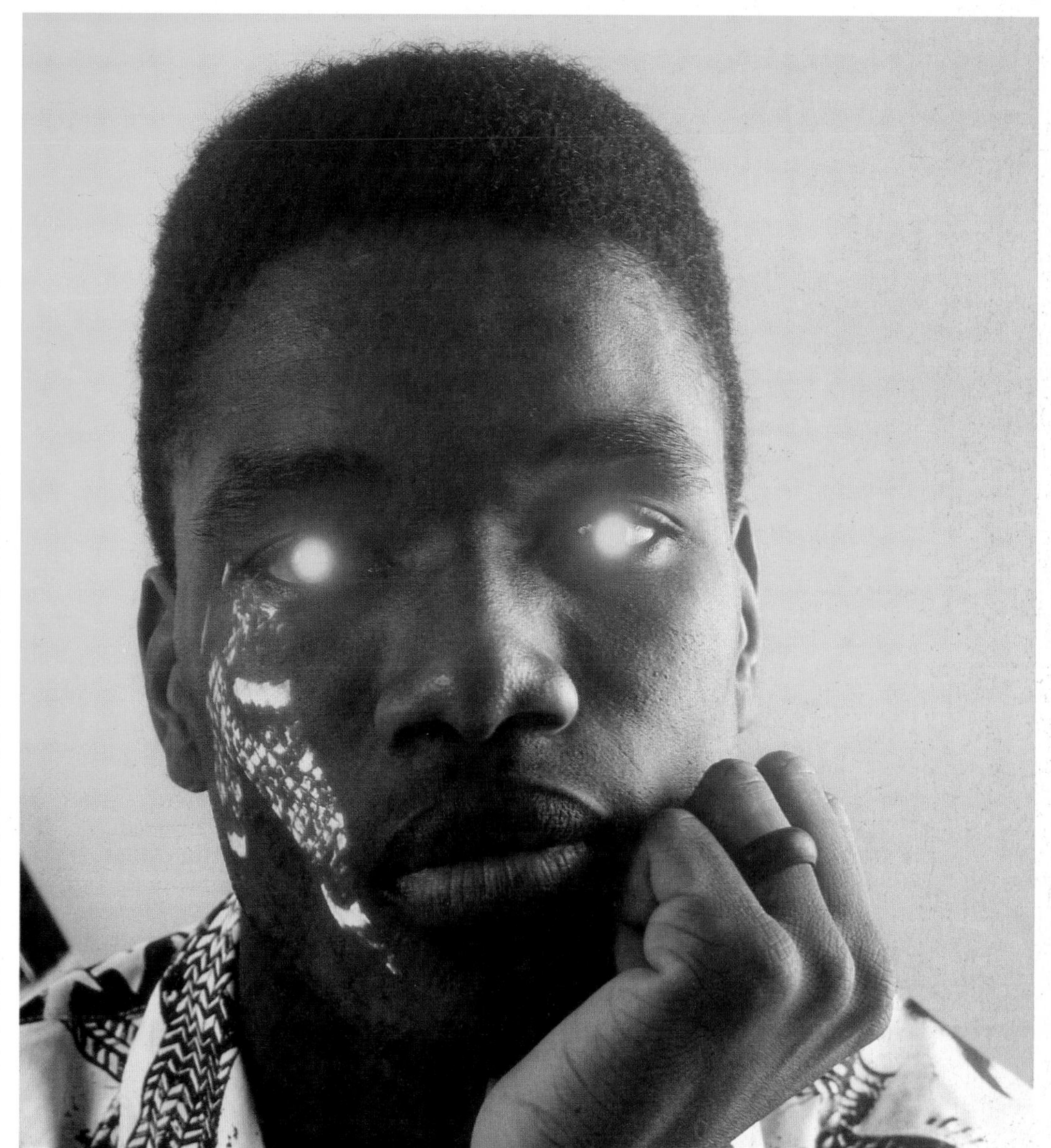

Individually engineered skin became fashionable in the 2460s. Here, taken from a family video archive, is Winthrop Davis after his graduation ceremony at UCLA in 2456. The voice over records that Winthrop had tactile scales with matching switch on/switch off glowing irises specially fitted for the occasion.

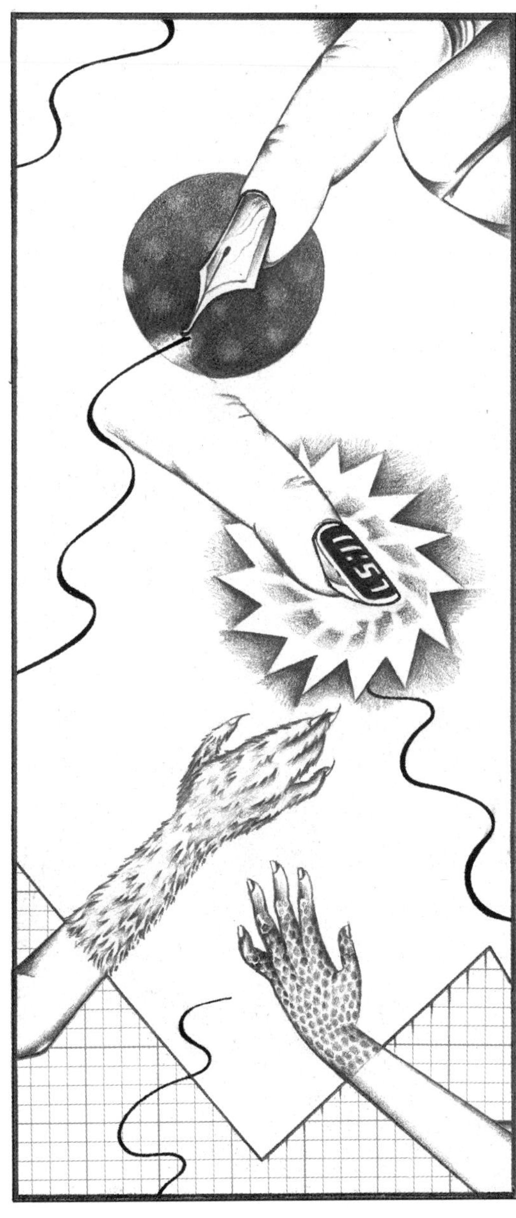

The Genetix cosmetic brochure for spring 2462 featuring the fingerpen, implant timepieces, retractable tiger claws, fur and scales.

their work, in their leisure, in their intimate relationships, and in themselves. They were restless in every sense of the word, moving from place to place and changing their personalities almost as often as they changed their clothes. They wanted to become social chameleons, able to blend with any background that fortune might provide.

Their attitude to the prospect of living for twice as many years – ultimately, perhaps, for *many* times as many years – was a cause of this general restlessness. Only versatility and variety, they believed, could make longevity bearable. They could point to an abundance of speculative fiction dealing with the prospect of immortality, whose interminably repeated message was that eternal life would be boring – burdensomely, hideously, intolerably boring. The social elite of the twenty-fifth century regarded their ceaseless pursuit of variety as a necessary antidote to their innate capacity for ennui.

Although they seem strange, perverse even, the attitudes of the twenty-fifth century had their own peculiar coherence. When we look at the novels and screen-dramas of the period it is easy to conclude that people found life desperately problematic and unsatisfying, but fiction always tends to deal with anxiety; there were probably a great many more contented folk than we imagine.

"Self-cultivation" for the new avant garde

The quest for "multidimensionality" was only one of the personal preoccupations of the Period of Transformation. As the twenty-sixth century progressed that keyword went out of fashion to be replaced by the jargon of "self-cultivation". The determination to live a varied existence is itself a form of self-cultivation, and one can find references to "cultivated" individuals in the literature of much earlier periods of history; but in the twenty-sixth century self-cultivation became more specific in its meaning.

An extensive use of "cosmetic biotechnology" for the adjustment of physical appearance was commonplace before 2400. Among the social élite, for more than three centuries no one had been fat, small or ugly (save, occasionally, for eccentric reasons). There had, of course, been changes of fashion in cosmetic biotechnology, but these had been mere ripples concerning skin-colour, hair-colour, breast-size and the like. No cosmetically-altered man or woman of the year 2400 would have looked out of place in twentieth-century New York. After 2450, however, a new *avant-garde* appeared, dedicated to more extravagant experiments in cosmetic engineering.

It began with skin – with the incorporation of metallic sheens, elaborate patterns, fur and scales. This was no mere rediscovery of the ancient art of tattooing and its associated aesthetics. Twenty-fifth-century biotechnologists had developed highly sophisticated techniques for the transformation of superficial tissues, and the range of possibilities was enormous. Trend-setters of the 2460s kept their cash, credit cards and cannabis derivatives in personal "kangaroo pouches" grafted into their arms or torso, and in extreme cases sported entire *trompe-l'oeil* suits of clothes which on close inspection proved to be the wearer's own skin. More practical was the popular retractable pen, built into the owner/wearer's index finger; the underworld version of this fad was a set of razor-sharp knives which popped out like tiger claws. The fashion had as much to do with tactile sensations as visual ones, and early members of this *avant-garde* proclaimed loudly that it could add an entire new dimension to the sensations of love-making. The words "new dimension" acted like a magnet.

It was not long before this play with skin-texture went a stage further, with new interest being taken in cyborgization, the building of mechanical systems into the human body, and vice versa. It had been possible for several centuries to build linkages between machines and human nervous systems via organometallic synapses. (These artificial nerves contained no iron but were jokingly known as "nerves of steel".) There had been many experiments in building artificial synapses into the limbs of humans so that they could plug themselves into machines and transmit commands direct from brain to machine via the motor nerves. For a decade at the end of the twenty-second century bionic scientists had foreseen a rosy future for this technique, but it had not materialized, simply because there was very little to be gained by linking machines directly to people's brains instead of letting their fingers manipulate keyboards. In fact, reasonably conclusive research at the University of Heidelberg proved that skilled fingers manipulating controls were more efficient than cyborg connections.

Cyborgized pleasure machines

In the late twenty-fifth century, though, bionic science became as lively an area of expertise as it had been in the brief years before technologies of tissue-regeneration had made artificial limbs and organs redundant. Self-cultivation was now extended to include artificial synaptic interfaces tastefully built in to cosmetically-patterned skin. Again, the leaders of this *avant-garde* spoke with unrestrained enthusiasm about the wonderful sensations to be gained by integrating oneself with various kinds of machines. The trend began with cars and looms, but before 2500 it had expanded to more bizarre adventures in man/machine "symbiosis". Numerous machines were manufactured for no purpose other than to link up with human nervous systems and provide new sensations. There was a plethora of "sex machines" for use by one person, couples or whole groups. The first of the so-called "psychedelic synthesizers", designed to provide a range of pleasurable hallucinations, appeared in the USA in 2487, reputedly invented by one Heinrich Traumer (an obvious pseudonym). For the first time there was a serious clash between the promoters of the new *avant-garde* and the Ethics Committees which were responsible for regulating human applications of biotechnology. Until now the Committees had turned a blind eye to what they regarded as harmless folly, but the psychedelic synthesizer was too much for them and was banned as a danger to health and sanity. It is difficult to estimate exactly how many deaths were caused by psychedelic synthesizers, but fatalities from the use of all machines designed solely to transmit electric charges into the human brain and body certainly added up to tens of thousands and many more suffered permanent disability.

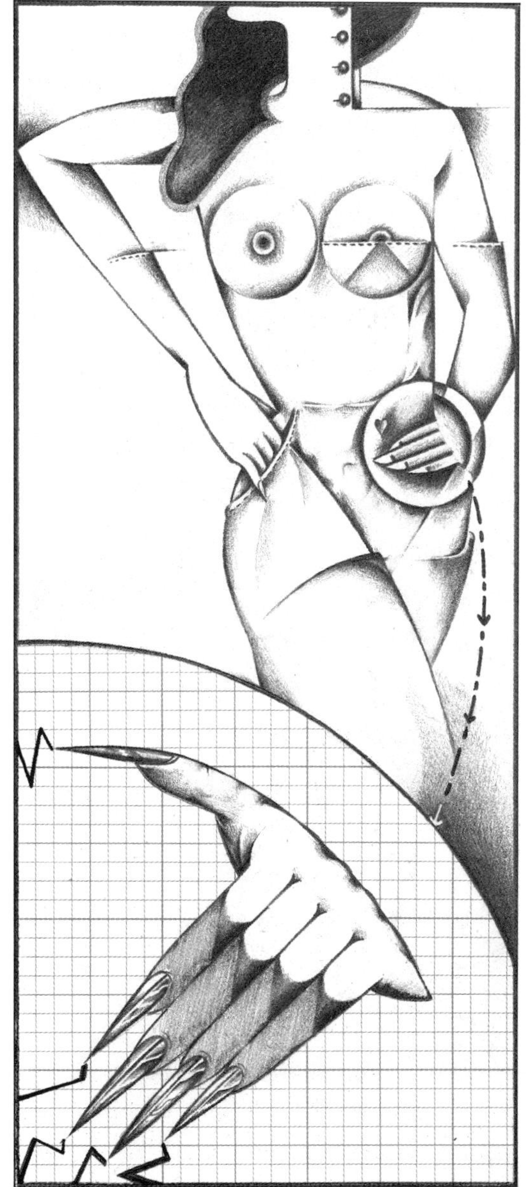

Genetix brochure, Christmas 2462, inviting the fashion-conscious to grow storage pouches, trompe l'oeil skin and protective talons.

The invisible avant-garde

Mention should be made here of the faintly ludicrous "invisible *avant-garde*" who had their senses subtly modified. A little work on the eyes allowed them to see further into the ultra-violet and infra-red than normal people (sometimes causing long-term retinal damage); cyborg implants could widen the frequency-range of hearing still more dramatically. "Silent symphonies" would throb with ultrasonic subtlety, appreciated only by the fiercely proud lite. Paintings and synthetapes in the school of Nonspectral Art appeared featureless – plain red or violet-bluish – to unmodified eyes. Exactly how many enthusiasts chose to extend their senses thus? The answer remains blurred by what was already known as the "Emperor's New Clothes Effect": people would praise subtleties they were incapable of seeing, and some critics insisted that unseen or unheard details still had their own validity.

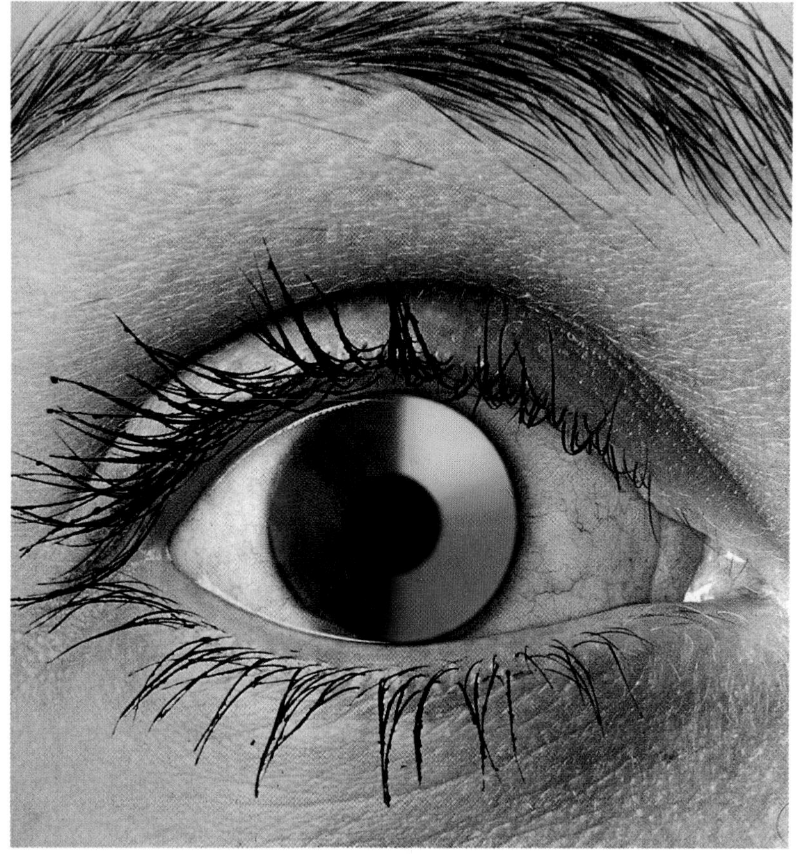

The rainbow-eye, a vital accessory for fashion followers of 2485, was a little disconcerting to watch for long. Usually the colours rotated slowly around the iris; but the wearer could speed them up.

By 2520 a backlash had set in against the *avant-garde,* and there was a counter-movement which foreswore the kinds of cosmetic biotechnology that had been commonly accepted for centuries. These "new Stoics" stood at one end of a well-filled spectrum which extended all the way to the champions of "total potential", who were determined to grasp as much of the gamut of potential human experience as they could cram into their lives. In spite of rejuvenation technology, total potential killed a great many people prematurely.

Sexual role reversal

It is difficult to say where the "centre" of this spectrum lay. Certainly in the richer nations by 2540 physical appearance was a major status symbol, second only to a person's house or houses. People used their epidermal adornment (including artificial synapses) as a signal of their financial means and cultural philosophy. Significantly, men took this more seriously than women. By now the establishment of child-licensing had brought about a role reversal between the sexes. Females no longer went in for extensive adornment in order to be attractive to male protectors. It was now the male who had to exaggerate his attractiveness, because he needed a co-operative female if he was to exercise his right of replacement. The Stoicism, insofar as it became a social movement, was very largely a female affair; while, according to several contemporary commentators, the self-destructive fringe of the total potential cult (which was almost exclusively a male preserve) represented a reaction to the increasing probability that a man would not be able to persuade any woman to bear a child on his behalf.

CHAPTER THIRTY-TWO

CITIES AND NATIONS UNDER ATTACK

The world's great cities, save for those which were flooded or bombed in the twenty-first century, survived – and many flourished – until well into the twenty-sixth century. The spread of the communications networks and the death of the commuter did not cause the widely anticipated disintegration of urban life. On the contrary, the dwindling of private transport consolidated the cities and inhibited the development of far-flung communities. Later on, in the Period of Recovery, the severity of land-use policies prevented any large-scale exodus from metropolitan areas. Only the large countries – the USA, the USSR and Australia – experienced a movement away from cities before 2500, and in the last case this emigration was balanced by immigration to urban centres from other nations.

Death of the city

In the course of the Period of Transformation, however, the long-heralded change finally came. The spread of artificial photosynthesis made agricultural activity much more economical in terms of land. The sophistication of building techniques, the maturation of the information networks and the constant quest for novelty combined to make an end of the huddling places where human herds had sheltered for thousands of years.

The great prophet and philosopher of "decivilization" in the USA was James Elvey, a black Baptist minister from Atlanta who mixed the ailing religious tradition of his people with a thoroughly modern ecological mysticism. He came from one of the last strongholds of Christian faith and, even here, Christianity was under severe test until Elvey revived the ancient evangelical method and took his new revelation to the masses. He was

Antinationalists and proponents of decivilisation of the late twenty-fifth century: Alkadi Nisreen, leader of the Indian sub-continent; José Araguex, radical anti-nationalist leader; Julius Luther King in the regalia of a disciple of James Elvey carrying his famous "blessing rod"; Dwidar Saad, antinationalist, known as the "Man with two brains" because of the cyborgised additions to his skull.

a tremendous showman. Indeed his detractors observed cynically that he was living proof that religion in America had become nothing more than a quaint backwater of the entertainment industry. But many people were deeply impressed by the sermons of his peak years, from 2468 to 2484.

James Elvey's creed of decivilization
Elvey presented the flight from the American cities as a crucial step in the spiritual development of the nation. For him, the cities symbolized many evil aspects of the past, especially oppression and injustice, and America was "ploughing under" its cities in order to put an end to those evils and enter a new era of peace, goodwill and justice. Although America was to become a *new* Eden, there was much nostalgia in his mythology – images of the ancient "unspoiled" America of "pre-frontier days" were cleverly built in to his speeches. Despite the eccentricity of some of his ideas he played a crucial part in the political success of Julius Luther King. King's "New American Dream" owed a lot to Elvey, and the presidential election of 2484 was, in a sense, the culmination of Elvey's ministry. Although he continued his work until his death from an inoperable deep-brain tumour in 2495, his crusade lost its force – displaced by the political schemes of the King administration.

Elvey's own creed never spilled over into other nations, but his example helped to persuade others to make decivilization a political cause. An important example is Alkadi Nisreen, who became a charismatic leader in the Indian subcontinent between 2475 and 2500, with his impassioned denunciation of the "seven cities of shame" that stretched in a twisted chain from Karachi to Rangoon.

Demands for the abolition of nations
There was a strong historical link between the decivilization movement and the antinationalist crusades of the twenty-sixth century. This can be seen in some of Elvey's more extravagant sermons, which made much of the image of a demolished New York. He depicted the death of New York City as a symbol of the destruction of the American State. This was never spelled out – and was, of course, greatly played down by Julius Luther King – but Elvey certainly believed that the injustices of the past should be laid at the door of the State, of which the cities were merely a symbol. Several of Elvey's successors switched their attack away from the cities (which were steadily emptying anyway) and began to criticize the existence of the USA itself, claiming that it was time to puncture the myth that Congress could ever truly represent the people, or ever had.

There was probably no nation on Earth which boasted so freely of its democratic traditions as the USA. Its statesmen had always called it the land of the free, but even a superficial study of its history revealed that (as with every other nation in the world) its governing élite had never been statistically representative of its people. It had elected black and Hispanic presidents, but an analysis of the Senate or the House of Representatives, over any period of time, showed that American politics had always been dominated by whites. The same was true of the USSR and Australia, while the political élites in India and China were just as easily identified as racial groups. In past centuries those who had considered themselves under-represented called for reform *within* nations. In the twenty-fifth and twenty-sixth centuries more and more spokesmen for "the power-deprived" began to call for the abolition of nations, demanding direct representation at international level, in a new, reformed UN.

States without boundaries
The antinationalist movement was not simply seeking a World State. Indeed, many leaders of the movement, including José Araguex and Dwidar Saad, stated bluntly that a World State which simply reproduced the iniquities of the nation-states on a huge scale would be a still worse abomination. Araguex, Saad and other radicals wanted to establish the right of individuals to shape their own political communities by voluntary association, with no regard for "lines on the map": to create, in short, states without boundaries. They argued that just as circumstances now permitted the break-up of the cities, so the time had come for the dissociation of political communities from geographical areas. They scathingly referred to "the eccentric chains of historical accidents which led to the boundaries that have divided true political communities since the twentieth century". It was, said Araguex in 2499, "time to rethink the map of the world".

Araguex and Saad were widely considered to be romantic anarchists, with no real political programme at all. There was, indeed, some uncertainty about their proposals, and they tended to retreat into destructive criticism of the *status quo* when asked what the map might look like after Araguex had rethought it. However, antinationalism attracted substantial numbers of converts who united their varied voices in a call for reform. This reflected widespread dissatisfaction with the organization of international politics. Over the years the more important the UN had become, the more resentments were felt among its member nations. Some very heavily-populated nations considered that they were not adequately represented – in particular India and China, which harboured more than a third of the world's populace but had nothing like a third of the UN's power. On the other hand, tiny nations like Vanuatu and Trinidad/Tobago felt ignored by the larger nations and were increasingly desperate to gain greater consideration and recognition.

While the governments of India and China had no desire to abolish their own power-structures, they sympathized with some of the antinationalist arguments, and supported many of their demands for "representative voices" in the world community. The governments of the three superpowers and the richer European nations found themselves under pressure within and without to justify their warrant to wield the power and influence they had inherited from an older and very different world.

Although the question of appropriate representation was raised continually, there were too many vested interests pulling in different directions within the UN Council for any settlement to be reached. When the colonies in space brought the problem of *their* status to the UN Council Chamber they found a position of stalemate surrounded by such confusion that they were hardly able to air their grievances. It was almost universally admitted that the status quo was irrational and unjust, but the weight of historical inertia was too great to permit much change.

Small nations unite

The only progress made in the twenty-sixth century was the union of several groups of smaller nations. Haiti and the Dominican Republic were fused into the new nation of Hispaniola in 2562, and in 2589 Hispaniola joined Cuba, Jamaica and other island nations in the Caribbean Confederacy. Only Trinidad/Tobago and Grenada remained aloof.

In Africa Western Sahara had been virtually united with Mauretania since the days of the ingenious President Calcar, and the other Saharan nations were joined in a loose "economic alliance". Many of the Tribal Republics created in the aftermath of the South African Revolution in the twenty-first century were reunited in 2600 as the Kalahari Republic, but an ambitious attempt by President Umundi of Zaire to create an African superpower stretching from the Sahara to the Cape of Good Hope failed. However, Zaire did absorb Rwanda, Burundi, the Congo, Gabon and Guinea to consolidate its status as the most influential African power.

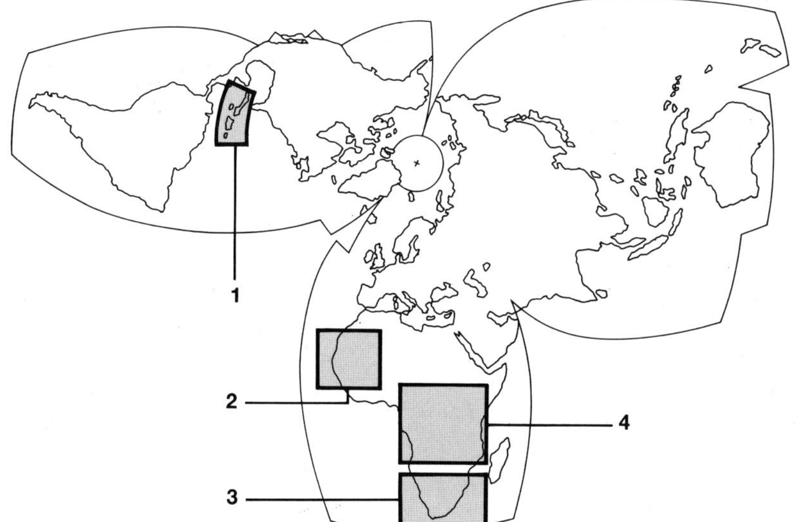

The unification of small nations
1 Caribbean Confederacy (2589): Hispaniola, Cuba, Jamaica and other islands.
2 Saharan nations united in unofficial economic alliance.
3 Kalahari Republic (2600): union of nine Tribal Republics.
4 Zaire after colonialist expansion (2612).

Internationalism becomes commonplace

None of these changes had much influence on the argument about representation, although they suggest a declining regard for national boundaries. The important change in the significance of national boundaries had happened much earlier, in the twenty-first and twenty-second centuries, when the spread of the communications networks began to erode intercultural enmity. By the time the antinationalist movement became vociferous, hostilities between countries had evaporated although the countries still existed by popular consent. James Elvey's hope that the death of the cities would lead to the end of oppression was over-optimistic, but not entirely unfounded.

CHAPTER THIRTY-THREE

THE ARTIFICIAL ECOSPHERE

The social movements that we have discussed typify the troubles and anxieties of the Period of Transformation, but like the Period of Recovery this was basically an era of optimism. By 2400 the world community had secured the goals that it had set for itself in 2180. As a result it lost some of its impetus and sense of direction, but it retained confidence in its own abilities. Nowhere was this more obvious than in the sphere of ecological planning, where great schemes like the reclamation of the world's deserts had made spectacular progress, and where equally grandiose projects were under discussion.

Even among the ecological planners, however, there was not the sense of common purpose that had been so evident in the twenty-third century. There had always been a spectrum of opinion represented on the UN's influential Land Use Committee (LUC), but in the twenty-third and twenty-fourth centuries the radical green-fringer had been content to keep a rein on what John Foden described as his "Edenic mysticism". After 2400, with so much achieved, the green radicals began to see themselves as a force for change and to push their ideas. Another faction, the self-styled Continental Engineers, also emerged with radical plans, beginning with the damming of the Strait of Gibraltar.*

Juliette Gautier's Garden Earth

These extreme ideologies caused such turbulence in the LUC that the moderates were forced to articulate their own philosophy with great cogency. This eventually became known as the "Garden Earth" ideology, after the title of a book published in 2470 by Juliette Gautier, who was to become the dominating force of the LUC between 2478 and 2519, and chairwoman for the last fifteen years of that period. With the exception of John Foden and Juliette Gautier very few leaders of the LUC ever attained world celebrity. The chairmen wielded great power, yet most of them remained almost anonymous. In his classic study of *Authority and Hierarchy* (2407) the sociologist V. V. Andreski observed that the contemporary UN bore a much greater resemblance to the medieval Papacy than to any secular parliament. He went on to say that if the UN Secretary-General could be regarded, by analogy, as sitting on the papal throne, then the Chairman of the LUC had a position not unlike that of the seventeenth- and eighteenth-century "black popes" – the leaders of the Jesuits.

There was, indeed, something Jesuitical about the UN ecologists of the Period of Transformation. They were zealous reformers, frequently ascetic in their habits and temperaments, with a strong interest in moral and ideological education. In their own minds, at least, they were the inheritors of a noble tradition, and were the saviours of the Earth. Many believed that it was their duty to set an example to mankind, demonstrating the errors of materialism so that paradise might one day be built on Earth. The garden metaphors which Juliette Gautier and others persistently evoked were mostly obvious and trite, but they had a power of the kind once possessed by ideas in religious mythology.

The essence of the Garden Earth approach to ecological planning was an appropriate balance between utility and aesthetics. In previous centuries necessity had obscured aesthetic considerations almost completely, although the planners had always done everything possible to preserve large tracts of wilderness and protect natural species from extinction. Now that the world's food supply was secured, and its population declining, the priorities changed. The gradual replacement of traditional agriculture by artificial photosynthesis, and the large-scale cultivation of the sea, released more land for new uses, and made it unnecessary to turn the reclaimed deserts into grain-fields. The scope of the planners was thereby enhanced.

The "new wilderness policy"

Juliette Gautier put enormous energy into promoting the "new wilderness policy", a scheme that encouraged governments to set aside large tracts of land so that species kept only in captivity or in seed-banks could be returned to the wild. The description of these new national parks as wildernesses was somewhat misleading, because constant interference and control were needed to sustain the equilibrium of their ecosystems. Many species had to be as zealously protected and nurtured in the "wild" as they had been in confinement. Those areas of "old wilderness" that had never been brought under human control were now left alone. The climatic changes caused by ecological engineering on a world scale had, of course, affected these places – just like everywhere else. They underwent drastic changes in the third millennium in other respects, but nature was allowed to take its course.

Ecofollies

It is perhaps unjust that the Garden Earth enthusiasts are remembered more for their

*Because more water evaporates from the Mediterranean than flows into it from its rivers, such a dam would have had the effect of lowering the level of the sea and increasing the land surface of southern Europe and North Africa.

The tiger rose that won the 2525 Chelsea Flower Show. Rules for engineered plants were very strict and deliberately ultra-conservative. Aesthetics were the only considerations: gimmicks of other kinds – flowers with claws for example – won no prizes.

follies and eccentricities than for their careful and substantial management of the ecosphere. Their small-scale enterprises, which permitted more extravagant and intensive ecological design, attracted constant attention from tourists and television cameramen. Few people appreciated the importance or the technical difficulties of the Great Australian Canal System, but many were ready to marvel at the Hanging Gardens of New Babylon at Toowoomba. To the general public the New Forests of Karakorum looked much like other forests and were therefore interesting, but the multicoloured lichen-covered mountain of Tienshui was a unique work of art constantly besieged by sightseers. The battle between engineers in Canada and New Zealand to construct the most spectacular waterfall in the world had a hint of the absurd about it even in its own day, but it was nonetheless noteworthy.

The poor grow fat and the weather grows calm

By 2500 the world food glut was such that crops were being left to rot in cultivated fields, and there was a possibility of the "new wilderness" emerging out of sheer neglect. The world's poor grew fat because their food credit entitled them to more than they could eat, while lack of flexible credit denied them both alternative pleasures and the medical care that would have saved them from obesity despite their diet. In the meantime, the prolific sowing of engineered kelps in deep water had begun to affect the great ocean currents and the surge of the tides; the world's climate was calmed and soothed by human endeavour even beyond the placidity that it had assumed when the greenhouse crisis ended. Although such phenomena as hurricanes and monsoons still occurred, they were now far less disruptive. By 2525 the LUC had achieved the dramatic cuts in world food production necessary to restore equilibrium, and had done much to introduce a proper balance into the geographical pattern of production. Even the least favoured nations could supply their own needs, and the most-favoured were no longer trying to export on such a vast scale.

Quasi-godlike exercises in creation

Inevitably, the ambitions of the controllers of the ecosystem grew. It was natural that people who became expert in balancing and maintaining complex combinations of natural species should begin to think about assembling whole ecosystems of genetically-engineered species: quasi-godlike exercises in creation. The green radicals on the LUC, who mostly professed some form of reverence for "Nature", were usually bitterly opposed to such projects, but there was no way of drawing a defensible line between such displays as the Hanging Gardens of New Babylon and the parks filled with genetically-engineered plants that began to appear in Australia in the 2530s. After all, gardeners had always used artificially-created plants even when the only means to such creation was careful selective breeding.

Juliette Gautier's successor, Ora Hummadi, gave his blessing to the Ecosystemic Creationists in 2532 when he persuaded the Federated States of Micronesia to surrender a dozen Pacific islets to scientists, so that they might show what they could accomplish.

Genetic art

Most of those involved in these projects had been dabbling in aesthetic genetic engineering for some years, often under the stern gaze of a disapproving public. Many had achieved dramatic transformations of flowering plants and invertebrate animals, but they had suffered the incomprehension often accorded to artists working in new media: what they were doing was considered vaguely improper and inherently repulsive. Just as, in earlier centuries, Paris had attracted *avant-garde* painters, Sydney became the adopted "home" of many of these genetic artists, and a Great Exhibition was mounted there in 2505. Film of the exhibits has been preserved and modern viewers can find much therein that is spectacularly beautiful, given the relatively primitive techniques. In 2505, however, the exhibition attracted far fewer visitors than it deserved, and exhibits were vandalized. One of the best of the aquaria was smashed on the second day, causing extensive secondary damage and drenching a score of bystanders.

The Creationists' "magic islands"

The "magic islands" of the Creationists were not built quickly or cheaply; but while the artists laboured the tide of opinion turned gradually in their favour. The Institute of Genetic Art in Sydney continued to hold exhibitions, and familiarity gradually bred content. By 2540 film crews were visiting the Creationists' islands occasionally to record the extremely slow progress. Observers quickly learned not to ask when the work would be finished. Questioners were advised to inquire instead when the projects might properly begin.

Not until 2580 were tourists allowed on any of the islands, and idle sightseers were never permitted to land on some of the more ambitious microworlds. Visitors were able to walk through an extensive labyrinth of hides on Nukuoro Atoll where Baumgarten and Klasinski showed off their magnificent neosaurians; but Jaggard and Raintree considered their giant insects of Bikini too delicate to be exposed to large numbers of visitors. Ironically, the whole set of islands was dramatically upstaged in 2610 when a huge team of Chinese scientists, which had been labouring for three generations, finally put on display the Imperial Dragons of Sinkiang. The Ecosystemic Creationists claimed that the Chinese were not playing the game – the dragons were not part of a balanced ecosystem – but their protests carried weight only with purists. The dragons were more colourful and more fabulous than Baumgarten and Klasinski's tyrannosaurs and brontosaurs, even if they did live on a special SAP-produced feed.

New life inside an asteroid

By this time a team of Russian genetic engineers were contesting Australia's lead in the genetic arts. They formed the Lysenko Institute for the purpose of hollowing out an asteroid and creating within it a new life-system which would stretch the capabilities of DNA to its limits. They spoke of "alternative meiosis" and "chromosomal versatility", and aimed to create a new genetic system that would be capable of evolution by the inheritance of acquired characteristics. In 2622 the Politburo censored the Lysenko Institute for publicizing past episodes which had been officially de-emphasized in the history books, but even within the USSR this was widely regarded as a touch of outmoded jingoism. In any case, a team of genetic scientists headed by Hu and Hora eventually left Earth in 2648 to begin the project.

Creationists keep genetic research alive

From 2550 onwards the Creationists and other genetic artists were the pioneers in biotechnological research. Utilitarian and commercial bioengineers no longer had any incentive to push back the frontiers of discovery. The Creationists, on the other hand, wanted to explore the limits of genetic engineering, and see just how far they could develop their technical finesse. For a hundred years the Creationists maintained progress in a discipline which might otherwise have stagnated for lack of demand. The refinements achieved by the Creationists were generally regarded as superfluous in their own time, but there would come a day when their importance would be very clear.

Pleasant "oases" in the Antarctic

While the Creationists made spectacular achievements which were of little use at the time, numerous other ecologists were steadily improving the environment in almost every part of the world. One of their projects caught the imagination of the people of the twenty-sixth century and still stands out: the Antarctic Improvement Scheme launched by Hothi Sohan Singh, who was chairman of the LUC from 2536 until 2551.

When people spoke of the Amazon rain forest as "the last great wilderness" (as they often did in Juliette Gautier's time), they were content to overlook the fact that Earth contained an entire wasted continent beneath the Antarctic ice. Even the Continental Engineers, with their dreams of damming the Strait of Gibraltar and the Bering Strait, never suggested that Antarctica be developed. The reason was simple. Knowing full well the devastating effects of a modest melting of the polar ice, no one was prepared to contemplate getting rid of the entire Antarctic ice-cap. Within the cycle of the usual seasonal variations the ice-caps had been stable since the middle of the twenty-third century, and everyone liked it that way.

Hothi Sohan Singh was in favour of keeping the Antarctic ice in the Antarctic, but he argued that there was no reason why it should not be rearranged slightly. He maintained that some of the potential of the neglected continent could be exploited without any risk at all: pleasant "oases" could easily be created in the desert of ice.

UN to move to Antarctica

Antarctica had never been completely ignored, even in the Period of Crisis. Indeed, the energy-starvation of that period had led several oil companies to brave the extreme conditions. A good deal of oil had been mined there, especially from the Ellsworth Land fields, between 2059 and 2138.

The UN's renewed interest in Antarctica in the 2540s was due to its being the "continent without nations". Centuries earlier, certain sectors had been assigned to nations as dependencies or protectorates, but as the UN had extended its dominion over the sea it had also – almost without anyone noticing, and certainly without anyone caring – inherited the fiefdom of Antarctica. Now the UN wanted to make part of Antarctica habitable, and comfortably so, in order to move its headquarters there. Antarctica was to be the first genuinely international territory. This was seen by some as a sop to antinationalist feeling, but it had little to do with antinationalism as such; it had much more to do with old-fashioned UN internationalism. Significantly, the lead was given by the LUC, and not the UN Council.

Like the Creationists, Hothi Sohan Singh did not realize his dream quickly or cheaply. He died in 2567 (despite rejuvenation he only lived to be 108) when work had barely begun at several locations, the most important being around Mount Erebus and at the South Pole itself. Amundsen City was not finally opened to immigrants until 2639, and for some years after that it was little more than a tourist centre whose domes and ice-tunnels became an eccentric playground. Still, the intention to move UN Headquarters to Amundsen City remained, and the first steps had been taken by 2650.

New volcano beneath Indian Ocean

It was not merely by what they built that the world's ecological planners demonstrated their worth in the Period of Transformation, and we cannot close this chapter without recording an incident which could so easily have become the major disaster of the period. In 2580 a rupture of the Earth's crust occurred deep beneath the Indian Ocean, a thousand kilometres north of Amsterdam Island. Although there was no land close to this new underwater volcano, the effects would have been catastrophic in earlier days. The warming of the ocean water disrupted the normally placid weather pattern, and brought freak conditions of drought to Madagascar and the African mainland. The vast sea-farming enterprises west of Australia were hard hit as the phytoplankton balance was thrown out. For the first time in nearly a century significant outbreaks of "rogue algae" attacked the sea-fields, and large areas of ocean surface became clogged with dead and rotting kelp. Food had to be shipped into southern Africa, and emergency irrigation works put in hand, but, despite this, the lives of the people in the tribal republics were, in real terms, hardly affected.*

Ecosphere in good repair?

Indeed, less disquiet was aroused by this incident than by the new virus disease that appeared in Ethiopia a few years later. The virus had such a short incubation period that it spread very rapidly, reaching distant parts of the world within a matter of days. But only in Africa did it lead to a significant number of deaths. Here again, the UN agencies proved their ability to respond to unexpected crisis, and managed to wipe out the disease within a decade. The fact that there was a substantial death-toll, mostly of infants less than two years old, led some critics to allege that the UN's guarantee of basic medical care for all could not be fully backed up. It is clear that these grousers were setting an impossibly high standard. Any unbiased observer, examining the way that the UN kept its vast house – the ecosphere itself – in such good order, would have been forced to the conclusion that this was one machine of government which functioned very well indeed.

*The twenty-eighth-century historians Wyhowski and Elliott tried to show that the subsequent union of smaller states into the Kalahari Republic was caused by the political squabbles over food imports in the 2580s, but as we have argued elsewhere their case seems weak.

Tyrannosaurus Rex, created for a life on Nukuoro Atoll in the Pacific, differed from its prehistoric forebear by being gentle, if clumsy, and a vegetarian. Baumgarten and Klasinski recreated 47 species of dinosaur and pterosaur, all of whom lived harmoniously together surviving on natural and biological vegetables.

CHAPTER THIRTY-FOUR

THE CONQUEST OF THE SOLAR SYSTEM

In space, as we have said, the largely unadapted humanity of 2400-2600 tended to lead a slightly sickly life, except in the big settlements which offered a reasonable level of natural or artificial gravity: Mars and Mercury, the Moon and other major moons, the best-established of the spinning microworlds. By a natural historical shorthand, it is widely believed that little real development of the solar system took place before space-adapted humans (ETs – see Chapters Thirty-five and Thirty-six) were well established, in the later twenty-seventh century. (Even more naturally, this version of events is popular among the spacefolk of today.) In fact, much was achieved by unaltered *Homo sapiens* – unfitted for long periods of free-fall, maybe, but carrying on regardless. As the notorious Geoffrey Fourmyle put it: "So it's killing me! Down Earthside the boredom would kill me and you'd never say a word; out here the Belt and the cosmics are killing me but I'm having fun, and that's what you neopuritans can't stand . . .".

Geoffrey Fourmyle, sketched by the robot artist Vango 38. This was one of the preliminary sketches for the children's synthetape feature *A Crack in Space.*

The cracking of Ceres

What drove such men on to their achievements? Beyond all the rhetoric and charisma of space messiahs was the patent fact that in space and only there, heroic achievements were possible – and possible without the well-meant but maddening delays of the UN Ethics Committee. One such "moment of greatness" was the cracking of Ceres by the *High Space* pioneer microworld, in 2433.

Ceres was then the largest asteroid of the Belt: a bare and desolate rock, at that time too large at 760 km radius to be conveniently hollowed out as a microworld, but too small to exert a healthy gravitational pull – about one-eighteenth of Earth's gravity was all. Its largely inaccessible mass, more than 10^{18} tons, attracted Captain Fourmyle and the *High Space* directorate. They sank deep shafts, hazarded their entire stock of fusion bombs intended for five years' asteroid-mining, and blew Ceres apart. In the expanding shell of massive debris there were rich pickings for the "miners" and others, of iron, nickel and chemically bound oxygen in particular – Fourmyle's gamble had paid off, and as a bonus his name flared into notoriety.

The greening of the Moon worried no one except, paradoxically, a few ultra-green cranks, but the cracking of Ceres caused a monumental commotion at the UN. For the first time, the greys ringingly said, humanity had made its majestic mark beyond Earth's orbit – with an unparalleled act of wanton destruction, retorted the greens. A perfectly good piece of cosmic real estate, familiar in our skies since 1801, historically important as the first asteroid ever discovered, had been wiped out! The reaction was perhaps exaggerated – few but the cataloguers of the asteroids had any real interest in the almost invisibly tiny light-point now no longer to be seen in the sky – but as a precedent Fourmyle's action was alarming. The UN made loud disapproving noises, solemnly condemned a scheme (somewhat far-fetched at the time) to crack Mercury similarly with the chaos bomb, and made some efforts to declare certain Frontier Zone features "special" and inviolate. This was more a pious hope than an iron law: it did, however, preserve the moons of Mars, so spectacular from the planet's surface, but such temptingly convenient sources of mass from close orbit.

The quest for mass

Mass and energy were everywhere the key to space. Energy could be had freely from the Sun if one did not stray too far away; otherwise, it could be obtained by reshuffling mass, as when light elements are combined in the cold-fusion process. Mass, though, was hard to find in space. So much of it had clumped together into stars or planets, too hot or too sunken in their own gravity wells for economic mining. The figures still surprise many planet-dwellers: the Sun aside, more than 70 per cent of the mass of the solar system is locked up in one huge, uncompromising lump called Jupiter, and the 70 per cent rises to over 99 per cent if we add the equally awkward gas-giants Saturn, Uranus and Neptune.

By the time of the Period of Transformation the territorial instincts of the microworld pioneers had changed. A place to live was not simply an area of land which, however abused, would always be there (the planetary view). Home was a flying lump of sculptured mass, and mass was a resource which could be used up. The tiniest course correction meant that part of the microworld's mass was thrown away at high velocity, via the plasma jets; serious travelling would cause home to dwindle visibly, spewed into space as almost irrecoverable electrons and nuclei. Mass in space is like water in the desert: thus no Belt dweller ever condemned Fourmyle's action (except through envy); and thus we still hear grisly folktales of microworlders desperately sacrificing their belongings, their food and their children to the plasma torch for the sake of a world-saving course correction. (The almost forgotten Earthside version of this myth concerns wolves and a sleigh.)

After leaving the Earth/Moon system with its home conveniences, such as lunar mass drivers, the seekers after f.i.s. (free in space) mass went first in the obvious direction, gravitationally "uphill" to the Belt. Mars was on that upward slope too, and beyond lay the inviting moons of Jupiter, and far beyond them again the rings of Saturn with their seemingly inexhaustible resources of water-ice and therefore fusion fuel. Furthest of all, spending most of their time beyond the planets and extending outward for lightyears – almost halfway to the nearest star – the Sun's immense family of perhaps hundreds of billions of comets offered hopeful star travellers a tempting last chance of mass-replenishment.

PAT adapted for Frobisher and Woo

It seems remarkable now that people so pitifully unready for the endless void of space travel, so shortlived in the days before universal NAR treatment and later the Zaman transformation, should have separated themselves so dramatically from the Earth/Moon centre to creep onward, and onward, and outward. One psychological buffer they did possess was the space-adapted version of a modern convenience we know well: PAT (personality analogue transfer).

Microworlds clustered in pairs, triplets and dozens near the Lagrange points of the Moon.

Frobisher and Woo, running the Ganymede Project in the 2460s, could not carry on "real" conversations with Earth owing to the maddening 35 to 50 minute travelling time – depending on the relative positions of Earth and Jupiter – of the communications laser. Instead they beamed data back to updated personality analogues of themselves "living" in the Earthside datanet: people on Earth spoke to these analogues with no time lag, and the same system in reverse gave Frobisher and Woo, and their team, the illusion of being in immediate contact with home. Such devices helped people at the furthest ends of the solar system and beyond to maintain contact. In the end this was not enough for Catryn Frobisher, who by the 2480s had become obsessed with her belief that somewhere amid the ammonia-and-methane slush of Ganymede there existed intelligent life. The Outer Belt Museum still preserves her pathetic collection of local chondritic rocks, which she was convinced showed signs of having been crafted by hand, into arrowheads and playing counters for a game resembling *Go*.

Ganymede as a filling station

But we remember the Frobisher and Woo team for their supreme achievement in the late 2460s, the "Jupiter Bridge" shuttle which opened up the first alternative source of fuel-mass. With the aid of an immense robot army they created and ran a fleet of shuttle-scoops which made daring hit-and-run raids into the fringes of Jupiter's atmosphere – indeed, into the fringes of Jupiter itself, since that planet has no true surface, no clear dividing line between atmosphere and solid mass. The big separator tanks on Ganymede and the Ganymede-orbit microworlds were fed with raw Jovian atmosphere, which they split into hydrogen (a fusion fuel), ammonia, and a scatter of trace gases. Ganymede became the standard "filling station" for transJovian travellers, and quantities of its precious fuels were sent coasting down the Sun's gravity slope to places where they were needed, in the Belt and further in. Frobisher and Woo grew rich, despite the hefty taxes imposed by the UN, which considered Jupiter a natural resource on which – like the oceans – it should charge rent.

(However, the UN's ability to collect tax on transactions so far away depended on their being funnelled through Earthside banks, the Bank of Luna or the Lagrange clearing houses, financial centres where the UN still held the purse strings. The Independent Banking Service of Pallas (IBSP), founded in 2501 on what was now the largest of the asteroids, helped many inhabitants of the Belt and points outward to avoid UN monitoring without resorting to plain barter. Later, of course, the IBSP was incorporated into the Free Belt Authority and began to impose taxes of its own.).

The cracking of Ceres, showing dramatic fusion fires splitting the 1000-kilometres in diameter asteroid. The blast was perfectly judged. Ceres came gently apart, a myriad boulders tumbling slowly toward the mass-hungry space miners.

The Hot Gang around Mercury

"Jupiter and the stars!" was the new cry of the space messiahs, who saw in those helium-3 resources the possibility of a nuclear-pulse space drive capable of crossing the interstellar gulfs at a respectable fraction of the speed of light. It was another of history's mild ironies that in the end – although at least one such probe was launched – the best way outward was to head inward. Inward to the sun-hugging orbit of Mercury, where microworlds were often one vast refrigeration system, and where in a hellish sleet of particles the "Hot Gang" was painfully developing the prototype of the hydrogen funnel.

The Hot Gang was a loose term, covering a miscellany of tiny groups: some of them UN-funded, some independent researchers, some eccentrics who demanded to "pit themselves against the limits of the possible" – none so eccentric as Pelham Brockway, who claimed to be questing for the perfect suntan and was subsequently treated for a variety of skin cancers. Saner folk found no place to hide so close to the Sun, where the sevenfold (relative to Earth's) flux of solar energy might be tolerable but the fast particles of the solar wind – hot hydrogen boiling from the Sun – were not. (Even now we tend to forget what dangers Earth's atmosphere shields us from.) Bases on Mercury itself, of which there were a few, had to endure this terrible onslaught for 176 days at a time, with no protecting atmosphere. The coolest place was the stable orbit in Mercury's shadow where Vulkan Station took shape, but even there the Sun is larger in the sky than the much closer Mercury, and is only partly obscured. "Just makes the difference between hell and purgatory," as Coris or his analogue liked to tell the Earth-side media.

The hydrogen funnel

Anatole Coris and John Eggar are usually considered to be the guiding spirits behind the hydrogen funnel, perhaps because the media like to focus on them as an old-fashioned married couple. Credit should be shared among a half a dozen more, prominently the theoretician Carole Mazidi who analysed the solar hurricane in terms of chaos physics and thus laid the foundations. Even hangers-on like Brockway played heroic roles as the impossibly fragile-looking funnel grid took shape in space. In 2486 the first successful test was made.

Coris and Eggar's original design for the hydrogen funnel. Stellar particles were sucked into the hungry well of electromagnetic forces. The road to the stars was opening up.

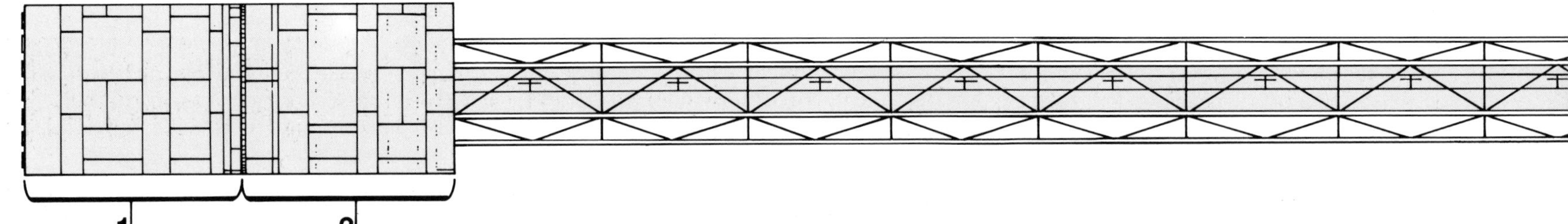

Its importance was not appreciated at first. Funnelling the solar wind into a condensed stream of hydrogen which was a usable source of mass (marginally) or fusion fuel was all very well; but Mercury was a long way downhill from civilization, and was a new mass-source really useful when the results needed to be boosted such an immense distance against the Sun's remorseless pull? The extravagant claims of Coris, Eggar, Mazidi and Rune in the academic synthetape *On The Amelioration of Mass Ratio Restrictions For Autonomous Space Vehicles* (2492) were chaffed as "science fiction".

By the beginning of the twenty-sixth century, though, a second-stage funnel was operating near Earth, a demonstration model whose far-reaching electromagnetic "fingers" provided another unexpected mass-source by trawling in a proportion of the thousand-odd tons of micrometeors which fall to Earth each day. This was a digression in funnel development, but attracted some attention during the construction of the third-stage model which was eventually installed in the experimental ship *T. E. Lawrence*. By the time of the *Lawrence's* 2512 trip, Mazidi had settled down as senior professor of theoretical physics in the O'Neill VII University, but the old team of Coris and

The Ramjet Starliner: the *T. E. Lawrence, above*, was a massive craft, larger than any structure built previously. The *T. E. Lawrence*'s features include:
1 In-system boost section
2 Hydrogen funnel and main engines
3, 4 Accelerator tubes and radiators
5 Cargo and command section
6 Rotating crew and passenger quarters
7 Erosion shield
Previous feats of engineering are shown to scale with the *T. E. Lawrence*, below. *Left:* an early space shuttle, *c.* 1990. *Centre:* a *Daedalus*-class robot starprobe, *c.* 2520, many of which – weighing some 50,000 tons at departure made one-way exploratory trips to the nearer stars. *Right:* Old Manhattan's Empire State Building in its nitrogen preserving dome.

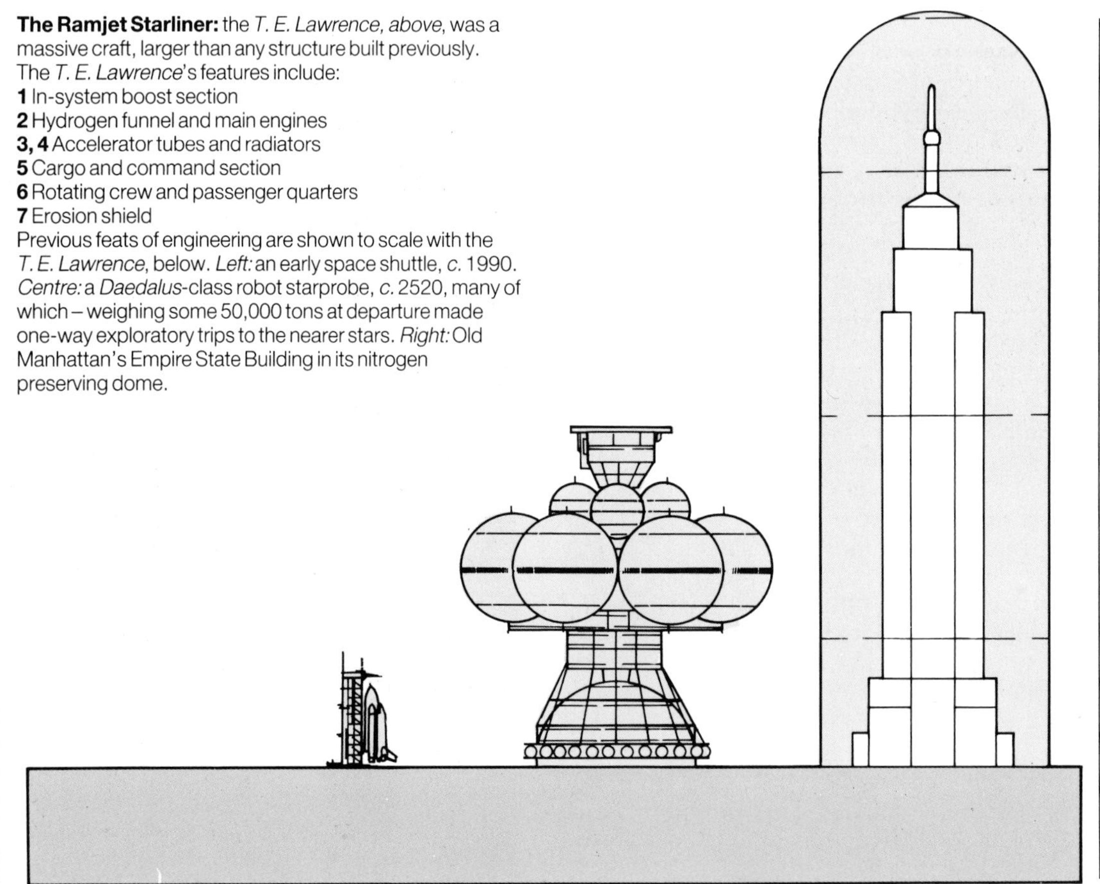

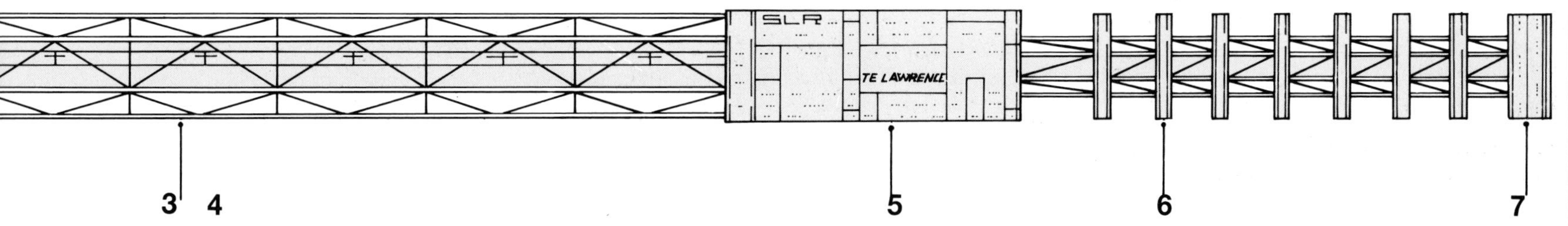

The laser lightsail was a starship without main engines. Some 60 of them were commissioned and used extensively in the twenty-sixth and twenty-seventh centuries. The vast "sail", some 1000 kilometres (620 miles) across was driven across space by the combined glare of the "trade lights" – ten laser stations in close orbit around the Sun, from which they derived the massive power required. Lightsails rode a lightyears' long searchlight of laser energy. Near journey's end, the outer ring detached and light from the target sun slowed the inner, payload sail to system-encounter velocity. The payload sail then navigated to its target world. The Earth-return sail was a mere 92 kilometres (57 miles) across. Lightsails travelled at more than half lightspeed. The *Medusa* took the Vega Riband with a top speed of 167,863 km/sec (104,328 miles/sec).

0 **160 km** (100 miles)

Outer ring detaches at journey's end. "Wind" from the target sun brakes inner sail. Complete sail at launch, 1000 km (621 miles) diameter.

System-encounter section, 320 km (200 miles) in diameter.

Earth-return sail.

Eggar were aboard for that historic journey around the Sun and back – the journey from which the *Lawrence* returned with greater fusion-fuel reserves than when it had set out.

Space travel revolutionized

With the funnel scooping in the tenuous hydrogen of space, travel within the solar-system was revolutionized. So many journeys had been a gamble with mass: the desperate choice between the alternatives of possibly running out of fuel or taking ruinously too much since each added kilogram had, itself, to be accelerated or decelerated with the ship/microworld until it was used. "You won't believe this," Coris exulted in an interview, "but way back in the twentieth century they worked out mass ratios for interstellar round-trips and got the same answers as the twenty-fifth century – tens or hundreds of times as much fuel as actual spaceship, maybe even thousands. John and I have made all that out of date, and squashed those kids-into-the-converter horror stories too."

(Coris was being a little disingenuous here, since the twentieth century also conceived an interstellar propulsion system called the Bussard Ramjet, which was supposed to function rather like a fifth-stage funnel – though without the chaos formulations, the proposed design would not actually have worked even if it could then have been built. Or so we believe.)

Improvements in the funnel made it theoretically workable even in the far lower hydrogen-densities between the stars, and – again theoretically – it seemed that a funnel-fuelled craft or microworld should be able, eventually, to approach the speed of light. Once a constant acceleration was possible without the awful burden of immense fuel tanks, the universe seemed to open up.

Probes reach Barnard's Star

Robot probes were heading out of the solar system as early as the 2520s, stripped-down devices consisting of a cold-fusion torch, a functioning artificial intelligence and a variety of sensors and communicators. Aimed at the nearer stars, these overtook the clumsier probes of previous centuries as they raced toward new potential territory.

The first signals returned from the Barnard's Star probes after 37 years (something had gone wrong with the first device targeted at the nearer Alpha Centauri), and Coris was duly feted. Always the showman in the past, he took little interest in the latest result of "his" achievement, having retreated into permanent melancholy in the late 2550s when his long-term partner's second rejuvenation, though not his own, had failed to "take", leading to Eggar's senescence and death. Even the news of a crude ecosystem on Barnard III meant little to the man after whom, by popular acclaim, the planet was named.

By now the space-adapted humans (ETs, see Chapter Thirty-six) were well-established and rapidly expanding their numbers. Colonies throve as far out as the moons and rings of Saturn, while pioneers – the trickle running ahead of the flood – had passed beyond the orbits of Pluto and Poseidon in largely abortive starflights, doomed to be overtaken by funnelcraft. Some of these turned miserably back to the comfortable pastures of the Sun; some, through pride, misadventure or communications failure, did not. One long-dead microworld, the *Skylark of Space*, passed through the Alpha Centauri system more than 250 years after its launch – stripped of surplus mass by the now mummified crew, and coasting on its own inadequate momentum.

Row over "ecological imperialism"

Could Venus be terraformed? And should it? It was too late to halt the second cargo of biocatalytic organisms when the debate began anew. "Ecological imperialism" was the rallying phrase used by the programme's opponents, and now they had a visible example, Mars. There, experiments aimed at engineering viable organisms for the arid and nearly airless Martian climate had proved all too successful: the spreading sand lichen threatened to convert the Red Planet to the Yellow Planet, and the tiny, deep-burrowing "Marsworm" was vilified as likely to displace putative Martian organisms from the one remaining ecological niche where they might exist. (A curious sidelight on the power of myth: almost without exception the media fastened on one junior member of the Marstech et Cie laboratory which engineered the Marsworm, and held him responsible. His name was Dr Vernon Frankenstein.)

But no "real" Mars life was ever found, nor has it been to this day – except in the eyes of Cowie's mid-twenty-sixth-century "Stars Are For Man League". The League argued that since humanity was "natural", then so were human actions, including the making of Marslife, which therefore became natural in itself. "A bird drops a seed on a barren island, and the barrenness is corrupted with life: entirely normal and natural, as you'll all agree. Now humanity drops a seed on the bare rocks of Mars, and – well, where is the difference?" Thus Akakia Cowie, in full sermonizing flight.

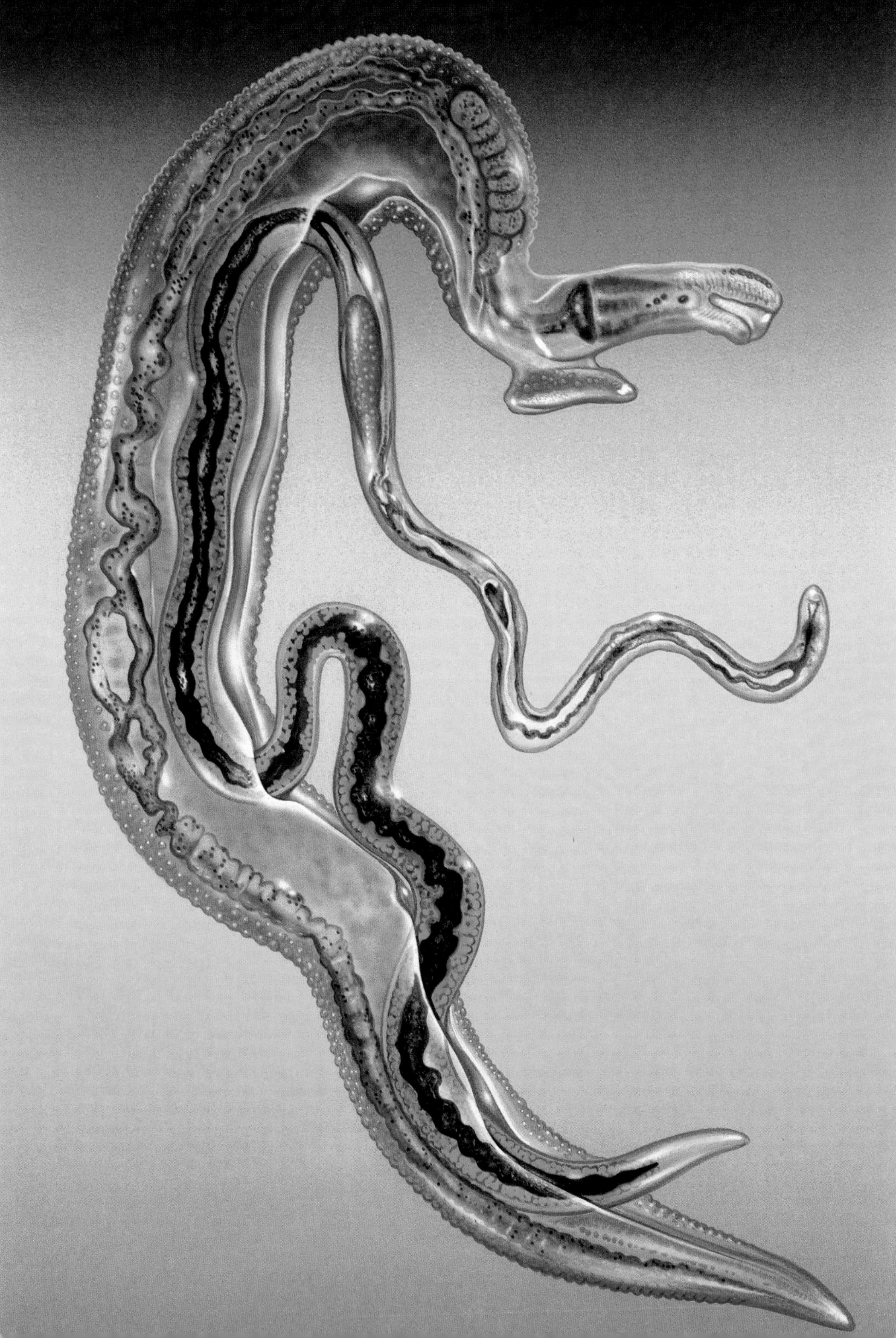

This perhaps futile debate went on. Is a self-programming, self-modifying species (like humanity) really in any sense natural? Such hairsplitting was for planet-bound dilettantes, said the ET pioneers and space messiahs, who now – with the destruction of the great barrier between us and the stars – were leaving the solar system in ever-increasing numbers. "Out of sight, out of mind": few of those who debated Venus or Mars had much concern to spare for the news, received in 2631, that the former ecosystem of the planet Coris (Barnard III) had been driven into a few remote enclaves by imported and genetically engineered Earth organisms. This was the result of a chance experiment of the microworld *Barnard or Bust*, rather than part of an intentional programme – but it prefigured the coming of the Arks.

The Marsworm, a deep-burrowing organism manufactured by the Genetix Corporation and designed to convert the Martian subsoil for Earth-style agriculture. This picture is highly magnified – the Marsworm is less than 5 mm long.

CHAPTER THIRTY-FIVE

THE STELLAR HORIZONS

The dead hand of Albert Einstein still blocked the road to the stars, with his now six centuries old relativity formulae which uncompromisingly laid down the absolute maximum speed limit in our universe. Information carried by massless photons can travel no faster than 300,000 kilometres per second, and actual mass – whether an atom or a microworld – can never quite reach this velocity. Nothing can pass between the Sun and the Earth in less than about eight minutes; between the orbits of Earth and Pluto in less than about five hours; between the Earth/Moon complex and Alpha Centauri in less than 4.3 years. In practice the early starfarers could only achieve a fraction of lightspeed.

An example is the portentously named *Columbus*, the first manned vehicle to orbit another star – it overtook several earlier "slowboats" *en route*, a few of which caught up decades or even centuries later. At the time, the mid-2560s, it was the last word in space technology: an entire midget microworld, almost exclusively ET-manned, with a fifth-stage funnel feeding a cold-fusion torch which also provided light to the immense manna fields (vacuum SAP-systems). Like its successors, *Columbus* began by following the sunward plunge of the *T. E. Lawrence*, taking advantage of dense solar wind at the closest possible quarters to fuel the initial acceleration before allowing the Sun's gravity to deflect it around and outward, on course for Barnard's Star. Continuous though low acceleration enabled it to average some 20 per cent of the speed of light over the journey, which thus took less than 30 years – reduced by several months from the travellers' viewpoint, of course, thanks to relativistic time-foreshortening.

Mapping the space lanes

Later starcraft improved considerably on this speed, due to the development of bigger and more efficient funnels – and to the gradual mapping of the "space lanes" or "currents of space". These are zones in which interstellar dust and hydrogen are denser than average, enabling the scavenging funnels to gather mass more readily: often the shortest route from A to B is by no means the quickest for a funnelcraft, if a more circuitous route will allow more fuel-intake and greater speed. The deep-astronomer Magda Saudek, who devoted much of her long life to spatial mapping, was fond of quoting a pre-atomic author named Chesterton: "The night we went to Birmingham by way of Beachy Head . . .".

Examining the nearest stars

Where was the most inviting territory for the colonists of the star-worlds? Their ancestors would have assumed Earthlike or near-Earthlike planets as the only possibilities – places with biosystems which were already hospitable or tameable. The microworld-dwellers of the twenty-fifth and twenty-sixth centuries were less choosy; all they asked were adequate supplies of mass and energy. They would bring their own biosystems with them. Thus the robot probes which went out to spy for us were not concentrated, as in previous centuries they might have been, on stars which resembled our Sun, or were thought to harbour planets, or both. Instead they were scattered indiscriminately to investigate the twenty or so nearest stars – and in the process found two more, the black dwarfs Ceres (named out of nostalgia, to replace the Ceres lost from the solar system) and Yang (after the founder of chaos theory).

Some of the names of the stars examined were more or less time-hallowed, and are still familiar in communications from the starfaring microworlds: Alpha Centauri, Barnard's Star, Sirius, Epsilon Eridani, 61 Cygni, Procyon and Tau Ceti. Others soon shed cumbersome numerals in the wear and tear of everyday usage – only the starchiest of astronomers insist on referring to Wolf 359, Lalande 21185, Groombridge 34 and so on. Still others were rechristened: Einstein, Foden, Gantz, Zaman and Gottløs were once called (for reasons known only to pre-Third Millennium astronomers) Luyten 726-8, Ross 154, Ross 248, Σ2298 and BD + 5° 1668. Each of these systems now has a fringe of energy-hungry microworlds; even the "useless" dead stars Ceres and Yang were successfully mined for their heavy metals, and are still occasionally helpful to followers of the space-lanes, who can make almost fuel-free course corrections by swinging comet-fashion through the dark stars' gravitational fields.

Early explorers: the stuff of legend

The first wave of manned starcraft comprised rather small microworlds, with complements rarely exceeding a few hundred, some of them mere ships rather than microworlds proper. Funnel drives for larger craft had yet to prove themselves, and the UN and many spaceborne authorities (for once in agreement) had in any case asked for restraint. Mass was apparently the point at issue: the smallest manned starcraft took several asteroids' worth of material with them, and there were worries – not merely from green parties – about ultimate depletion of the solar system's f.i.s. mass. The concern proved exaggerated, and many believe it to have been a political ploy, an attempt to slow and delay the star-fledglings' inevitable escape from the nest to far-off independence.

Stories of those first explorers are still among the most popular works of historical fiction and synthetape drama, especially in the "off-planet" communities (moons and microworlds) of our system. Actual events were varied and wonderful enough, the stuff of legend. The desperate improvisations after a partial biosystem failure on the *Duke of York* microworld, and Captain Fothergill's suicidal remorse after five years of controlled cannibalism on the last leg of that microworld's journey to Episilon Indi – only for the *Duke of York* to find itself in second place, overtaken by the faster *Lone Star*, launched fifteen months later. The turning aside of the Chang Commune expedition to investigate an anomalous radiation source, and discovering it to be a new wonder of the universe: the remnant of an antimatter planetoid, passing through our galaxy from God knows where, eroded by each particle of interstellar dust in a flash of gamma rays as normal matter and antimatter annihilated each other. The tragedy of the Free Belt Ship *Infinity*, whose funnel mysteriously blew apart in a freak accident just past the halfway point of its Sirius journey: the sister-world *Serendipity* was able to decelerate, the *Infinity* could not and whipped helplessly on past its destination at approximately eight-tenths the speed of light...

Just a toehold in the galaxy

This last gives us a measure of our influence in the galaxy today, at the beginning of the Fourth Millennium. If the *Infinity* is still travelling, and it probably is, it will now be a little over 300 lightyears out. No later spacecraft is at present likely to catch up on its head start (unless the Vega Community carries out its wild plan to send a relativistic microworld to the galactic core, a 30,000 year journey to be reduced to a subjective couple of hundred years by pushing close to the speed of light); and it's doubtful that any other craft has gone further than 180 lightyears from Earth. Yet the *Infinity*'s awesome 300 lightyears is only the distance to the bright star Beta Centauri, one of our astronomical neighbours; Rigel and Betelgeuse are twice as far away; their distance is less than 0.2 per cent of the diameter of our galaxy. Trivial calculations like this can make us seem very young and inexperienced, rather than the wise old race we tend to consider ourselves.

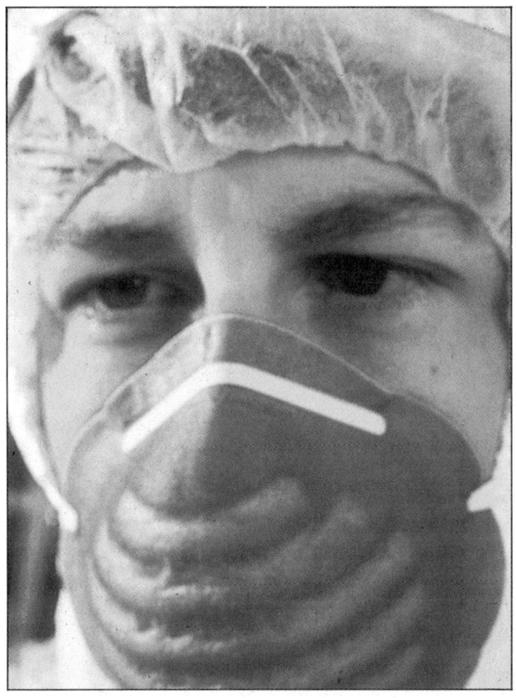

Captain Fothergill of the *Duke of York* microworld. The primitive mask was a necessity in the last stages of the voyage to Epsilon Indi, when bio-system breakdown encouraged the spread of deadly viral diseases aboard the craft. A small fraction of the pioneers survived the journey due to well-planned cannibalism.

Could there still be living people aboard the *Infinity*? The last glum messages were heard more than a century ago. Remembering the sad fate of the *Duke of York*, it is perhaps wiser not to speculate.

Sirius: beautiful but "too damned crowded"

Of course, many voyaging microworlds did not stop at one destination. Director Karla Zogov, of the *Serendipity*, is supposed to have said, "It's getting too damned crowded out here," when the third manned microworld arrived in the Sirius system, with more promised in the next five years. After exchanges of information, supplies and aid – not to mention a few people, for relationships had time to form while the *Serendipity*, the *Amalthea GmbH* and the UN Observer Community *Chruschik* shared a wide orbit round the Sirius binary – Zogov's microworld moved on and was next seen at Epsilon Eridani, a relatively nearby star, the first space habitat to visit three suns.

Sirius was and is worth visiting, as centuries of transmitted pictures have shown. Its dwarf companion provokes and attracts great flares of hot gas from the Sirian photosphere. These are sometimes very spectacular indeed and have been dubbed another wonder of the universe, on the scale of the rings of Saturn and that remarkable antimatter planetoid named (by its discoverers) Mao. The wild dance of Sirius and its companion makes the

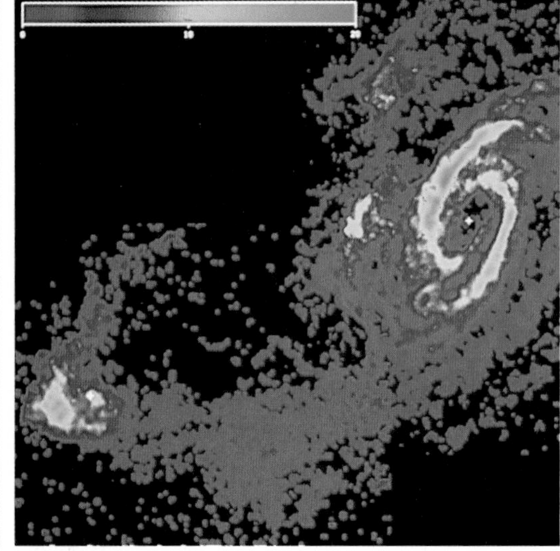

Galactic hydrogen clouds, fuel for interstellar ramjets which increased velocity as they traversed each cloud.

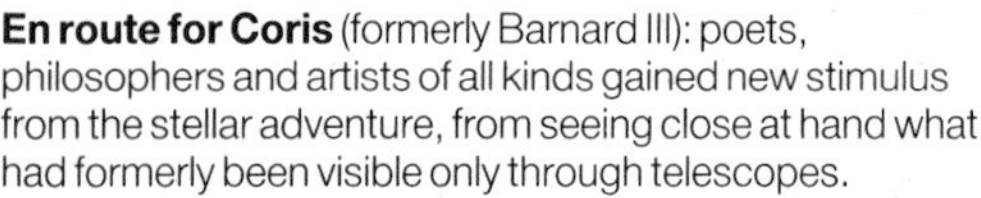

En route for Coris (formerly Barnard III): poets, philosophers and artists of all kinds gained new stimulus from the stellar adventure, from seeing close at hand what had formerly been visible only through telescopes.

system extraordinarily rich in fuel-gas passing from the larger to the smaller star. One simply steers one's starcraft through the thickest "turbulence": a daring novelty when first tried by Bruce Illawalli with the *Woomera* in 2648, but later a routine and highly practical manoeuvre for visitors to the Sirius System.

Universe thought barren

On one front, the initial discoveries of the starcraft were sparse. The pseudo-algae and pseudo-protozoa of Barnard's Star had, it turned out, been something of a lucky find. From system after system the reports came in: "nothing", "nothing", "perhaps in another million years", "nothing". Several near-habitable planets were located but, in this period, only one more with even primitive life-forms. On the fourth planet of Hawking (mildly notable as the first sun to be explored by a secondary expedition rather than directly from the solar system), the USS *Libertarian* came across the most depressing find of all: an ecosystem which had long ago faltered into extinction without getting beyond the equivalent of the single-celled level. It began to seem, on this first evidence, that our universe was a very bleak place. "Alone, alone, all, all alone, Alone in a wide wide sky!" said (or rather, paraphrased) Secretary-General Thayer as, back in the solar system, the negative reports accumulated. He was, however, premature.

Arks to the stars

If the universe was nearly barren, the messianic and pioneering fringes of humanity were already prepared to do something about it. In the third and fourth decades of the twenty-seventh century, the larger relativistic microworlds called Arks were beginning with slow acceleration to leave the solar system. Their names alone are significant even without the later accretions of history: the *Go Forth and Multiply*, the *Promised Land*, the *Sower of the Systems*, and several with Biblical names like – inevitably – *Ham*, *Shem* and *Japhet*. The Belt provided some less solemnly named Arks, among them the *Population Explosion* and the *Fascist Imperialist*.

An Ark was a kind of super-microworld, peopled by thousands of the space-adapted, crammed with the latest in physical and biological technology. It was ready to cruise virtually forever at near-lightspeed on its Funneldrive (one or two members of the original wave are probably still travelling), and it carried a special cargo. The earlier explorers had travelled as nomads or sightseers, living much the same spaceborne existence in no matter what new solar system, and spawning new microworlds of fly-by-nights like themselves. The Ark-riders had a mission, and carried millions on millions of frozen zygotes of Earthly and Earth-developed creatures – flora, fauna, and sapients. It has been rightly said that the only cargo which can be economically transported between the stars is pure information. Those compact coils of DNA contained the most condensed life-building information the Ark-riders could imagine; and their computer banks held the rest of human knowledge. They were ready to engineer tailor-made "Earth" creatures even for the not quite habitable worlds. "We have a mission – to give the priceless gift of life where the womb is barren," was the sententious phrasing of Rachel al'Mutasim of the *Promised Land*.

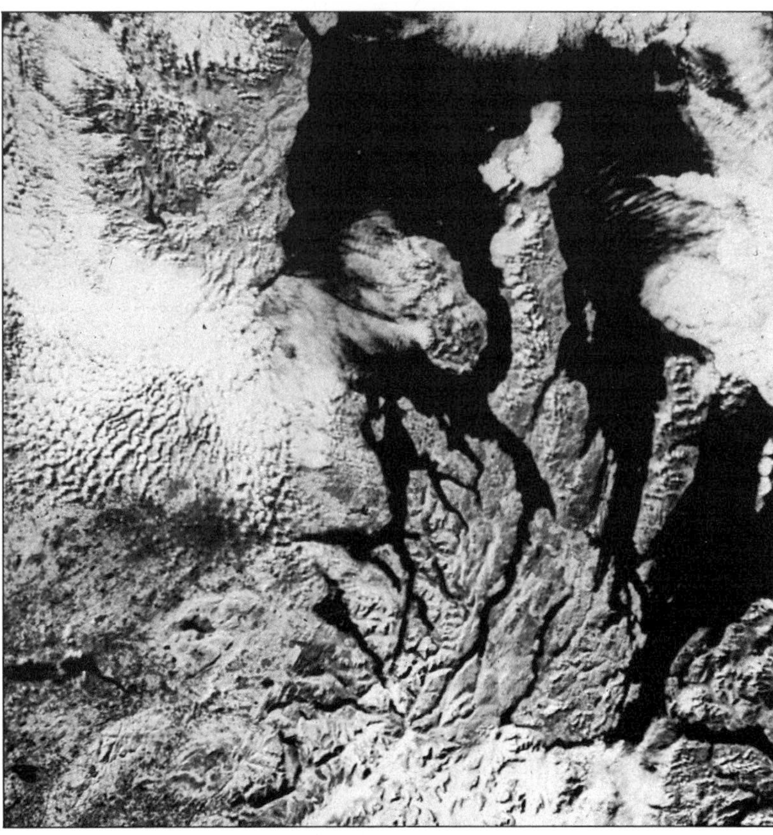

Coris (formerly Barnard III), seen from the flightdeck of the *Columbus*. Primitive algae and protozoa lived in the swirling waters of Coris when *Columbus* arrived, but soon afterwards, organisms released from the *Barnard or Bust* proved tougher than the natives. Within a decade the invaders from Earth had destroyed the planet's ecology.

Stars beyond UN control

Again, on Earth, the weakly querulous cry of "ecological imperialism" went up. The issue was confused, though, by the prevailing – though as it turned out, not quite typical – lifelessness of the universe so far inspected by humanity. It was difficult to refute the argument that anything must be better than this desolation. On the other hand, there was the fate of the Barnard's Star ecology to consider – boding ill for any other functioning ecosystem which might get in the way of the Arks' "zygotic evangelism". Let Secretary-General Tchernavin, speaking in 2649, have the final word:

"It is not only the cream of bioengineers and physicists who have left us as they voyage on their Arks. With them has gone the initiative; they have taken the power of final decision with them in their luggage, to the stars. We would do well not to shriek after them like foolish and possessive parents, and instead set our own lands in order."

These words ushered in the modern era.

CHAPTER THIRTY-SIX

THE DIVERSIFICATION OF MAN

During the second half of the twenty-fifth century attitudes to genetic engineering changed markedly. As cosmetic engineering became commonplace, the public's view of human engineering inevitably relaxed. The more sweeping the tissue-transformations indulged in by adults, the easier became the argument in favour of ambitious modifications of human ova.

The first radically modified human beings

In spite of this relaxation of the taboo, the first significant attempt to create radically modified human beings was carried out in secret. The Australia-based Coral Sea Investments commissioned a team of human engineers – including Helena Andrianou, Omar de Maroussem and Mirafza Khan – to adapt a group of six human embryos, three male and three female, for an amphibious existence. These adapted people were to have: gills as well as lungs; physiological protection against caisson sickness; skin designed to resist the corrosion of salt water; an extra layer of subcutaneous fat; webbed flipper-like feet; a lateral-line system of chemoreceptors to "smell" dissolved compounds in the water; and an echo-location system like that used by dolphins. The original ova and sperm used to fertilize them were donated by the senior members of the team of engineers, who exercised their right of replacement in order to demonstrate their commitment to the project.

The six children were delivered from their artificial wombs between February and May 2485. It is known that one of the males died shortly afterward, but the records fail to indicate how many embryos were "spoiled" in the early stages of the experiment. This unusual lack of data illustrates the caution with which the project advanced. Secrecy was maintained for many years as the children grew up in artificial lagoons among the islands of the Great Barrier Reef. The first official announcement was delayed until January 2500, although some UN officials were already fully informed.

The news did not quite provoke the anticipated storm of controversy. There were attacks on the corporation, the Australian government and the engineers themselves, but they came from predictable sources and failed to arouse any upsurge of public anger. Many people, in fact, were totally disinterested – there had been talk of adapted humans for so long that their arrival seemed inevitable.

The merpeople multiply

The real test of the project's success came in 2503, when Leonie, one of the three females of the new species (the media, of course, instantly christened them merpeople) became pregnant. Ova had already been removed from all three females for eventual *in vitro* fertilization, but these remained in cold storage while the scientists monitored Leonie's natural pregnancy. When she was delivered of a healthy baby girl, who retained all the features of the new race, the engineers claimed complete success. The number of embryos that had later to be aborted when ectogenetic reproduction of the new species became routine suggested that Andrianou's team – and Leonie – had been somewhat fortunate; and this was underlined in 2509 when Viola, the eldest of the group, died after miscarrying her second child.

Despite this inherent vulnerability the merpeople multiplied. By 2540 there were ninety-two, more than half of whom were less than twenty years old. They lived in an extensive, specially designed underwater habitat north of the Great Barrier Reef. All were employees of CSI, and their work – exploring and helping to exploit the undersea – was proving useful, if far from profitable. However, by this time arguments between the merpeople, their creators, and the corporation were becoming embittered. Niall, who became spokesman for the original group when Viola died, claimed that the support given to his species to build their underwater homes was inadequate. There was much angry debate as to whether CSI had intended to create a race of slaves, and what obligations they had to their creations. The conflicts continued after Niall's death in 2547, following a failed attempt at NAR-rejuvenation. It became apparent then that the merpeople were less robust than their parent race.

Merpeople become renegades

The merpeople could not maintain an extensive underwater technology of their own, and their undersea "city" was therefore entirely dependent on support from the land. This they resented. Although there was useful work to be done beneath the sea for which they were uniquely equipped, they had no real bargaining power. In 2555 thirteen of them left CSI to work for one of its rivals, and in 2560 a further seventeen emigrated to a spot near the island of Espiritu Santo in Vanuatu, where they claimed food and housing credit while trying to establish an independent lifestyle.

By then, CSI had closed the project and no more merpeople emerged from its artificial wombs. However, representatives of the new species went into an Australian court in 2563

Merpeople swimming in their native habitat. A sapient diver can be seen in the background. The brain coral was engineered to live up to its name, acting as an intelligent warning system, part of the defences around Neptune, the merpeople's Pacific capital.

The bubble domes of Neptune, *far right*, kept technical equipment dry. The merpeople have, of course, proliferated a great deal since the twenty-sixth century. At least one community is now settled beneath the effervescing seas of the planet Perrier, orbiting the star Gottlos. Against many predictions, their water-filled microworld completed the journey with barely a leak.

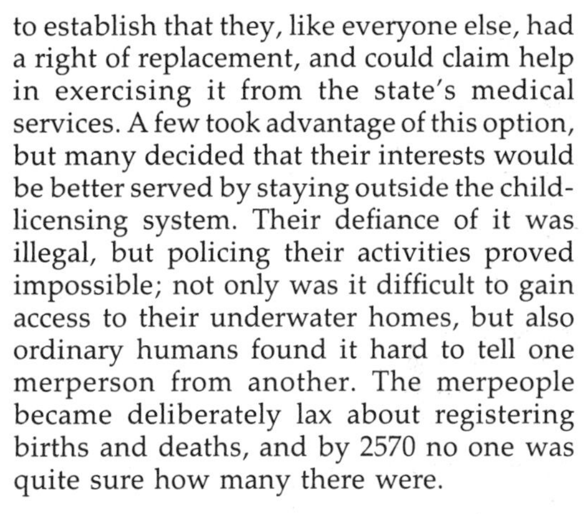

to establish that they, like everyone else, had a right of replacement, and could claim help in exercising it from the state's medical services. A few took advantage of this option, but many decided that their interests would be better served by staying outside the child-licensing system. Their defiance of it was illegal, but policing their activities proved impossible; not only was it difficult to gain access to their underwater homes, but also ordinary humans found it hard to tell one merperson from another. The merpeople became deliberately lax about registering births and deaths, and by 2570 no one was quite sure how many there were.

Birth of the ETs

Despite the problems encountered by CSI's project other adaptation schemes began soon after its announcement. Sperling's plan for adapting men to live in low-gravity conditons was simpler than Emerich's (see Chapter Twenty-nine) but for some reason, now unclear, Emerich's was developed first. An American team headed by Stephen Jesperson, and a Soviet one led by Vadim Radekoff and Kiril Khial, began work before the end of 2502. By 2510 nearly a hundred infants were growing up in a variety of extraterrestrial locations. The inhabitants of these space colonies had little time for the legal niceties so scrupulously observed on Earth, and by 2525 second-generation children were being born in some profusion. Even at this early date the second new race (dubbed ETs by the media) outnumbered the first ten-fold.

Spaceships manned entirely by ETs came into regular service in 2528, and the first communities of such people appeared on the moon and in the asteroid belt before 2540 while the "elder statesmen" of the new race

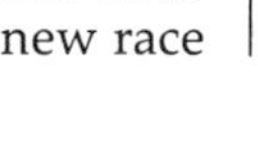

were still in their thirties. ET women found pregnancy easier than merwomen, and it was apparent by 2560 that ETs had a conventional human life expectancy. The merpeople had one advantage over their cousins: they could enter the habitat of their creators and walk upon the land. The ETs, on the other hand, could not come down into Earth's gravity-well, not so much because their adapted lower limbs could not give them the necessary support, but because the physiological adaptation of their circulatory systems made them vulnerable to heart attacks and breathing difficulties. (Ordinary people who lived in space for a long time often had similar problems on return to Earth.)

The heirs of space

By 2600 there were nearly 3000 ETs in the solar system. They had access to all the technology enjoyed by their ordinary neighbours, and had adapted most of it to their own needs. Their superiority, especially when working in zero-gravity, was manifest. Although at this stage there were 300 ordinary humans outside the Earth for every ET, many people could see that – as Emerich had postulated – the ETs were the inevitable heirs of most of the human enterprises in space. Other planets would undoubtedly prove as inhospitable to them as Earth, but the regions between were their domain. It seemed that the day was approaching when all new spaceships would be designed to be crewed by ETs, even if they also provided accommodation for ordinary passengers. Unlike the merpeople, the ETs were not inclined to be assertive about their rights and needs. They inherited their attitudes largely from the people of the space colonies, and this generated some obvious cultural differences. Nevertheless, the attitudes of Earth-dwellers to ETs was coloured by their knowledge of the merpeople. Ordinary people tended to lump the two together as "others".

ETs suffer unfairly

In 2604 a group of merpeople petitioned the UN suggesting that the oceans should no longer be regarded as the property of the world community, but rather as the nation of the merpeople. The audacity of the claim led to it being discussed more widely than it deserved, and this sparked off fears of what would happen if the ETs were to demand the whole solar system as their native territory.

Leading spokesmen for the ETs, notably Edward Zain, did their best to gain a favourable public image in the world's media, but they were unable to quell the gathering apprehension. In 2615 a group of merman extremists sabotaged a Filipino sea-harvester in the Celebes Sea. They did little damage and caused no casualties, but people immediately began to talk about the ease with which a spaceship could be sabotaged, and the extent of the tragedy that could be caused. When the Soviet spaceship *Potemkin* suffered a serious mishap early in 2161, with the loss of a hundred lives, rumours of ET involvement were rife. They were utterly without foundation, but attained such currency that they almost caused the anger and resentment within the ET community that was imagined to exist already. The fuss died down when the Supreme Soviet published its report on the *Potemkin* disaster, but the affair left a legacy of bad feeling.

Creationists look to the stars

By this time plans to create other human races, adapted for life on other planets, were being developed. Of the few life-supporting worlds so far discovered in other solar systems, none were places where ordinary human beings could live comfortably. However, some offered scope for specially-adapted species – indeed for entire artificial life-systems which could be integrated into the native ones. Creationists now raised their sights from Micronesia to the Milky Way, hoping to find a new dimension for their artistry. It seemed more sensible, of course, for any such adapted humans simply to take SAP-systems and tissue-culture farms into their new worlds, leaving living organisms behind as superfluous; but the vaulting ambition of the genetic engineers would not be stayed by such vulgar practical considerations. At first the UN was cool toward plans of this kind, but financial support was given to the development of a viable ecosphere on Venus – a first step along the engineers' desired road.

The experiments in human engineering, that followed closely after the creation of the ETs, did not lead immediately to any further new species. Many "optimized" children born from artificial wombs were unable to reproduce with naturally-born humans, but this was not sufficient to establish them as a new species. Besides, for the most part, they could not have children with one another either.

New species of talking chimps

In 2551 Roberto Inacio brought his experiments in the augmentation of animal intelligence to fruition. In previous centuries scientists had explored and exploited the potential of chimpanzees and dolphins to communicate with humans, and it seemed at first that Inacio's engineered chimpanzees

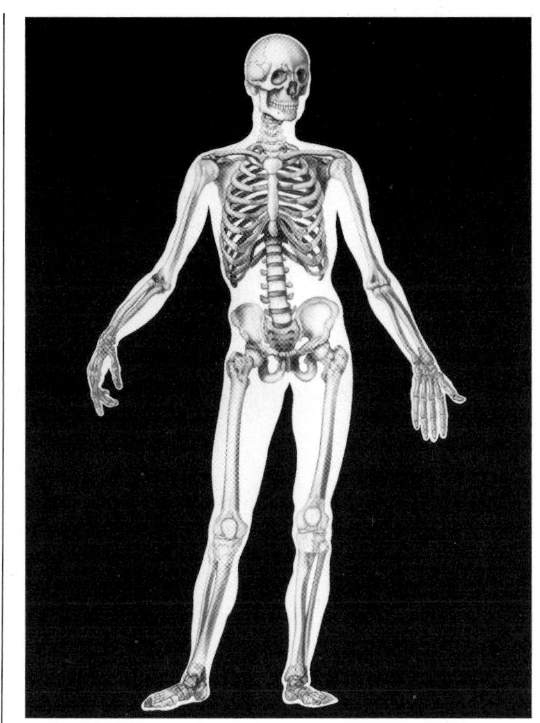

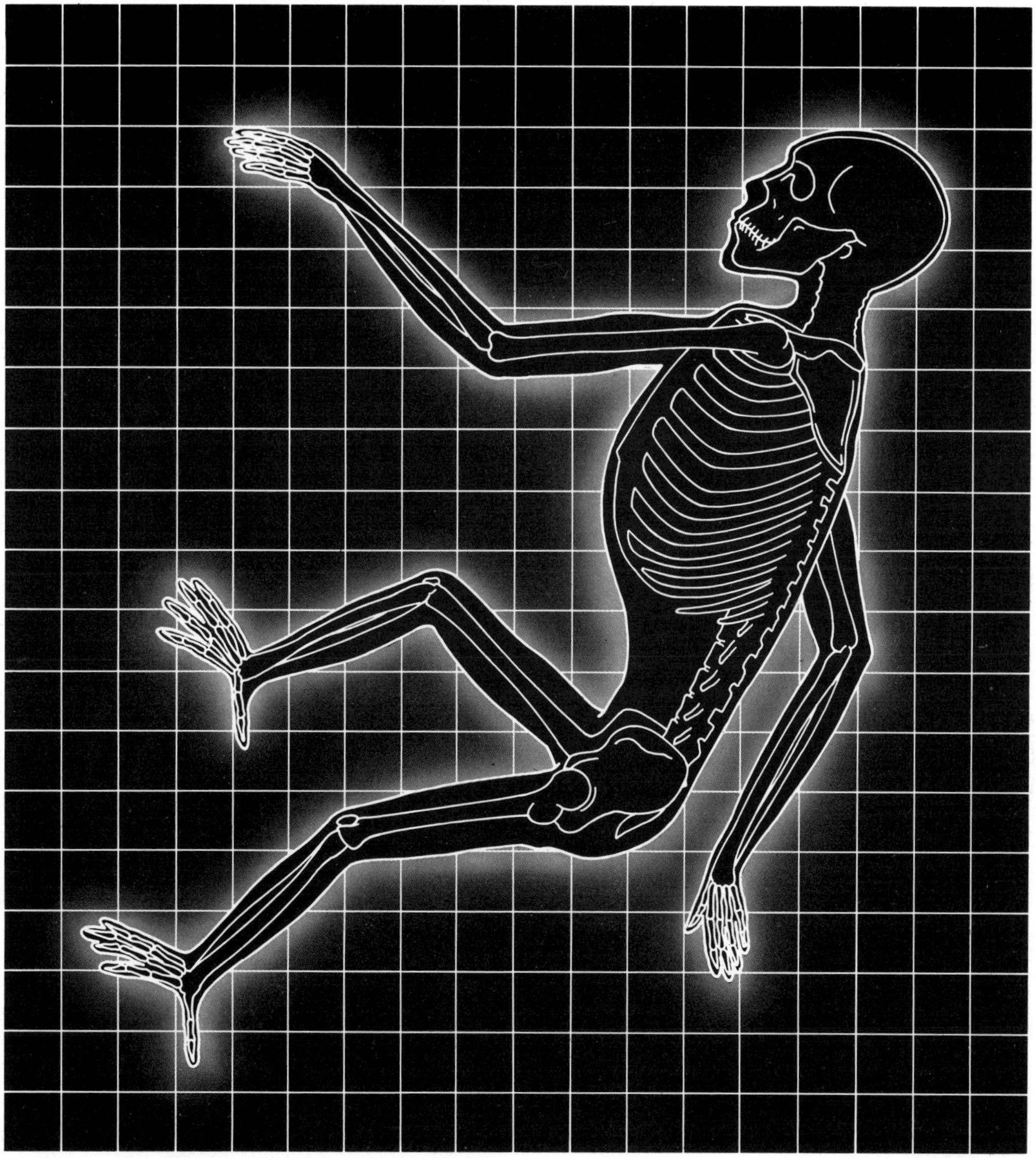

Skeleton of ET, or faber, compared with that of Sapient or Ordinary Man: the principal skeletal features of fabers are long arms, short legs, an extremely supple spine and grasping hands instead of feet.

were scarcely cleverer than those that had previously learned to construct sentences in sign-language. It quickly became apparent, though, that the difference was significant. Inacio continued to experiment, and in the years after his rejuvenation produced several generations of engineered chimpanzees, each marginally cleverer than the last. By 2590 he had a family group whose members could pronounce most of the syllables used in human speech, and whose mature intelligence was that of the average human eleven-year-old. These chimps were clearly a new species – they were different and they could breed with one another, but not with ordinary chimps.

Inacio's work stimulated some experiments in augmenting the intelligence of human babies by fetal engineering, but the results were unimpressive. Inacio was making chimps more like humans – to whom, after all, they were fairly closely related genetically. The human engineers had no ready-made model to work toward.

Sad deaths of the "chimpmen"

Inacio seemed capable of duplicating in a short period the long process of evolution by which man had evolved from apelike ancestors, and this was disquieting to many people. Chimpanzees, of course, were not very like the apes that were their own and man's ancestors, but it was nonetheless likely that in a few more generations Inacio would produce individuals who could communicate with men on equal terms. Without necessarily looking like humans, although that too might be arranged, they would have all the attributes previously reserved to the human species. Like the artificial intelligences, Mac, Lev and Ito, they would be

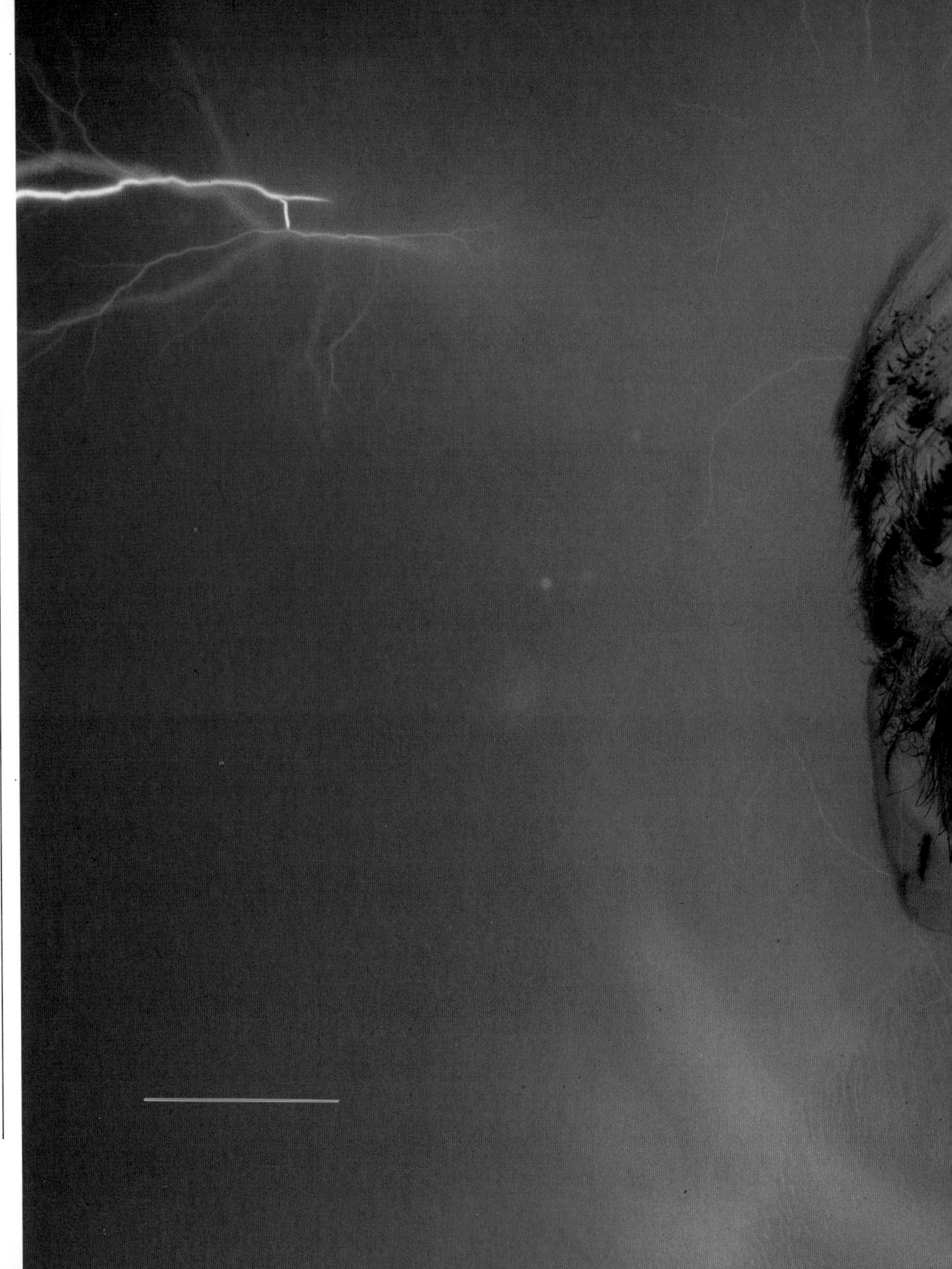

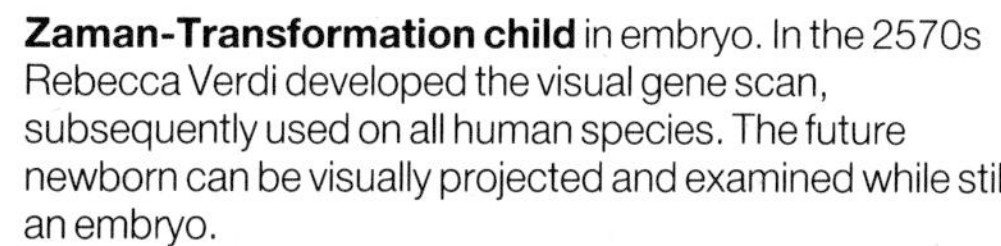
Zaman-Transformation child in embryo. In the 2570s Rebecca Verdi developed the visual gene scan, subsequently used on all human species. The future newborn can be visually projected and examined while still an embryo.

"human analogues", but with the vital difference that they could reproduce themselves naturally. In 2595 the UN's senior Ethics Committee responded to public pressure by prohibiting further transformations on embryos taken from Inacio's family of "chimpmen".

Marianne Tovali's book about Inacio's last family, *The Severed Link* (2614), describes a history as tragic as that of the human analogues. Her account is over-sentimentalized – she puts words and thoughts that were really her own into her subjects' mouths and minds – but one can sympathize with her argument. She gives lengthy descriptions of the chimpmen trying to come to terms with the fact that as they approached their intellectual peak they were already becoming senescent. Inacio was forbidden to try rejuvenating this last family, and they were separated in 2601 to prevent their having natural offspring. Inacio and Tovali both called this genocide. They may well have been right.

Cloned infants ill-treated by radicals

Like the mechanical human analogues, Inacio's approach to the production of human beings was not quickly repeated. Four "hominid" children displayed on the telescreens of the world in 2636 were not, as alleged by the Zairean government officials who "discovered" them, the result of illegal engineering of ape embryos. They were cloned human infants derived from an early embryo which had suffered accidental chromosomal fragmentation. Why the four fetuses had been allowed to come to term in their artificial wombs was never made clear, but the subsequent disgraceful treatment of these unfortunate children occurred while they were being fostered by a radical group campaigning for a total ban on human engineering. When the pretence was exposed the infants became wards of the Zairean state, but none survived to adulthood.

The Zaman-Transformation children

Although no progress was made with Inacio's methods, techniques developed by other animal engineers were elaborated for use on humans. The most significant by far was the lifespan-extension technique developed in 2461 by Ali Zaman. As already noted (see Chapter Thirty), the initial response to Zaman's discoveries was unenthusiastic, and attempts to apply his methods to humans were actively discouraged. Because existing methods of human rejuvenation had proved their worth, few were willing to fight for the right to use Zaman's unproven one.

Following the 2465 judgment against him, Zaman maintained silence for twenty years. He continued his animal experiments, refined techniques and improved his results. When he again applied to work with human engineers, in 2485, opinion had changed. Zaman moved to Australia, where legislative reforms carried through by Edric Haylor guaranteed the legality of his work. There he collaborated with Rebecca Verdi, formerly an assistant to his old friend Helena Andrianou. Verdi was a brilliant theoretician but lacked practice (she was thirty years Andrianou's junior). The project therefore took time to get properly under way, and the first group of Zaman-Transformation (ZT) children was not born until the autumn of 2489. All of them were to prove sterile – they could not breed with ordinary people nor with one another – and hence were not a new species.

ZTs show no signs of old age

By its very nature, the Zaman/Verdi experiment would not bring in any results for a very long time. The Sapporo tests had begun with men and women who were already old, and Toshiko Hiroshita had been able to produce an interim report after only thirteen years testifying that they had been made young again. Ali Zaman had to wait far longer to see whether his technique worked. He did his utmost to see the project through – he was twice rejuvenated and lived to be 140 – but when he died in 2550 the oldest of the ZT children was only 61. He did, indeed, seem young, but many decades would pass before he could demonstrate his longevity.

Zaman and Verdi did publish an interim report in 2540, stating that their creations were showing no signs of old age, but it created little excitement. When the ZT children made the news it was usually due to their arguments with their makers – a pale echo of the coverage given to the conflicts between Andrianou's team and the merpeople. Before he died, Zaman wanted to try a second experiment. He was convinced by then he could produce children who would not be sterile – who could, at least, reproduce with one another. He was blocked again by the UN Ethics Committee, despite his Australian support.

A superhuman species

Rebecca Verdi was left to engineer the second group with new co-workers, in 2562. In 2581 Jessica Sidney became the first ZT woman to become pregnant by a ZT man, establishing that the ZTs were – like the merpeople and the ETs – a new human species. At last the world paid attention, realizing that the new ZTs were not just a new human species, but might even be regarded as a superhuman species. Exactly how long they would live still remained to be seen; members of the original group, now in their early nineties, looked as fit as ever. The eldest, having achieved a slightly belated celebrity, boasted that he would not need rejuvenation until he was 150, and that with the aid of rejuvenation he expected to live to be 300. He was over-optimistic, but only because his rejuvenation did not take as well as it should have.

By 2650, the ZT children had proved Zaman right. Humans could be engineered for longevity. The doubling of the lifespan that NAR-technology had made possible was, after all, only the beginning. This prospect was welcomed by many, but voices were raised against it, on the grounds that it now seemed that, while the ETs would inherit space, the ZTs would inherit the Earth itself. What, then, would be the future for *Homo sapiens*, "ordinary man"?

CREATION OF THE NEW WORLD

2650 TO 3000

We do not mean to imply by calling the years from 2650 to the present day "the modern period" that little has happened since that date, or that today's world is no different from that of 2650. Those who remember the last half of the twenty-seventh century, although their memories have faded considerably, confirm that much has changed: death was a much more familiar and unwelcome event; some of the frenetic restlessness of the Period of Transformation lingered; the human community was virtually confined to the solar system, and was much less varied in its member species.

In 2650 the UN took a decision, the staggering importance of which it did not perhaps fully appreciate. In effect it determined the subsequent evolution of the various human species. And this was one of the few occasions when the UN Council took the lead in settling a controversial matter.

In the early twenty-seventh century several parents, mostly in the USA, demanded government-subsidized Zaman transformations for their unborn children, but were ruled out of order. The attitude of the governments concerned is easily understood – no nation had remotely sufficient resources of equipment or expertise to open the floodgates to this kind of demand. Some persistent parents followed a slow and tortuous path through national and international courts, looking for clarification of the legal position.

Law Lords guarantee longevity to embryos

Everywhere the courts procrastinated until April 2650, when a group of British Law Lords, renowned for their independence of spirit, found in favour of two plaintiffs and directed the British Ministry of Health and Longevity to provide a Zaman transformation for their child, free of charge.

Right-of-Replacement key, twenty-seventh-century from Spain. At that time the right of replacement was contained in a disc, issued at birth, unique – save in the case of identical twins – because it carried the owner's DNA pattern. The disc was often enshrined in jewellery, and frequently in a key which on surrender symbolically "unlocked" the way to parenthood.

even on the wording of an innocuous resolution expressing support for the principles of the Christmas Charter. However, influential members of the various UN agencies – which were not, of course, represented in the Council Chamber – pressed Secretary-General Nikolai Tchernavin to adopt a strong line. The confusion both between and within the nations seemed to offer the UN an opportunity to assert its authority.

2651: birth-rate plummets in every nation

In the later months of 2650 it was not clear how much support the revived Chartists had; the matter had blown up so quickly that many suspected the crusade to be a brief fad. Despite the apparent advantages of ectogenetic development many parents still thought it repugnant, and the great majority of children were still born naturally. Although 300 years had passed since the mere idea of human engineering generated the horror that fuelled James Lyndhurst's Crusade for Moral Rearmament, many people still felt that the old-fashioned way of having babies was the proper way. If the new Chartists were to have their way, the world would have to provide for every human child conceived outside the womb, subjected to massive genetic engineering, and brought to term in an artificial womb. If all parents did this, *Homo sapiens* would become extinct. A new species would inherit the Earth.

Some argued in favour of guaranteeing parents the right to choose ZT children, on the grounds that not many would exercise it, and that therefore the cost would be containable. As 2651 wore on this argument weakened; from the beginning of March – hardly ten months after the British Law Lords' pronouncement – the birth rate in every single nation on Earth began to drop, and by the end of summer it was falling steeply. The world's would-be parents were hesitating over the exercise of their right of replacement. This might have been a brief trend, caused by the enormous attention given to the issue, but Tchernavin and his advisers took it very seriously.

Superpower leaders meet in Amundsen City
In October 2651 Tchernavin made the extremely unusual move of inviting the premiers of the three superpowers to a face-to-face meeting in Amundsen City. It was by no means rare for one world leader to meet another in private, instead of using the communications network, but three- or four-cornered discussions were almost always by telescreen. Precisely what occurred remains unknown, but Tchernavin certainly received pledges of support from Premier Zukarov and from the newly-elected Australian prime minister, Lance Sheihan. President Oakley gave no such pledge, but his subsequent behaviour suggests that he favoured the course taken by Tchernavin.

2652: the UN's historic resolution
In April 2652, after much more work by Tchernavin and his allies behind the scenes, the UN passed its most important resolution, stating in very strong terms that the UN deemed the Charter of 2442 to apply to engineered longevity as well as to adult rejuvenation. In two subsidiary resolutions the UN resolved to divert vast funds to two massive projects: expansion of facilities for cryonic storage of sperms and ova, so that anyone might defer indefinitely the exercise of their right of replacement; and the development of human engineering facilities on a large scale throughout the world, including the training of personnel and the building of vast "womb-factories". All this was to be handled by UN agencies, with all nations allowing the UN to levy taxes directly on their citizens to pay for these programmes. The UN's plans would not create the necessary technological resources until well into the twenty-eighth century, but the new gene-banks allowed people to postpone having children until a Zaman Transformation could be made available – even if this was impossible during their lifetime.

Radical reconstruction of world political hegemony
The consequences of these decisions were even more wide-ranging than anticipated. Although the 2652 resolution concerned the particular matter of longevity engineering, it represented a reconstruction of world political hegemony. In one sense, the UN had been a *de facto* world government for many centuries, but it had been so inhibited by national governments and global corporations as to be virtually powerless. The resolution of April 2652 – particularly its subsidiaries – cut the Gordian knot and gave the UN council genuine authority. From then on, not just Land Use was planned at world level, but all the matters of life and death which affected the world's people. When, in 2671, the Council moved into its new permanent chamber in Amundsen City a new era in world politics had already begun.

The end of family life on Earth
The consequences for world society of the decision encapsulated in the resolution were dramatic enough in themselves. Although the birth-rate rallied a little in 2653, it never again reached a fifth of the rate recorded three years earlier. It was not that large numbers failed to exercise their right of replacement, but simply that the children of any given generation were spread over a much greater period as people lived longer, and as it became more common for them to exercise their right posthumously.

Attitudes to human engineering changed abruptly. By 2665 most people felt that it was a poor mother who would deny her child the gift of extended life by insisting on carrying and bearing it herself. A preference for natural pregnancy came to seem perverse, and even the desire to have one's children while one still lived was suspiciously selfish. While the waiting-lists for Zaman transformations remained very long, there was a certain sense in this latter attitude, but the suspicion lingered even in later centuries, when the techniques became available more-or-less on demand. In the 2650s, therefore, the world virtually abandoned what was left of the old-style "family life".

"Humanists" pledged to preserve Homo sapiens
Those who dissented quickly found it politic to band together in the face of criticism, forming their own aggregate households and, later, entire communities. The dissenters realized that the future of *Homo sapiens* as a species depended on them, and

they made rhetorical capital out of this. It became their mission – their chosen destiny. Many called themselves "humanists", implying subtly that the new race of ZT children who would soon have dominion over the Earth and its colonies in space were somehow not quite human. The outrageous piety of some of these sects earned them the nickname, Neanderthals. Although the original supporters of such movements had been labelled "dark grey", it became apparent that the humanists were mostly radical greens. Along with Zaman transformations they proscribed all other forms of human engineering; and some of the more determined groups began to reject other kinds of technology. Many joined forces with the survivors of older anti-technological cults, retiring to the "unspoiled islands" where they could live as they imagined their ancestors once had. Cynical observers suggested that these islands might one day become cages in a kind of zoo, where immortal tourists would come to marvel and laugh at the "living fossils" of *Homo sapiens.*

Majority of children born to deceased parents

World population continued unstable for more than a century, and it was not until 2800 that a new equilibrium was reached at just below 2.5 billion. It has not varied by more than a few per cent since. Average life-expectancy at birth was then officially estimated at 180 years, though the figure was entirely speculative. Gradual refinement of the Zaman transformation has prevented demographers from fixing an accurate figure, but their estimates climbed throughout the twenty-ninth and thirtieth centuries. Applications for desterilization fell as life-expectancy increased, and by 2800 the majority of the children born from the world's artificial wombs were the issue of deceased parents. Aggregate households adopted children for rearing without paying much attention to biological parenthood.

Family life thrives in space colonies

We should not forget that aggregate households have undergone considerable evolution since the twenty-fifth century. Obviously the age-structure of the average household altered considerably, as a result of Zaman transformations. In the latter half of the twenty-seventh century it became clear that either the size of the average aggregate would grow or many more households would be childless. Statistics from contemporary social scientists in the USA reveal that after a period of uncertainty, during which so many households fragmented that it seemed there might be a return to isolated or monogamous living, aggregates formed again at much the same population-levels (usually between nine and twelve individuals). The difference was that most of them were childless for long periods.

However, after 2650 a sharp division of life-styles opened up between Earth and the space colonies. It was not that the people living outside the Earth were dissenters from the use of human engineering – indeed, their dependence on technology was so great that the idea of extreme humanism taking root on the Moon or Mars was absurd. The difference was one of *lebensraum.* The extraterrestrial colonies were expanding and growing rapidly in number. They therefore required a constant flow of personnel, which was assured partly by emigration from Earth and partly by sustaining a high birth-rate.

The colonies were already better-equipped with the technologies of human engineering than the nations of Earth, because their capacity had been rapidly built up for the adapting of humans for low gravity life. ETs could bear ET children naturally, but they had no prejudice against artificial wombs, and neither had the ordinary humans who lived and worked alongside them. With relatively small populations and booming economies, the major space colonies were able to guarantee their people access to ZT techniques much more quickly than the nations of Earth. On the Moon and Mars it never became normal for people to postpone their replacement until after they were dead. Outside the Earth family life did survive, and aggregate households had to adjust to an *increasing* proportion of young members. By 2700 statisticians were playing games with graphs, attempting to predict when the birth-rate outside the Earth would grow to match the birth-rate on it. They also tried to guess what proportion of those children would undergo each combination of transformations.

Space begins to attract social elite

In theory, emigration to the space colonies had always been an option open to anyone on Earth who did not like the way things were developing there. Before the twenty-eighth century, though, there had been little to make the space colonies seem a real alternative. It had always been expensive to leave Earth's gravity-well, and the richest people had rarely been attracted by the opportunities in space. After 2700, though, it grew much more difficult to become or remain rich if one stayed "Earthside", where UN taxation and creeping egalitarianism were rapidly eroding economic differences. For the first time, the outer reaches of the solar system began to seem attractive to members of the world's social elite. All the talk of new frontiers and the pioneer spirit finally began to mean something.

There is a less cynical explanation for the spectacular upsurge of interest in the space colonies after 2650. The constant flow of news from outside the Earth, and the record of human achievements in space, were intrinsically exciting. People were at last beginning to realize how small the surface of their planet really was, and what a restriction of opportunity its lack of *lebensraum* imposed. Even those people of earlier centuries who had been forced to tolerate a natural lifespan of seventy years had found it necessary, as soon as they attained control of their food and energy supplies, to restrict their breeding stringently. Now, as people were beginning to live much longer, they were forced to contemplate restrictions so extreme as to render the whole world almost childless. Many were perfectly willing to adapt to this, but even they felt happier knowing that they still had a choice in the matter. The solar system was there, and beyond it, the galaxy. Instead of thinking of outer space as a dreadful cage of darkness around the fragile biosphere, people began to think of it as territory, to be claimed and used.

Amundsen City in the twenty-eighth century: crystal and duralite spires sparkle in the icy glare of the long Antarctic afternoon. Amundsen City was built for the UN as a self-sufficient archology complex, from raw materials mined from the continent far below and from Gantz products. Many inhabitants never left the domes, living a life of ease and warmth within the city. Others, like the person in the foreground, used the frozen environment as a playground. SAP-skins, bio-engineered to keep out the cold, enabled them to live outside with little or no regard for the sub-zero temperatures. Bulky clothing was a passing fashion trend, not a functional necessity.

CHAPTER THIRTY-EIGHT

ADAPTATIONS TO LONGEVITY

The early rejuvenates of the Period of Transformation scarcely changed their lifestyles as a result of their longevity. Nucleic Acid Renewal gave them an extra stretch of life which they used as best they could, never quite sure how long their borrowed youth would last. In the modern period, though, adjustments have been necessary at the psychological and social levels. Modern man has been forced to reassess the human condition, and to take up a very different attitude to it.

Even early rejuvenates encountered some of the more basic difficulties of longevity – particularly the problem of memory. It had always been the case, of course, that memories faded even in a lifespan of seventy years, but in general people who lived for that short period had no difficulty in keeping a sense of personal coherency and continuity. They retained enough impressions of their early years to maintain a sense of connection with their earlier selves. Rejuvenates often lost this sense of connection. They found that, as they carried their active lives forward into a second century, the extent of their forgetting bred a sense of existential unease, which was magnified as soon as they became conscious of it. Even before 2650 there was talk of "dissolving identity" and "pernicious amnesia", and in the later twenty-seventh century numerous fads surfaced offering anxious rejuvenates some compensation for their loss.

Rejuvenates struggle to remember their childhoods

Memory-training hypnosis became popular in the USA in the 2670s, after several centenarian telescreen stars claimed to have rediscovered their childhood memories with the aid of an amiable psychotherapist named Samuel "Svengali" Lu. It is doubtful whether Lu's techniques really achieved what he claimed; probably the "memories" in question were fabricated illusions. The treasure-houses that he unlocked, however, were comforting.

The next craze, for so-called "memory boxes" – electronic data-stores which could be hooked up to the brain and fed with thoughts and visual images – brought no such satisfaction. The boxes worked – that is to say, a person equipped with artificial synaptic interfaces could, indeed, store impressions in them for later recall – but they failed to restore the sense of personal continuity. People who played back last year's "deposits" from their memory boxes found them frequently incoherent, almost always uninteresting, and seemingly alien. Despite this the boxes were still selling well into the twenty-eighth century, as adults pressed them upon the children in their care, convinced that in a hundred years' time the deposits that such children reluctantly made would be among their most valuable possessions.

Another disadvantage of the memory boxes was their scope for illegal use. A black market in stolen and decoded memories sprang up overnight: see how A really thinks, learn how to blackmail B, check out the affections or business secrets of C! "Hot tapes" of highly-spiced memories circulated, as they still do: find how the other sex feels when making love, revive the delights of being a 20-year-old stud, even – with "snuff tapes" – experience death. In the Theodore White case of 2688, the defendant was accused of hiring a software pirate to break into and modify White's memory record, hoping to alter his personality and cause him to rewrite his will. The successful suit was brought under "invasion of privacy".

Memorative drugs also enjoyed a vogue, though most were highly dangerous and universally banned from use or sale. Over the previous six centuries biotechnology had produced a vast "psychotropic pharmacopeia" – literally millions of organic compounds which stimulated the brain to produce phenomena like euphoria, hallucination, intoxication or depression – but only a few interfered with the process of memory-storage and recall and the great majority of those were amnesiacs, destroying memories rather than facilitating their retrieval. Those which did promote recall normally affected short-term memory. There was no known compound that would have achieved what the uneasy rejuvenates wanted – the renewal of their memories to match the renewal of their tissues by NAR-treatment. Rumours that such drugs existed, or had recently been discovered, circulated widely in the memory-box era of 2690-2740, and many people were taken in by confidence tricksters.

Many converts to the new Stoicism

Eventually the long-lived had to accept that there were no easy answers, and that they would have to come to terms with their unease. The generations of psychotherapists which succeeded the colourful Mr Lu adopted a new approach, suggesting that their patients' anxiety was unnecessary and inappropriate, and that what they were losing was not a "treasure" after all. An old cliché resurfaced in this new context: "You can't take it with you." Some therapists even argued that the unease was not caused by failures of memory, but should be regarded as a neurotic side-effect of the quest for personal "multidimensionality".

It was not surprising that this new attitude became widespread, because multidimensionality rapidly went out of fashion in the early twenty-eighth century and by 2740 was a thing of the past. The belief that tedium could only be kept at bay by continual change and that variety was the essence of life became rare. The new Stoicism – initially part of the backlash against the wilder excesses of cosmetic biotechnology and sensational cyborgization – gained many converts in the twenty-eighth century, in all the hyperdeveloped nations.

Although the new Stoicism took its name from the ancient Hellenic school of Zeno and Chrysippus, the similarities were few. The new Stoics resembled the old, however, in their insistence on leaving the pattern of their experiences largely to the dictates of providence, and in their belief that one should be content with the range of human experience that naturally presented itself. The relentless pursuit of exotic sensations was condemned as puerile.

New attitude to sex

An interesting corollary of this concerned the neo-Stoic attitude to sex. The dominant view of the twenty-seventh century had been that sexual intercourse was simply a form of play – an attitude which fitted well enough with the circumstances: sterility was the norm and the link between intercourse and procreation had long been severed. The neo-Stoic attitude, though, was that sex should be taken seriously, as love-making in a literal sense. It should be a profound experience, the pleasure of which was far from superficial; and, although its pattern need not be stereotyped,

Memory box equipment was popular right up to the twenty-eighth century. The best monitors, such as this one displayed by a bicentenarian female, projected holo-images of the user's memories.

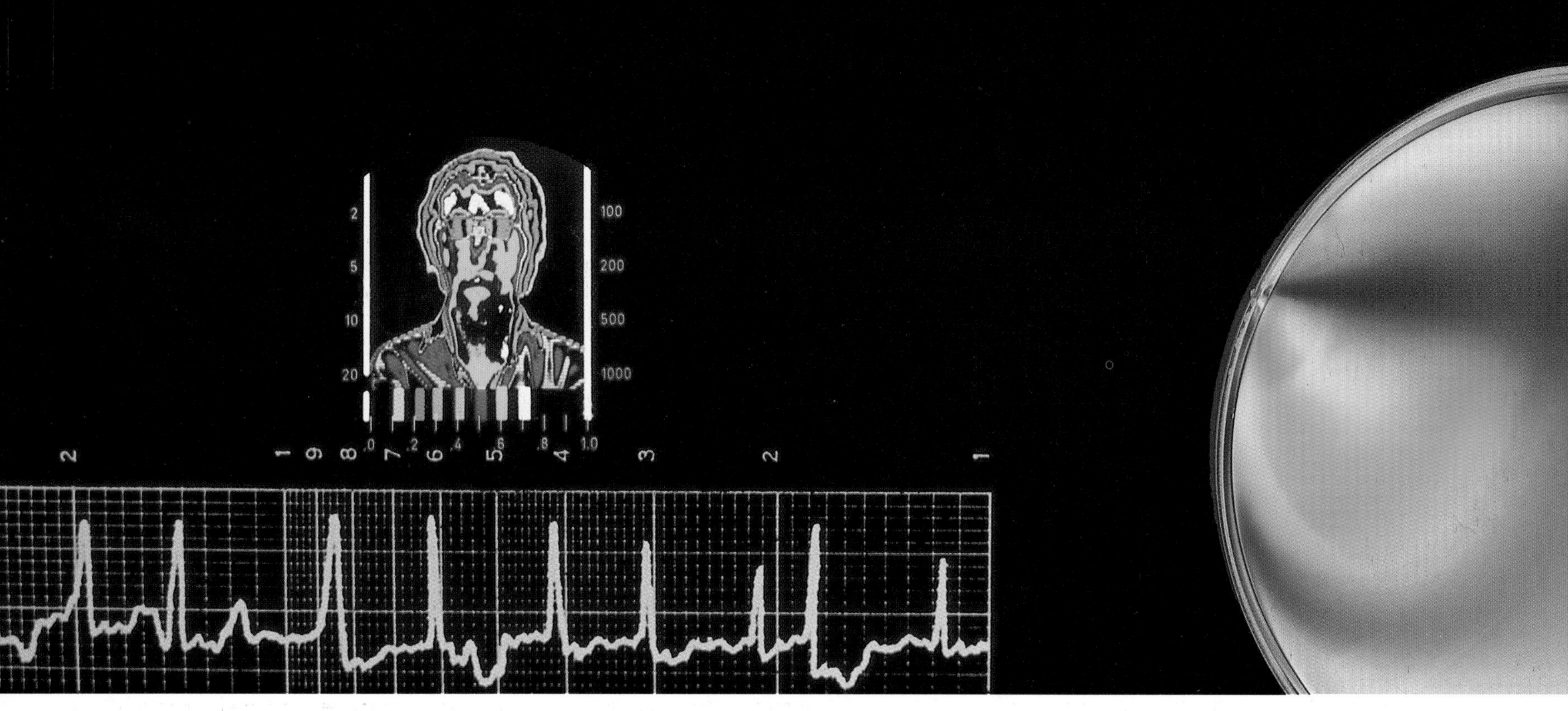

NAR memoflash, of the type used in the early twenty-seventh century, part of the all-important and delicate process of monitoring NAR treatment.

it should not be subjected to the bizarre decorations associated with cosmetic transformations and cyborg accessories.

Once regarded as moral reactionaries, too inhibited to accept the carefree hedonism of the age, the new Stoics had acquired a serious following by 2735, by which time leading exponents – including Louise Toussaint and Linda Lydka – had attained a level of celebrity rare among philosophers.

It was clear that the vast majority of converts to the new Stoicism were rejuvenates, who felt that they had passed through the hedonic phase of first adulthood to a further maturity. Or, to put it more simply, they had become bored with the constant struggle to hold boredom at bay. They were satiated with variety, and had resolved to discover virtue in constancy. Many were readily convinced that the idea of the hideous tedium of extended life was a chimera, and that what long-lived people needed was tranquillity and calm of mind.

The old inherit the world

By this time, virtually all power was in the hands of rejuvenates. It was not that the old had inherited the world, but rather that they had hung on to it as they had grown old. In 2500 less than 5 per cent of the seats in the UN Council Chamber were occupied by people who had undergone NAR-treatment. By 2600 the figure had risen to 50 per cent; by 2700 it was more than 99 per cent. In 2740 there was hardly a position of influence anywhere in the world that was not occupied by a centenarian. In view of this it is not surprising that the period once seen as the prime of life – the years between 30 and 60 – was now widely described as "secondary adolescence". The rejuvenates defended their position by asserting that it was only after revitalization that a person became truly capable of wisdom. Thus they rationalized the methodical squeezing of the under-60s out of power. Their adoption of the new Stoicism was fundamental to that rationalization; it was the symbol of their superior maturity.

New Stoics under attack

Inevitably, as the new-Stoicism developed from a cult to become the "religion" of the time, the movement fragmented into rival groups which modified its original ideas. The most serious of these schisms came in 2747, when Ahmed Perez and Karl Kramin broke with Toussaint and Lydka after bitter accusations had been made regarding the attempts of these two males to "masculinize" the philosophy. (In the beginning, it will be recalled, the new Stoicism was predominantly a female movement. When its appeal became universal the originators feared that their influence might be hijacked by zealous male converts.)

By the end of the twenty-eighth century the Stoic traditionalists found themselves faced on the one hand by the self-styled neo-Epicureans, and on the other by the Xenophiliacs. Jordan Harrison and Jai Ramcharon popularized the neo-Epicurean school of thought, which took its name from the principal opponents of the original Stoics. The Xenophiliacs were led by the effervescent Michi Okuyama, an Australian genetic artist who criticized his opponents for trying to salvage ideas from the cradle of philosophy, and promoted his own thinking as the only authentically modern philosophy.

Neo-Epicureans influence the arts

Harrison and Ramcharon questioned the Stoics' opposition to hedonism and their belief that providence could supply all the experience that a human needed. However, they did not defend the excesses of the past, nor did they make any concessions on the matter of wisdom being the prerogative of the rejuvenated; but they were more generous in their definition of maturity. They were the champions of "careful hedonism", and argued that judicious activity rather than passive reliance on providence leads to worthwhile experience. They agreed that sexual intercourse should be an expression of love, but they had a more liberal definition of love. They mocked the Stoics' earnest, metaphysical image of love, and developed a more romantic ideology which stressed the boundless joy of "sexual friendship". Predictably, neo-Epicurean philosophy had a greater impact on the arts than neo-Stoicism. The greater lyric poets of the early twenty-ninth century, who breathed new life into an art-form which had been moribund for hundreds of years, all owed their inspiration to Epicurean ideas. Urashima's *Sonnets* (2803) and Stephen Rorison's *Pleasures of Methuselah* (2811) are supreme examples of this.

Michi Okuyama's Xenophilia

However, the importance of the neo-Epicureans can be overestimated. In fact they did little more than provide the rejuvenate elite with an excuse to adopt a more relaxed image. Okuyama was right in saying that his Xenophiliac philosophy was more radical and of more immediate relevance. His fame grew after publication of his slim volume of polemic, *Xenophilia*, in 2765 (he had been rejuvenated for the first time in 2752), and he maintained his reputation as a brilliant speaker and charming iconoclast for an unusually long time. He was one of the very few people to benefit from a third rejuvenation, and lived until 2890, failing by only a month to reach his two hundredth birthday.

Okuyama was always willing to mock the idea of a "further maturity" for the rejuvenated, arguing that a new maturity had yet to be created, and that when it was it would be available to anyone. He put this case so cleverly that in his early days he attracted both those who had not yet been rejuvenated and the ever-increasing legions of the Zaman-transformed. Later, of course, the ZTs made him their guru, and he was widely (though falsely) credited with inventing the name which they preferred: "emortals".

Okuyama also mocked his rivals for their preoccupation with sex, and their insistence that sexual intercourse was fundamental to feelings of love. This had probably been true in the past, he said, but there was no virtue in clinging to old ideas that circumstances had rendered irrelevant. He maintained that in the modern world sex *was* playful, and thus peripheral to the real business of life. Love, by contrast, remained central to human experience, and what modern man required – emortal man in particular – was a new capacity to love. The xenophilia from which his philosophy took its name was an inversion of the ancient xenophobia – the fear of those who had differently coloured skin or who followed a different way of life – but

Michi Okuyama, philosopher and author of *Xenophilia* (2765), pictured in 2886 at the age of 196. Okuyama responded well to rejuvenation treatment, receiving it successfully three times.

there was more to Okuyama's thinking than that. He suggested that humanity was in deep need of a desire to embrace and welcome human strangeness; and he went beyond simply advocating that ordinary men should live in harmony with ETs and merpeople, to suggest that only through some mysterious sharing of experience by the different human species could an authentic maturity be achieved.

Learning to love all human species

The Xenophiliacs not only applauded the new diversity of mankind, but interpreted it as part of a noble and essential purpose. They considered it part of the destiny of ordinary people to create extraordinary people; to take control of and responsibility for the future of many human species; and to love them all with the kind of fervour that Christians had once credited to their imaginary creator.

One might cynically suggest that such a philosophy was bound to be popular, because it merely insisted that what was happening in the world ought to be happening, and that everyone should be enthusiastic about it. Certainly those who embraced Xenophilia were simply learning to love the inevitable, but learning to love a person, let alone another species, is not easy, and the large numbers who could honestly call themselves xenophiliacs at that time are therefore historically significant. Today we are all xenophiliacs of some description, and we take so many of Okuyama's ideas for granted that it is difficult to imagine that they were once fiercely disputed. We can recapture a sense of the bitterness of the initial debate, though, from the recorded telescreen dialogues of 2771 and 2772, featuring Okuyama, Jordan Harrison, Linda Lydka and Karl

Kramin. (The heavily edited version which concentrates on Okuyama's exchanges with Lydka, titled *Xenophilia versus Zenophilia*, is as unsatisfactory as the silly play on words implies.)

Critics of xenophilia argued that it simply opened the door again to the excesses of the twenty-fifth and twenty-sixth centuries. The idea of "total potential" did indeed reappear, and certainly a vulgar variety of xenophilia that was little more than exotic sensation-seeking became briefly fashionable with rejuvenate socialites. The ancient dictum of "Do What Thou Wilt" was adopted by some would-be prophets of the new era, including Christian Device, the self-styled Archimage of Abdera. Few people took Device seriously while he was alive, but after his death following an ill-judged experiment with an illegal psychedelic synthesizer, he became a cult-hero who had died attempting to push back the horizons of human experience.

Rejuvenation rejected by Homo sapiens

Another twenty-eighth-century cult had no leaders and was restricted to a vanishing minority. After the UN resolution of 2652 the number of *Homo sapiens* births remained small by comparison with earlier days, but it was by no means negligible even outside the ranks of the Humanists. These were the "disinherited children" who found themselves excluded from positions of power in a world run by rejuvenates. Many, of course, were content to wait until their rejuvenations to have their chance, but those born after 2700 soon realized that by the time they reached their majority the balance of power would be changing again, with emortals rather than sapients in the ascendant. They reacted by embracing a peculiarly aggressive pessimism which led them to reject not only the values of the rejuvenates, but also rejuvenation itself. In hundreds and thousands they decided to die instead of claiming their second term of youth, often applying for euthanasia even before senescence. This group gave itself no name, but others called them "Thanatics". Their views became well-known, although they had no spokesmen to debate on the screen with the likes of Michi Okuyama and Jordan Harrison, because of a profusion of telescreen dramas featuring conflicts between such people and other members of their households – there was a rich vein of sentiment to be exploited here.

Death welcomed by the long-lived

Thanaticism died out – literally – before 2800, but it left a legacy by accelerating the change in attitudes to death. Paradoxically, the idea of death as a "reasonable alternative" made considerable headway as life-expectancy dramatically increased. One of the corollaries of the universal availability of rejuvenation treatments was a widespread horror of senility. When the initial onset of old age could be defeated by artifical renewal of youth, the idea of being old seemed doubly strange and intimidating. The feeling that, when rejuvenation could no longer hold old age at bay, one should accept death rather than submit to its ravages became increasingly common.

For centuries a majority of people had been able to choose the moment of their death, opting for painless suicide rather than suffering. Usually, though, people had clung hard to life until it really became unbearable. After 2780 a much more modest reduction in the quality of life was regarded as justification for voluntary euthanasia. The long-lived – naturally enough – presented this as one more facet of their new maturity, and they made a show of welcoming death when they decided that the time had come. It had become conventional to exercise the right of replacement posthumously, giving directions for the use of cryonically-stored sperms or ova in one's will. Many of the long-lived now declared that in accepting death they were making room for their descendants. Thus suicide became a kind of inter-generational politeness.

The future belongs to the emortals

.Whether the Thanatic attitude to death was reasonable or not, they were correct in anticipating that power would pass to the emortals. In 2750 less than 5 per cent of the seats in the UN Council Chamber were occupied by emortals, but by 2850 this had become 50 per cent and by 2950 it was 99 per cent. Xenophiliac ideas certainly contributed to the ease with which this take-over was achieved, but it was inevitable in any case. It was to the emortals that the future really belonged, and it was for them to shape it.

CHAPTER THIRTY-NINE

THE MEEK INHERIT THE EARTH?

The gradual soothing of the characteristic restlessness of the Period of Transformation had repercussions on patterns of work and on the economic fortunes of whole nations, as well as on personal philosophies of life.

One consequence was the decline of the construction and development sector of the world economy. As the movement of households slowed down, so the casual erection and demolition of buildings, once part of the routine of the hyperdeveloped nations, became a thing of the past. By the end of the twenty-seventh century most groups who commissioned the building of a new home insisted that it should last at least a lifetime – which meant for two centuries and more.

World slump in twenty-eighth century

For a few decades after 2700 the fragmentation of aggregate households sustained the ailing construction industry, but as new and more stable groups formed there was a dramatic slump. Since most of the workers held other jobs as well, there was no significant increase in unemployment. In any case job specialization was becoming common again and resentment over loss of income was somewhat muted. This remained the case even when the sales, marketing and service sector of the hyperdeveloped economies began to slide, due to a new utilitarian attitude to purchasing brought about by the new philosophies. As lifestyles became less varied and less colourful the market in luxury goods faded away.

All the hyperdeveloped nations suffered equally from this slump. In theory, the post-Communist economies should have been able to accommodate dramatic changes in consumer demand better than the post-Capitalist economies. In fact, the ideological differences between the two had long been merely cosmetic. The USSR was just as badly affected by the "flexible credit crash" as the USA, and their finance ministers conferred regularly over means of fighting the problem.

The Chichikov Solution

Eventually, the Russian economist Pavel Ivanovich Chichikov proposed a "solution" – by propounding quite simply that there was not a problem. He argued that, in the past, wholly irrational patterns of demand had sustained an "artificial economy" devoted to such imbecile ends as conspicuous consumption and the acquisition of status symbols. Now, the world was becoming mature (it need hardly be added that Chichikov was a rejuvenate) and was putting aside such follies. The hyperdeveloped nations were abandoning their hyperactivity and returning to "normality". People wanted less and therefore needed less employment. In short, the slump was not a slump, but merely a return to the necessary and sensible level of economic activity, following an unnecessary and prolonged boom.

Whether or not Chichikov's interpretation was any more than convenient sophistry is hard to say; but it was accepted with enthusiasm by Stoically-inclined individuals and by governments, who could now cease the unequal struggle for growth and make into official policy what was happening anyway – namely deflation and the shrinking of their economies. Thus, the depression was allowed to bring a slow death to the global corporations, which had long depended for their profitability – and their power – on those very sectors of the world economy that were in decline. The flexible credit which they had long controlled and manipulated shrank, while the UN used its new powers to appropriate much of what was left in order to finance the universal right to emortality.

Nations economically equal

A dramatic worldwide equalization of economic opportunity ensued. The differences between rich and poor nations - as well as individuals – had dwindled during the Period of Transformation, but the gap had never seemed likely to close entirely. It had been sustained largely by merchants, who had always been able to create demands for themselves to supply. Such people had survived the free availability of food and – partially – of housing, communications and medicine. They had kept their markets healthy even though the supply of necessities was a marginal and unprofitable part of their business. They might even have survived the fashionability of Stoicism, but too many vultures were waiting to pick the bones of their corporations. The widespread acceptance of Chichikov's theory ensured that they got no help from the governments that had always protected them in the past.

Other trends, too, helped to destroy the distinctions between the rich and poor nations. As SAP-systems had become more efficient and versatile, industry had migrated from the temperate zones to the tropics. The guarantee of universal access to NAR-treat-

The evolution of global equality. The vast gulf between rich and poor in the first centuries of the millennium gradually eroded so that now the peoples of the world and the solar system have roughly equal shares. This is, of course, the result of numerous factors, but principally: the worldwide banishment of poverty; the spread of SAP systems to poorer countries; the industrialisation of space which brought benefits to all nations; and the growing power of the UN with its policy of redistributing wealth.

The world economy

Product per capita for eight nations of planet Earth: dollars adjusted for inflation

Country	*Year* **2000**	**2200**	**2400**	**2600**	**2800**
USA	*119*	*164*	*350*	*252*	*201*
USSR	*49*	*129*	*298*	*240*	*187*
Australia	*85*	*147*	*337*	*244*	*203*
France	*83*	*85*	*159*	*198*	*197*
Algeria	*13*	*18*	*53*	*146*	*187*
Chile	*13*	*25*	*72*	*181*	*195*
China	*5*	*14*	*66*	*100*	*184*
Nepal	*1*	*3*	*28*	*91*	*177*

Dallas Schuller, pictured by a securicam on his emigration run to Titan. Security before the dome colony went "open" (see caption on facing page) was strict, aiming to catch potential domebusters well before they had a chance to do any damage.

ment had promoted the equality of technological resources between nations. By 2800 it made little sense to speak of hyper-developed nations, and the notion of the USA, the USSR and Australia as "superpowers" reflected a political hegemony based on tradition alone. These nations had even lost their primacy in scientific research and technical innovation, because so much experimental work now took place outside the Earth, in the furtherance of man's expansion into the greater universe.

Money ceases to matter

The differences between rich and poor individuals were not eroded to quite the same extent. Individuals were still rewarded according to the kind of work they did, and although people could no longer make fortunes from entrepreneurial activity the most skilful or talented earned substantially more than the average. However, the sophistication of the communications network had led by now to virtual equality of opportunity: comparable education was available to all.

Of course, by the twenty-eighth century equality of income had ceased to be an issue of importance. In previous centuries wealth had been the criterion by which nations had been broken into social classes, but by 2700 there were much more obvious status groups which had nothing to do with income or flexible credit: the rejuvenate and the non-rejuvenate; the emortals and the sapients. By 2800 the world had passed through the Age of Avarice, and was embarked on the Age of Abundance. Money no longer mattered.

Virando and Schuller: latterday capitalists

Although it was praised by the new Stoics, the neo-Epicureans and the Xenophiliacs alike the social change of the twenty-eighth century had its critics. The majority accepted Chichikov's view that this was progress towards a new maturity, but there was a minority that saw it as a slide into decadent senescence. Some of those who took this line did so out of self-interest, like the Martian separatist Stefan Solarski, whose objective was to emphasize the dynamism of the developing extraterrestrial cultures and to secure their full political independence. On the other hand there was a group of Earth-bound social scientists, led by the Americans Mark Virando and Dallas Schuller, who regretted the decline of the profit motive in human affairs. Virando was the leading proponent of the theory that greed was the main motive force in human affairs, and that satiation of desire would lead to a "lotus eater society". In *The Politics of Content* (2763) Schuller argued that social solidarity could only be maintained by a widespread sense of threat, and that the banishing of anxiety would be fatal to the quality of life on Earth. Both men looked back with nostalgia to the dire days of the twenty-first century when the world faced a serious crisis and wealth "really meant something".

Dallas Schuller emigrated in 2787, going first to Mars and later to the Titan colony. Virando became Professor of Sociology at Harvard in 2795, at the age of 76, and remained there until he died, still complaining about the world's surrender to tedium, in 2863. "The meek," he once observed with characteristic bitterness, "have inherited the Earth."

The theories of Virando and Schuller were probably the last significant expression of the attitude that was commonplace before the extension of the human lifespan was actually achieved: that centuries of existence in a relatively stress-free world would become depressingly boring, and that life would lose its savour. In our view Virando and Schuller have been proven wrong. Nothing has replaced greed and fear as forces of human motivation, but that is because they needed no replacement. The people of the modern world have not found it difficult to do without them. (To be fair, we should note that Mark Virando, were he still alive, would not be impressed by this dismissal of his views. After all, the authors of this history are ageing emortals: we are the meek who inherited the Earth; we are the lotus eaters – how else could we be expected to think?)

The Icehouse Crisis

Virando and Schuller would likely have gained renewed optimism from the news transmitted back to Earth from Solar Research Station 1 (commonly known as the "solarion") in January 2905. A group of astronomers, including Motshubi, Rikkerink and Yip, had analysed changes in the solar corona which suggested that the level of radiation reaching Earth was falling, and would fall far enough to trigger a fresh Ice Age. As we know, their predictions have been borne out: during the last century sea level has fallen and the ice-caps have spread, particularly in the north. The media was quick to dub this gradual change the "Icehouse Crisis", and it seemed for a time that the sense of threat might indeed reassert itself amid human affairs.

On the other hand, Virando and Schuller would probably have been disappointed by our calm in the face of the slow march of the glaciers. After a brief period of alarm, the world community rapidly recovered its self-confidence. The spirit of Chichikov rose again, the UN Council taking the view that the best way to deal with the problem was simply to declare it non-problematic. It might be necessary, of course, for a few hundred million people to migrate into the tropics, but there was plenty of time for that. And if some people preferred to stay put – why not? It was, of course, supremely fitting that the UN Council Chamber stood almost exactly upon the South Pole; the very existence of Amundsen City proved that the new world had nothing to fear from ice. Temporary winter might grip the planet, but a race that was armed with nuclear fusion and sophisticated biotechnology could clearly cope with ease.

Human failing prevents Utopia

The political and economic developments of the early part of the modern period have led to what people of earlier ages might have described as a Utopia; but no one who has lived in the last two centuries would describe the world so. Even the most convinced opponent of Virando and Schuller would not claim that the modern world is perfect. In terms of political boundaries – the "lines on the map" which José Araguex loathed so much – the world remains an inglorious patchwork, the product of thousands of historical accidents and compromises. No one asked to design a sensible and viable political community, let alone a perfect one, could possibly have produced such a curious conglomerate. The instruments of world government lack symmetry, sleekness and perhaps even sanity. Nor can it be said that people are totally content, "lotus eaters" or not. Even the emortals retain the human tendency to complain.

Indeed it is difficult to imagine the human community of Earth *ever* arranging its affairs without some disorder and dissent, if only because it is so large and varied. Bioengineering may produce many new species of human, but it will surely not create people so perfectly in tune with the needs and desires of their fellows that they could build a Platonic Republic or a Campanellan City of the Sun. To be human is to be imperfect; and it is reasonable to hope that our failings will save us from uniformity, and from the decadent senescence feared by Virando and Schuller.

Materialistic motives have been largely replaced by aesthetic ones, and there may be people, even today, who think that this is a trivialization, rather than a maturation, of culture; but no one can honestly regret that our material needs are well satisfied and that we are free to indulge the playful side of our nature.

Titan Town in 2998, *overleaf.* Originally built under an airtight membrane in a deep fissure on Titan, moon of Saturn, the town has been open to the sky since the terraforming of Titan was completed in 2871. The magnificent view of Saturn's rings has long attracted lovers from all over the solar system.

CHAPTER FORTY

HORIZONS OF THE HUMAN ENTERPRISE

When the modern period began there were four distinct human species: *Homo sapiens*, the ancestral species, which was still commonly described as "ordinary human", although its members were already becoming known as sapients; ZT people, who were eventually to be called emortals; those adapted for life in space, for whom the name faber had supplanted the ethnocentric term ET; and the merpeople, who retained their original name.

Creation of the Starpeople

More species were created early in the modern period: notably the emortal fabers, usually known as "starpeople", who were the result of a variant of the standard Zaman transformation applied to faber children. The extended lifespans of the starpeople made them ideal personnel for Arks taking many years – or centuries – to reach destinations among the stars. Because they lived in artificial environments, highly dependent on technology, the fabers were quick to adopt ectogenetic reproduction universally; by 2720 they had taken the lead in human engineering from the Earth-based sapients. Axel Vanninen and others improved on the original faber transformation in 2732, and refined the special Zaman transformation which had created the starpeople. Technically, the original fabers were extinct by 2800, and the fabers then living belonged to four distinct species. By then, though, the definition of a "species" had become blurred.

An alien sun rises over Maya, the first world to be colonised by specially adapted humans.

The human species interbreed

Traditionally, two humans were of the same species if they could produce fertile offspring in the natural fashion. By the end of the twenty-eighth century, though, children were hardly ever produced in such a way. Certainly, all faber children were born from artificial wombs. At the same time members of different human species *could* have children; either the sperm or the egg would be engineered for compatibility. Thus a faber and a sapient could have a child of either species, which could eventually have children with members of its own or another species. Due to biotechnological ingenuity, therefore, the human species were *not* distinct – but then, with the aid of genetic engineers, sheep could interbreed with goats. The concept of "separate species" was losing its ancient meaning.

On Earth sexual intercourse between members of different human species remained rare. It was almost unknown for land-dwellers and merpeople to seek biotechnological aid in order to have children. Like so many taboo relationships, though, the idea of intense love-affairs crossing this particular species boundary exerted a tremendous imaginative fascination, reflected in countless works of romantic fiction – including Dana Coughlan's *Yet the Sea is not Full* (2717) and *Those in Peril on the Sea* (2802) by Dorothy Wingard. This suggests that, while opportunities for land-dwellers to meet merpeople were very restricted, moral commitment to Xenophiliac philosophy still required symbolic expression.

Matters were different in space, where humans and fabers lived and worked side-by-side, and where intercourse between species was commonplace. It was by no means unusual for faber children to have one ordinary parent. There was relatively little epic romantic fiction featuring fabers – indeed, novels and screenplays created by fabers tended to play down erotic relationships in favour of the exploration of the universe.

Fabers and starpeople outnumber "normals"

The increase in the numbers of fabers and starpeople was so rapid that by 2780 there were many more adapted than ordinary humans in the asteroid belt. Like the Earth, the colonies on the Moon and Mars were inherited by emortals, but the other colonies with a reasonable level of gravity – including those on the large moons of Jupiter and Saturn – were as well-suited to fabers as to people with legs. It was taken for granted that the permanent stations that were being established on the smaller satellites of the outer planets would be starpeople territory. The vitally important construction and equipping of the Space Ark microworlds in the outer reaches of the solar system had to be entrusted to faber hands.

Relations between the species living beyond the Earth's atmosphere improved steadily after the years of friction at the end of the Period of Transformation. There was nowhere that Xenophiliac philosophy was more necessary than on Mars and the Moon, and fortunately there was nowhere that Okuyama's ideas took stronger root. It is probable that by 2750 the emortals of the Moon had fewer prejudices against fabers than against those of their own species who lived in Earth's gravity-well. Certainly they had the waspish criticisms of their own Abhrim Yomi and Mars's Stefan Solarski to encourage a contempt for Earth-dwellers while they learned to like and respect their four-handed neighbours.

Most of those who lived further from Earth found the idea that it was their "home" somewhat ludicrous. The shipbuilder Hans Hamersvelt was an ordinary man – not even an emortal – but three generations of his ancestors had been born outside the Earth. In his autobiography he said that he had always considered the stars to be "nearer" than the Earth, meaning that they had greater relevance to him. He had his children adapted to be starpeople, though their mother was not a faber. In the twenty-eighth century one of the most widely-read books in the outer solar system was *The Legend of Earth* (2731) by Wu-Yao Lua, a native of Titan. It it a witty satire discussing, in mock-solemn style, the "myths" which space-dwellers had supposedly invented to account for their origins on an imaginary and improbable world.

Earth irrelevant to space-dwellers

Many "citizens of the solar system" found the historical, political and biological bonds tying them to the Earthly lotus eaters an embarrassment which they quietly resented. The UN was a distant irrelevance, and history began with the Promethean pioneers who had planted civilizations in the wastelands of space. There was a large measure of ingratitude in this stance; after all, not until the late twenty-eigth century were the major space colonies able to supply the needs of the smaller ones while remaining self-sufficient themselves. By 2800, of course, the colonies would have been undisturbed if all life on Earth had suddenly ceased.

In that year there were about 500 self-sufficient human communities in the solar system, and a handful already *en route* to other systems. It must be remarked that there is more to self-sufficiency than possession of a fusion reactor, a source of fuel, and a collection of SAP-systems, even if many colonies endowed with such things liked to boast of their independence. On the other hand, many spaceships a fraction of the size of the great space arks could sustain themselves as closed systems for hundreds – perhaps thousands – of years, and could therefore with some justification be considered as independent microworlds.

By 2900 the 500 had grown to 2000, and the handful had become 200, though most of these "human worlds" had populations of less than 1000. In terms of worlds rather than individuals, the starpeople rather than the ordinary emortals were the principal human species by 2900.

Arks reach other solar systems

By then more than a dozen space arks must have reached their destinations in other solar systems: worlds where suitably adapted people might live "freely", as they do on Earth. This estimate is imprecise because information concerning their arrival could, of course, only return at the speed of light; furthermore, as they attained speeds close to that of light the sense of duration became distorted aboard the arks themselves. By the time news of an ark's arrival reached Earth, the work of the settlers was well-advanced. Ordinary people had been brought out of cryonic suspended animation to work on the surface of the raw planet, and had already built cities, SAP-factories and hatcheries crowded with artifical wombs, from which eventually would emerge the new indigenes, designed to leave the domed cities to build their own civilizations.

The people of Earth felt isolated, by time as much as by space. It was difficult for them to celebrate the news that men were walking for the first time upon a new world, when they knew that, as they raised a cheer, third-generation colonists were being born. The ever-expanding catalogue of names – of ships, of worlds and of human pioneers – quickly became more than memory could cope with, and lost its significance. Only a few stayed in the mind as memorable firsts: Maya, the first alien world to be colonized by adapted men; Hyperborea, whose lush life-system caused such problems that the human invaders were almost wiped out; Faraway, where the physical environment was so exotic that the new natives were the first humans with the power of independent flight.

News of the disembarkation on Maya reached Earth in 2840, and enthralled the ancestral world. After that, all else was repetition. Information from Maya and its solar system always held a certain freshness, because this was where the pattern was first laid down. The colonization of Maya itself was only one of the tasks undertaken by the people of the ark *Adventure*; they set up communities of emortals on other, less hospitable planets in the system, and starpeople established themselves on and in the smaller bodies. Indeed, it is doubtful whether *Adventure*'s crew of starpeople ever regarded Maya as their main objective. As starpeople they probably thought of planets – even Earthlike ones – as hellish places unworthy of serious attention. On the other hand, for the biotechnologists Maya was a wonderland – an alien ecology with its own system of genetic transmission, utterly different from the DNA common to all forms of life owing their origin to the Earthly biosphere.

The Mayans visit Earth

In 2938, almost a hundred years after news of the *Adventure*'s arrival reached Earth, a starship from Maya arrived in solar space. The Earthly media referred to this as a homecoming, but this offended the voyagers. Naturally, the crew were starfolk whose notion of "home" was unconnected with particular planets or stars, and the Mayan passengers – ambassadors of goodwill who brought samples of Mayan life-forms for the delight of Earthly biologists – had no doubt that they had come *from* their home to visit a strange and alien place. The moment when the UN Secretary-General, Nolo Sequeira, shook hands with the heavily-suited Mayan Gerd Steinhardt on a balcony in Amundsen City was strangely moving for most of those who watched. They were struck less by the symbolism of the handshake than by the awkwardness of the tall, silver-clad figure whose face was barely visible through the plastic of his visor. The viewers staring at their wallscreens were forced to ask themselves whether there was any meaning left in the idea of the human community. In what sense, if any, did these two men belong to "the same world"?

By chance, Steinhardt and his fellow Mayans visited the solar system just as the so-called Venus controversy was developing. The artificial biosphere established on that planet centuries earlier had changed atmosphere and surface conditions considerably; and many scientists felt that it was time for further intervention. However, there were fierce arguments about the ultimate goal of this gradual transformation. On one side was the proposal that Venus be "terraformed": that an oxygen/nitrogen atmosphere should be established to make it ready for colonization by adapted humans. Several Creationist groups, on the other side, felt that this was inappropriate: that humanity did not need yet another home. Some of these wanted to make Venus into a vast exercise in genetic art, a huge version of one of the old Creationist islands; others favoured using it for the most ambitious experiments in the adaptation of life-forms yet attempted, and did not, therefore, want the physical conditions to become too Earthlike.

The potential to conquer the universe
The arrival of the Mayans was felt to be relevant to this debate because in Steinhardt and his kindred the people of the solar system could see the seed of a possible future: the distribution of descendant species of *Homo sapiens* throughout the galaxy, and perhaps ultimately the universe. Those who favoured the terraforming of Venus felt that a crucial principle was at stake – nothing less than humanity's potential conquest of the universe – and they believed that human destiny would be betrayed by the use of Venus as a Creationist playground rather than a human environment. Steinhardt himself was reluctant to take sides and, when pushed, managed to offend everyone by suggesting that it did "not matter very much".

In the years after 2940 the more ambitious Creationists gained a great deal of support and seemed to be winning the argument. Their proposals had grown more varied and fantastic, and their horizons had quickly broadened. One group, led by Ellen Quartermaine and Nils van Klaveren, even approached the colonists on the satellites of Jupiter for financial support for the creation of life-forms to populate the desolate outer regions of the Jovian atmosphere.

Setbacks for the Creationists
The towering ambition of this new generation of Creationists was a response to what they felt to be an unfortunate accident of circumstance. They were disappointed because a thorough exploration of the solar system had revealed that none of its worlds except Earth harboured any life of any kind. The nearest alien life was tens of light years away, and the samples that Steinhardt had brought from Maya were considered meagre crumbs of comfort. These biologists felt that they had exhausted the secrets and possibilities of Earth's biosystem, and that the continuing existence of their science depended on their finding opportunities to deal with *new* kinds of life. Adapting humans was no longer a challenge.

In 2956 Quartermaine and van Klaveren released a number of artificial organisms into the atmosphere of Jupiter, intending to provide the basis for a complex biosystem. The project failed – by 2960 no trace of the seeded organisms could be found. When a conservative augmentation of the Venerian life-system was finally implemented in 2963 that, too, went wrong. The Creationists found themselves in disarray, having apparently over-reached their abilities.

Encounters with aliens
The wider argument, about humanity's role in the universe, was further confused in 2967 when news arrived that a robot probe had been intercepted by alien sentients some seventy-five light-years from Earth. The ensuing ripple of excitement was tinged with anxiety: the encounter had taken place seventy-five years ago, and by now the aliens might be much closer to the solar system. A face-to-face meeting might soon follow.

And indeed this proved to be the case; the Starship *Pandora* effected a rendezvous with an alien starship a mere thirty light-years from Earth, even before news of the first encounter got back. Word of this reached Earth in 2981. Curiously, the content of the report seemed anti-climactic, despite the inevitable attempts by the media to dramatize the story. When the rhetoric and hyperbole were pushed aside, the simple truth was that the starmen aboard the *Pandora* had exchanged innocuous greetings with other starmen – beings, at least, who resembled them more closely than they resembled the other species of adapted men. The "original" aliens, who had created their own starmen just as we had created ours, could not have been mistaken for *Homo sapiens* – they were different in dozens of minor ways – but if one were ever to visit Earth, silver-suited and plastic-visored, he would seem no stranger than the Mayan Gerd Steinhardt. The aliens, it seemed, were alien only in a technical sense. They were the products of a different evolution, but having taken control of their own evolution just as humanity had, they had made the differences irrelevant. "Form follows function".

For a brief period there was much talk of "the galactic community", and some discussion of establishing a "United Nations of the Stars", but the absurdity of this was quickly appreciated. Interstellar distances are too great to sustain any meaningful communications, let alone communities. It is now widely accepted that there will be no union between the star-worlds, whether inhabited by "humans" or "aliens". There can be no galactic empire, or federation, except in the sense that when we look up into the starry night we are conscious that it is full of life.

Alien planetary system. Holograph taken in 2938 by a crew member of the *Age of Aquarius*, one of the few starships to have completed more than one round trip back to the solar system. The holographer is standing on a moon of an as yet unnamed planet of the star Algol, in the constellation of Perseus. Algol is a double star – the red dwarf is shining in the sky, the brighter type B star, not in picture, illuminates the strange cracked moon. An intensely-cold helium sea extends to the horizon.

EPILOGUE: THE END OF PROGRESS?

In the first chapter of this history we noted the fascination that large round numbers excite in the human imagination. The people who lived in the small, enclosed world of Christendom found it easy to believe that the year 1000 AD would provide a climax in their affairs. It did not seem ridiculous to imagine that Christ would come again and that the dead would rise from their graves to be judged, so that all the miseries of Earthly existence could be set to rights once and for ever. For those who were alive in the year 2000 AD numbers had lost much of their enchantment. Nevertheless, apocalyptic anxiety stirred restlessly in their imaginations too. The end of the world may not have seemed inevitable, but it certainly seemed – and was – possible.

It is easy for us, in the year 3000 AD, to consider such fears foolish. An emortal, living in a world long-since pacified, cannot readily enter the mind of a twentieth-century factory-worker. We know that the Kingdom of Heaven never was supernaturally established in Dark Age Europe and that the all-consuming nuclear holocaust never came; and this knowledge is a barrier preventing us from understanding how such people really felt. They could not know the future, and their ignorance provided perfectly rational grounds for their fears.

As humanity awaits the beginning of the Fourth Millennium, we could argue that we, glorying in a maturity of knowledge and feeling beyond those of our ancestors, have a genuinely realistic view of the prospects of mankind. However, we feel compelled to distrust our sense of certainty in this respect. The horizons of the human enterprise now stretch to infinity, but that does not mean that we can see all that lies within them.

We have our own "end of the world" to look forward to, just as our ancestors had. We face a new Ice Age, perhaps as bad as any the Earth has experienced. That we are not in the least worried by this prospect is one measure of our success as a species. We do have anxieties about the future, but they concern what is within us rather than without. It has become fashionable to speak of "the end of progress", and the popularity of the phrase might be seen as our concession to the magical fascination of large round numbers: our expression of the sense of finality which so variously, but inevitably, affects people contemplating the close of their millennium.

We do not mean by the end of progress that the story of the *Oikoumenê* is finished. The *Oikoumenê* has shattered already; there is not one human world but many – but that is certainly no ending. Nor do we mean that our maturity represents the limit of human potential; we call ourselves emortals but there may come a day when our descendants will laugh at us for such pretentiousness about a lifespan as brief as three or four centuries. Nor does "the end of progress" imply that we have found out everything that can be discovered by scientific enquiry. It is true that we have unearthed no fundamental laws for many centuries, and this suggests that we have uncovered every secret of the universe that human perception can reach. Even so, we know well that human perceptions can be changed or augmented in numerous ways; and we may therefore still be blind to undiscovered truths.

What is meant by "the end of progress" concerns social rather than scientific possibility. We have a sense of having come as far as we need to go, of having lost our impetus. We have inherited, so the fashionable argument goes, a special kind of freedom. We can do as we wish to do, be as we wish to be. It seems that further discoveries will serve no human purpose, and that an aesthetic value is their only form of worth. The "end" of progress, in this way of thinking, is an end not in the sense of "finish" but in the sense of "achievement". The implication is that progress has brought us to the goal for which we were always aiming.

Certainly, we have not fulfilled all the dreams that our ancestors entertained. We have not acquired telepathic communication or the ability to move objects by the power of the mind; nor have we found the trick of travelling faster than light. In our maturity we have put such dreams away; we accept their impossibility and no longer make them objects of desire.

Nonetheless, we are anxious and this, paradoxically, is because we have run out of needs. There is scope for everyone on Earth to design and attain their own personal, perfect world. And yet we remain restless while not knowing where to go, because all possible destinations seem to be already here.

"The horizons of the human enterprise now stretch to infinity, but that does not mean that we can see all that lies within them."

Furthermore, we feel we no longer have any excuse for dissatisfaction.

It may be that, after all, we are more like our ancestors in the tenth and twentieth centuries than we think. Perhaps they too thought that the ends of progress were within their reach, yet like the food of Tantalus could not quite be consumed. Perhaps they too felt that they knew how life ought to be lived, and that they should be able to live it thus, and yet somehow could not do so. If so then our vision of "the end of progress" may be false and we are in no position to say whether we have reached such an end, or whether we ever shall.

We cannot summarize the achievements of the Third Millennium in a single paragraph. However, by referring to one result of those achievements, we can illuminate the argument of this epilogue. What we now call our anxiety as we contemplate the end of the Millennium is but the palest shadow of the tortured state of mind in which our ancestors approached the end of theirs. We know full well what they could hardly dare to believe – that we *can* hope, just as we *must* fear.

The authors gaze into the universe and contemplate "the end of progress"? In fact, they are at home in Langford's recreation area, examining a holo-projection of the sky as viewed from Epsilon Eridani, to which they will begin to journey shortly after publication of this history.

POSTSCRIPT

From *The White Stone* by the nineteenth- and twentieth-century French writer Anatole France, published in France in 1905 and, translated by Charles E. Roche, in the United Kingdom in 1909.

"Few are those who have sought to know the future, out of pure curiosity, and without moral intention or optimistic designs. I know no other than H. G. Wells who, journeying through future ages, has discovered for humanity a fate he did not, according to every indication, expect... All the other prophets of whom I have any knowledge content themselves with entrusting to future centuries the realization of their dreams. They do not unveil the future, being satisfied with conjuring it up.

"The truth is that men do not look so far ahead without fright. Many consider that such an investigation is not only useless, but pernicious; while those most ready to believe that future events are discoverable are those who would most dread to discover them. This fear is doubtless based on profound reasons. All morals, all religions, embody a revelation of humanity's destiny. The greater part of men, whether they admit it to, or conceal it from, themselves, would recoil from investigating these august revelations, to discover the emptiness of their anticipations... They dare not confess to themselves that morality, which has continually changed with manners, up to their own day, will undergo a further change when they have passed out of this life, and that future men are liable to conceive an idea entirely at variance with their own as to what is permissible or not. It would go against the grain with them to admit that their virtues are merely transitory, and their gods decrepit... They fear disgracing themselves in the eyes of their contemporaries in assuming the horrible immortality which future morality stands for. Such are the obstacles to a quest of the future."

INDEX

Figures in italics refer to illustrations

ACKNOWLEDGEMENTS

Photographs supplied by
The British Army
Daily Telegraph Colour Library
The Disney Corporation
European Space Agency
Michael Freeman
Matt Irvine
David Jefferis
MARS
NASA
Science Photo Library

Illustrations by
John Bavosi
Jillian Burgess
Rob Burns/Drawing Attention
Lynne Duncombe
Eagle Artists
Hayward Art Group
Gavin Page Designs
Graham Palfrey-Rogers
Michael Roffe

Shuckburgh Reynolds Ltd would like to give special thanks to
Michael Freeman for his original creative photography, much of which was specially commissioned for this book.
Thanks are also due to the following individuals and organizations who supplied assistance and reference material:
BBC
John Brown
Mark Hewish
Dick Leech
Mai Graphics
Ann and Paul Meacher
Alan and Graham Norris
Roger Pring
Anna Willson